The New Era of Global Competition
State Policy and Market Power

The globalization of the economy and the conservative agenda of governments affect every aspect of Canadian society. A worldwide reorganization of markets poses new challenges for domestic industry while continental trade initiatives threaten the livelihood of Canadian workers and communities in all regions of the country. Environmental quality has been put at risk by development strategies driven more by the possibility of short-term gains from export sales than by attempts to achieve long-term sustainability.

In considering these changes, the contributors to *The New Era of Global Competition* first analyse recent public-sector initiatives – monetarist macro-economic policies, a trade deal with the United States, and the increasing use of the Charter of Rights and Freedoms to make regulatory decisions – that have altered the Canadian economy and transformed Canadian society. They then consider the consequences of these changes for some of Canada's key industries and for Canadian social policy, noting the conservative agenda's effect on workers' incomes, work conditions, collective bargaining, and social benefits as well as on the role of the state in the economy. The final chapters explore possible alternatives and the real and hard choices that Canadians must make in determining economic and social policies for the future, focusing on macro-economic management, employment, industrial strategy, and the environment.

Daniel Drache is a member of the Department of Political Science, Atkinson College, York University.
Meric S. Gertler is a member of the Department of Geography, University of Toronto.

The New Era
of Global Competition

State Policy and Market Power

EDITED BY DANIEL DRACHE
AND MERIC S. GERTLER

McGill–Queen's University Press
Montreal & Kingston • London • Buffalo

© McGill-Queen's University Press 1991
ISBN 0-7735-0817-1 (cloth)
ISBN 0-7735-0818-x (paper)

Legal deposit first quarter 1991
Bibliothèque nationale du Québec

Printed in Canada on acid-free paper

Publication of this book has been assisted by a grant
from the Canada Council through their block grant
program.

Canadian Cataloguing in Publication Data

Main entry under title:
The New era of global competition

ISBN 0-7735-0817-1 (bound). –
ISBN 0-7735-0818-x (pbk.).
1. Canada – Economic conditions – 1971–
2. Canada – Economic policy – 1971–
3. Canada – Social policy.
I. Drache, Daniel, 1941–   . II. Gertler, Meric S.
HC115.N393 1991   330.971'0647   C91-090008-6
                        7079

Typeset in Bembo 10/12 by Caractéra inc.,
Quebec City.

Contents

Acknowledgments

Many people have helped in the preparation of this volume. We wish to thank Professors Carlo Casarosa and Carluccio Bianchi of the University of Pisa who were the co-organizers with Daniel Drache of a joint Canada-Italy conference on state policy and uneven development held in Pisa in April 1989. Many of the chapters of this book were first presented in draft form at this conference. We are grateful in particular to Atkinson College, York University, and the Canadian Academic Centre in Rome for assisting in the organization of this international workshop. We also wish to acknowledge the support given Meric Gertler during his sabbatical stay in the Department of City and Regional Planning at the University of Wales, Cardiff, and in the School of Geography at Oxford University. Both the Department of Political Science at Atkinson College and the Department of Geography at the University of Toronto provided much-needed logistical support while we worked on the manuscript. Finally, the difficult editorial task of co-ordinating a collection of this size has been greatly eased by the fine staff of McGill-Queen's University Press. Special thanks are due to Philip Cercone for his enthusiastic commitment and wise counsel from the very beginning. Joan McGilvray was extremely patient and helpful in answering our endless questions about the editorial process and production details. As well, we owe a special thank you to Diane Mew, our superb editor; all the contributors have benefited from her watchful eye and sharp pencil. Needless to say, the editors accept all responsibility for the errors which remain. Finally, we are in debt to our wives and children who gave much needed support and criticism throughout. But the last word has to go to the contributors who made this book possible. They were gracious, kind, and co-operative partners in this project.

Preface

Globalization is a powerful force changing the fundamental relationship between markets and states. Countries are looking to market forces to put their economies back on the rails. This newfound faith in markets reflects a willingness to accept the lead of the world economy while the national economy follows.[1] As trade barriers fall, societies are impelled to alter their institutions radically to accommodate the dramatic changes in world trade. Indeed, the growing pressure to harmonize has already led to the erosion of existing social programs and social security nets. This offensive comes at a time when corporations have reorganized to become more powerful, with new abilities to influence state policy in unprecedented ways. These companies have also pursued employment relations that give them greater flexibility in deploying their workforce. The trend to smaller workforces points to the profound change in labour markets that these strategies have brought about. More competitive labour markets mean not only fewer jobs but lower pay and insecure employment for young people, for women in the service sector, and for older workers in mature industries.

These dramatic changes to work, state policy, and markets constitute the broad themes of this book. The authors – political scientists, economists, geographers, and sociologists in the main – come from an uncommonly broad range of social science disciplines and share a common belief that the concept of globalization embraces three elements. First, larger markets: the nation-state can no longer satisfy the accumulation needs of transnational and corporate players, so markets need to be enlarged by integrating national markets into larger trading areas.

Secondly, increased capital mobility: as world trade has continued to increase faster than domestic production, corporations have exhorted individual nation-states to dismantle trade barriers; this has accommodated both the meteoric growth of the international finance economy and the drive towards increased flexibility of production systems. Lastly, greater specialization: as world trading intensifies, countries seek to concentrate on those industries in which they are most competitive while abandoning firms in mature, high-cost sectors. Thus, in the new global economy nations are struggling to find new ways for state policy to enhance their economic performance. Decision-makers in Ottawa have responded to this need by relying solely on passive, market-liberalizing approaches. The state has embraced a fundamentalist version of export-led growth, in which exploitation of natural resources is being pursued with newfound vigour, but with questionable returns both to the economy and the environment. Ottawa's new commercial policy has paid few dividends economically. In the space of one year, Canada has lost more than seventy thousand jobs and its record merchandise trade surpluses of the last decade have evaporated overnight.[2]

These dismal results have not deterred the government from pursuing its business-oriented strategy that intends to manage the economy in much the same way that corporate Canada runs the private sector. Price competitiveness focuses on short-term advantages from selling more by price-cutting. With its look-alike industries selling look-alike products for export in the United States, Canada has a limited and declining capability to increase its share of the American market by producing innovative new goods. Therefore the long-term prospects for a better economic performance are dim indeed.

The more immediate problem is that, for the better part of a decade, Canadian exporters have been losing their share in the American market.[3] The productivity of Canada's branch-plant economy is poor by international standards and a large number of small indigenous firms do not have the resources to acquire the latest information-based computerized production technologies.[4] What is more, Canada lags far behind the other Western countries in the use of labour market training, apprenticeship training, and on-the-job training.[5] Thus, a business-as-usual approach is not likely to solve Canada's poor performance. Even the Canadian Manufacturers' Association has been forced to admit that Canada's business culture cannot cope with the challenge it faces. It appears that neither government nor business knows how to plan for long-term growth or to rebuild Canada's productive capacity in an era of global trade. This failure stems from the longstanding reliance of the Canadian state upon a policy of growth led by staples exports. This strategy naively assumes that trade is beneficial regardless of its costs, and that industrial adjustment is a trivial problem. Not surprisingly, it sadly underestimates the complexities of state action required in a time of market reorganization and trade intensification.

A NEW POLITICAL ECONOMY OF GLOBAL CHANGE

The contributors to this volume have taken up the challenge to flesh out a more complete strategy for state action. They have adopted a theoretical focus that marks a new departure in Canadian political economy.[6] In the seventies and eighties, Canadian political economists paid less attention to analysing the global dynamics of change and more to nationally bounded issues. Questions such as gender, state policy, the labour process, social policy, economic dependency, multinational enterprise, and growing regional disparity were at the top of the research agenda. Canadian theorists looked inward to explain the dynamics of Canadian growth, the role of the state and, to a lesser degree, sexual inequality. Theoretical issues must now be rethought and the boundary lines of political economy redrawn. And the evidence is that Canadian political economists now see the importance of integrating the best of European and North American theory into a Canadian perspective. What is unique about this development is that English-speaking Canadian political economists have tended to look toward France rather than England or the United States for new theoretical direction.[7]

The most prominent example of this is the theoretical framework of the Paris-based Régulation school of political economy. As developed by Robert Boyer, Michel Aglietta, Alain Lipietz, Pascal Petit, Benjamin Coriat, and Danièle Leborgne, it addresses the fundamental dynamic of change in late capitalist society. The importance of this school has grown because it provides a powerful alternative to a narrowly focused marxism, with its excessively deterministic emphasis on class. It also transcends the empty neo-classical economic belief that individuals pursuing self-interest will produce socially optimal outcomes.

The most original contribution the Régulation theorists have made so far is their insight into the importance of institutional ordering to explain the strength and viability of democratic societies in the postwar decades. In North America, Europe, and Japan, the growth and long-term stability of Western capitalist societies required major reforms that went beyond the establishment of Keynesian social income programs for those at the bottom of the income pyramid. The reform which radically changed industrial society was the new status and importance accorded to collective bargaining in the late 1940s. The modern collective bargaining regime created, in effect, an institution that would become a wage-setting mechanism for the entire society. It accorded workers and unions a new standing in the workplace and increased influence on state policy-making.

In theoretical terms, the regularization of collective bargaining in North America as well as Western Europe meant that while the arrangements and the policies varied from country to country, as a general principal wages would no longer be determined mainly by the market. Instead, wages would be loosely linked to productivity growth. This gave Western industrial society the possibility of achieving both rapid economic growth and social stability in the workplace, with far-reaching consequences for both consumers and for the industrial working class whose class identity and consumer interest would for the first time be inextricably linked. The spread of collective bargaining resulted in an upward pressure on wages, thus ensuring a higher standard of living for those in the core sectors of the economy as well as for those in other sectors benefiting from the flow-on effects. This wage revolution was pivotal in changing the material well-being of the industrial working class; within a generation it would transform consumption norms and enable workers to buy homes, own cars, and support mass production industries through mass consumption.

This profound change from competitive to regulated capitalism was a revolution but not of the kind that marxists had predicted. True, the state became an instrument for correcting the market and setting society's social and economic agenda, but there was no revolution of a more fundamental kind. Markets were only administered by governments. Wages were taken out of competition but wealth was not noticeably redistributed. Private property remained the basis of the transformed order. Most critically, the economy rested in private hands. In the final analysis, Keynesian policies were not designed to address the growing distributional inequality between regions or between classes.

Since the late 1960s this sytem of institutional ordering has been fundamentally challenged due to the deep-seated changes occurring in labour markets, trade, state policy, and industrial organization. This is what the Régulationnistes describe as the post-Fordist crisis. This also constitues the sub-text to the present volume: the demise of full-employment capitalism and the state's new role in economic life.

The search for a new institutional order between the state and the market is now at the centre of the policy agenda of governments. The Mulroney government sees Canada's economic salvation in the release of unfettered market forces. The idea is that markets have some natural form, that their structure and rules of operation define themselves most efficiently when left to their own dynamic. This newfound belief in market liberalism now grips the 1990s in the way Keynesian policies stirred the imagination of postwar policy-makers. But, like any creed, it is difficult to separate fact from fiction.

Almost a half century ago, Karl Polanyi definitively settled the historical claim that a laissez-faire market system could ever be spontaneous. With characteristic eloquence, he wrote: "The road to the free market was opened and kept open by an enormous increase in continuous, centrally organized and controlled interventionism ... Laissez-faire was planned; planning was not."[8] This volume shares his well-grounded scepticism, contending instead that markets continue to exist only as the product of active social construction through the interaction of business, the state, and working men and women. Markets for labour, capital, land, commodities, and services are grounded not in the invariable laws of supply and demand but in institutions that have their own logic and history. Similarly, outcomes are determined not by faceless actors but, in a myriad of ways, by the political and economic interaction between the corporate élite, organized labour, and the state. In a world dominated by the three hundred leading banks and industrial transnationals, the theory of the firm has given way to power politics and mega-economics. Freedom of choice means little more than individual market freedom for the chosen few.

THE MARKET: TOWARD A NEW THEORETICAL PERSPECTIVE

This volume takes its theoretical point of departure from the essential insight of the late C.B. Macpherson, one of Canada's most original political theorists and thinkers. He saw the historical evolution of the market from the seventeenth to the nineteenth century as a gigantic mechanism of social order and social dislocation which, as such, was capable of transforming the most fundamental of economic arrangements no less than the whole of civil society. Everything would be subjected to this vast, fully extended universalization of the commodity-form.

Today, the market is once again the primary institution shaping history from East to West, and it is assumed that market freedom can be reconciled with individual choice and political pluralism. This tension between market liberalism and a revolutionized society is always problematic and, in the end, unmanageable. The deeper reality of market-driven change is that the continuing drive for maximizing accumulation, whether for the few or in the name of national development, leads step by step to a crippling social dependency for the many. Liberal society has no way to redress the fundamental inequality in the transfer of power and wealth that results when private property is made sovereign. Thus at the centre of even a reborn, postmodern liberal society there remains a chronic, deeply rooted instability. Market rights work to suppress the democratic and libertarian possibilities inherent in liberalism. In Macpherson's words, a resurgent market liberalism has no way "to reconcile the claims of the free market with the claims of the whole mass of individuals for some kind of equality."[9] It is this challenge that Canada has to face. Dramatically new political and economic circumstances confront the industrial working class in late capitalist society. It is these emerging realities that are front and centre in this volume.

Part One examines what is different about the world economy and Canada's macro-economic performance as it enters the 1990s. Drache and Gertler show that a policy regime of trade-led development constitutes a fundamental rupture with Keynesian policies. Society's agenda is now to be set by its narrow pursuit of commercial interests. Donner reviews Canadian macro-economic policy and the overall performance of the economy. He makes the central point that the Canadian economy never fully recovered from the 1982 recession and, more importantly, that there has been a significant redistribution of wealth within Canadian society. The high interest rates and tough new measures in the labour market have had an unprecedented impact on wages and income level of workers everywhere in Canada. As Donner argues, monetarism in Canada was not only a way to control inflation but, more fundamentally, to create a new regime of capital accumulation. Increased capital mobility is the most visible sign that the trade in money, currency and services drives the global economy. The consequences of these changes in political economy have forced a radical change in Canadian economic and social policy.

Part Two addresses the dominance of Canada–United States relations in determining the path of future Canadian economic development. Under Trudeau, Canadian state policy vacillated between pursuing stronger links to the United States business cycle and charting a more independent and multilateral course. Clarkson contends that Canada has embarked unambiguously on the former course, signifying a dramatic break with the past. This has far-reaching implications for Canadian society, already deeply marked by regional and social inequalities. Mandel analyses the importance of the Charter of Rights as a new form of state power that will be used increasingly by Ottawa to enhance business power, socially and economically. It creates an American-style legal system that enshrines process over outcome and favours private sector rights over public accountability. Therefore it is also necessary to determine to what degree the growing asymmetry in power between Canada and the United States will create severe problems of adjustment for industries, regions, and communities. Cohen challenges the conventional wisdom that trade theory supports a non-interventionist state. The other side of this coin is the growing importance of regional trade blocs such as Europe 1992 and the free trade agreement. Comparing these two examples, Wilkinson demonstrates that these institutions are not simply economic entities but a political means to structure markets. In his detailed comparison he reveals that while these prototype agreements may have the same goals, they are very different mechanisms for achieving market reorganization. On this point, Europe 1992 has clearer safeguards for national autonomy than the North American variant.

Part Three focuses on the industrial restructuring that the global economy has already brought about in key economic sectors. Will firms reinvest their earnings in technologically advanced work processes or milk existing plant capacity while diverting profits elsewhere? Will they operate from a single establishment, as multiple establishments within Canada, or as a multinational enterprise with branches in Canada or elsewhere? Finally, businesses must choose between a co-operative approach to labour relations, in which they invest in the future potential of their workforce, and a more traditional adversarial or paternalistic employment relation.

What becomes clear in the case of two dominant, mature industries – automobiles (Holmes) and steel (Masi) – is that the significant restructuring experienced here has been facilitated by the state, which has successfully intervened to reshape market forces. Furthermore, while both sectors can be described in conventional terms as "success" stories, it is clear that success has been achieved at considerable cost to former and current workers. Some of this is due to a new wave of foreign direct investment from Japan (Morris), and nowhere are the contradictions and conflicts inherent in contemporary capital accumulation more evident than in those Canadian industries experiencing significant "Japanization." Canadians have long dreamed of moving their economy away from traditional sectors such as resource exploitation and mature manufacturing. As Phillips demonstrates, Canada now faces a major crisis in many of its resource sectors because of corporate Canada's failure to participate in a worldwide restructuring of production methods.

Part Four examines the consequences of restructuring for people, their work experience and social programs. From their respective viewpoints Drache and Mahon address the proposition that workers no longer have the option as to whether to embrace technological change. The key question is rather how labour can intervene to influence decisions made about new work processes, social policy, and macro-economic management. Unions have to devise new strategies to combat management's drive to expand its powers. In this regard, Bakker warns that employers' heightened pursuit of flexibility in the workplace is a threat to the existing levels of net public expenditures that benefit workers – the social wage. Also under attack has been the publicly owned corporation, a key instrument of Canadian economic development. As Laux emphasizes, the outcomes of private-led development will not be as equitably distributed as the returns from state-owned enterprises.

The spectre of skewed and uneven growth patterns raises the issue addressed in Part Five: should the state actively encourage the further coalescence of economic power within the hands of fewer and fewer private actors, or should it promote more democratic forms of economic activity? Similarly, will the state see global competition as a mandate to pursue narrow economic efficiency at all costs, or will fairness and distributional concerns receive their due? This is the question addressed by Myles's analysis of alternative scenarios for a post-industrial society. In a low-wage economy, the working poor subsidize managers' incomes and owners' profits. In a high-wage economy, workers share in productivity gains. In Cox's far-reaching analysis of the choices facing industrial nations, countries have to choose between two fundamentally different macro-economic strategies in the global economy. The hyperliberal approach defines a country's competitiveness in terms of corporate needs and market power. The alternative to a return to nineteenth-century laissez-faire policies is the state-capitalist approach. This strategy is premised on the idea that states intervene not only to enhance a nation's industries but also to link productive effort to protecting the welfare of the principal social groups. Industrial policy could be one of the key instruments to manage the restructuring of the Canadian economy and its constituent industries. Gertler stresses that Canadian business has, left to its own devices, performed poorly in developing indigenous high-technology industry. He reviews the options for a Canadian industrial policy, calling for a significant reorientation of current practice.

With global specialization and trade bound to intensify, risk of greater environmental degradation becomes heightened. Thus in the final section Tester makes a powerful case that existing models of development must be rejected if countries are to take seriously the search for a "dark green" alternative. Rotstein and Duncan show how communities and individuals can reassert some degree of monetary insulation from worldwide forces by turning to non-money alternatives. Finally, Cameron challenges the traditional distinction between a productive private sector and an unproductive public sector, arguing for a rethinking of the relationship between states and markets in a way which empowers society's subordinate groups. Like Rotstein and Duncan, Cameron's policy agenda proposes an expanded role for institutions in the popular sector that operate on a cost-recovery rather than profit-maximizing basis.

In editing this book, it is our hope that those who read it will become convinced that liberalized trade and the harsh winds of global change will destabilize societies, rather than bring prosperity to all. Indeed, these forces will accentuate the differences that already divide us. To believe otherwise is to subscribe to the illusion of export-led growth and insatiable markets. Alternatives do exist but more are needed to build a stronger, more democratic Canada for the 1990s and beyond. Governments are faced with a basic choice: either to create a macro-economic climate that simply lets business decide when and where to invest, or to promote economic renewal by means of active, co-ordinated policy management and a national consensus. Countries must choose between the confrontational hyper-liberal policies of a Reagan or Thatcher, and building a new national consensus to manage the adjustment process in a power-driven world economy.

Developing an industrial policy that is not simply market-driven is a daunting task. The recent New Democratic Party election victory in Ontario presents that government with an unparalleled opportunity to create Canada's first coherent industrial strategy worthy of the name. In doing so, they may wish to draw on the contributions to this volume for the analysis of how governments have failed in the past, and the ideas for future action. In particular, they will want to consider the complex relationship between productive efficiency and social policy. While the Rae government's ability to implement its social welfare agenda may ultimately depend on the productivity of the economy, the very foundations of a productive economy must be seen to rest upon just and equitable policies for labour markets and income redistribution.

D.D. and M.G.
Toronto, October 1990.

NOTES

1 There is an immense literature on the impact of the global economy. For a recent introductory analysis, see Susan Strange, *States and Markets* (Oxford: Basil Blackwell 1988).

2 *Financial Post*, Special Issue, "Free Trade Pact One Year Later," 2 January 1990. While estimates of the actual number of jobs lost vary considerably, there is general agreement that the extent and number of jobs lost in auto, resource, electrical, and food-processing industries was beyond anything that either business or labour could have predicted.

3 Ontario, Ministry of Industry, Trade and Technology, unpublished special study, November 1989.

4 For a useful study of the high cost of adopting new process technology, see D.G. McFetridge, *The Distinguishing Characteristics of Users of New Manufacturing Technologies* (Ontario: Ministry of Industry, Trade and Technology February 1989).

5 Canadian Labour Market and Productivity Centre, "Review of Education and Training in Canada," Spring 1989.

6 See Daniel Drache and Wallace Clement, eds., *The New Practical Guide to Canadian Political Economy* (Toronto: James Lorimer 1985); Wallace Clement and Glen Williams, *The New Canadian Political Economy* (Montreal: McGill-Queen's University Press 1988).

7 Gérard Boismenu et Daniel Drache, eds., *Politique et Régulation* (Montréal: Méridien 1990).

8 Karl Polanyi, *The Great Transformation* (Boston: Beacon Hill Press 1957), 140.

9 C.B. Macpherson, *Democratic Theory: Essays in Retrieval* (Oxford: Oxford University Press 1973), 173.

PART ONE

The End of the Remarkable Eighties: Crisis and Change

1 The World Economy and the Nation-State: The New International Order

DANIEL DRACHE AND MERIC S. GERTLER

The drive to compete has forced all industrial states to take bold initiatives to create a new framework of public policy. The free trade agreement (FTA) is but one symptom of this search for alternatives; Europe 1992 is another. Both are typical of the new policy environment pushing states to adopt market-based and trade-centred policies in the 1990s.

With corporate concentration on the rise, business élites have welcomed the prospects of unleashing the market on a world scale. They want new rights to invest and divest with minimal restriction and establish their businesses without regard to borders.[1] Where existing programs are perceived as barriers to business, they have to be modified so as not to impede the trade in goods and services. If present standards stand in the way of harmonization and competitiveness, new standards have to be imposed, even if it means overturning existing national programs. Most importantly, firms and states are under pressure to institute greater flexibility in wages and benefits by deregulating the labour market. Wages are no longer to be linked to productivity growth through collective bargaining, but allowed to drop to their so-called natural level.[2]

These changes in the social and economic order have powerful distributional consequences for both workers and states. As firms strive to enhance their global competitiveness, they are under pressure to adopt productivity-enhancing technologies. Often this involves labour-shedding, a slowdown in the growth of employment, and a reinforcement of management's power over the workplace. As business increasingly looks outward, the resulting transformations will feed back to produce even larger economic impacts. Pushed by technological innovation, the increase in trade in goods and services has already affected the way institutions and businesses operate.

What happens to Canada as it throws its markets wide open? What choices does it have in striving to maximize its economic strengths? What kinds of policy instruments create economic leverage in the global economy? How will existing employment prospects, economic productivity, and industrial organization be reshaped by private initiative reinforced by state policy?

The answers to these questions are anything but simple. Yet one fact is clear. In a trade-dominant world, the pursuit of "insatiable export markets" remains a dangerous illusion. Under a system of free trade, complying countries are required to open their markets regardless of the cost to their industrial competitiveness and despite what other countries may actually be doing. This kind of political economy is based on a country having a competitive price advantage. Driving down costs becomes the single most important priority for business and the state. With many industries past their prime, a regime of pure trade liberalization is an unrealistic goal for most Western capitalist governments.[3] But it is, nonetheless, the kind of myth that governments and business find sufficiently compelling to justify rejecting the existing framework of state macro-policy of the last three decades.

THE DEMISE OF FULL-EMPLOYMENT
CAPITALISM

Western democracies used to be committed to a macro-policy framework characterized by a virtuous circle of economic growth based on price stability, a surplus on the current account, a rapidly expanding economy, and a corresponding growth in productivity and real wages.[4] Full employment capitalism, the term coined by Kalecki, was synonymous with a commitment to manage the economy in the full sense of the term. Under these conditions, the state would secure full employment by the cumulative impact of the government's fiscal, monetary, and labour market policies. The vision was revolutionary. No longer would the market have the sole, or even principal, responsibility to allocate resources. In its place, the state would direct investment, subsidize consumption, manage trade within a broad commitment to gradually lower tariffs, organize the labour market in order to ensure stable growth, and increase the general standard of welfare for all.[5]

Kalecki was far-sighted. Keynesian planning heralded an era in which capitalism was no longer subject to the crises of overproduction and underconsumption which had brought the capitalist economies to a standstill in the Great Depression. In this vision, the role of the state was to be pivotal. Keynesian policies were aimed at controlling the level of unemployment and the distribution of income by deepening the national market by a judicious use of managed trade and a commitment to the gradual lowering of tariffs worldwide. Not only would it regulate the macro-side of the economy by creating social programs to act as income safety nets; it would also channel and manage social conflict, particularly in the workplace, through a whole variety of institutions. It is these institutional forms of workplace control linked to a new social structure of accumulation and a much-deepened norm of consumption that ultimately transformed the social fabric of industrial societies, enabling capitalism to experience three decades of unparalleled growth and prosperity.

In fact, postwar reality was more complex than Kalecki's theory allowed. Western countries without exception repeatedly failed to overcome the harsh recessionary effects of persistent economic crises. Yet crude competitive capitalism was a thing of the past; a transformation had occurred. Though many of these changes today seem like mild reforms, structurally capitalist society had been permanently altered at a deep level. A new economic dynamic had been unleashed that provided Western industrial democracies with the means to manage wholesale adjustment and change. While trade would be essential, given the volatility of the international economy, the need to export could not be allowed to set the agenda for industrial society. Rather, it was to be only part of the ensemble of state policy instruments. The more important dimension would be to deepen the domestic market by tariffs or other elements of an industrial strategy and to strengthen consumer demand largely by the spread of collective bargaining. To the extent that countries would open up their borders to international competition, trade would only be a logical extension of domestic production needs.

The Paris-based Régulation school of political economy helps illuminate the complex link between the volatile nature of the world-trading system and the need to maintain high levels of domestic demand in a country's mass production industries.[6] It offers a tightly argued explanation of why foreign markets have proved neither the only nor the best way to organize production or the work process. The reason why growth cannot be solely externally driven had its origins in the Great Depression, which eventually forced industrial nations to strike a different balance between the international economy, domestic growth, and capital accumulation.[7]

For these theorists, laissez-faire capitalism was based on the principle of comparative advantage that assumed that growth is largely driven through trade and specialization rather than internally generated. In the three decades prior to World War One, the volume of world trade had grown by an average of 40 per cent per decade. But by the thirties, it had dropped drastically to 14 per cent per decade.[8] The unstable nature of global markets had triggered the collapse of capitalism in the 1930s as goods went without buyers. The world trading system had been brought to its knees by beggar-thy-neighbour policies and the wholesale dumping of goods by the leading industrial nations when the United States raised its tariffs by 60 per cent. These actions were not motivated by the desire to nurture and protect infant domestic industries, but were largely predatory. Nevertheless, they failed to rescue domestic industries from the dramatic fall in domestic spending.[9] This kind of retaliation inevitably encouraged reciprocal action by other countries on an unprecedented scale. The resurgence of this short-sighted, bellicose form of protectionism stopped the wheels of international commerce and precipitated an ever deeper crisis of underconsumption brought about by falling wages. The reasons are important to recall because they foreshadow the kinds of changes that governments in industrial countries would be forced eventually to introduce when World War Two ended.

In the twenties and thirties in most Western countries, wages in the mass production industries did not keep pace with the growth in productivity. Employers regularly cut the wages of their workforce, as few industrial unions in the smokestack industries had won the right to bargain collectively. Thus, the gap between productivity and real earnings widened in the twenties and worsened by the mid-thirties. With demand fluctuating, a worker's ability to buy essential goods and services was limited and consumption norms were narrowly based.[10] In the United States, for instance, total income in the form of profits, interest, and rent soared by over 45 per cent during the decade of the twenties. By comparison the real wages of factory workers barely grew by 2 per cent. This contrasted with the top 1 per cent of the population which increased its share of the national income from 12 to 18 per cent while the top 5 per cent saw its wealth increase from 24 to 33.5 per cent.[11]

This chronic structural weakness of competitive capitalism was overcome, in large measure, after World War Two when liberal democratic governments took the unprecedented step of linking the organization of the workplace to the macro-economic management of the economy. The most important feature of the new institutional ordering was the legal recognition of unions and the spread of collective bargaining,[12] which would serve as a wage-setting mechanism for both the organized and the unorganized. More than any other single factor, the spread of modern collective bargaining schemes in the smokestack industries transformed existing consumption norms. Regular wage increases meant that workers would become consumers, and mass consumption would fuel internally generated growth by creating jobs and expanding domestic industries. The consequences of this Fordist regime of collective bargaining were enormous for industrial society. With collective bargaining creating constant pressure on employers to be efficient, industries could no longer rely on low wage costs for their comparative advantage. In the scheme of things, it required countries to become competitive by constantly innovating and using the stick of higher wages to force industry and the state to adopt industrial strategies.

The success of these institutional arrangements can be seen in the fact that businesses in the industrial world were prepared to tolerate these new rights in return for a profitable environment. By 1973 output in the advanced capitalist countries was 180 per cent higher than in 1950. Under this sytem of managed capitalism, more was produced in this quarter-century than in any comparable previous period in human history. Thanks to its increased power at the bargaining table and its strike power, labour saw its living standards rise dramatically as the growth in real wages and social benefits made people twice as well off as their parents and four times as well off as their grandparents. The secret of labour's new standing was that under the institutional arrangements of regulated capitalism, wages, profits, and productivity rose in parallel fashion until the mid-seventies when this model of accumulation peaked as growth slowed and commodity prices fell.[13]

THE THEORY OF LAISSEZ-FAIRE STATE POLICY IN THE 1990S: BRINGING THE STATE BACK IN

The prospect of relying on trade rather than deepening domestic demand as the foundation of public policy for industrial societies signals the end of Fordism in its present form, as defined by the Régulation approach. As such it constitutes a definitive break with the economic growth model of the last three decades. As states seek to reduce barriers to investment as the principal way to create an environment favourable for world commerce, the return to the raw principles of neo-liberalism requires a realignment of labour markets to better fit the new regime of accumulation. Market forces are to be free to pursue their immediate private interests subject only to minimal government regulation. In theory, the stated aim of market liberalism is to confine the state to a rigid political shell within which "flexible market forces will generate the social order."[14] In fact, the pressures on the state are more complex.

Keynesian and Fordist policies always needed and indeed depended on the state to act autonomously in the national interest. The state had to have sufficient room to manoeuvre in order to keep in check rogue employers who did not see the virtue in social safety nets and rising income levels. Neo-liberal governments, committed to competitiveness at all costs, now want to intervene across a broad front. They want to be simultaneously more non-interventionist *and* instrumentalist. This apparent contradiction stems from the deep-seated conflicting demands inherent in a trade-driven model of development.

Competition, be it national or international in origin, has inevitably harsh and dislocative effects. This is particularly the case given the volatile nature of international financial markets and the dynamics of global commerce. In a post-Keynesian world, the rules of commerce have been so dramatically altered by governments to facilitate capital's freedom to invest and divest without regard to national boundaries. This had made the accumulation process highly unstable and unpredictable. In the current world economy, capital movements, exchange rates, and credit flows operate almost independently from the flow of goods and services. Thus all countries are subject to inflationary price movements, as capital movements criss-cross the globe looking for short-term speculative investment.

On the goods side of the economy, adjustment problems are no less severe. As countries trade more, this will tend to accentuate their sectoral specialization and, inevitably, there will be winners and losers. Industries that are more competitive will expand and gain new markets; others will suffer declining markets, layoffs, plant shutdowns, and face an uncertain future. Thus, the effects of trade liberalization are inevitably uneven, varying across industries and regions and between firms. Herein lies a difficult truth for policy-makers. In terms of macroeconomic policy, even when a country is exporting more by volume and by value, it is not necessarily winning new markets, producing goods with higher value-added or becoming more competitive by selling semi-processed resources and sub-component parts internationally. Thus, for many countries, the long-term effect of a trade strategy based on comparative advantage is to lock a country into a trade pattern that reinforces the structural weaknesses of the economy regionally, between industries and between workers. This is certainly the case for the United States, which is a powerful competitor globally.

Contrary to the promise of globalization and open markets, increased competition has had devastating effects on American industries. In the early eighties more than a million and half jobs have been lost from the manufacturing sector. Under the banner of increased capital mobility, corporations are able to shift production from one region or country to the next. In a world with fewer classical trade barriers, increased capital mobility gives corporations the leverage to control future investment. Countries increasingly behave like unions forced to bargain with powerful groups of capital to attract investment and prevent widespread disinvestment in a nation's industrial capacity. In theory, "disinvestment is supposed to free capital and labour from relatively unproductive uses in order to put them to work in more productive ones."[15] In fact, this is not happening. Corporations are milking their older facilities as "cash cows," letting them deteriorate until they are no longer seen as profitable in light of the larger corporate strategy.[16]

This kind of structural change in the process of capital accumulation gives the corporate élite vast power to demand concessions and other forms of direct capital subsidies. In such an environment, it is global capital which sets the market signals that establish product prices, wage rates, and returns on investment. With capital ever more mobile, the old pressure to compete by upgrading domestic industry through innovation and application of new technologies is greatly reduced. In addition, business can move offshore or tie investment decisions not to the adoption of best-practice technology but to tax credit schemes and other forms of short-term speculative activity. Thus, in a situation where the nation-state badly needs a hedge against increasing competition, in the absence of co-ordinated industrial planning, the state has less and less autonomy. Competitiveness becomes defined narrowly on the terrain staked by private sector actors, who want a state strong enough to discipline the workforce and constrain wage movements but one which is increasingly liberal in providing industrial subsidies, tax concessions, and tax expenditures. In such an economic climate, in the words of Stephen Clarkson, "governments are forced to reorient their whole approach to governing." For the foreseeable future they will be at the mercy of the market, without the benefit of a secure national base.

As countries find it increasingly difficult to accept at face value the idea that world-scale economic forces transcend the nation-state, it becomes imperative that policy-makers provide escape valves in order to pursue trade liberalization strategies. Accordingly, trade-led development is only viable as a macro-policy if it makes allowances for industries seriously injured by tariff reduction or the use of non-tariff barriers.[17] In these conditions, the state will be called upon to find ways to compensate industries and provide transitional support for workers who are victims of the global economy.

For the 1990s, industrial policy debates will return with a vengeance to the top of the economic policy agenda as countries face the decision to shape or be shaped by markets.

INDUSTRIAL POLICY IN THE NINETIES

For states that want to exploit global change as opportunity, many will adopt active strategies of the kind used with great success by such diverse countries as France, Sweden, Germany, and Japan. All have relied on industrial policies to restructure their industries in ways that pursue new market opportunities by creating more efficient plants, better technology, low-cost pools of risk capital, and a highly trained workforce. Sweden has pioneered one approach in terms of its labour market and industrial strategy. Successive governments have accepted the argument of Sweden's powerful trade union movement that trade-led policies accelerate the rate of structural change and therefore ought to be rejected. Thus the Swedish state has fashioned its own variant of export-led growth. It has combined trade liberalization with generous and comprehensive adjustment policies for workers, communities, and industries. These policies are devised to overcome firm- or sector-specific job skills, and the costs associated with job search and change in a geographically extensive economy. By mounting extensive worker retraining programs, labour relocation assistance policies, and even capital grants and subsidies to speed the flow of investment into new enterprise, the Swedish state shoulders much of the costs to the benefit of private business. But even this so-called forward-looking policy of industrial restructuring is under attack today from business and from sectors of the labour movement.[18]

In contrast to the carefully planned Swedish approach, other governments such as the United States also accept the need to act as buffers between the nation-state and the global economy, but the scope of their intervention is qualitatively and quantitatively different. The American strategy uses protective action to bolster market forces.[19] In the quest to be competitive, the hyper-liberal state's role is largely limited to those actions that grease the wheels of private market-led industrial change. Key policy support is to go to business rather than to aid workers and their communities hurt by a system of liberalized trade. Despite the neo-liberal rhetoric about the primacy of market forces, the state decides when it is necessary to move people and resources out of industries which it deems are no longer socially necessary or economically viable. Sick industries are usually allowed to die but, as Reagan's bail-out of Chrysler demonstrated, American governments are committed to protecting core industries and firms from what they construe to be unfair trade practices abroad. To this end the United States has pioneered this kind of targeted relief, and now has an arsenal of trade instruments and statutes to minimize the dislocation caused by international competition. It has effected micro-change at the industry level by a combination of policies, including special tax breaks, low-interest loans, rationalization of product lines, and inter-firm co-ordination. Most recently, the US Department of Defense has gone much further and set in motion a plan which, many observers believe, is the forerunner of a more sophisticated industrial policy: it has organized a cartel of micro-chip producers in apparent violation of American anti-trust law, citing national security reasons for its dramatic intervention. Adjustment assistance is also backed up by tough, far-reaching us trade laws to harass foreign competitors in the American market. In the name of promoting trade liberalization, these statutes provide for escape clause relief, voluntary restraint agreements, orderly marketing accords, or unabashed protectionist measures to protect the jobs and industry of trade-battered communities.[20]

In sum, then, states that want to exploit global change for their benefit must have a broad range of measures from which to choose. While the spectrum of choice runs the gamut from left to right, what these responses share is a simple idea: no country can afford to give more than it is getting from a more open system of international commerce. They cannot allow their firms to compete completely unprotected. Countries that want to position themselves better in the world market have to make strategic choices that conflict with the bare-knuckled logic of the free trade doctrine.

NEW DANGERS AND NEW CHALLENGES FOR CANADA

The tensions and contradictions of a return to market liberalism create new pressures on Canada with its open economy, fragmented political system, and an economic élite overtly international in its aspirations.[21] With their export-oriented policies, Canadian governments have always been attracted to the older idea of competitive capitalism as the appropriate macro-policy for growth. Now that Ottawa has committed itself to removing the remaining tariff walls, the dislocation and pressures are likely to be acute. More and more the state is leaving it up to Canadian-owned industry to restructure and acquire sophisticated means of production, this despite the fact that Canadian industry, dominated by small firms, does not have the funds to restructure, let alone be at the cutting edge of technological innovation. Overall investment growth remains volatile and uneven. If these trends continue into the 1990s, Canadian industry is not going to remain competitive in an increasingly trade-oriented world. Therefore Canada must consciously formulate a strategy to deal with three emerging challenges: growing regional disparities, Quebec's nationalist aspirations, and the erosion of Canada's social welfare system.

Province-Building in a Continental Economy

The first challenge is to confront regional inequalities which have been on the rise throughout the 1980s. Economic growth has become more unbalanced and, not surprisingly, the benefits from greater trade dependency on the United States are not being shared equally. Ontario registered the strongest productivity growth and had the lowest rate of unemployment. Quebec turned in the second-best performance in terms of its productivity growth but faced double-digit unemployment for the entire decade. Both British Columbia and the prairies with their resource-based industries have been subject to the worst effects of the boom/bust export-led growth cycle. Unemployment rates there are almost twice as high as they were at the beginning of the decade, while productivity growth has been slowed to a standstill and, in the case of British Columbia, has even been negative. Strikingly, Quebec appears as the big loser in the race to become more competitive. Despite a strong recovery, its workforce suffered one of the largest declines in real wages in Canada between 1980 and 1988.[22]

These kinds of economic indicators point to a more fundamental problem. The pursuit of export markets also brings about widespread reorganization of industry. Frequently, this will lead to significant production and employment losses.[23] Industry is forced to restructure at a time when a combination of high interest rates and a soaring Canadian dollar has increased the uncertainty on Canada's trade front. For Canadian-owned firms, the bilateral trade agreement established to confront and help resolve trade problems between the two countries has had the opposite effect. Small firms have had to compete directly with already much larger American firms which, at least on price terms, hold a substantive advantage. But the largest impact of the FTA still has yet to be felt in its entirety.

In recent years some Canadian-owned operations, such as Dominion Textiles, Bombardier, and Northern Telecom, have become global competitors. But these Canadian giants are now producing less in Canada and employing fewer Canadians than ever before. Northern Telecom is typical. Sixty-five per cent of its revenues come from its American operations. Fifteen years earlier two-thirds of its sales were made in Canada. Employment patterns have followed the same course. The Northern Telecom production workforce at its Brampton plant has been cut from four thousand to twenty-four hundred workers. Future employment growth is expected to occur in the United States as a result of expansion and acquisitions there.[24] Significantly, this growth will increasingly include R&D personnel. The direction is clear. Canadian multinationals want to be thought of as American multinationals and relocate in the American market to the extent that it is necessary and feasible.

The out-migration of Canadian multinationals has become a crucial factor destabilizing the adjustment process at the regional level. Yet despite the celebrated examples just cited, most Canadian firms are not going global. This is not the route that reordering and restructuring has taken. By contrast, the FTA has given new impetus for many American firms to re-examine their commitment to having a Canadian manufacturing operation. Already Inglis, Bendix Safety, Gerber, Fiberglas, Galtco, Consumer's Glass, Burlington Carpet, Sklar-Peppler, Outboard Marine, Toro, Bovie, Kimberly Clark, Campbell Soup, Gilette, Schlegel, Leviton, Coleman, United Maple, ITW, Picker, Hartz, Kelsey-Hayes, Ivaco, and Sysco have announced plant closures.

With capital increasingly free to move across national boundaries, foreign investment is particularly threatening for Ontario, which has the largest number of branch plants in Canada. In recent years, there has been over twenty-five hundred takeovers in Canada. Ontario faces the sharpest adjustment, yet neither the Ontario nor federal governments have adequate adjustment programs in place.

Canadian industries nationally and regionally face a troubled future. It is estimated that 80 per cent of foreign subsidiaries in Canada have no global mandate permitting specialized product design, production and exporting within an internationally organized spatial division of labour. Branch plants spend half as much as do domestic firms on research and development. American subsidiaries in the labour-intensive industries are not innovative or technologically driven. Two-thirds of foreign subsidiaries have no exports at all from Canada. Clearly, these "structured pygmies" never will be world-class competitors. Nonetheless, for many American corporations their branch plants perform a key role of buying sub-components and sub-assemblies from the parent organization. It is estimated that, in recent times, 56 per cent of Canadian exports was in the form of tied trade between entities of American multinationals. In reality this figure understates the case. According to American estimates, 75 per cent of their exports to the three hundred largest companies in Canada originates from the demand generated by Canadian subsidiaries.[25]

This kind of trade-distorting relationship dramatically reduces regional or provincial possibilities for developing strong competitive industries. Given the highly integrated relationship between parent and subsidiary firms, the crucial question is whether the branch plants will receive the green light from their American corporate parent for new investment and export mandates – in other words, will such corporations restructure their operations to integrate Canadian plants into an internationally defined division of labour? The evidence thus far is not very encouraging. Despite the announced shutdowns of many American-owned branch plants, no major influx of foreign firms establishing new or expanded plants as part of a restructured corporate division of labour has been documented.[26] Indeed, while Holmes (this volume) shows how such a new spatial division of labour emerged within the automotive sector, he underscores the *managed* nature of the agreement which led to this state of affairs – a circumstance that does not exist in other sectors.

QUEBEC NATIONALISM VERSUS CANADIAN NATIONALISM

For Quebec, the new political order of laissez-faire poses a second, equally difficult, challenge. In a tightly knit interdependent world, it needs to rely on greater state intervention both to protect its industries and to modernize them. Yet the act of creating a North American-wide market will have the reverse effect and impose new and far-reaching restrictions on Quebec's fundamental policy goals to safeguard its language, culture, and economy from assimilationist pressures. Canadian federalism has given provincial governments substantial control over their economic development. For Quebec, this has meant using the state to develop programs which discriminate in favour of Quebec capital against out-of-province or out-of-country firms. Quebec, like other governments, has exercised these powers extensively to promote domestic natural resource industries by a variety of programs, including tax rebates, processing allowances, and special taxes on the export of unprocessed resources. Hydro Québec has played a particularly dynamic role in promoting manufacturing companies in Quebec. It has paid up to 10 per cent more for equipment from Quebec firms. But despite these "very good results" in attracting business to the province, these businesses have tended to be assembly operations.[27] According to a Hydro Québec vice-president, the state enterprise plans to use its $48 billion capital spending program over the next ten years to promote full-scale indigenous companies.

In the important area of investment, Quebec has been a leader promoting the growth of home-grown firms and financial institutions mainly through the Quebec Stock Savings Plan and the Caisse de Dépôt et Placements. With assets of over $32 billion, Quebec governments have relied on the Caisse to attract new industry to the province and/or create an indigenous class of entrepreneurs. Over two decades, it has grown to become the forty-seventh largest investment institution in North America.[28]

Prior to the signing of the FTA, these programs were not regarded as constituting an unfair trade subsidy. Rather, Quebec's élites justified support for local enterprise on the grounds that Quebec's developmental needs could not be met by federal policies. For that important reason,

Quebec's non-tariff barriers were not seen as distortions to the market in Canada but, rather, a necessary correction against the economic bias of federal programs which frequently favoured Ontario-based manufacturing at the expense of the rest of the country.[29] It is doubtful, for instance, that Hydro Québec will be allowed indefinitely to shape the market to the benefit of Quebec-based firms without running afoul of the many provisions of the FTA designed to rein in interventions by Canadian governments.

As a front-line supporter of the FTA, Quebec has made itself more vulnerable to American trade law. Quebec business believed that it had come of age – that it no longer needed the degree of state support that it had received in the past. Bourassa accepted Mulroney's assurance that Quebec's special language legislation would not be discussed in the negotiations. But a reading of the FTA shows that Quebec gave up more, and in vital areas, than it got. As a matter of public policy, Quebec's authority to use its powerful instruments of state-led development will be much reduced. This will unquestionably limit the ability of the Quebec government to manage the economy strictly in its national interest. More importantly, the power of American trade law will be brought to bear directly on Quebec's institutions with respect to the creation of new state enterprises, nationalization, or screening of foreign takeovers.

Bourassa has accepted the logic implicit in the FTA, which is to acknowledge the primacy of economics over political or cultural objectives. This can be seen from key articles in the agreement. Article 103 diminishes provincial authority to regulate provincial and local economic activity. Article 2010, dealing with the power of public monopolies, also curbs provincial powers to create state enterprises in the area of public housing, non-profit services such as day care, resource management and cultural policy. Article 1603 prevents a Quebec government from demanding performance requirements, job or production guarantees from US firms. Further, any control that Quebec introduces must not be "a disguised restriction on trade" when it legislates to correct a market failure, alleviate regional disparities, or regulate foreign ownership. The magnitude of this kind of provision is intended to enhance corporate freedom and sharply reduce the ability of future Quebec governments to intervene in the management of the economy broadly defined.

With more tariff-protected industry than in any other part of Canada, Quebec will suffer the most economically from a regime of trade-led development. While over 85 per cent of Canada's exports to the United States are already tariff-free, major Quebec industries such as textiles, apparel, leather products, and footwear enjoy tariff protection three to four times the national average. These industries will experience severe adjustment problems and labour-shedding.[30] In addition, many of Quebec's branch plants are less efficient than Ontario's, suggesting that Quebec's plants will lose out as their parent operations rationalize North American production. For the one-quarter of Quebec workers who are presently employed in its goods-producing industries, their job prospects are poor, particularly when corporations are searching for low-cost/high-quality locations for technologically advanced industries.

In accepting the need for old-fashioned trade liberalism as a growth strategy, Quebec's business élite understands that long-standing cultural and linguistic policies are second-order items compared to the top priority of forcing Quebeckers to compete in a more open and English-dominated trading world. The principal concern of Quebec's economic élites is to make money in an unregulated North American way without regard to national borders or the employment prospects of Quebec workers.[31] Significantly, Quebec's corporate élite sees no further need for state-directed nationalism. Provigo, Bombardier, Télémedia, Lavalin, Bell Canada, Merrill Lynch, Sécor, the Quebec Chamber of Commerce, the Montreal-based Hudson Institute, all have strong links to the North American market and actively supported the FTA. In the new Quebec, business wants to operate without the constraints of nationalism but with the full backing of the provincial government.

For Quebec nationalists, these sweeping changes pose a fundamental problem. As supporters of Mulroney in the 1988 election, they endorsed closer ties with the United States because they thought that the deal was strictly economic, that Quebec's social programs were exempt, and that Quebec-based business would be better positioned in the American market. This calculated risk was justified on the shaky grounds that it is an alternative to doing business with "hostile anglo Canadians," but it makes no strategic sense in either the short or the long term.

Quebec nationalists, in accepting the pro-market policies of a trade-centred regime, have backed themselves into a corner. The social democratic foundation of modern Quebec nationalism has been replaced by the ideology of free market competition. The irony of this situation is that many of the new economic élite owe their present stature to the very interventionist policies that they now reject. For the long-term survival of Quebec as a distinct society, the danger of opening its borders regardless of the costs and consequences are real. Without a strong economy, what future, is any, does Quebec have if it does not have the means to strengthen its economy against strong external pressures and influences?

At the same time that Bourassa has compromised provincial authority to direct its economic development in an autonomous way, Quebec's political leverage within Canada has never been more uncertain. Canada's Charter of Rights and Freedoms has struck a blow against Quebec's language policy, the cornerstone of what Quebec sees as its linguistic survival. The court has restricted present and future governments' ability to implement measures to strengthen French as the majority language in the province. The recent Supreme Court ruling striking down sections of Bill 101, Quebec's language laws, will also prevent Quebec from protecting its language and culture from the forces of assimilation.

In the face of these developments, English Canadians are now less sympathetic to Quebec's aspirations than at any time in recent history. Dramatic evidence comes from the failure of English Canada to endorse the distinct society clause at the heart of the Meech Lake Accord. Much of this sentiment comes as a backlash against Bourassa's use of the notwithstanding clause. The mood change represents a dramatic swing against Quebec. In the words of former Ontario Premier David Peterson, Canada is "more fractured, more mean, more hard on its minorities than it has been in a long time."[32] With all these pressures building, a reinvigorated market liberalism can only make it more difficult for Quebeckers to protect their culture, institutions, and identity. At the very least, the large-scale erosion of the French fact requires a new political awareness on the part of Quebeckers. With the end of the social democratic nationalist project that once formed the basis of a political consensus among a majority of Quebeckers, Quebec is in for a rough ride. It no longer has the state to protect it from the massive structural change that the global trade imperative demands. The leadership of the nationalist movement is increasingly drawn from the conservative-minded business élite. As the assimilationist pressures of being an American nation mount, Quebec faces an increasingly uncertain future. Even if the indépendantiste movement has gained new momentum from the formation of the Bloc Québécois, the province's economy seems less capable of supporting the nationalist goal of sovereignty than its supporters care to admit. But for the business élite this is not a worrisome prospect. In an era of open borders, symbolic gestures serve an important ideological function – symbols count more than substance.

DEFENDING THE SOCIAL CONTRACT

The final challenge is to forge a new social consensus on how best Canadians can accommodate the adjustments brought about by the highly volatile global economy. In the space of six years the Mulroney government has introduced more changes to existing programs and policies than any other government in the last forty years. No area of government policy has been spared. Across a broad front that includes not only trade but regional development, tax and fiscal policy, old age pensions, family allowance, labour market policy, social income programs, and collective bargaining, the government has moved persistently and systematically to reshape the institutional and legislative character of Canada. Its strategy is to water down Canadian redistributional programs so as to make them equivalent to the (American) lowest common denominator, and to cut the direct and indirect labour costs to business.

Since coming to power in 1984 Mulroney, backed by the recommendations of the MacDonald Commission, has singled out social policy as *the* strategic area requiring the greatest amount of redirection. Social spending as a percentage of gross domestic product declined from 8.1 per cent in 1984/85 to 7.1 per cent in 1989/90.[33] All programs have suffered cutbacks, budgetary restrictions, and underfunding. Only old age pensions have received an increase in funds. Family allowances, unemployment insurance, the Canada Assistance Plan, and the Established Programs Financing to assist provinces pay part of the cost of health care have received no increases in funding or have declined somewhat. The February 1990 budget introduced further stiff cuts in social transfers to the provinces, to the tune of $2.5 billion over two years.

At the same time that the government has reined in its spending, it has introduced a series of tax hikes that have hit low-income earners the hardest. Average taxes paid by a working poor family with an income of $24,000 from two income earners with two children have risen by 60 per cent from 1984 to 1991. This compares with a tax hike for upper-income families of only 11.2 per cent, resulting in a perverse inversion of the Keynesian redistributive principle. The boldest attack on Canada's social programs is the government's draconian revision of the Unemployment Insurance Act, which reduces the level of benefits and makes it harder for unemployed workers to qualify. The federal government has also withdrawn its annual contribution of two billion dollars. These changes to the UI system will have profound effects on the Canadian labour market, making it more competitive, but rendering workers more pliant and unions less powerful.

The weakening of national programs and institutions creates new economic stresses and heightens regional divisions. The mood of the country may be changing but Ottawa's perspective has not. In the words of Bob White, leader of the Canadian Auto Workers, "the thinking in Ottawa seems to be that we can solve everything by being competitive at any price. Everyone seems to be going their own way without a national plan or consensus."[34]

None of this bodes well for Canada's future. A return to the principles of market liberalism will not give Canada the kind of economic leverage it requires. How then should countries strike a better balance between trade and economic growth? Is there a way for all Canadians to benefit from a regime of trade-led development?

SHAPING COMPARATIVE ADVANTAGE: THE LIMITS TO FLEXIBILITY

The alternative is to opt for a different relationship between the market and the state, in which governments actively influence the direction of economic development. All countries employ some form of industrial policy, either wittingly or unwittingly. Even the United States, long claiming to be the stronghold of free enterprise, has implemented a form of industrial strategy consisting of the Reagan defence buildup, coupled with various admittedly piecemeal protectionist measures. An industrial strategy worthy of the name requires a systematic approach to direct industrial restructuring, rather than relying on *de facto* measures. Anything else will not do. Independent companies operating in unco-ordinated "free markets" cannot create a long-term, viable competitive edge. In an era where the aim of trade is to take over the market share of rivals by tough aggressive measures, countries can no longer afford to subscribe to the ideology of free market competition.

When trade sets the economic agenda for a society, a society is also letting market forces set the social and political agenda. Employment standards, union viability, and wage levels will necessarily follow a downward curve. This is because a society that puts competitiveness ahead of any other single concern is prevented from dealing with the challenges posed by a labour surplus economy and by its need to harmonize its public policies with those of its trading partners. To prevent the growth of short- and long-term unemployment and the worsening of wage and household inequality, innovative measures are needed to create a fundamentally different policy mix.

The central challenge for Canada is to develop an industrial strategy that maximizes its commercial leverage globally, insulates it (to the extent possible) from the sharp and unpredictable downswings of the business cycle, delivers a reasonable standard of living to its workers, and protects its capacity to set its own standards. While all countries want to trade and participate in the world economy, Canada has to plan carefully to ensure that a gulf does not develop between the highly competitive but relatively few internationally oriented sectors, on the one hand, and the remaining sectors fighting for a declining share of the domestic market, on the other. As well, productivity growth cannot be confined to a few highly specialized trade-oriented sectors of the economy, thereby benefiting only the privileged and best-situated workers or regions. Finally, when Canada seeks to compete head-to-head with the newly industrializing countries (NICs) or the new cheap-labour periphery of Eastern Europe, it cannot engage in the practice of "dismantling many labour standards, cutting real wages and fringe benefits savagely and imposing rigid controls over union activity."[35] Such labour market policies, often allegedly justified in the name of achieving greater flexibility, are, in fact, nothing less than an organized offensive against workers. This is not the kind of future that most Canadians seek.[36] The challenge is to find a coherent way to link economic restructuring to the reorganisation of the labour market and to facilitate the adaptation of new and different kinds of production technologies.

The first principle of an industrial strategy is that goods production remains essential to a country's economic well-being. This sector's importance to the economy is measured not simply by the number of workers it employs directly, but by the infrastructure, research capacity, and the many service sector jobs which are dependent on it.[37] And yet, to avoid direct competition with the NICs, Canada will have to concentrate its efforts on the high-productivity, skill-intensive activities that can support a high standard of living. This requires new investment capital, modern technology, and increased state assistance. Long-term stability depends on creating a strong group of indigenous firms. Many will be small or medium-sized. Size alone is no longer the key criterion to compete globally. Rather, the more important requirements are that indigenous Canadian firms have access to financial assistance to underwrite the cost of high-quality service inputs, the right mix of technology to allow them to tailor products to changing demand, and support from the state or local authorities. And here, the relationship between labour and capital in and out of the workplace will be crucial in reshaping the system of labour education and training, and indeed in defining the entire social and political agenda for development. Any change in the relations of production also affects consumption norms and questions of distribution. The wage-setting process determines what people are paid and their ability to buy what is produced. Collective bargaining allows workers to share in economic growth by negotiating rates of pay and conditions of work.

The introduction of new production methods has had far-reaching consequences for the workforce. Industrial workers are shrinking in numbers and power. At the same time, the growth of the service sector is creating new employment conditions for women, youth, and immigrants in both the public sector and in the world of private sector subcontracting. The wage structure is being revised downwards. Well-paying blue-collar jobs are becoming more scarce, and low-paid work more abundant. In these new circumstances, one way to compete is on the basis of price and cheap labour inputs. The aim is to drive down labour costs with the support of restrictive collective bargaining practices. This kind of strategy, in which investment is short term, looking for immediate results, is dominant in Canada and the United States. By contrast other countries, such as Japan, Germany, and Sweden have responded to the new competitive pressures by means of a state co-ordinated industrial policy. Competitiveness is largely determined by industries and firms investing in products, research and development, service and marketing strategies. With wages comprising less than 15 per cent of total manufacturing costs in most industries, a highly skilled, well-paid workforce is a reliable asset and not a liability.

A second component of an industrial strategy has to change the rules and the way the labour market operates: what is needed is to have programs to improve income distribution while protecting individuals from the uncertainty of the global economy. This requires not only a co-ordinated industrial policy and strengthened job security but, what Standing refers to as, "the citizen's right of income security."[38] This involves a sweeping reform to social income policy. All existing benefits would be replaced by a guaranteed annual income to be paid to all individuals regardless of sex, marital status, and age. Other details would have to be worked out in conjunction with a progressive reform of Canada's income tax act. The need to provide comprehensive income security arises because, as employers rely more and more on part-time, casual, and contractual labour, individual employment in the world of part-time work is incapable of generating adequate income security for a majority of the population. The proposal for a comprehensive income security package may sound utopian today, but it stands a good chance of becoming tomorrow's reality. Its appeal is that it would facilitate employment mobility for a large part of the workforce. It would make it easier for people to work part-time, to continue working after retirement; and, most importantly, it recognizes the reality that the more a society wants to participate globally, the more it will have to create new institutional arrangements to support this goal. Recognizing this need for change will depend on developing different investment strategies, upgrading human resources, learning to diffuse technology more rapidly and effectively, increasing co-ordination between the principal social actors in society and, significantly, discarding the outdated idea that technology on its own is the most important determinant of success.

The final component is to decide which kinds of technologies are most suitable for Canada's industrial structure. Corporations have the power to decide whether to rely principally on traditional Fordist techniques of mass production in large, centralized plants requiring a largely unskilled workforce, or on decentralized production in multiple smaller plants utilizing flexible machinery and employment relations. While the former option has traditionally been associated with strongly organized workforces, the latter option has the potential to support a shorter work week, flexible working hours more closely tailored to workers' needs, and a system of self-management rather than a despotic factory regime. The attraction here is that self-directing workers are, in the end, not only more productive and more efficient[39] but the more involved the workforce is in decision-making, the greater potential it possesses to influence outcomes in the workplace.

There are other choices to be made as well. Decentralized production can be implemented in smaller enterprises with extensive worker participation in a union setting; but it can also be done through the contracting out of sub-assembly units and component parts to small marginal non-union factories, where business can rely on traditional means of sweating their workforce to cut costs and to maintain price advantage. In these enterprises, there are few limits on the arbitrary power of management. Or producers can take advantage of a new kind of spatial reorganization based on just-in-time production methods. Supplier-firms need to be closer to an assembler whose inventories are reduced to a minimum. Priority is given to continuous production and rigorous quality control. For these fragile clusters of enterprises to work most effectively, they require the co-operation of their employees to ensure a minimum of disruption to the production process. Thus, they work best with a modern regime of collective bargaining and a strong labour presence.

But the most important decision facing Canada is whether to let itself be shaped by the global market or whether, through an innovate state policy, Canadians will determine their own future. The choice is essentially a political one. If governments do not invest in people and protect their citizens from the uncertainty of global competition, positive economic change will not happen on the ground where is counts most. No amount of persuasion will convince people to accept change as a normal part of modern economic life, let alone accept the need for greater flexibility in the workplace and outside of it. In the new era of global competition, knowing how to maximize a country's economic leverage by shaping market forces is, in the final analysis, what ultimately matters.

NOTES

1 Liberalization in trade in services creates many problems for countries. See the North-South Institute, "Trade and Investment in Services: An Issue for the 80s," briefing notes, no. 10 (Ottawa 1984).

2 See André Gorz, *Adieux au Prolétariat* (Paris: Éditions Galilée 1980).

3 Daniel Drache, "Canada-u.s. Free Trade: Not a Muddle, Not a Mess, but an Unparalleled Disaster," *The Round Table* 307 (July 1988).

4 For an excellent overview of the new order see P. Armstrong *et al.*, *Capitalism since World War II: The Making and the Breakup of the Great Boom* (London: Fontana 1984), 167.

5 M. Kalecki, "Political Aspects of Full Employment," *Political Science Quarterly*, 14; no. 4 (1943): 322.

6 Of the Paris group, at this time Alain Lipietz comes closest to focusing on the importance of international markets. See his "The Globalization of the General Crisis of Fordism 1967–84" in John Holmes and Colin Leys, eds., *Frontyard Backyard* (Toronto: Between the Lines 1987).

7 The literature on regulation theory is extensive. A useful introduction to the Paris-based perspective is Robert Boyer, *The Theory of Regulation: A Critical Analysis* (New York: Columbia University Press 1990). For a Canadian perspective see Gérard Boismenu et Daniel Drache, eds., *Politique et Régulation; Modèle de Développement et Trajectoire Canadienne* (Montréal: Méridien 1990).

8 Susan Strange, *States and Markets* (New York: Basil Blackwell 1988), 167.

9 Robert Lawrence and Robert Litan, *Saving Free Trade* (Washington: Brookings Institution 1986), 35.

10 See Robert Boyer, "Wage Formation in Historical Perspective: the French Experience," *Cambridge Journal of Economics* 3 (1979); Melvyn Dubofsky, "To What Extent Was the u.s. Fordist?" Maison des Sciences de l'Homme, GEMDEV/Paris and Fernand Braudel Centre Binghamton, 8–10 juin 1988, Paris.

11 The figures are taken from Mike Davis's review of Michael Aglietta's "Régulation et crises: L'expérience des États-Unis," *Review* 2, no. 2 (Fall 1978): 224.

12 For the US story see Samuel Bowles, David M. Gordon, and Thomas E. Weisskopf, *Beyond the Wasteland* (New York: Anchor Press 1983).

13 Armstrong *et al.*, *Capitalism since World War II*, 167–68.

14 Robert Jessop, "Thoughts on Flexibilisation Strategies" in O. Jacobi, B. Jessop, and H. Kastendiek, eds., *Economic Crisis, Trade Unions, and the State* (London: Croom Helm).

15 See B. Bluestone and B. Harrison, *The Deindustrialization of America* (New York: Basic Books 1982), 16.

16 For a discussion of Canadian de-industrialization see Daniel Drache, "New York Processes, Unregulated Capitalism and the Future of Labour" in Gyorgy Szell, *et al.*, *The State, Trade Unions and Self-Management* (New York: Walter de Gruyter 1989).

17 Robert Z. Lawrence and Robert Litan, *Saving Free Trade*, particularly chapter 2.

18 Gosta Esping-Andersen, *The Three Worlds of Welfare Capitalism* (Cambridge: Polity Press 1990).

19 For a general account of US trade adjustment policies see Lawrence and Litan, *Free Trade Ideal*.

20 In the last three decades Congress has increasingly used its power to restrict imports which cause or threaten serious injury to domestic production. As US industries have faced increased competition Congress has eased the test for industries to obtain relief. These changes have made it easier for American firms to demand that the state increase tariffs. In the seventies, the success rate for industries demanding safeguard protection was nearly 30 per cent. By the eighties that rate had doubled.

21 For a detailed analysis of the impact of the new regulatory order see Gérard Boismenu, *La Vraisemblance de la Problématique de la Régulation pour Saisir la Réalité Canadienne: Étude des Indicateurs Économiques en Moyenne Période*, Cahiers du GRETSE (Université de Montréal, juin 1989). See also Diane Bellemare et Lise Poulin Simon, *Le Défi du Plein Emploi* (Montréal: Éditions Saint-Martin 1986); and Robert Campbell, *The Grand Illusion, The Politics of the Keynesian Experience in Canada 1945–1975* (Toronto: Broadview Press 1987).

22 Toronto Dominion Bank, *The Economy* 12, no. 1 (Summer 1989): 6.

23 Conference Board of Canada, *Adjusting to Free Trade: What Do the Numbers Tell Us?* (Toronto March 1988), 12.

24 David Robertson and Jeff Wareham, *Changing Technology and Work: Northern Telecom*, CAW Technology Project (October 1989), 26.

25 Stephen Clarkson, *Canada and the Reagan Challenge* (Toronto: James Lorimer 1982), 98.

26 "First year of free trade: time for review," *Globe and Mail*, 2 January 1990.

27 Ibid., 19 October 1989.

28 Christian Rioux, "La Machine à millionnaires," *L'Actualité*, juillet 1989.

29 Canada, Royal Commission on the Economic Union and Development Prospects for Canada, *Final Report*, vol. III, 1985: 132.

30 Department of External Affairs, *Canadian Trade Negotiations* (Ottawa 1987), 48.

31 See Philip Resnick, *Letters to a Quebec Friend with a Reply by Daniel Latouche* (Montreal: McGill-Queen's University Press 1990).

32 *Toronto Star*, 22 July 1989.

33 The figures in this section are taken from National Council of Welfare, *Social Spending and the Next Budget* (Ottawa February 1989).

34 Quoted in *Toronto Star*, 22 July 1989.

35 Guy Standing, "European Unemployment, Insecurity and Flexibility: A Social Dividend Solution," World Employment Programme Research, Working Paper 19 (International Labour Organization July 1988).

36 For an elaboration of these issues see M.S. Gertler, "The Limits to Flexibility: Comments on the Post-Fordist Vision of Production and its Geography," *Transactions, Institute of British Geographers* new series 13, no. 4 (1988): 419–32.

37 See M.S. Gertler, "The Service Economy: Prospects for Urban Growth and Employment" in M. Lyons, ed., *Manufacturing Matters: Conference Proceedings and Research Papers* (Toronto: Industrial Development Institute of Metropolitan Toronto 1989), 68–80.

38 Standing, "European Unemployment, Insecurity and Flexibility."

39 For the evidence in support of this statement, see chapter 6 in Bowles, Gordon, and Weisskopf, *Beyond The Wasteland*.

2 Recession, Recovery, and Redistribution: The Three R's of Canadian State Macro-policy in the 1980s

ARTHUR W. DONNER

The Great Recession of 1981–82 marked an important structural turning point for the Canadian economy. The downturn was traumatic for organized labour and major industrial sectors of the Canadian economy. The rise of unemployment which followed shifted the balance of power away from organized and unorganized labour towards the corporate sector. Federal and provincial government policies supported the shift, partly because of fears of rising fiscal deficits, partly in response to a growing conservative tilt to economic policy in the United States.

Nevertheless, once the trough of the recession was reached in December of 1982, the Canadian economy embarked upon one of its lengthiest recoveries of the postwar period. Indeed, that upturn continued on into 1989. Despite the durability and the strength of this recovery, large sectors of the Canadian economy have remained in an almost continuous crisis situation in the 1980s. Two focal points for this crisis are the public sector and the labour market. Federal and provincial governments have been hamstrung by large fiscal deficits and the high cost of servicing the public debt. Labour's crisis is reflected in the legacy of unusually high unemployment rates in most parts of the country, a sharp decline in market power of employed workers, lack of real wage growth (defined as money wages adjusted for the rate of inflation), and increased regional differences within labour markets in Canada. The problems facing both sectors converge in the empirical observation that the average duration of unemployment increased markedly, particularly for older workers, in the 1980s. It is evident that the federal government has moved towards the European view of accepting long periods of unemployment as normal and at the same time accepted long-term change in income and salary levels.[1] This shift in fiscal and labour market policy is disturbing and points to a fundamental change in the way the government intends to manage the economy in the future. This paper examines the lengthy economic recovery which emerged out of the 1981–82 recession and the particular long-term redistributive effect that labour market policy has on wage and income levels. It draws attention to the costs of monetarism and the difficulty of achieving any real sense of balanced growth within the Canadian economy.

THE REMARKABLE 1980S

By most conventional economic indicators, Canada's experience in the 1980s was quite remarkable. As in the United States, a seven-year recovery (dated from the end of 1982) took place within an environment of fairly stable inflation and declining unemployment rates. At a national level the Canadian unemployment rate reached a peak of 12.8 per cent in December 1982 and consumer price inflation nearly reached 13 per cent during the middle two quarters of 1981 even as the economy was plunging into the steepest contraction of any industrial country at that time. The wrenching economic adjustment following the recession seemed to stabilize Canada's inflation rate between 4 and 4.5 per cent between 1982 and 1988. Inflationary pressures started to rekindle again in Canada in 1989, as inflation shifted up from a 4.1 per cent pace in 1988 to 5 per cent in 1989.

While economic growth resumed at a fairly brisk clip after 1982, in many respects developments since have been disappointing. Economic projections published in May 1990 by the International Monetary Fund (IMF) do not tell the full story of the prospects for an international economic growth slowdown in 1991.

The real Canadian picture, however, is somewhat worse than that reflected in these projections. In fact, the odds have sharply increased that the Canadian economy slipped into a made-at-the-Bank-of-Canada recession in 1990. There has been a major escalation in interest rates in the United States and Canada during 1989 and 1990, and recently matters were made even worse because of the 2 August 1990 international oil price shock and the added risk of a US recession. Indeed, one can no longer as easily discount for Canada the possibility of a rerun of the steep 1981–82 recession in the early 1990s (see tables 2.1 and 2.2).

Monetary policy concerns were at the forefront of the fears relating to a 1990 made-in-Canada recession. Indeed, the prime lending rate at the Canadian chartered banks had climbed to 13.5 per cent in March 1989 and remained at that level for a full eleven months. The bank prime

Table 2.1
Industrial Countries: Real GNP 1972–91
(annual changes in per cent)

Real GNP*	Average 1972–81	1982	1983	1984	1985	1986	1987	1988	1989	1990ᶠ	1991ᶠ
Canada	4.4	−3.2	3.2	6.3	4.8	3.1	4.5	5.0	2.9	1.6	3.1
United States	2.7	−2.5	3.6	6.8	3.4	2.7	3.7	4.4	3.0	1.7	2.3
Japan	4.6	3.1	3.2	5.1	4.9	2.5	4.6	5.7	4.9	4.4	4.2
France	2.9	2.5	0.7	1.3	1.9	2.3	1.9	3.5	3.4	3.1	3.1
Germany F. Rep	2.4	−1.0	1.9	3.3	1.9	2.3	1.7	3.6	4.0	3.5	2.7
Italy	3.7	0.3	1.1	3.0	2.5	2.6	3.0	4.2	3.2	3.0	2.9
United Kingdom	1.6	1.7	3.6	2.1	3.7	3.6	4.8	4.4	2.3	1.1	2.2

SOURCE: IMF, *World Economic Outlook* (May 1990), 130.

* Real GDP for Canada, France, Italy, and the United Kingdom

rate then increased further to a 1990 peak level of 14.75 per cent between April and June of 1990. The Canadian economy received an incredibly heavy and drawn-out dose of tight money in 1989 and in 1990. Nevertheless, the Canadian economy finished up in 1989 with a surprisingly robust 3 per cent expansion in real GDP, though economic growth slowed sharply towards the end of 1989 and in early 1990.

A close examination of the statistics suggest that the deceleration of economic growth in late 1989 and in early 1990 would likely reduce Canadian economic growth far below the increases projected by the IMF for 1990 and 1991. There is little doubt that unemployment rates in Canada will start rising again in the early 1990s. Unemployment tends to lag behind the business cycle in Canada, so the relatively low national unemployment levels recorded during the early months of 1990 could easily mislead federal policy-makers in terms of the continuing strength of the economic expansion. The 7.3 per cent unemployment rate which was reached in January 1989 represents the lowest national figure for the 1980s.

Indeed, the inflationary pressures which the Bank of Canada was pointing to in 1989 to justify its restrictive measures only truly escalated in response to tax-induced consumer price index hikes. As Chart 2.1 indicates, consumer price inflation in Canada remained more or less in the 4 to 4.5 per cent range over the six years ending December 1988.[2]

On a deeper level, however, the lengthy economic recovery barely papers over a series of structural problems which have plagued the economy in the 1980s. The fact that many of these structural problems

Table 2.2
Consumer Price Inflation 1972–91: Industrial Countries
(annual changes, in per cent)

	Average 1972–81	1982	1983	1984	1985	1986	1987	1988	1989	1990ꜰ	1991ꜰ
Canada	9,1	8.7	5.0	3.1	2.6	2.4	4.3	4.1	4.9	4.0	4.7
United States	7.8	6.5	3.8	3.8	3.0	2.6	3.1	3.3	4.2	4.1	4.1
Japan	7.4	1.9	0.8	1.2	1.4	1.8	−0.3	0.6	1.5	1.9	1.5
France	10.4	11.7	9.7	7.5	5.8	5.1	2.9	3.1	2.7	3.3	2.8
Germany F. Rep	4.9	4.4	3.3	2.0	2.2	3.1	2.0	1.4	2.5	2.9	3.0
Italy	15.8	19.0	14.9	11.4	9.0	7.6	5.9	6.2	6.3	6.5	4.9
United Kingdom	14.2	7.6	5.3	4.6	5.6	3.5	4.9	6.6	6.7	5.1	6.5

SOURCE: IMF, *World Economic Outlook* (May 1990), 132.

seem an acceptable price to pay to the national authorities is equally disturbing.

One of the key structural problems of the 1980s has been high real interest rates. This problem is not uniquely Canadian, nor is there any one generally accepted explanation for its emergence. Nevertheless, its ramifications for the performance of the economy are severe, and play a part in the increased competitive difficulties facing the Canadian economy.

When the Canadian inflation rate was very low in the 1950s and the 1960s, ordinary market (or nominal) interest rates were a fairly reliable indicator of the how the financial markets and monetary policy were affecting the economy. However, when both price inflation and interest rates escalated in the 1970s, but at uneven paces, market interest rates no longer conveyed the same meaning for understanding the economy, or for judging the effects of interest rates on borrowers or lenders. In a nutshell, real interest rates were unusually low in the 1970s and unusually high in the 1980s.

The real interest rates traced out in chart 2.2 are calculated as the simple difference between long-term Canadian government bond yields and annual increases in the consumer price index. Most economists would admit that this is an imperfect measure, since it uses the current rate to represent future expected inflation rates. Moreover, these calculations are on a pre-tax basis, and obviously do not take into consideration the importance of taxes in spending and saving decisions. Nevertheless, as imperfect as this method is, it highlights some dramatic shifts in real interest rate levels since the 1970s.

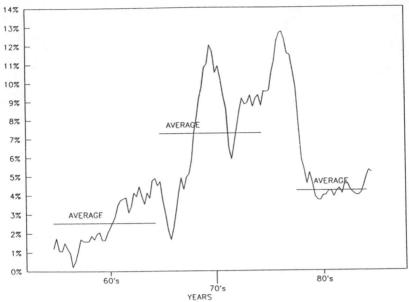

Chart 2.1.
Canadian Consumer Price Inflation

The chart indicates that real interest rates were quite stable in the 1960s when inflation itself was rather stable. That is, the economy rewarded lenders with a fairly stable 3 per cent real rate of return in the 1960s. All of this changed in the 1970s with the acceleration of price inflation. Indeed, during a surprisingly long span within the 1970s real interest rates were negative – which means that the financial markets rewarded borrowers and severely penalized savers. That is, during much of the last decade market interest rates were too low relative to the rate of inflation to provide lenders with a positive real rate of return. An historical low level was reached with a negative real rate of return of 3.1 per cent during the fourth quarter of 1974.

Negative real yields are unhealthy, and of course, they are unsustainable. Yet the negative real returns of the 1970s provided a strong stimulus to economic growth by spurring on the expansion of the capital goods sectors and the housing markets at rates which were far faster than normal. After all, borrowing money at negative real interest rates has to be the bargain of the century. But the financial markets completely reversed themselves in the 1980s. Real interest rates rose to "more normal" levels during the 1981–82 recession, and then moved slightly higher over the last five years. The 1980s peak in real interest rates occurred in the second quarter of 1984 at 9.1 per cent. This 1980s

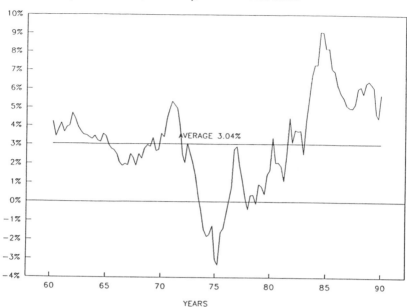

Chart 2.2.

Real Interest Rates (ten year bond yield minus CPI − % CHG)

pattern of unusually high real interest rates has benefited savers, but has been very painful for borrowers.

It is doubtful whether governments or the monetary authorities can have much direct effect on underlying real interest rates. The inflation premium in interest rates can only be affected by government policies over a very long period, if at all. Indeed, interest rates in Canada are more responsive to developments and policies in the United States than to specific Canadian factors. To the degree that the Bank of Canada can affect interest rates, its influence is limited to nominal, shorter-term financial contracts. The long-term government bond yields which were used in the accompanying chart's real interest rate calculation are hardly affected at all by Canadian central bank policy.

By historical yardsticks real interest rates in Canada are already too high to ensure a continuation of strong economic expansion in 1990.[3] Indeed, one has to be somewhat puzzled that the Canadian economy was able to perform so well in the 1980s considering that real interest rate levels were two to three times higher than the full capacity growth rate of the economy. This phenomenon of high real interest rates has two other important impacts within the economy: it contributes to a shift in the distribution of income towards rentiers, and it increases the cost of servicing the government's debt, which is one of the justifications behind the federal government's longer-term pursuit of fiscal restraint.

STRAINS WITHIN THE LABOUR MARKET

In previous decades Canada and the United States used to post practically identical inflation and unemployment rates. Yet when Canada's unemployment rate was 7.6 per cent in February 1989, the American rate had declined to 5.1 per cent, its lowest level since 1974. Indeed, since the last recession ended Canada's unemployment rate has been consistently higher, the difference ranging from two to three percentage points or more. This development represents a clear sign that Canada's economic policies have failed Canadian workers. The fact that unemployment rates in Canada still tend to move in the same direction as those in the United States suggests that American influence on the Canadian economy remains strong. Nevertheless, the fact that a wide spread remained in the late 1980s suggests that, at the margin, Canada has been pursuing less expansive policies than the United States in the 1980s. A complicating issue is the fact that the Canadian economy contracted further than the American during the 1981–82 recession, so Canada had much further to go in terms of job creation simply to catch up.

Perhaps what is more important, though, is that Canadian government officials are simply willing to accept higher unemployment levels in the 1980s than they would have in the past.[4] Indeed, as in other countries, official prognostications on what constitutes acceptable unemployment has changed in Canada over the past twenty-five years. In 1966 Canada recorded 3.4 per cent unemployment, yet the Economic Council of Canada then maintained that 2 per cent inflation and 3 per cent unemployment were achievable objectives for the 1960s. Now the conventional view in Ottawa is that a 7.6 per cent unemployment rate is dangerously low, and close to setting off an inflationary spiral.

Finally, since 1982 Canada's labour market has not performed well on two important fronts. First, marked differences in regional unemployment rates are a long-standing feature of the Canadian economy, a situation which didn't improve in the 1980s despite the economic recovery. On the surface it seems odd that Quebec, which is geographically close to Ontario, should record a 9.2 per cent unemployment rate in December 1988, when Ontario was able to keep its rate to 5 per cent. Similarly the British Columbia and Newfoundland unemployment rates, at 10.3 and 13.3 per cent, were sharply higher than the levels recorded in southern Ontario. The main point is that whatever equilibrium mechanism there is between the labour markets of the different

Table 2.3
Unemployment and Job Vacancy Rates, Canada and Regions: 1974, 1981, 1987

	1974	1981	1987
CANADA			
Unemployment rate	5.3	7.5	8.9
Job vacancy rate	4.4	3.5	3.8
U–V equivalence rate	4.7	5.1	5.5
ATLANTIC			
Unemployment rate	8.0	11.5	14.1
Job vacancy rate	3.6	2.4	3.3
U–V equivalence rate	5.3	6.5	7.5
QUEBEC			
Unemployment rate	6.6	10.3	10.3
Job vacancy rate	5.3	3.4	4.1
U–V equivalence rate	6.3	6.4	6.5
ONTARIO			
Unemployment rate	4.4	6.6	6.1
Job vacancy rate	3.5	3.0	4.3
U–V equivalence rate	3.7	4.3	4.8
PRAIRIES			
Unemployment rate	3.4	4.5	8.6
Job vacancy rate	3.4	3.2	1.6
U–V equivalence rate	3.1	3.6	4.0
BRITISH COLUMBIA			
Unemployment rate	6.2	6.7	12.0
Job vacancy rate	5.6	6.7	2.9
U–V equivalence rate	5.4	6.3	7.1

SOURCE: Canadian Labour Market and Productivity Centre, *Quarterly Review* (Spring 1988), 33.

regions of this country, it obviously was not working very well. This failure also represents a severe indictment of Ottawa's task of evening out economic opportunities across the country. Secondly, the degree of mis-match between those who are unemployed and firms with unfilled jobs has been rising. This has occurred both within and between provinces. The number of unfilled jobs are surprisingly high considering the numbers of individuals who are unemployed or drawing unemployment insurance benefits. The main point is that these regional unemployment rate differences are far too high for a country with a strong central government and numerous government programs geared specifically to lessening the unemployment and job vacancy discrepancies. (see Table 2.3)

Table 2.4
Unemployment Rates by Age and Sex, Selected Years, 1976–89 (% *labour force*)

	Average 1976–80	(%) 1981	1982	1983	1988	1989
BOTH SEXES – TOTAL	7.7	7.5	11.0	11.8	7.8	7.5
Youth	13.5	13.2	18.7	19.8	12.0	11.3
Prime age (25–44)	6.1	6.2	9.4	10.4	7.2	7.2
Older workers (over 44)	4.6	4.4	6.7	7.4	5.7	5.4
MALE – TOTAL	6.9	7.0	11.0	12.0	7.4	7.3
Youth	14.0	14.1	21.1	22.3	12.9	12.4
Prime age (25–44)	5.1	5.3	9.1	10.3	6.5	6.6
Older workers (over 44)	4.2	4.1	6.6	7.3	5.2	5.2
FEMALE – TOTAL	8.9	8.3	10.9	11.6	8.3	7.9
Youth	13.0	12.3	16.1	17.0	11.0	10.1
Prime age (25–44)	7.9	7.5	9.7	10.5	8.0	7.9
Older workers (over 44)	5.6	4.9	6.9	7.6	6.4	5.7

SOURCE: Department of Finance, *Quarterly Economic Review* (June 1989), and *Canadian Economic Observer* (June 1990).

An important by-product of the failure in labour market policies since the recession ended can be seen in the increased duration of unemployment in the 1980s. When an individual becomes unemployed, the odds of short-duration unemployment converting into long-term chronic unemployment are fairly clearly documented in the labour market statistics. Two dimensions of the unemployment experience are important: the incidence (or risk) of unemployment, and its duration. The proportion of the labour force that experiences some unemployment in any particular year and the duration of that unemployment varies considerably with age and sex. Young people have continuously higher unemployment rates than older workers, though young people also experience rather short unemployment spells between jobs. The figures in tables 2.4, 2.5 and 2.6 summarize how the unemployment experiences of different age and sex groups in the Canadian labour force has shifted around since the mid 1970s.

Even though the probability of experiencing unemployment was lower in the late 1980s than in the 1970s for virtually all age and sex groups, once some unemployment occurs the chance of re-employment has worsened for the entire labour force. The key point which emerges from the figures in tables 2.5 and 2.6 are that workers over forty-five became far more vulnerable to chronic unemployment in the 1980s than they were in the 1970s.

Table 2.5

Incidence of Unemployment by Age and Sex, Selected Years, 1976–89 (% labour force)

	Average 1976–80	(%) 1981	1982	1983	1988	Q1 1989
BOTH SEXES – TOTAL	27.2	25.9	33.2	28.2	22.2	21.0
Youth	55.2	53.0	63.3	55.9	52.0	
Prime age (25–44)	20.6	20.3	26.9	23.3	19.2	
Older workers (over 44)	13.0	11.8	17.0	14.5	11.3	
MALE – TOTAL	24.0	22.7	32.1	26.9	19.4	19.2
Youth	57.5	54.7	69.0	60.1	54.6	
Prime age (25–44)	16.7	16.1	25.3	21.4	16.2	
Older workers (over 44)	11.2	10.3	16.0	13.9	9.2	
FEMALE – TOTAL	32.1	30.5	34.8	30.3	25.6	23.4
Youth	52.6	50.6	57.0	51.6	49.8	
Prime age (25–44)	27.0	26.6	29.4	26.4	23.2	
Older workers (over 44)	16.5	14.7	18.8	15.7	15.0	

SOURCE: Department of Finance, *Quarterly Economic Review* (June 1989).

The related public policy dilemma is that the longer an employee is unemployed, the more his or her skills and knowledge are lost. Economists describe this as a labour market de-skilling phenomenon (or hysteresis). Where hysteresis is prevalent in Europe, one observes that high unemployment also breeds further high unemployment. If hysteresis is a problem in Canada, it is more likely to exist in the Atlantic provinces and in the northern half of the country. Indeed, these economically depressed regions of Canada have developed an intricate economic culture that revolves around high unemployment and the Canadian social security safety net, particularly the use of unemployment insurance.

PRODUCTIVITY AND EMPLOYMENT TRADE-OFFS

Since 1982 unemployment in Canada has never returned to former, more comfortable levels, and has not restored a normal balance with comparable United States rates. The loss in jobs might have been acceptable if the overall economy had gained sufficiently on the productivity front to expand the resources available to help the unemployed. But this clearly has not occurred. Throughout Canadian history productivity growth has enabled Canadian industry to pay high real wages and to remain competitive with other countries. However, as the figures in

Table 2.6
Average Duration of Unemployment by Age and Sex, Selected Years, 1976–89 (weeks)

	Average 1976–80	1981	1982	1983	1988	1989
BOTH SEXES – TOTAL	14.7	15.2	17.2	21.8	18.3	17.9
Youth	12.7	13.0	15.4	18.4	12.0	11.3
Prime age (25–44)	15.5	15.9	18.1	23.1	19.4	19.0
Older workers (over 44)	18.6	19.3	20.5	26.7	26.1	25.4
MALE – TOTAL	15.0	16.0	17.8	23.3	19.7	19.0
Youth	12.6	13.4	15.9	19.3	12.3	11.5
Prime age (25–44)	15.8	17.1	18.7	25.0	20.9	20.2
Older workers (over 44)	19.2	20.6	21.3	27.5	29.1	28.3
FEMALE – TOTAL	14.5	14.2	16.3	19.8	16.8	16.6
Youth	12.8	12.6	14.7	17.1	11.5	11.0
Prime age (25–44)	15.1	14.7	17.2	20.6	17.9	17.8
Older workers (over 44)	17.5	17.4	19.0	25.3	22.3	21.4

SOURCE: Department of Finance, *Quarterly Economic Review* (June 1989), and Statistics Canada.

Table 2.7 illustrate, manufacturing productivity growth in Canada and the United States has been virtually at the bottom of the international pack. Moreover, productivity growth has declined dramatically in all industrial countries in the 1970s and the 1980s. This means that Canada's ability both to pay higher real wages and to remain competitive has been under severe strain.

One of the ingredients in this picture is the fairly rapid growth of the Canadian labour force, certainly by European standards. The Canadian labour force is expected to increase by about 1.6 million individuals over the next five years. This means that the economy will have to create at least that many jobs simply to absorb all of the new entrants into the labour force. In addition, if one believes that economic policy should attempt to mop up at least another 250,000 of the current unemployed, we will have to expect considerable job creation from an economy already experiencing fierce competition from abroad and continued job displacement.

On the face of it, then, there appears to be a contradiction between two worthwhile public policy objectives – job creation and productivity growth. Few countries seem to have arrived at a comfortable balance between productivity and job creation. Compared to European standards, both Canada and the United States have been able to generate fairly rapid rates of job creation but rather low rates of productivity growth. The economic implications of such differences can be easily seen in the following hypothetical example. Let us assume a world

Table 2.7
Annual Percentage Changes in Manufacturing Output and Employment,
Seven Countries, 1960–87

Year	United States	Canada	Japan	France	Germany	Italy	United Kingdom
Output							
1960–67	3.4	4.3	8.7	3.9	3.0	4.9	1.3
1960–73	4.8	6.5	12.8	7.2	5.2	7.3	3.0
1973–87	2.2	2.3	5.1	1.0	1.1	2.7	−0.3
1973–79	1.9	2.5	3.6	2.6	1.7	3.1	−0.7
1979–87	2.4	2.1	6.2	−0.2	0.6	2.4	0.0
1979–85	2.0	1.5	7.6	−0.6	0.5	1.9	−0.9
1986	2.3	2.6	0.6	0.6	0.7	3.3	0.2
1987	4.3	5.4	3.4	1.1	0.7	4.3	5.4
Employment							
1960–87	0.5	1.1	1.6	−0.3	−0.4	0.1	−1.6
1960–73	1.4	2.0	3.3	1.3	0.4	1.6	−0.5
1973–87	−1.2	0.0	0.0	−1.0	−1.3	1.3	−1.4
1973–79	0.8	0.8	−1.5	−1.0	−1.6	0.3	−1.4
1979–87	−1.2	0.0	1.0	−2.4	−1.0	−2.5	−4.2
1979–85	−1.4	−0.8	1.6	−2.4	−1.6	−3.0	−4.9
1986	−1.4	2.8	−0.3	−2.5	1.6	−1.2	−2.3
1987	0.4	2.3	−1.1	−2.5	−0.1	−0.8	−2.0

SOURCE: US Department of Labor, *Monthly Labor Review* (December 1988), 29.
NOTE: Rates of change based on the compound rate method.

composed of two countries, each recording 3 per cent real growth in
GNP (i.e., the sum of output per worker and the growth in employment).
In country A all of the GNP growth is accounted for by employment
gains, in country B by productivity gains with no increases in employment. Country A experiences declining unemployment rates, but those
who are employed receive no real wage gains. In addition, country A's
international competitive position deteriorates, unless a currency devaluation occurs. Country B generates higher real wage gains for those
who are newly employed, but national unemployment escalates.

While these examples are exaggerated, they represent the important
employment and productivity differences between Europe and North
America. West European countries have opted very much for the type
B version of economic growth. That is, European markets and government policies emphasize productivity growth rather than job creation,
and in the process the unemployed pay a high price. Canada and the

Table 2.8
Annual Percent Changes in Manufacturing Productivity, Seven Countries, 1960–87
(output per hour)

Year	United States	Canada	Japan	France	Germany	Italy	United Kingdom
1960–67	2.8	3.3	7.7	5.0	4.4	5.7	3.7
1960–73	3.2	4.5	10.3	6.4	5.8	7.5	4.2
1973–87	2.5	2.1	5.3	3.7	3.2	4.0	3.2
1973–79	1.4	2.1	5.5	4.6	4.3	3.3	1.2
1979–87	3.3	2.1	5.1	3.0	2.3	4.6	4.7
1979–85	3.4	2.4	5.8	3.0	2.9	5.4	4.7
1986	3.3	0.3	1.7	3.0	0.0	0.8	2.7
1987	3.4	2.4	4.1	3.2	1.4	3.2	6.8

SOURCE: US Department of Labor, *Monthly Labor Review* (December 1988), 28.
NOTE: Rates of change based on the compound rate method.

United States, by contrast, fit the A version of economic growth, which stresses job creation over productivity and counts on currency devaluations to remain internationally competitive. These two extreme cases focus directly on difficult public policy dilemmas. Obviously the ideal solution is to generate both high real wage growth as well as sufficient job creation to employ everyone. The way out of this dilemma is to encourage a more rapidly growing economy. If the two mythical economies expanded at an annual rate of 5 per cent rather than 3 per cent, for example, the economy could generate a combination of higher employment and productivity growth, each advancing 2.5 per cent annually – possibly the best of both worlds.

Some countries have been able to strike an easier balance between productivity growth and job creation than Canada, but those countries rely heavily on consensus mechanisms to achieve their aims. Thus, there is considerable irony in these figures. Western Europe requires a more generous social assistance system than we have in Canada in part because of the far heavier emphasis on productivity expansion. The North American economies, by engineering poorer productivity growth, in essence practice a kind of job sharing as their own version of social welfare.

REAL WAGES AND INCOME DISTRIBUTION

One of the by-products of the incomplete recovery from the 1982 recession is that real wages in Canada, were actually lower in 1988 than they were when the recession began in 1981. An even more pronounced problem exists in the United States, where the national unemployment rate is considerably below Canada's. In that country average hourly earnings on an inflation-adjusted basis have not increased above the level paid out in the early 1970s even though the economy is currently in the midst of a major re-industrialization boom.

In the United States considerable effort has gone into studying the job quality issue, but surprisingly little consensus has emerged on its cause. This is reflected in a recent article by two economists who observe that the good job–bad job debate in the United States has crystallized around four competing explanations.[5]

A structural change in labour demand has occurred resulting in a rising proportion of low wage jobs. According to this view a long-term restructuring of the American economy has resulted in a shrinkage of the number of high-paying manufacturing industry jobs and an expansion of many low-paying jobs in the service sector. Supporters of the structural demand explanation often advocate industrial policies designed to save high-wage manufacturing jobs.

Changes in age composition has resulted in a rising proportion of low-wage jobs. The premise behind this explanation is that weak real wages primarily reflect labour supply factors. The baby boom of the 1970s propelled a large number of young people with little work experience into the labour force, which expanded the ranks of unskilled, low-paid workers. The increased participation of women in the labour force, who on average earn lower wages than men and who often prefer part-time employment, has also tended to skew the workforce in the low-wage direction. This explanation implies that time will cure the problem.

The increased proportion of low wage jobs is a temporary phenomenon, related to the business cycle. The US Department of Labor, which takes no formal position on the job quality issue nevertheless attributes many of the recent problems to the severity of the 1981–82 recession and its echo effects. The main policy direction from this eclectic view seems to be "wait and see."

Low-wage growth is related to poor productivity, not to structural factors. This argument starts with the premise that job quality really has not changed but labour productivity growth has sharply slowed down. As a consequence, the only way to increase real wages at a faster pace is to find measures which boost the productivity of labour and capital.

Despite the apparent contradictions inherent in these different explanations, Loveman and Tilly observe that there is at least some agreement on the empirical facts. There is broad agreement that there has been an unusual decline in real wage growth, an increase in the proportion of

low-paying jobs for full-time workers, and an increase in wage inequality both within and between American industries and occupations.
Whether the low-earnings proportion of all jobs has increased remains
a serious point of contention.

Since the Canadian economy is closely tied to that of the United
States, it is not surprising to discover that there is a Canadian counterpart to this story. At an aggregate level most Canadian employees are
earning less today in real terms (after accounting for inflation) than they
were in 1982. This picture is intimately associated with the shifts in
market power and also with the observation that productivity gains of
the workforce in Canada remain low by the standards of the 1950s and
1960s, and quite low relative to most other countries. New studies have
documented the dramatic changes to Canada's wage structure. A recent
Statistics Canada report traced the growth of labour income since the
mid 1980s in real and nominal terms.[6] It grouped these changes into
two primary components: wages and salaries, and supplementary labour
income (which includes employers' contributions for health and welfare
schemes, pension plans, workers' compensation, and unemployment
insurance). It found that in nominal terms labour income per Canadian
employee rose by 140 per cent between 1975 and 1987 but in real terms
the increase was only 1.5 per cent. All the real growth in average labour
income occurred on the supplementary income side (up 32.7 per cent);
real average wages and salaries were lower in 1987 than back in 1975.
Construction and forestry workers experienced the largest declines in
total average real incomes over than period – 16.3 and 15.5 per cent
respectively. The winners on the industrial wage front were employees
in financial services and communications, with total real income gains
of 16.8 and 13.1 per cent respectively.

Income distribution re-emerged in the United States as an important
public policy concern in the 1980s. It is almost inevitable that similar
concerns would surface in Canada as well. An article by Frank Levy
captures the spirit of the unusual shifts in income distribution that have
occurred in the United States: "Since the 1973–74 oil price increase, [US]
income growth has stagnated while mobility within the income distribution has diminished. To this point, we have been able to maintain
the [US] middle class dream through demographic adjustments – more
two-earner couples, postponed marriages, and low birthrates. These
adjustments can take us only so far. If we do not return to a healthy
economy with rising real wages, the middle class, and with it, the
nation's social fabric, will come under increasing strain."[7]

Once again there seems to be a Canadian counterpart to this story,
but its empirical dimensions are far from resolved. Statistics Canada
reported on a special survey of work history for two specific time per-

iods, 1981 and 1986.[8] The income distribution shifts over that five-year period were calculated by distributing the employed Canadian labour force into ten groups based on average earnings. Accordingly, the bottom wage earning group was paid $5.24 per hour or lower in 1986, the next level up was paid between $5.25 and $6.76, while the top paying employment group was paid at rate of $19.62 or more per hour. The advantage of using ten groups is that it is far more precise than the typical division which is based on simply three classifications – low, medium, and high. This study found that between 1981 and 1986 there was a modest decline in the share of Canadian employment in the middle of the wage distribution picture caused primarily by the changing wage structures *within* given industries and occupations. That is, "wage shifts within occupations and industries had more influence on the wage distribution than did changes in occupational and industrial structure over this period."[9] The most interesting finding was that key occupational and industrial changes which have altered wage distribution have impacted heavily on young people. It found that the most dramatic change relates to a decrease in the relative wages paid to young workers and an increase in the relative wages of middle aged and older workers. This downward wage shift for young people occurred across the whole spectrum, and was independent of the level of education.

Another surprising feature is the observation that Canadians are much less dependent today on wages and salaries than at any time over the past seventeen years. This jumps out of the personal income figures presented in Table 2.9. Back in 1970 wages and salaries accounted for just under 72 per cent of personal income in Canada; in 1989 wage and salaries accounted for less than 65 per cent. The proportion of personal income flowing out of investments has practically doubled since 1970, from 7.4 to 14.1 per cent of personal income in Canada. At the same time government transfer payments to individuals have increased from about 10 per cent of personal income back in 1970 to a peak of 14.6 per cent in 1984. Indeed, it is not so much that labour income has increased slowly as that investment income has soared. For example, labour income rose sixfold over the past seventeen years, from roughly $50 billion in 1970 to close to $300 billion in 1987. Investment income rose from about $5 billion in 1970 to about $60 billion in 1987, a twelvefold expansion. Similarly, government transfer payments to individuals increased close to tenfold since 1970.

What factors explain these unusual personal income shifts? Demographics and the aging of Canada's population clearly play some role. The number of savers and investors in Canada has been expanding with the increase in the average age of the population. Young people generally spend in excess of their incomes to finance their housing and other heavy

Table 2.9
Trends in Major Components of Personal Income in Canada since 1970

	Percentage Shares of Personal Income				
Year	Interest and dividends and other investment income (1)	Wages salaries etc. (2)	Government transfer payments to persons (3)	Personal savings (4)	Investment income and government transfer payments (1 + 3 = 5)
1970	7.4	71.8	10.2	4.5	17.6
1971	7.1	71.4	11.0	5.5	18.1
1972	7.9	70.6	11.7	7.0	19.6
1973	8.5	69.6	11.3	8.6	19.8
1974	9.0	69.8	11.7	9.1	20.7
1975	8.6	69.7	12.5	10.2	21.1
1976	8.7	70.8	12.4	9.4	21.5
1977	8.7	70.8	12.4	9.4	21.5
1978	10.2	69.1	12.9	10.2	23.1
1979	11.3	69.1	12.2	10.6	23.5
1980	11.9	68.9	12.4	10.9	24.3
1981	13.8	67.5	12.0	12.2	25.8
1982	14.6	65.1	13.7	14.4	28.3
1983	13.2	64.7	14.9	11.7	28.1
1984	13.7	64.2	14.6	11.9	28.3
1985	13.5	64.3	14.6	10.5	28.1
1986	13.3	64.3	14.5	8.3	27.8
1987	13.0	64.7	14.4	7.2	27.4
1988	13.4	64.7	14.1	7.7	27.5
1989	14.1	64.7	13.8	8.5	27.9

SOURCE: Statistics Canada, National Income and Expenditure Accounts (13-001)

start-up costs, while older Canadians are the savers. As well, the importance of company pensions plans and RRSPs has been increasing over time. Increased use of private pension plans for saving purposes has been deliberate public policy, and was sparked by changes in provincial and federal legislation.

What all this seems to imply is that buoyant job creation statistics disguise some very important market power shifts in the Canadian economy in the 1980s. Organized and unorganized labour have lost market power to corporations, and both groups have lost market power to rentiers – those who benefit directly from high real interest rates. The shift in labour market power towards management is also reflected in the growth of numerous new small firms. In many instances it is cheaper and more efficient for larger companies to contract out services which they were previously providing internally. There is also the tendency of the non-unionized, smaller firms, to pay lower wages than larger businesses.

THE FISCAL POLICY DILEMMA

Whereas high real interest rates have helped alter the distribution of income within Canada, they have also worsened the Canadian government's fiscal position. The government is a major debtor, with its net debt outstanding amounting to about $380 billion in 1990. Even after six years of fiscal restraint under the Progressive Conservatives, Canada still has a budget deficit in the $30 billion range for fiscal 1990–91. Approximately 27.8 per cent of total budgetary expenditures were allocated to service the public debt in fiscal 1990–91. The other part of this story is that the shrinking deficit to date hardly slowed the rapid growth of the government's overall indebtedness.[10]

Canada's budget deficit reached an all-time high of $38.3 billion back in fiscal 1984–85. Since then the combination of spending curbs, slashed programs, increased taxes, and strong economic growth reduced and then held the nominal deficit level to $28.1 billion in fiscal 1987–88 and to an estimated $30.5 billion in fiscal 1988–89 and a projected $28.5 billion in 1990–91. It is widely realized that unless new taxes are raised or programs are sharply slashed further, the early 1990s economic slowdown trashes the federal government's fiscal plans to reduce the deficit. Yet fiscal austerity and frugality was the name of the game for much of the Mulroney government's mandate. For example, spending on all statutory programs only increased at a 2.8 per cent annual rate between fiscal 1984–85 and 1988–89, which is considerably below the rate of increase of consumer prices. Indeed, expenditures on two important statutory programs, established program funding and family allowances, have hardly increased at all.

The federal government's real financing problem resides in its huge debt. Ottawa was required to spend $41.1 billion on interest payments in 1989–90 simply to service the debt. Indeed, the federal government's interest payments are nearly three times as large as the government's defence expenditures, and are more than twice the amount of all of the revenues generated through the corporation income tax.

The main point is that even with nearly six years of economic restraint, the federal government's total debt has continued to rise.[11] Critics like to point out that the public debt increased by about $90 billion during the Tory restraint phase. The federal government's debt, whether viewed on a per capita basis or relative to GNP, outstrips the debt burden of most other industrial countries by a wide margin. Indeed, with the sole exception of Italy, Canada has the largest central

Table 2.10
Major Industrial Countries: Central Government Fiscal Balances and Impulses, 1982-91
(per cent of GNP)*

Fiscal Balance (+ surplus, − deficit)	1982	1983	1987	1988	1989	1990F	1991F
Canada	−5.4	−6.2	−4.2	−3.4	−3.6	−3.4	−3.1
United States	−4.6	−5.2	−3.6	−3.0	−2.9	−2.3	−2.1
Japan	−5.2	−5.0	−2.2	−1.3	−0.8	−0.5	−0.3
France	−2.7	−3.2	−2.3	−2.0	−1.7	−1.6	−1.5
Germany, Fed. Rep.	−2.4	−1.9	−1.4	−1.7	−0.9	−1.2	−1.0
Italy	−13.0	−13.9	−11.6	−11.5	−11.1	−10.8	−10.4
United Kingdom	−2.7	−2.7	1.4	0.8	−0.1	−0.6	−0.9
Seven major countries	−4.7	−5.0	−3.4	−2.8	−2.5	−2.2	−2.1

Fiscal Impulse (+ expansionary, − contractionary)	1982	1983	1987	1988	1989	1990F	1991F
Canada	1.3	0.6	−0.1	−0.3	0.2	−0.5	−0.2
United States	1.1	0.8	−1.0	−0.2	−0.1	−0.6	−0.2
Japan	−0.2	−0.4	−0.9	−0.7	−0.3	−0.3	−0.2
Seven major countries	0.4	0.4	−0.7	−0.2	−0.1	−0.3	−0.2

SOURCE: IMF, World Economic Outlook (May 1990), 139.
* GDP for Canada, France, Italy, and the United Kingdom

government deficit relative to the size of the economy of the seven major industrial countries. Moreover, as the IMF figures presented in Table 2.10 illustrate, the fiscal impulses of the recent Canadian budget have been restricting economic growth, yet critics of the government argue that budgetary policy must be tightened up further.

Canada also can no longer claim with comfort that its debt is completely internalized. Indeed, about 20 per cent of Canada's debt was held abroad in 1989, and that ratio will likely grow further in coming years. Federal government debt is now competing with private sector and provincial government debt in both domestic and foreign markets. The volatility of capital flows into Canada increases because of this increased propensity to fund the government's debt abroad.

The plain facts are that it doesn't matter whether I happen to believe that the public debt is a problem; the point is that the financial markets believe that Canadian government deficits of these magnitudes (even though they are nominal rather than real problems) are destabilizing, and they can destabilize the economy by either forcing higher interest rates or a lower currency value. In addition, the high nominal budget

Table 2.11
Business Investment (Excluding Institutions) by Major Regions
Percent of National Total (current $)

Year	Atlantic	Quebec	Ontario	Prairies	B.C.	Total West
1980	5.7	18.9	29.4	30.7	13.5	44.2
1981	5.6L	16.7L	29.0L	32.7H	13.3	46.0H
1982	7.3	16.9	29.4	30.6	12.3	42.9
1983	8.1	17.4	31.1	31.1	12.1	43.2
1984	7.4	18.9	32.8	26.2	11.3	37.5
1985	7.3	18.6	35.2	26.2	10.7	36.9
1986	6.7	19.6	40.7	22.6	9.2L	31.8
1987	5.9	21.0	41.1H	21.7L	9.6	31.3L
1988	5.9	20.4	40.1	22.6	10.3	32.9
1989	6.1	21.4	40.0	20.4	11.1	31.5

SOURCE: Statistics Canada

L = Low point since 1963; H = High point since 1963

NOTE: Ratios do not add up precisely to 100 because "other areas" are not included.

deficit clearly limits the government from undertaking worthwhile initiatives either in a counter-cyclical sense or even on a longer-term planning basis.

REGIONAL FRAGMENTATION

Canada does not have one labour market operating efficiently across the country, but rather a series of markets, each more heavily oriented to regional developments than to the national economy as reflected in GNP statistics. The current manifestation of fragmentation can be traced through a recent and continuing bout of investment spending.[12]

Business investment in plant and equipment has always been an important dynamic driving the Canadian economy. Private investment only represents some 10 to 15 per cent of GDP, but because of its volatility it can at times account for as much as 50 per cent of economic growth, or more than 100 per cent of a slowdown. Because of Canada's heavy natural resource endowment, capital investment cycles are often set off by movements in international commodity prices; and since natural resources are unevenly spread across the country, investment cycles usually have distinct regional dimensions in Canada. The Canadian economy started to accelerate after 1985, and business investment also picked up. Unlike the last business investment cycle which peaked in the early 1980s, the current investment cycle is predominantly an eastern phenomenon, centred in Quebec and Ontario.

The figures in Table 2.11 illustrate that the four western provinces accounted for 46 per cent of all private investment spending in 1981;

this represented their highest proportion over the past quarter-century. Business investment flowing to the same western provinces declined to a quarter-century low point in 1987. While Ontario's share of business investment fell to a twenty-five-year low in 1981, its share also climbed to a quarter-century peak in 1987. The figures underscore than even in this period of relatively hard times, the West has been far more successful than Quebec in terms of attracting new investment. Western Canada's total population is only slightly larger than Quebec's, yet in 1990 it is still expected to attract about one-third more business investment than Quebec. What seems to be happening is that over longer periods business investment is attracted by internal migration and rapid increases in population and employment. On balance, the regions with the fastest relative population gains and the lowest rates of unemployment have been the Western provinces and Ontario. Indeed, the high-unemployment regions have been furious with the central government for imposing tight monetary conditions right across the country. Monetary policy is a blunt instrument, as the same interest rates affect all regions of the country. In a period of tightness economic growth is curbed not only in tight markets such as Toronto, but also in the high-unemployment areas such as St. John's, Calgary, or Edmonton.

CONCLUSION

Canada has now experienced eight years of uninterrupted economic growth with relatively stable price inflation. Despite a solid growth performance in 1988 and 1989, the Canadian economy, and to a far lesser extent the United States economy, has had to digest some steep interest rates in 1989 and in 1990. Not surprisingly, therefore, both economies began to experience slower economic growth in the second half of 1989 and in the early months of 1990.

It is generally recognized that the Canada's economy will have a series of difficult structural problems to overcome in the 1990s. A somewhat extended phase of slower economic growth is expected because of the coming together of a series of negative factors – including a softening or possible end to the recent phase of strong business capital spending in 1991, the introduction of the 7 per cent Goods And Services Tax (GST) in 1991, and the related probability that monetary conditions will remain very tight prior to and following the introduction of the GST.

The Bank of Canada has embarked upon a major anti-inflation crusade since early 1989, and the governor of the Bank continues to warn that zero inflation is his real objective. Even if this objective is only partly rhetorical, it suggests that many of the structural problems noted above will likely become worse in 1990s. A tight Canadian monetary posture almost guarantees the continuation of high interest rate spreads relative to the United States, although US policies and other external events will continue to determine the general path of Canadian interest rates. If there is a risk in this scenario, the risk is that the monetary squeeze in Canada will be carried too far, and that the widely expected recession of 1990 will turn into a lengthy economic downturn such as the Great Recession of 1981–82.

Aside from the macroeconomic policy challenges stemming from the likelihood of somewhat slow growth and unacceptabley high inflation (at least to the governor of the Bank of Canada), there are four important structural issues which will affect the Canadian economy in the 1990s. On the international front, there are only glimmers of the future shape and the direction of new tradings blocks which are starting to emerge. While Canada is firmly anchored into the United States block, there is considerable uncertainty about the prospects for North American trade under the Free Trade Agreement and continued harassment of Canadian firms and governments. Further, there is always a possibility of Mexico entering this North American trading bloc at some time in the relatively distant future. Secondly, there is the whole issue of labour market policy in the 1990s, and grappling with continuously high levels of structural unemployment across the regions. The federal government has been attempting to disengage itself from its responsibilites for unemployment insurance and for structual imbalances within the economy. Thirdly, there is the isse of how industries can and will restructure in the 1990s, and what role federal and provincial governments will continue to play in this process. And finally, Canada–US economic relations will continue to be strained as the Canadian public and politicians come to realize that the Free Trade Agreement has probably forced faster industrial change than they would desire, and has constrained both provincial and federal governments in terms of the kind of adjustment assistance which is required.

NOTES

1 There are some parallels with the Thatcher conservative policy direction in the United Kingdom. The parallels come ever closer when one considers the monetary-fiscal policy mix, and the difficulties that arise when governments attemps to promote domestic and balance-of-payments objectives which may be incompatible. See David Vines, "Is the Thatcher Experiment Still on Course?" *The Royal Bank of Scotland Review* 164 (December 1989), 3–14.

2 The Bank of Canada has been very uneasy about even such periods of inflation stability. For an interesting discussion of such concerns, see R.F. Lucas, "The Bank of Canada and Zero Inflation: A New Cross of Gold?" *Canadian Public Policy* 15 no. 1 (March 1989), 84–92.

3 Expectations of considerably slower economic growth for the Canadian economy in 1990 became fairly widespread in 1989. For example, see the chapter on Canada in the *OECD Economic Outlook* 46 (December 1989), 81–85.

4 For an explanation of why this is the case see Canada, Royal Commission on the Economic Union and Development Prospects for Canada; *Final Report*, Vol. 2: 279–81. This small section of the report explains the differences which exist among mainstream economists with respect to stabilization policies.

5 Gary W. Loveman and Chris Tilly, "Good Jobs or Bad Jobs: What Does The Evidence Say?" *The New England Economic Review* (January/February 1985).

6 Statistics Canada, *The Labour Force* (September/October 1988).

7 Frank Levy, "The Middle Class: Is It Really Vanishing?" *The Brookings Review* (Summer 1987), 21.

8 Statistics Canada, *The Labour Force* (September/October 1988).

9 Ibid., 100.

10 See C. Bloskie, "An Overview Of Different Measures of Government Deficits and Debts," *Canadian Economic Observer*, Statistics Canada (November 1989), 3.2–3.20.

11 The Macdonald Commission report explains the mathematics of this problem. That is, "The debt/GNP ratio will rise as long as the ratio of the deficit to GNP exceeds the rate of growth of GNP multiplied by the ratio of the outstanding debt to GNP." See *Final Report*, Vol. 1: 295.

12 R. Paul Shaw observes that chronic unemployment can be directly traced to the mix of industries in a particular region. See "The Burden of Unemployment In Canada," *Canadian Public Policy* 11, no. 2 (June 1985), 143–47.

PART TWO

Freer Trade and Economic Integration

3 Regional Trading Blocs: Fortress Europe versus Fortress North America

BRUCE W. WILKINSON

Two major trade and commercial policy initiatives got under way in the second half of the 1980s. One of these was the Canada–US free trade agreement (FTA) for which negotiations were formally commenced in the spring of 1986 and concluded in early October, 1987. The other initiative was the decision by the member countries of the European Community (EC),[1] to complete the liberalization of trade and economic integration among them by the end of 1992.

This chapter considers the implications of the two agreements on each other and the longer-run identity of the nations within each of the two blocs. Four key conclusions emerge. First, although the two trading blocs may appear somewhat like large fortresses designed to protect their own constituent countries and corporations, neither bloc could afford or would want to be responsible for the destruction of world trade that would result if they became extremely inward-looking and protectionist. Secondly, conflicts are likely to arise increasingly between the owners of capital and managers on the one hand, and the other members of the labour force on the other hand, particularly those less well educated. Because of the institutions and processes involved in Europe 1992, it is probable that the implications for the labour force may be less adverse in the EC than in Canada. Thirdly, political union of the nations involved in each bloc is a real possibility. Although such a possibility is being openly discussed in the EC, it is not something that receives explicit attention in Canada and the United States. In fact, discussion of it is essentially taboo. Fourthly, even if a political union does not occur in North America, it is clear that Canadian institutions are not well protected by the FTA. The nature of the agreement is such that American influence is overwhelming, whereas in the EC national rights and identity are better protected because no single nation is able to control the course of events. Also, the domination of corporate interests over those of the rest of Canadian society is apt to be much greater than in the EC.

THE EC AND CANADA–US: A STATISTICAL OVERVIEW

Although the EC has 20 per cent more people, its gross domestic product (GDP) is still only 88 per cent that of Canada–US, and per capita income on average is only 72 per cent of the North American countries (see Table 3.1, section I, C). The two blocs also differ greatly in the extent to which one nation is dominant. In the North American case, the United States accounts for 90 per cent of the population in the trading area, 90 per cent of the labour force, and about 92 per cent of GDP. In contrast, West Germany, the most powerful nation in the EC, is only 19 per cent of the EC population, 20 per cent of the labour force, and 26 per cent of GDP (Table 3.1, section I; B, C, and D). Even with all of Germany united, it would only account for 23 per cent of total EC population – still a far cry from American domination of the FTA.

With regard to foreign trade, the EC is much larger than Canada–US, particularly if trade (both merchandise and services) among the individual countries in each bloc is counted (Table 3.1, section I, E 1a and 2a). Even when such trade is excluded, the EC still exports nearly 90 per cent more merchandise than does North America. On the import side, however, the huge United States merchandise inflow brings the two blocs much closer together, with the EC being only 4 per cent larger.

The nature of trade dependence of the individual nations upon other members of the two trading blocs varies as well. Several of the countries in the EC export nearly as large a proportion of their goods to the remainder of the EC nations as Canada does to the United States, and import nearly as much from other EC nations in total as Canada does from the United States (Table 3.1, section II). In Canada's case the dependency is entirely upon trade with one nation, whereas the comparable trade for each European nation is spread among eleven other countries. In addition, the United States trades far less with Canada (even though Canada is its largest trading partner) than any nation in the EC trades with the rest of the EC. The nearest equivalent in the EC is that between Ireland and the United Kingdom: Ireland ships 34 per cent of its exports to the United Kingdom and receives 42 per cent of its imports from the same source, whereas only about 4 per cent of

Table 3.1
The EC and the Canada–US Trading Blocs: A Statistical Comparison: 1987

I.	EC	Can.–US	EC: Can.–US
	(1)	(2)	(3)
A NUMBER OF COUNTRIES	12	2	
B POPULATION	325 millions	270 millions	1.20
Population of the dominant	61 millions	244 millions	
country	(West Germany)	(USA)	
Dominant country as proportion of total bloc	18.8%	90%	
C GROSS DOMESTIC PRODUCT (GDP) ($US)	$4,303 billion	$4,912 billion	.88
GDP of dominant country as proportion of the total	26.3% (West Germany)	91.5% (USA)	
GDP per capita ($US)	13,095	$18,144	.72
D LABOUR FORCE	138 millions★	135 millions	1.02
Labour force of dominant coutry as proportion of total	20.0%	90.0%	
Average unemployment rate	11.7%★	5.7%	
E INTERNATIONAL TRADE			
1 Merchandise			
a) Incl. trade among and between countries Within each trading bloc			
– Exports	$951 billions	$337 billions	2.82
– Imports	$950 billions	$509 billions	1.87
Balance (x–m)	−1 billion	−172 billions	
b) Excl. trade among and between countries Within each trading bloc			
– Exports	$396 billions	$209 billions	1.89
– Imports	$395 billions	$363 billions	1.04
Balance (x–m)	+1 billion	−72 billion	
2 Services			
a) Incl. trade among and between countries Within each trading bloc			
– Exports	$440 billions	$201 billions	2.19
– Imports	$411 billions	$198 billions	2.08
Balance (x–m)	+29 billions	+3 billions	

Table 3.1
(continued)

II. Trade Dependency

A TOTAL TRADE OF EACH COUNTRY IN EACH TRADING BLOC	Exports to members of trading bloc as a percent of total exports (%)	Imports from within the trading bloc as a percent of total imports (%)
1 Canada–US Trading Area		
Canada	76	68
United States	23	17
2 EC		
Netherlands	75	64
Belgium–Luxembourg	74	73
Ireland	74	66
Portugal	71	64
Greece	67	61
Spain	64	55
France	60	61
Italy	56	58
West Germany	53	52
United Kingdom	49	53
Denmark	47	52

B THE LARGEST TRADING PARTNER FOR EACH COUNTRY IN THE EC	Exports		Imports	
	Country	% of Exports	Country	% of Imports
Ireland	UK	34	UK	42
Netherlands	West Germany	27	West Germany	27
Belgium-Luxembourg	France	20	West Germany	24
Denmark	West Germany	16	West Germany	24
Greece	West Germany	24	West Germany	22
Italy	West Germany	19	West Germany	21
France	West Germany	17	West Germany	20
United Kingdom	West Germany	12	West Germany	17
Spain	France	19	West Germany	16
Portugal	France	16	West Germany	15
Germany	France	12	France	12

SOURCES:

– Population, GDP and Services Trade: International Monetary Fund, *International Financial Statistics: Yearbook* (Washington, DC, IMF).

– Merchandise trade: OECD, Department of Economics and Statistics, *Foreign Trade by Commodities* vols. I and II (Paris, OECD 1987).

– Labour force: EC.　　*Eurostat* V (Brussels 1988).

　　　　　　　USA.　　*Survey of Current Business* (Washington DC 1988).

　　　　　　　Canada. *Bank of Canada Review*, June 1989.

* 1986 numbers

British exports and imports are to and from Ireland respectively. However, Ireland does not have to negotiate with the United Kingdom alone on matters of dispute between them; the other ten nations of the EC will be involved as well.[2]

The final observation to be made from Table 3.1 is that West Germany, in addition to being the largest nation in the EC, is the most important trading partner within the EC. Apart from the United Kingdom's leading role with respect to Ireland, Germany is the number one source of imports for all nations in the EC, and the main market for a majority of the EC nations' exports (Table 3.1, section II, B).

With these basic facts in mind, let us consider briefly the background to these two large liberalization initiatives, and the main economic rationale for them.

THE INCENTIVES FOR GREATER ECONOMIC INTEGRATION

Canada–US

A variety of studies done in Canada over the years provided an economic rationale for an FTA with the United States.[3] Foremost among the reasons given were the achievement of greater economies of scale in manufacturing, leading to greater efficiency and lower average costs of production; the exposure of Canadian industry to greater competition so that a variety of other efficiency-improving measures would occur, including additional research and development and more rapid dissemination of new technology; and secured access to the huge United States market (i.e., exemption from American countervailing duties and anti-dumping laws), especially in the event that American protectionism were to increase. Early estimates of the gains to Canada were frequently in the range of 7 to 10 per cent of GNP, with employment increasing about 5.5 per cent.[4] However, as additional studies were undertaken and more realistic assumptions were built into the models, the projected benefits to Canada became progressively smaller. The most recently published works suggest that the net rewards could be close to zero or even negative.[5] And if one allows for the full range of commitments beyond the reduction of tariffs which Canada bound itself to in the agreement, and which are not provided for in any of the models, the likelihood of negative gains to Canada becomes even greater.

The most recent research on Canada–US productivity differences suggests that in 1982, in a majority of cases, Canadian manufacturing efficiency or productivity was already superior to that of the United States![6] We should therefore be suspicious of estimates suggesting that the benefits to Canada from new economies of scale and other productivity improvements will be substantial.

The United States news media hardly considered the negotiations with Canada worthy of mention. (This was true after the agreement was concluded, too.) Yet concomitantly the US ambassador to Canada and other authorities were encouraging Canadian business leaders and others to take action. Repeated warnings that the window of opportunity for Canada would be closing soon made it appear that haste in negotiating a deal was essential. In addition, much overt as well as behind-the-scenes pressure by the powerful Canadian Business Council on National Issues[7] convinced Ottawa not to wait for the completion of the multilateral GATT Uruguay Round in 1990 as the means of achieving Canadian efficiency-improving objectives. For their part, the United States authorities made it clear that they wanted substantial changes in Canadian policies in order to achieve far fewer restraints upon and greater opportunities for American firms in the Canadian market.[8]

Given the inflated initial Canadian estimates of gains, the popular Canadian view that the nation had no alternative but to negotiate a deal, and the Canadian failure to recognize that it had more to lose because its tariffs were on average greater than those in the United States, placed the Americans in a strong bargaining position. They thus achieved the majority of their objectives. As for Canada, although all tariffs are to be removed over time by both countries, discussions regarding subsidies and related issues are to continue for another five to seven years beginning January 1989.[9] Hence, Canada's major objective of attaining restraints on the application of United States contingency protection was not met.

The EC

The incentives for the White Paper of 1985 and the Single European Act (SEA) of 1986 were both economic and political. On the economic side, Europeans were aware that although tariff removal internally had already been achieved,[10] trade among member countries was greatly hampered by hundreds of non-tariff measures (NTMs), some of a longstanding nature and others that had been quietly introduced during the economic downturns of the 1970s and early 1980s. The objectives of the original 1957 Treaty of Rome had never been attained with regard to the removal of these barriers to trade, or with regard to the liberalization of service trade (including banking, insurance and securities, labour movements, or capital flows).[11]

A commitment was therefore made in the White Paper to make the EC a genuine economic community where goods, services, and factors of production would be able to move freely across national borders within that community. It was believed that opportunities for lower costs and the spur to efficiency and technological advance that the removal of all NTMs would provide would stimulate investment and break the relative economic stagnation that Europe found itself in, thereby augmenting economic growth and increasing incomes and employment. At the same time the enhanced market integration by 1992 was envisaged as a means of enabling the Community to regain the international competitiveness lost during the early 1980s to the United States, Japan, and the newly industrialized countries (NICs) in both domestic and world markets, especially in advanced technology industries, but also in other sectors such as foodstuffs.

At the political level, a more closely knit and economically stronger Community meant for many in Europe that the EC would be a more effective counterforce to the United States (and Japan) in the councils of the world. Although not all members favoured political unification, Britain being the least enthusiastic, many of the bureaucrats in Brussels as well as the politicians viewed a United States of Europe as the logical, desirable, and irreversible next step to full market integration.[12]

There has not been nearly as much research on the possible economic gains to the EC as on the Canada–US agreement. The most recent and comprehensive study is the Cecchini Report[13] which makes both microeconomic and macroeconomic estimates of the net benefits. The microeconomic forecasts set the gains at between 4.3 and 6.4 per cent of GDP, or an average of 5.3 per cent. The net macro-improvement in GDP over the longer term was calculated at between 3.2 and 5.7 per cent of GDP or an average of 4.5 per cent. Short-term employment is, however, expected to decrease significantly, particularly in some sectors such as in customs work (as border controls are removed) and as a result of corporate mergers and acquisitions (which invariably mean layoffs) and the closure of those firms unable to compete. Over the longer term, employment is projected to increase between 1.3 and 2.3 million, or 1.8 million on average – providing the anticipated efficiency improvements occur. Other projected benefits are for consumer prices to diminish by about 6 per cent, along with some modest improvements in governmental budget positions and the net external balance. To the extent that these results permit greater scope for *wise* macroeconomic policy initiatives, the projected gains could be as high as a 7 per cent increment in GDP and employment expansion of 5 million.[14]

These numbers must be treated with caution. If the situation evolves anything like it did for the Canada–US agreement, we can expect to see the estimates of net economic gains become more modest as time passes. Nevertheless, they will undoubtedly be quoted frequently in order to sustain the momentum that has been created in the drive toward Europe 1992.

The major differences between the Cecchini Report and studies of the expected effects of the Canada–US agreement are threefold. First, the gains are all based on the removal of the non-tariff measures whereas the focus of the Canadian studies was on the removal of tariffs. Secondly, the exploiting of scale economies accounts for about 40 per cent of anticipated gains in Europe, whereas for Canada they are expected to produce nearly all the benefits. Thirdly, the European work is more comprehensive in the sectors it includes, such as services and factor of production flows, than are Canadian studies.[15]

The studies are similar, however, in that they represent possibilities more than probabilities, economic objectives rather than accomplishments. The actual results in each trading block and the broader implications of these initiatives will much depend on the nature of the liberalization measures themselves and the institutions created to respond to them.

MARKET INTEGRATION MEASURES

Initially, the EC White Paper called for some three hundred measures to be taken towards the liberalization of the European internal market, later reduced to 279. These were classified under three headings:

1 *the abolition of technical barriers*: the free movement of persons, capital, and services; the opening up of government procurement; the harmonization of standards and laws; and commercial and industrial provisions for greater co-operation among firms;
2 *the removal of physical barriers*: particular emphasis on border controls on all types of goods, services, and people; and
3 *the removal of fiscal frontiers or barriers*: especially increased harmonization of excise and value added taxes.

By 1 April 1989 83 per cent of the proposed liberalization mesures had been submitted by the European Commission to the Council. By the June 1989 summit meeting of the European Council, well in excess of 50 per cent of the required proposals had been passed. The best progress has been made on the technical barriers, especially those related to manufactured goods, services (including financial ones), capital flows, recognition of professional qualifications, and government procurement. The areas of least progress have been animal and plant health controls, free movement of people, and fiscal harmonization.

At first glance, it may appear that the plans for Europe 1992 market integration are much more extensive than anything negotiated in or envisaged for the Canada–US relationship. Initial impressions are misleading. In many ways the FTA is very similar to EC 1992 in scope and purpose, covering most of the same areas and providing for similar degrees of consonance. Also, for a variety of sectors the extent of integration between the two nations even prior to the FTA was far more than has occurred in the EC since its formation in 1957. In these sectors EC 1992 will simply bring the EC closer to where the Canada and the United States already are. In other spheres, harmonization within the FTA is proceeding more rapidly than in the EC and for a number of sectors where the planned integration within Europe appears to be greater than in the FTA, the FTA provides for additional negotiations, or the United States has itself legislated that there should be additional changes in Canada to bring Canadian policies in line with American interests, or there is likely to be pressure by big business in Canada to bring the Canadian business environment more into line with the American environment. The remainder of this sector develops these statements.

Before the FTA, a wide range of equipment of an electrical, electronic, or otherwise technical nature already reflected similar standards in the two countries. And under the FTA the two nations have agreed to make their technical standards more compatible where they are not already, and to recognize each other's laboratory testing and inspection systems. Also, short-term capital flows and long-term debt capital movements by individuals and institutions have moved freely between Canada and the United States for many years – in contrast to a variety of exchange controls and other restrictions that have plagued the EC. Direct investment flows across the Canada–United States border have also long been extensive, even though both nations have had legislative or regulatory means of restricting takeovers on occasion. Under the FTA both nations are committed not to increase these, and Canada is phasing out many of its screening provisions on direct and indirect acquisitions by US firms.

National treatment rules are endorsed for businesses as well (article 1602). It is noteworthy too that the United States legislation to enact the FTA calls for the removal of remaining Canadian requirements for the screening of foreign direct investment, including the energy and cultural sectors which were excluded from the FTA liberalization measures. It also calls for an end to Canadian technology transfer and performance requirements regarding foreign investment in Canada, and it wants disputes regarding investment matters to be subject to the chapter

18 dispute settlement mechanism which will require arbitration. The aggrieved party (likely to be the United States) will have the right under the FTA to retaliate.[16]

With regard to banking services, the most important changes under the FTA have been the liberalization of Canadian rules to exempt United States banks from restraints that existed on foreign ownership of Canadian bank shares and on the market share of foreign forms.[17] Both countries will permit banks from the other to be established in their territories, (although because of current US laws, Canadian banks in the United States do not have all the privileges that American banks will enjoy in Canada). There is as yet, however, no provision in the FTA for some of the integrative measures that the EC Commission is proposing to the Council such as the "introduction of a single licensing system for financial institutions" and "common rules on the supervision and regulation of financial institutions."[18]

In the transport sector, although the EC was in some ways less open than the Canadian–US border (for example, fuel in transport trucks had to be measured and taxed at the borders), it is moving to greater liberalization than will occur under the FTA. A key objective is for non-resident firms to be able to provide transport services in other member states. Although there were provisions initially in the FTA for moves in this direction (with regard to shipping, for example), they were deleted at American insistence before the agreement was formally signed in December 1987.

In both the EC and the FTA there will be some opening up of the telecommunications services markets, although neither agreement will prevent state monopolies over basic telephone services. In broadcasting, the EC is striving for greater freedom to "receive and retransmit radio and television programmes."[19] Considerable freedom already exists between Canada and the United States in this area. More important from a Canadian perspective is the fact that the exceedingly high proportion of programs on Canadian television originating in the United States, as well as the overwhelming extent of American content of other Canadian cultural industries (97 per cent of movie screen time, over 75 per cent of book and magazine sales)[20], means that these materials and the values that they represent will continue to permeate Canadian society in a far greater way than the cultural materials of any one country in the EC will permeate any one other nation there, regardless of the extent of liberalization that may occur.

The FTA also provides for liberalization measures for a wide range of other services, movement towards "mutual recognition of licensing and certification requirements" (article 1403–3), and subsequent extension of the agreement to services not yet covered. The EC has initially reached agreement on inter-country recognition of architects' qualifications "and most of the medical and paramedical professions."[21] Architects are also the group specified in the free trade agreement where the development of common professional standards will first occur. In the case of medical and paramedical people, over the years the persistent movement of them from Canada to work in the United States reflects that at least implicitly some agreement on standards has been in existence for a considerable time.

With respect to intellectual and industrial property rights, the EC is attempting to move ahead to harmonize trademark and patent law, and to protect copyrighted materials. This area was left out of the FTA at this time, as apparently the demands by the United States were more than the Canadian negotiators were prepared to accept. Nevertheless, prior to the completion of the FTA negotiations, the US government pressured Canada into giving greater patent protection to US pharmaceutical companies and reducing the market in Canada for much cheaper, generic pharmaceutical products. Canadian copyright laws were also amended to give American originators of new information greater protection in, and revenue from, the Canadian market.[22] In addition, the American legislation bringing the FTA into effect specifically calls for further negotiations with Canada on these matters. It would appear that Canadian concessions to American interest in this area are not yet finished.

Less progress was made on government procurement matters in the FTA than is apparently occurring in the EC, although for the sectors previously covered by the GATT code the threshold value for items that will now be included has been reduced.[23] More significantly, the FTA does provide for a continuation of negotiations on this issue within a year after the conclusion of negotiations on procurement in the current Uruguay Round in GATT (article 1307). Even more important, the US enabling legislation specifically provides for such negotiation particularly regarding telecommunication products.

As for the areas where the EC has been making the least progress, the FTA shows mixed results. With regard to plant and animal health, where real difficulties at reaching agreement have arisen in the EC, both Canada and the United States have already committed themselves "to harmonize their respective technical regulatory requirements and inspection procedures" (article 708–1–a), and to this end have set up eight working groups (article 708–4). In this area the FTA is moving ahead more rapidly than the EC appears to be doing at this time.

Another area of limited EC advance has been over restrictions on the movement of individuals over national borders. The Canada–US agreement provides for increased freedom of movement of professionals and business people, both self-employed and employees of corporations, so as to facilitate commodity and service trade, the establishment of new businesses, and corporate movement of employees. The movement of persons that are liberalized are supposed to be "temporary," but this can mean a several-year period. There is also provision in the agreement for additional negotiations (article 1503). Although at this juncture there is no evident consideration being given to unrestricted migration between the two nations, as seems to be the objective of the EC, subsequent sections of this paper will indicate that it could be an item on the table in the future.

The final area in which the EC is having difficulty getting measures changed is in the harmonization of value added and excise taxes. This was apparently not an item discussed in the Canada–US negotiations. Nevertheless, there tends to have been pressure on Canada over the years not to deviate too far from United States taxation measures, and on occasion to modify Canadian rules to reflect the American approach, at least with regard to corporations (for example, the change made back in 1971 to let Canadian firms deduct takeover costs for income tax purposes because this was allowed in the United States). Furthermore, the removal of many of the remaining barriers to trade and factor flows between the two countries implies that the fiscal regimes are likely to become more similar, with Canada moving closer to the American model. It was no surprise to see the 1989 report of the Advisory Council on Adjustment (the de Grandpré report), *Adjusting to Win*, recommending that the Canadian tax system should be in line with the nations "major competitors" (p. 89), which of course means the United States.

This increasing degree of conformity by Canada to the American model will be further enhanced by several additional aspects of the Canada–US relationship under the FTA. In particular, Canada has provided the United States privileged access to all its resources and resource products.[24] Articles 409 and 904 of the agreement provide that in the event of shortages, or should Canada for other reasons wish to place restrictions on the export of its resources, it will have to export to the United States the same proportion of its total domestic supply (whether it comes from domestic production or imports) as it has supplied over the previous thirty-six-month period. And even if the products have been subsidized by Canadian taxpayers (as in the case of oil and gas production from the frontier areas), Canada will not be able to charge the United States a higher price than Canadians are charged for those products. This provision goes much beyond what Canada and the United States and the European countries are committed to under the International Energy Agreement, or what the EC nations are committed to with one another under their own treaty, and clearly entails a new dimension of economic integration between the two countries. This type of guaranteed access to Canadian resources at prices no higher than Canadians pay (so there will be little economic reason for the processing of the resources to remain in Canada) has been an American objective for several decades, even though it was not widely discussed during the FTA negotiations.

A common external tariff is currently an accepted aspect of the EC but is not a requirement of the FTA. Many advocates of the FTA have insisted that because it did not specifically require a common external tariff, the pressures for integration would be less. The fact is, however, that strong pressures do exist for Canada to move towards the US tariff structure on a wide variety of products if Canadian firms are to compete with American producers who have access to machinery and equipment as well as components and parts and other intermediate products (such as textile materials) available to them from third countries (such as the LDCs or the NICs) at lower tariffs than do the Canadian firms. This pressure will increase as the agreed Canada–US tariff reductions are increasingly activated. Unlike the EC case, it will not be a situation where the high-tariff country lowers its tariffs somewhat and the low-tariff nation raises its tariffs somewhat. Instead, it will simply be another example of Canadian rules being altered to conform to those of the United States.[25]

LEVERAGE AND DISPUTE RESOLUTION MECHANISMS

It should be clear by now that the United States exerts much greater leverage over Canada than vice versa. This is not only because of its greater size and Canada's dependence upon trade with it, but because its own legislation has been designed to give it a more powerful position in the FTA. A good example of this is the "fast-track" legislation under which the FTA was approved by Congress. It required that any agreement endorsed under this legislation had to have a six-month termination date. Hence the FTA contained such a provision (article 2106). Canadian negotiators and politicians have applauded this clause by indicating that if at some future point Canada does not like the FTA it can withdraw from it at six months' notice. But this is a short-sighted view. Once Canada has restructured its industry on a north–south basis and become even more dependent upon trade with the United States, it will not be in a position to terminate or threaten to terminate the agreement. The United States, however, will more readily be able to do so in order to get its way in subsequent negotiations.

A further example of the leverage given to the American negotiators by legislation follows directly from the preceding example. The US act passed to bring the FTA into effect specifically states that if Canada and the United States are not able to reach agreement within seven years from 1 January 1989 regarding the rules on the use of anti-dumping and countervailing duties, then the president of the United States must justify to Congress why the FTA should be continued (section 410). The pressure will therefore be on Canadian negotiators and the government to comply with American wishes on these matters, so as to avoid termination of the agreement.[26]

The US enabling legislation also provides for a variety of other negotiations to be conducted by the President's Office to gain further concessions from Canada. These include increasing the value of Canada–US inputs to automobiles from 50 to 60 per cent (thus reducing Canada's capability to import from Japan, Korea, or other countries); limiting Canada–US trade in potatoes (a product in which Prince Edward Island has a major comparative advantage); challenging Canadian export controls on unprocessed fish; and restricting Canadian steel exports to the United States.

Finally, the United States did not exempt Canada from its 1988 protectionist trade act, even though this was given as an important reason for Canada to secure the free trade pact. Thus Canada will now be even *more* vulnerable to American actions than other nations because of the manner in which disputes under the FTA are to be settled. Panels are to be appointed to resolve difficulties, but they are only binding on the two countries if they involve safeguard measures which are not resolved under chapter 18, or if the two nations agree to make a particular panel's decision binding. Otherwise the outcome will be based on further bilateral bargaining and/or one nation retaliating. Once again the United States, because of its much greater size and lesser dependence on Canada than Canada has on it, is in the stronger position.

By contrast, the decision-making procedures in the EC are markedly different. Power is much more evenly spread between the twelve constituent countries. Furthermore, the various governing institutions accommodate regular inputs from directly and indirectly elected representatives (through the European Parliament and the Council of Ministers respectively), from bureaucrats (through the Commission), from appointed judicial representatives (at the Court of Justice), and from a broad variety of interest groups, including workers, small business, farmers, professional groups, and consumers, in addition to the usual industry lobbies (through the 189-member Economic and Social Committee). Thus, outcomes are not subject to undue influence from a single country.

For example, in order to defeat proposals to Council that seek to enhance the internal integration of the market, a minimum of three nations must be opposed.[27] Hence, although new integrative measures can still be prevented, on a wide range of issues one nation alone no longer has the power to do so. At the same time, for changes to be instituted, at least seven nations must be in favour of them.

While the Council remains the key decision-making body within the Community, the 1986 SEA includes a range of clauses which constrain the Council's scope of action and enhance the visibility, status, and authority of the European Parliament. The Parliament is made up of 518 members directly elected every five years by voters in all twelve countries.[28] Frequently, as is currently the case in the United Kingdom, those joining the Parliament may have quite different views from the governments in power in their home countries. This provides a further counterbalancing influence from a body whose recently enhanced role includes the power to withhold approval on measures to bring about complete integration of the internal European market, the admission of new members to EC, or the establishment of agreements with outside countries (articles 18, 8, and 9 of the SEA).

Likewise, the Economic and Social Committee provides an opportunity for various interest groups to have some input into the policy decisions of the Community. The 1987 SEA (article 18) has enhanced the role of the Committee: all new directives passed by the Council which have as their purpose the complete liberalization of internal Community markets by 1992 must be referred to this Committee for its opinion. This means that at least interest groups like labour have a recognized and accepted channel for their views to be inserted into the decision-making process as the Community marches toward integration. They do not have to fight for a hearing, nor are they to be ignored.

These broadly representative institutions have been accorded increasing authority by the EC's member countries, and may eventually come to supersede their counterpart institutions in the individual states. For example, the judgments of the European Court of Justice already take precedence over the courts of the member nations, and have on occasion helped to reduce the protectionism of individual member states.[29]

THE EC AND THE FTA: SOCIAL AND POLITICAL DIMENSIONS

It is appropriate at this point to examine the way the liberalization process is being handled in these two large trading blocs, and the broader political implications of the integration now occurring.

Social Dimensions

The nature of the economic changes proposed under the Europe 1992 liberalization plan is been quite different from what has gone on in North America under the FTA.

The 1986 SEA added a new section to the Treaty of Rome, entitled Economic and Social Cohesion. This section commits the members to "reducing disparities between the various regions and the backwardness of the least-favoured regions" (article 130A) and to co-ordinating their economic policies to achieve these objectives (article 130B). The use of the European Regional Development Fund "is intended to help redress the principal regional imbalances in the Community" and to assist "in the conversion of declining industrial regions" (article 130C). Amendments are to be made in the operating rules of this fund as well as the other structural funds of the EC so that they would have more funding and be better able to achieve the desired objectives (article 130D and the declaration on article D:64). In the process there are to be inputs by the European Parliament as well as the Economic and Social Committee.

In another addition to the 1957 treaty, the Community committed itself "to preserve, protect and improve the quality of the environment; to contribute towards protecting human health; [and] to ensure a prudent and rational utilization of natural resources" (article 130R–1).

The 1986 amendments also included changes to existing sections of the EC treaty to emphasize the importance of developing "the dialogue between management and labour" which could lead to decisions "based on agreement." Attention was also given to improving working conditions, especially regarding "the health and safety of workers" (article 118A–1), and ensuring that "administrative, financial, and legal constraints" would not discourage the development of small and medium-sized businesses. This concern for small and medium-sized firms was also reflected in the provisions for additional research and development (article 130F–2).

More recently the Commission produced *The Report on Social Developments: Year 1987*, which reviewed a wide range of social policies and concerns relating to unemployment, poverty, education and training, health, industrial relations, working conditions, and social support systems generally.

In May 1989 the Commission introduced a preliminary Community Charter of Fundamental Social Rights, reflecting the significance which the previous two European Council meetings had attached to ensuring that the achievement of the liberalized internal market was accompanied by responsible and compassionate social policies throughout the Community. This charter had sections on fair and equitable wages; improved living and working conditions; adequate social protection; rights of association and to engage in collective bargaining; rights of information, consultation, and participation of workers in business decisions affecting employment and working conditions; and the protections of particular disadvantaged groups in society such as the disabled and the elderly.

At the Council of Ministers meeting of 12 June 1989, eleven of the states (the United Kingdom being the exception) approved the charter, and it was agreed that discussions should be continued with a view to bringing about its adoption as soon as possible. The European Council, meeting at Madrid on 26–27 June, agreed that work on this "social dimension of the Single Market" should be continued, and specifically stated that "in the course of construction of the single European market social aspects should be given the same importance as economic aspects and should accordingly be developed in a balanced fashion" (p. 5). The European Council also agreed that a European Environmental Agency should be established.

These measures reflect not only the growing strength of socialist and environmentalist political representatives in the European Parliament,[30] but also the lengthy, broad, and inclusive process of discussion and consultation that has been established in moving towards 1992. From the time that the White Paper came out in mid 1985 until 1992, there will have been more than seven years for interested parties in each country of the EC to examine the implications of what is happening, and raise significant concerns about the process and its effects.

The way that Europe 1992 was negotiated is in stark contrast to the approach taken to construct the FTA. The US "fast-track" legislation required that an agreement be reached by 4 October 1987 for it to be approved under this legislation. This meant that less than eighteen months elapsed from the time negotiations commenced until they were completed. As well, the negotiations were cloaked in secrecy so that interested groups in society had no firm idea as to what was being discussed, and therefore had little opportunity until after the agreement was announced to consider the wider social and other implications of the arrangement.[31] By that time, under US law, the agreement could not be altered; it was a take it or leave it proposition.

The clear message was that the social implications of the deal could be safely ignored. This view was manifested in the Canadian government's assertion that the agreement would make Canada economically stronger and thus better able to strengthen its social and regional development programs.[32] And during the debate in Canada on the FTA, the government repeatedly claimed that Canada's regional development programs, health care system, and other social support programs would not be affected by the agreement.

Consequently, instead of containing the wide range of measures to cope with regional disparities, environmental issues, the interests of small business, and the working conditions, health care, and other social concerns of the population as the EC provisions have, the FTA is silent on these matters.

This does not mean that these matters are not on the table. The US implementing legislation, as well as its 1988 Trade Act to which Canada is subject, has gone on record against all Canadian development grants which, in its view, subsidize Canadian exporters to the United States.[33] In areas of environmental concern, the United States has often been slower than Canada in recognizing the need to act on certain environmental matters such as acid rain. In terms of social programs, in spite of all its wealth, the United States stands near the bottom of the list among developed countries regarding broad social programs such as health care and unemployment insurance.[34] In addition, the orientation of American big business, which heavily influences Canadian business attitudes, is towards reduced social programs, lower wages, and weaker and fewer unions generally.

It is evident that, by signing the FTA, Canada has committed itself to be drawn more and more into the United States economic and social vortex, where the interests of big business prevail over broader societal interests. As Eric Kierans and Walter Stewart have observed, the system is one of "corporatism, not capitalism."[35] Corporate interests dominate. We can expect that this process will continue as the remaining trade barriers between the United States and Canada come down. Even the Advisory Council on Adjustment which was appointed in 1989 by the Canadian government to consider the opportunities available under the FTA, as well as the adjustment issues that might be involved, had a strong big-business orientation, and showed little of the social consciousness of the EC's Community Charter of Fundamental Social Rights.[36]

In fairness we might note that the federal government has taken to encouraging small and medium-sized businesses to begin exporting, and, rather belatedly, it has established certain consultative mechanisms involving labour and other groups in society.[37] But the nature of the FTA, and the characteristics and dominance of the United States' economic, political, and social systems, are likely to mean that the Canadian system will become increasingly like the American one over time, rather than retaining a social orientation that in the past has had much more in common with the nations of the EC and the approaches they are emphasizing today.

Political Dimensions

Discussion of the EC evolving into a politically unified Europe after 1992 is open and unabashed. One of the preparations being made for this is to bring about a complete monetary union. The SEA included a chapter in the 1957 treaty which provided for the "convergence of economic and monetary policies" (article 102A). At the EC summit in

Madrid in June 1989 it was decided that the Community should move to end exchange controls and other blockage to community-wide banking and financial services.[38] Some observers and participants see this move as being the crucial one in subsequently bringing about fiscal harmonization and eventual political union.[39] The United Kingdom is still much against the monetary union, and as yet has not committed itself to the next two steps entailing the establishment of a common currency for all member countries and a regional central bank for the EC. As this is one area where each nation has a veto, it is difficult at this time to know what will transpire in the future, given the intense feelings on the part of France and some other European nations in favour of greater monetary and eventual political union and Britain's reluctance to move in this direction. Yet the pressures now being placed upon the Community members by the bureaucrats in the Commission and some of the leading member states such as France and West Germany remind one of the pressures by committed people, including Prussian civil servants, that resulted in all the states in the Zollverein except Luxembourg forming into Germany as we knew it prior to World War One.

With respect to the United States and Canada, monetary union involving a single currency and a unified central banking system for the two nations is not currently being considered by either country – even though on occasion Canada has been referred to as the thirteenth Federal Reserve District of the United States because of the marked tendency of the Bank of Canada to follow policies similar to those of the US Federal Reserve system.

The possibility of eventual political union is not being openly discussed either. It is as though there has been implicit agreement among politicians and the news media not to do so. This complete absence of discussion may be for one of three reasons. First, it is possible that the idea is believed to be simply too ludicrous or absurd to deserve serious consideration in either nation. Those who hold this view in Canada may well be content to believe that Canada is a sovereign nation which will continue to be able to exercise its sovereignty regardless of the nature of its ties with the United States and the far greater economic and political clout that country enjoys in the bilateral relationship. The American rationale may simply be that it has no desires along this line and that it is not an option that it would wish to entertain. Thus, no further discussion is warranted.

The second reason is that both governments recognize that eventual union is a realistic, if not an inevitable, possibility, but they would prefer to let it occur gradually with as little political debate as possible until the two nations are so harmonized in their policies and so irreversibly intertwined that the tying of the final knot looks to be the only logical and sane course of action. The United States may hold this view because to make union an explicit policy might alert Canadians too soon to what was happening and thus generate a strong Canadian backlash against such a move with much ill-will ensuing. Concurrently, it would place the United States in an unfavourable light internationally, for it would be seen to be following the same type of imperialistic policies that it pursued in the decade before the turn of the twentieth century when it unilaterally "absorbed" Hawaii, Guam, the Philippines, Puerto Rico, and Wake Island.[40] From the Canadian side, the government and its supporters in the business community and elsewhere may also see that a premature pursuit of such a policy could lead to the government's downfall should voters show a strong sentiment to preserve the Canadian identity and Canadian self-government. Hence it is content to wait for the opportune moment before openly discussing and explicitly moving towards some form of union with the United States.

The third reason may well be because, although such a union is a realistic option, it is quite unnecessary. From the American perspective several of its major objectives vis-à-vis Canada have already been achieved – such as the removal of Canadian tariffs over time, guaranteed access to Canadian natural resources at prices no higher than prevail in Canada, reduction in Canadian constraints on foreign direct investment, and the emasculation of the auto pact. The FTA also provides for continued negotiations over the next few years which are likely to produce additional limitations on Canadian regional development, trade, investment, and cultural and social policies, as well as further bilateral harmonization of standards and policies in a number of sectors. Hence the probability is high that the United States view of how the bilateral relationship should evolve will come to pass.[41] Pressures by the corporate sector in both countries, especially with regard to taxation, social support systems, and other relevant programs, are also likely to result in Canadian policies being brought increasingly into conformity with those in the United States. From an American perspective, therefore, effective control of Canadian political decision-making, insofar as it in any way affects the interests of the United States, largely will have been obtained. The United States will have the control it desires without having to bear the political responsibilities for the impact of its actions on the Canadian people, and without having to face the legislative pressures that would come from having additional states in the union with their share of congressmen and senators participating in the debate and log-rolling that occurs in Washington.

On the Canadian side, the foregoing type of arrangement may be quite acceptable to the federal politicians and bureaucrats. It gains for them the fatherly approval of the United States authorities and at the same time preserves the appearance that significant economic and political decisions are being made in Canada. With any luck, the arrangements may minimize the objections of those Canadians concerned about the future of Canada as a separate entity. This stance could, of course, backfire if the arrangements result over time in Canadians becoming relatively less well off – and this could occur if there was a major exodus of manufacturing or service functions to the United States and/or a reduction in the social support systems to which they had become accustomed. At the moment, however, those in authority, if they have any qualms about the future course of events, seem willing to submerge them and gamble on the outcome being favourable for them, even if it may not be for Canada as a whole.

IMPLICATIONS OF THE EC AND FTA FOR WORLD TRADE

Once most of the barriers to flows of merchandise, services, capital, and, to a significant degree, labour are removed within the EC and between the United States and Canada, two closely related questions arise: what will be the relationship between these two huge trading blocs? How will they affect world trade?

With regard to the North American bloc, the dominance of the United States implies that the international effects will depend primarily on what its stance happens to be. Canada is unlikely to have any determining role.[42] For its part, the United States is likely to have little interest in pushing the system to a point of collapse by becoming an inward-looking trade fortress as a consequence of a trade war with Europe post-1992. As the world's largest international debtor it continues to face large annual merchandise trade and current account deficits which are augmenting that debt by over $100 billion annually. If it ever hopes to reverse this situation, it will have to have a liberalized trading world for its exports. Massive increases in protection by the United States would only invite retaliation by other nations and bring world trade to a virtual halt. Thus, although it can bluster and threaten, the United States is not really in a position to go the ultimate step of closing its doors completely to trade. Also, that country's current goods and services exports amount to about $500 billion or over 10 per cent of its GDP. A major disruption of such trade would have a severe adverse impact on the US domestic economy.

In addition, given the tremendous power and influence of the huge corporations in the United States, and noting that it is not in their interest that world trade be stymied, businessmen are likely to put serious pressure on their government to keep trade flows relatively open. With relatively few exceptions, these corporations are already international in their operations, and would only be hurt by a major trade war. For example, in 1988, American corporations had $327 billion of foreign direct investment, 39 per cent of it being in the EC alone. Also, many American firms that currently are not in the EC are now planning to invest there, rather than merely relying on exports to the EC. This has undoubtedly been in part stimulated by the EC plan to have all products which satisfy the technical standards of one member be entitled to circulate freely in all member countries. Again, American corporate subsidiaries abroad are major exporters back to the United States and would suffer greatly from large increases in protectionism. Fully 30 per cent of Taiwan's trade surplus with the United States and 40 per cent of Japan's can be accounted for by the exports of American subsidiaries in these countries back to the United States.[43] Increased US protectionism is not in their interest.

There are, of course, some large American firms which are basically import-competitors rather than international in scope. These will continue to seek import protection when the competition is severe: this has occurred vis-à-vis Canada, despite the FTA, for lumber, steel, potash, processed pork, and a variety of other manufactured products. But such moves are nothing new, have little to do with internal market liberalization envisaged by Europe 1992, and are unlikely to override completely the broader international interests of the majority of large American corporations. In general there would seem to be little cause for international concern about the trade implications of the FTA.[44]

As for the EC, it is not likely that the removal of internal non-tariff-measures will result in a Fortress Europe mentality and a decline in world trade. Such a scenario goes against the main motivation of those spearheading EC 1992, which is to enable European businesses of every size to compete more effectively with the United States, Japan, and the NICS. The very concept of Fortress Europe also goes against the EC's commitment to adhere to GATT and to continue negotiations in the Uruguay Round for lower barriers on goods and services. The EC authorities have also pledged themselves not to take away the rights of foreign firms already in the EC. Similarly, European subsidiaries of foreign firms have been guaranteed the same access to public procurement as EC-owned firms, provided the sectors involved are covered by the GATT procurement code.[45]

Moreover, the fortress concept is also contrary to the perceptions and plans of the corporate sector in Europe. Over 60 per cent of all firms surveyed, both in manufacturing and services, see their reorganization in Europe as but part of a *global* strategy. For some sectors, such as computers, mechanical engineering, and telecommunications, the percentage is over 80.[46] Accordingly, horizontal (as opposed to vertical) mergers and diversification are popular acquisition strategies in the EC, as are joint ventures and other such alliances, including the licensing of technology, particularly among European- and Japanese-owned firms in the EC. Even small and medium-sized firms which are planning to compete successfully by finding market niches for themselves are no longer looking at mere national markets, but at Pan-European ones as a minimum.[47] Furthermore, with the advent of modern production and communication technology such as computer-aided design and computer-aided manufacture (CAD–CAM) and fax machines, "Giant companies may no longer enjoy a competitive edge, except in capital-intensive sectors such as aerospace." More important than size is simply the geographic spread of operations and the ability to coordinate supplies and production to satisfy the preferences of local markets.[48]

Finally, European firms in both the manufacturing and service sectors are expanding their investment in other nations, not just within the EC but in the United States in particular. In 1988 there were US$ 194 billion of foreign direct investment in the United States from corporations in the EC, amounting to 59 per cent of all such investment. United Kingdom companies alone spent US$ 32 billion on takeovers in the United States in 1988.

To summarize, then, it appears overly pessimistic to think that the two large trading blocs in North America and Europe would begin to withdraw into themselves as fortresses with accompanying highly adverse consequences for themselves and world trade generally.

There are, however, several aspects of Europe 1992 which do give cause for concern to other nations. EC firms will likely be more competitive, not only in Europe, but also in the United States, Japan, and throughout the world. Secondly, the EC has already indicated that some protectionist measures which have hitherto been on a national basis within the EC, such as import quotas on some industrial goods from Eastern Europe, Japan, and under the Generalized System of Preferences, will be replaced by EC-wide quotas and uniform rules of access. The bargaining power of the EC on such quota negotiations will thus be greater than before.

Thirdly, and of greater significance, the EC is going to be emphasizing "balance of mutual benefits and reciprocity." In other words, the EC is not about to give unilaterally to other nations the benefits of full access to the liberalized EC market beyond what they have now without getting something in return. This will be true for financial services, transport, telecommunications, and public procurement.[49] If foreign firms want to enjoy such benefits, their home countries are going to have to provide similar privileges to EC firms in their countries.

This is where it becomes difficult for United States, which does not have a consistent position on such issues as national treatment and reciprocity. It wants the national treatment principle extended to its firms in foreign lands, so that they may enjoy the same rights as domestic firms to bid on government procurement contracts. Yet Washington refuses to accept the same principle on patent rights. If a nation prefers not to provide patent protection to any domestic or foreign firms, that nation can be punished according to US trade law as passed in 1988. That is, countries other than the United States are not even allowed to decide for themselves what patent rules they want; they must either conform to the American view or be liable to retaliation.[50] Canada has already experienced the full force of this viewpoint.

As for the reciprocity principle, the United States simultaneously holds inconsistent positions. It endorses the principle that foreign countries should give US firms the same access to their domestic telecommunications market as it provides foreign firms in its home market. Yet in an area such as banking, it is not prepared to provide the same access to foreign banks that many foreign countries provide to their banks operating in those foreign countries. American state and federal laws greatly restrict the cross-state operation and types of transactions that banks can use. If other nations were to use the principle of reciprocity that the United States has now made law with respect to intellectual property rights, they would be justified in punishing the United States or withdrawing privileges from its banks operating in their countries.[51] Perhaps the United States is apprehensive that the EC will move in this direction.

We may ask, therefore, whether America may be attempting to raise the spectre of Fortress Europe from time to time to divert attention from its own inconsistent policies designed to protect the interests of American corporations wherever they are.

LOOKING TO THE FUTURE: WHITHER CANADA?

Let us now review the major insights arising from the preceding analysis. First, the Canada–US free trade agreement is close to being as comprehensive and integrative in nature as is the EC 1992 objective. The agreement covers nearly all the same areas, and provides for a wide range of harmonization measures similar in nature to those being adopted in Europe. In a number of areas the degree of integration that existed between Canada and the United States even before the FTA was greater than existed in the EC after nearly thirty years. This is true for such items as capital flows, many product standards, and the reliance of Canadian news media and the cultural industries generally on American material and productions. Hence the EC 1992 measures in these areas are basically a catching-up process in comparison with the long-standing Canada–US situation.

In other areas the FTA is currently moving more rapidly towards integration than the EC appears to be – for example, with regard to the "temporary" movement of business people and firms among countries. In areas where the FTA currently does not envisage as extensive an integration as under the EC 1992 proposals, there are either (1) provisions for further negotiations in these areas for greater liberalization (as with services and government procurement); (2) the US implementing legislation specifically calls for further liberalization in accord with American interests (as with the remaining Canadian restrictions on foreign direct investment inflows and accompanying performance requirements, the protection of intellectual property rights, and government procurement, especially in telecom products); or (3) there is likely to be pressure by Canadian business to harmonize Canadian laws with those of the United States (as with taxation).

Additionally, provisions giving the United States guaranteed access to Canadian resources go far beyond resource agreements in Europe or elsewhere. In return for these giveaways, Canada has failed in its bid to secure exemption from American protectionist actions. Furthermore, mechanisms for governance and dispute resolution, coupled with a markedly larger economy, give the United States much greater leverage over Canada than that which is exerted by any single European nation over its EC partners. While this may not ultimately lead to the kind of outright political union being openly considered in Europe, powerful pressures for harmonization of regulatory frameworks, industrial assistance, regional development, and social programs will make Canadian sovereignty increasingly hollow.

This discussion also suggests that concern about the two large trading blocs of Europe and North America squaring off against one another in a global trading war in the 1990s is misplaced. Rather, countries need to be more wary of the growing international power of large business corporations of whatever nationality, the increasingly large influence they are having on the policies and politics of nations, and the potential for conflict which is developing between these powerful entities and society generally as they move their operations around the world.

NOTES

1 In the past it has been customary to refer only to the 1957 treaty establishing the European Economic Community (EEC). There were, in fact, two other treaties establishing Communities in Europe: the 1951 Paris

Agreement when the European Coal and Steel Community (ECSC) was formed, and the 25 March 1957 treaty in Rome (the same date as the EEC treaty) when the European Atomic Energy Community (EAEC) came into being. It was decided in 1965 to merge the administrative institutions of these three organizations, and this took effect in 1967. Today, therefore, it is customary, and appropriate, to refer just to the EEC or, as the Europeans prefer to think of it today, the European Communities (EC). The EC includes the original six nations which formed the EEC in 1957 (Belgium, Luxembourg, France, West Germany, Italy, and the Netherlands); the three which joined 1 January 1973 (Denmark, Ireland, and the United Kingdom); Greece, which became a member in 1981; and Spain and Portugal, which entered on 1 January 1986.

2 In addition, the long-standing hostility between Ireland and the United Kingdom means that Ireland is unlikely to be absorbed into the United Kingdom or come to accept arbitrary British decisions on disputes involving the two nations.

3 See Bruce W. Wilkinson, "The Canada–US Free Trade Negotiations: An Assessment," in David L. McKee, ed., *Canadian–American Economic Relations: Conflict and Cooperation on a Continental Scale* (New York 1988), and Brian Copeland, "Of Mice and Elephants: The Canada–US Free Trade Agreement," *Contemporary Policy Issues* 7, no. 3 (July 1989): 42–60.

4 See, for example, Richard Harris, "Jobs and Free Trade," in D.W. Conklin and T.J. Courchene, eds., *Canadian Trade at a Crossroad: Options for New International Agreements* (Toronto, Ontario: Economic Council 1985.)

5 See Druscilla K. Brown and Robert M. Stern, "Computable General Equilibrium Estimates of the Gains from US Canadian Trade Liberalization," in David Greenaway, Thomas Hyclak, and Robert J. Thorton, eds., *Economic Aspects of Regional Trading Arrangements* (New York: Harvester Wheatshead 1989), 69–108; Randall Wigle, "General Equilibrium Evaluation of Canada–US Trade Liberalization in a Global Context," *Canadian Journal of Economics* 21, no. 3 (August 1988): 539–64; and Fred Lazar, "Survey of Ontario Manufacturing," *Canadian Public Policy* 14, no. 1 (March 1988): 78–91.

6 Tim Hazeldine, "Is There a Canada/US Productivity Gap?" paper presented to the Canadian Economics Association Meetings, Quebec City, June 1989.

7 The Business Council on National Issues, consisting of the chief executive officers of 150 of the largest corporations in Canada, is without doubt the most powerful economic lobby group in Canada. For a discussion of its origins and early part in bringing the free trade deal to pass see Dave Langille, "The BCNI Calls the Shots," *The Facts* 10, no. 2 (Spring 1988): 102–7.

8 These included reductions in provincial liquor board mark-ups on US alcoholic beverages, in Canadian controls on foreign direct investment

inflows, in restrictions regarding the cultural industries, in certain Canadian standards and testing requirements, in US banking activities in Canada, on service trade generally, and on Canadian Wheat Board restrictions regarding US grain and grain products imports; as well as greater discipline over the Canadian use of subsidies; and enhanced protection of their intellectual property rights in Canada (e.g., Office of the US Trade Representative). See Duncan Cameron, ed., *The Free Trade Papers* (Toronto: James Lorimer 1986).

9 One modest gain for Canada was that it is less likely to be adversely affected (as it was hitherto) if the United States uses its safeguard laws to restrain imports from third countries.

10 Except for the most recent members such as Spain and Portugal.

11 See the treaty of Rome, Title I, "Free Movement of Goods," especially chapter 2, "Elimination of Quantitative Restrictions Between Member States," and Title III, "Free Movement of Persons, Services and Capital."

12 See, for example, Commission of the European Communities, *Completing the Internal Market: An Area Without Internal Frontiers* (Brussels 1988).

13 The first study was by Data Resources Inc. in 1987. Its full results are not available to other than the firm's clients. But it is known that projected benefits are far from spectacular – a gain in GDP by 1992 of about one-half of 1 per cent, and an expansion of employment by 1995 of only 300,000. (See Michael Calingaert, *The 1992 Challenge from Europe: Development of the European Community's Internal Market* [Washington: Brookings Institution 1988], 67). There was also the 1988 report by Jacques Pelkman and Alan Winters, *Europe's Domestic Market*. But rather than being a quantitative economic analysis it is simply a discussion and assessment of the white paper and the measures necessary to reach the European objectives.

14 Paolo Cecchini, *The European Challenge, 1992: The Benefits of a Single Market* (Aldershot, England: Wildwood House 1989), chapter 10.

15 The Canadian government published a series of studies after the FTA was negotiated which looked at implications of the agreement for a broad spectrum of industries, including services, agriculture, and other resource sectors. But they were more in the nature of apologies for rather than careful analyses of the agreement and its full consequences.

16 United States, A Bill to Enhance the Competitiveness of American Industry and for Other Purposes (the Omnibus Trade and Competitiveness Act, 1988, section 304).

17 For example, the United States is now exempt from the rule that no more than 25 per cent of a Canadian bank's shares can be held by foreigners. Also US subsidiaries will no longer be restricted by the rule limiting the foreign sector of the banking industry to 16 per cent of total banking assets (article 1703).

18 Commission of the European Communities, *Completing the Internal Market*, 18.

19 Ibid., 19.

20 David Crane, "Canada–US Free Trade Negotiations and the Cultural Industries: a Canadian View," notes for a presentation to the Council on Foreign Relations, New York, 26 March 1987.

21 Commission of the European Communities, *Completing the Internal Market*, 17.

22 See Roy Davidson, "Patents and Copyright: The Tilt in the Level Playing Field," *Policy Options* 11, no. 1 (January–February 1990): 24–30. He discusses the concessions made in the Canadian Patent Act of November 1987, and the Copyright Act of 1988.

23 From about c$200,000 to about c$30,000.

24 The agreement is reciprocal, but the issue involved is most likely to arise with regard to the supply of Canadian resources to the United States, not the other way around.

25 Members of the European Free Trade Association may also have to conform increasingly to the common external tariff of the EC and to whatever harmonized taxes may evolve in the EC. This is because many of them already have tariff-free access to the EC, and as the huge EC internal market becomes more integrated, their own competitiveness will require such conformity (See Jeffery Harrop, *The Political Economy of Integration in the European Community* [Aldershot, England: Edward Elgar Publishing 1989], 15). The principle here is identical to that of Canada conforming to the large US internal market arrangements.

26 Another example of where US law has taken precedence in Canada–US negotiations is the potash settlement in late 1987, after American allegations of Canadian dumping. The agreement that resulted involved Saskatchewan conforming verbatim to US law regarding the pricing of foreign products alleged to be dumped in US markets. See Bruce W. Wilkinson, "The Saskatchewan Potash Industry and the 1987 US Antidumping Action," *Canadian Public Policy* 15, no. 2 (1989): 154–61.

27 In the qualified majority procedure, each of the four largest nations – France, Italy, the United Kingdom, and West Germany – have ten votes. Spain has eight votes. The next four countries – Belgium, Greece, Netherlands, and Portugal – each have five votes. Both Denmark and Ireland have three votes, while Luxembourg has two. For a measure to be passed, it must receive fifty-four of the seventy-six votes. Policy areas where qualified majority voting will henceforth be used include amendments to any Commission proposals (providing the Commission and the European Parliament approve) (article 7); the altering or suspending duties of the common external tariff of the Community (article 16); the improvement and harmonization of conditions in the working environment regarding health and safety measures (article 21); detailed implementation of research and technological development programs (once the broad principles have been

unanimously agreed to) (article 24); and the funding of Euratom (article 28).

28 The distribution of representatives by countries is: eighty-one from each of France, Italy, West Germany, and the United Kingdom, sixty from Spain, twenty-five from the Netherlands, twenty-four from each of Belgium, Greece, and Portugal, sixteen from Denmark, fifteen from Ireland, and six from Luxembourg.

29 Calingaert, *1992 Challenge from Europe*, 17–18.

30 In the May 1989 EC elections the Socialist parties gained the largest proportion of seats they have ever had – 35 per cent, or 182 of the 518 seats. Those parties with a particular focus on environmental issues (the Rainbow Group) gained twenty-three seats, up from 20 in the previous Parliament. And if the UK had had some form of proportional representation, additional seats for this group would have been gained from there as well. Commission of the European Communities, *Fourth Progress Report of the Commission to the Council and the European Parliament* (Brussels 1989).

31 Sectoral Advisory Groups on International Trade (SAGITs) were established by the Canadian government to be in liaison with the Trade Negotiations Office. But they were made up primarily of those with strong initial biases in favour of a deal, and were not oriented towards the broader social issues associated with any agreement reached.

32 Canada, External Affairs, *The Canada–U.S. Free Trade Agreement Synopsis* (Ottawa 1987), 1.

33 The US implementing legislation provides for the president to *negotiate* the FTA with Canada so as to bring about greater discipline over the use of subsidies by federal or provincial governments which, in the US view, have adverse effects upon American producers of similar products in the markets of the United States *and Canada* (my italics) (section 409, a, 2, A, ii). Notice that this statute covers not only goods exported to the United States but goods *produced and sold in Canada* with which US products exported to Canada would have to compete! The US Omnibus Trade Bill of 1988 goes on to define subsidies as including government grants, loans, and loan guarantees that are not at commercial rates, the provision of services or commodities of any type at less than full market prices, the forgiveness of debts, and the covering of production or distribution costs by governments (section 1312). There is no exception made for grants or any other assistance which might be given in Canada to offset the costs of locating an industry in a region which Canada would like to assist but which from a purely business perspective may have cost disadvantages. Moreover, the 1988 US Trade Act states that "Nominal general availability... is not a basis for determining that the bounty, grant, or subsidy is not, or has not been, in fact provided to a specific enterprise or industry, or group thereof" (section 1312, 5, B). That is, even though the govern-

mental assistance may be available to all firms in an area, this is no reason *not* to count it as assistance to the particular firm whose products are being labelled as subsidized. Recall that even before the FTA and the 1988 Trade Act, the US International Trade Administration had concluded that Canadian regional development grants were subsidies to Atlantic ground fish production against which countervailing duties should be applied. The ITA actually found fifty-five of eighty-five federal and provincial programs to be subsidies on Atlantic ground fish production and export; see Economic Council of Canada, *Reaching Outward* (Ottawa 1987), 48. Clearly, the US objective is to act against Canadian regional and other development programs involving government aid to industry in any form. This is quite different from the EC, where the regional development and other assistance funds are to be augmented to assist backwards regions or disadvantaged groups!

34 "Of the twenty four OECD countries, in 1986 only three nations, Spain, Luxembourg, and Japan, have lower government social expenditures as a per cent of GDP than does the United States. Canada stands thirteenth. Again, health care in Canada is universal, whereas in the United States about 35 million people have no medicare or medical insurance. Also, a far lower percentage of the unemployed in the United States are entitled to unemployment insurance benefits than is true for Canada. See Economic Council of Canada, *Reaching Outward*, 50–53.

35 Eric Kierans and Walter Stewart, *Wrong End of the Rainbow: The Collapse of Free Enterprise in Canada* (Toronto: Collins 1988).

36 This is not surprising given that four of the five Council members represented big business. Only one of them was from labour and no one represented other groups in society. Although the report contained a few recommendations for steps to be taken to protect workers more effectively when layoffs or bankruptcies occurred, the majority of the recommendations regarding the labour force had to do with preparing it better to serve the needs of business. These included greater outlays for education and training and a definite shift away from safety-net types of expenditures for unemployed people. Another host of recommendations had to do with additional support for big business in the way of more financing of universities by provincial governments so better-equipped workers would be available, increased tax breaks for business if they meet training commitments and do more R&D, and more government procurement contracts for business (such as in the high-tech defence industries) so as to encourage more R&D. The report made little of the fact that employers in Canada spend a far smaller proportion of the sales on training than does business in many other countries, that industrial research and development performance of big business in Canada is far less than in other advanced nations, and that foreign-owned entreprises in Canada are the poorest performers in this latter regard. Nor does the report take any cognizance of

the fact that it is not big business that creates the jobs in Canada (especially not foreign-owned big business which has frequently reduced employment in Canada) but rather small businesses of fewer than twenty employees, and thus did not give any special attention to the needs of such businesses. See Report of the Advisory Council on Adjustment, *Adjusting to Win.*

37 For example, the newly instituted Labour Force Development Strategy will involve consultation with thirteen national organizations via six task forces. It commenced in July 1989. The focus of these consultations is much along the lines of the recommendations of the Advisory Council on Adjustment.

38 The United Kingdom, although it has not been in favour of monetary union, nevertheless has agreed to join the European Monetary System (a system of fixed exchange rates among the members) providing the above liberalization measures were completed and the country's inflation rate was "reduced significantly" from its 1989 rate of 8.3 per cent.

39 Note the viewpoints expressed in Canada, External Affairs, *1992 Implications of a Single European Market* (1989), 119. The entire section B.12, Banking and Finance, of this report is relevant.

40 See Bruce W. Wilkinson, "Canada–US Free Trade Negotiations: An Assessment," in D.W. Conklin and T.J. Courchene, eds., *Canadian Trade at a Crossroad: Options for New International Agreement.* (Toronto: Ontario Economic Council 1985).

41 The FTA even now provides that if either nation should wish to enact policies which prejudice or reduce the advantages which the other country believes it is entitled to under the FTA, there must be negotiations. The aggrieved nation could retaliate if it is not satisfied with the other nation's response to its allegations. Hence again, the United States, because of its size and the threat of abrogation in six months, has the stronger position.

42 Canada's role will continue at best to be one of reacting to American decisions, and on occasion taking the lead among non–US and non–EC nations – as it has done in recent years with regard to agricultural matters – in submitting proposals for the resolution of differences between the United States and the EC.

43 Robert Reich, "Corporation and Nation," in *Dialogue* 83, no. 2 (1989): 1–6.

44 An exception to this would be Japan, which has reason to be upset about the deal that the United States struck with Canada regarding the treatment of Japanese automobile companies under the FTA.

45 Delegation of the Commission of the European Communities, "Europe 1992: Europe World Partner," *News* (Ottawa, 10 October 1988).

46 Canada, External Affairs, *1992 Implications of a Single European Market. Part 1: Effects on Europe* (Ottawa 1989), 52.

47 Ibid., 26–29, 34–35, 42.

48 Ibid., 14–15. Many Canadian economists, and other supporters of the FTA who argued that the achieving of new economies of scale was the key reason for Canada to enter the FTA, overlooked this point.

49 Delegation of the Commission of the European Communities, "Europe 1992: Europe World Partner," 3, 4, 5; ibid., "A Europe without Borders by 1992: Answers to Some Questions," News (Ottawa, October 1988), 4, 5.

50 Raymond Vernon, "Can the US Negotiate for Trade Equality?" Harvard Business Review 89, no. 3 (May–June 1989): 96–103; and John F. Magee, "1992: Moves Americans Must Make," ibid.: 78, 84.

It is also worth recalling that traditionnally, extending back into the nineteenth century, the United States has not been a respecter of the intellectual property rights of other nations, such as publications, for example. Only now, when the United States believes it has more to lose than to gain by nations not respecting intellectual property rights, has it come out strongly in favour of international agreement on appropriate rules.

51 Ibid.

4 Exports, Unemployment, and Regional Inequality: Economic Policy and Trade Theory

MARJORIE COHEN

In an era of global competition, the importance of trade to Canadian economic growth is not in question. Rather, the focus of debate should be on whether exports should lead growth strategies and whether trade should provide a larger portion of the national income than it does now. Since the 1960s export-led growth in Canada has been successful in the sense that exports have risen dramatically. While in the early 1960s exports accounted for about 20 per cent of the gross national expenditure, they rose to about 25 per cent in the 1970s and have been closer to 30 per cent in the 1980s. Canada is more export-dependent than most industrialized countries.[1] However, the export-led growth strategy has failed in that export growth has accentuated structural problems which already existed. This paper will focus on how the pursuit of increased exports has failed to generate an economic structure which would support greater regional balance and full employment.

The failure of export-led growth strategies results in a poor integration of economic sectors and a poor potential for growth in industries other than those dependent on resource-related exports. It will be argued that trade liberalization, most specifically the Canada–US free trade agreement, is an export-led growth strategy which indeed targets specific industries, but that this initiative by government on behalf of particularly dominant economic interests fails because it cannot pursue the potential which could be realized when dynamic, rather than static, efficiencies are the object of economic policy.

This paper will advocate neither a self-sufficient economic strategy nor a closed-economy approach to development. Rather, it will recognize that there are important distinctions to be made between an export-led strategy, where trade is the major source of growth, and an open-development strategy in which trade is an element of growth.[2] In an open-development strategy in which trade is not the focus of growth but a part of it, other economic objectives (such as a more balanced economy with full employment and better distribution of income between groups and regions) which may make more sense in the long run, can dominate economic policy.

EFFECTS OF EXPORT-LED STRATEGIES

Export Growth

The most significant indicator of the success of an export-led growth policy is the change in the structure of demand for domestically produced products. Export-led growth policies are pursued because of the recognition of extraordinary success which some countries have experienced using this strategy.[3] This is a demand-oriented strategy which relies on the export rather than the domestic market for innovation and industrial growth. But it also has implications for supply. Efficient production of goods destined for export is seen as critical to the performance of the economy as a whole. The underlying premise of the export-led growth approach is that increased foreign demand will result in production efficiencies arising from the positive relationship between the rate of growth of output and the rate of growth of productivity.[4]

The pursuit of growth as a response to foreign demand has traditionally been considered preferable to attempts to increase domestic demand as a stimulus for growth for several reasons. First, it permits wage increases to lag behind productivity increases without affecting the level of demand. When money wages do not keep pace with productivity increases and the source of demand is domestic consumption, there can be serious problems with under-consumption. However, the gap between money wages and productivity can be extremely beneficial when demand is external. Costs will fall and the country's exports will grow quickly because they will be more competitive.

Secondly, some public policy dilemmas become apparent when growth relies on domestic consumption rather than exports. For example, efforts to increase investment, which will result in a shift of resources from consumption to investment, can lessen the inducement to invest since reduced consumer demand will ultimately mean fewer sales. With demand led by exports, this contradiction does not arise.

A third reason why export-led growth is considered to have greater potential for increasing the underlying growth rate relates to the

Table 4.1
Structure of Demand in Real Terms, 1960–88
(category as a % of the gross domestic product)[1]

Year	1960	1965	1970	1975	1980	1985	1988
Personal expenditure on goods and services	58.3	55.0	53.9	56.7	55.8	54.9	55.3
Current public expenditure on goods and services	18.6	18.8	21.4	21.1	19.5	18.8	17.6
Gross formation of fixed capital							
Total	19.7	20.4	19.1	20.7	22.4	21.5	25.4
Public sector	3.9	4.2	3.7	3.4	2.6	2.8	2.7
Non-residential	11.1	11.6	11.0	12.1	14.4	13.0	15.9
Housing	6.4	6.1	5.5	6.0	5.6	5.6	6.8
Variation in stocks	1.2	2.4	0.7	0.9	0.1	0.6	−0.2
Imports of goods and services	15.8	16.0	18.7	21.8	25.0	27.6	32.5
Total internal demand for domestically produced goods and services	82.0	80.6	76.4	77.6	72.8	68.2	65.6
Exports of goods and services	17.3	18.8	25.0	22.2	27.0	31.8	34.0

SOURCE: Statistics Canada, *National Account of Revenues and Expenditures*, Catalogue 13-001;
Department of Finance, *Revue économique trimestrielle: Tableaux de référence annuels*, June 1989,
Table 6.
[1] According to 1981 prices by category.

structure of domestic consumer demand and the possibilities for economies of scale with export production. It is held that productivity
growth, as a result of economies of scale, is best realized in the manufacturing sector.[5] Since there is likely to be less demand for manufactured goods in the domestic market, the possibilities for
productivity growth are higher if exports as a proportion of national
income expands.[6]

As can be seen from Table 4.1, the effect of greater trade liberalization
has been to increase the level of both export and import demand. Foreign demand for Canadian goods and services has grown substantially
and steadily since 1960. The consequence of a more liberalized trading
system is not simply that exports have become more significant for
producers in Canada, but that as Canadians buy more goods and services produced in other countries, the demand for domestic goods and
services dropped dramatically, from 82 per cent of total demand in 1960
to about 65 per cent in 1988.

The extroverted nature of the economy has made Canada extremely
vulnerable to external forces.[7] When things go wrong, as they do per-
iodically when the international market is considerably less than efficient, the impact on Canada can be extreme. The most recent example
was the global downturn in the early part of this decade. Canada felt

Table 4.2
Economic Indicators for Seven OECD Countries

	rate (%) by year					
	1979	1981	1983	1985	1987	1988
GROWTH IN GNP/GDP*						
United States	2.5	1.9	3.6	3.4	3.4	3.9
Japan	5.2	3.7	3.3	4.9	4.4	5.8
Germany	4.0	0.0	1.9	1.9	1.8	3.4
France	3.2	1.3	0.7	1.9	1.9	3.4
United Kingdom	2.2	−1.1	3.9	3.7	4.6	4.5
Italy	4.9	1.1	1.1	2.9	3.1	−
Canada	3.9	3.7	3.2	4.8	4.5	5.0
Average	4.3	2.2	2.9	4.2	4.1	−
EMPLOYMENT GROWTH						
United States	2.9	1.1	1.3	2.0	2.6	2.3
Japan	1.3	0.8	1.7	0.7	1.0	1.7
Germany	1.4	−0.7	−1.5	0.7	0.7	0.6
France	0.1	−0.7	−0.3	−0.2	0.1	0.4
United Kingdom	1.3	−3.4	−0.2	1.4	2.1	2.1
Italy	1.0	0.5	0.6	0.8	0.2	0.8
Canada	4.1	2.8	0.8	2.8	2.8	3.5
Average	2.5	0.9	1.2	1.7	2.2	2.1
UNEMPLOYMENT RATE†						
United States	5.8	7.6	9.6	7.1	6.2	5.5
Japan	2.1	2.2	2.7	2.6	2.8	2.5
Germany	3.3	4.6	8.2	8.3	7.9	7.9
France	6.0	7.6	8.4	10.2	10.5	10.3
United Kingdom	4.5	9.1	11.2	11.6	10.3	8.5
Italy	7.2	7.9	9.2	9.3	11.0	11.1
Canada	7.4	7.5	11.9	10.5	8.9	7.8
Average	5.0	6.4	8.3	7.1	6.7	6.1

the impact first, experienced it harder, and took longer to recover than most other industrialized nations.[8] But what is equally clear is that trade liberalization, and greater reliance on trade, has not reduced the structural imbalances of the Canadian economy, or lessened the country's economic problems.

At this point it is necessary to clarify what is meant by a successful economy and to identify Canada's most serious economic defects. By most success indicators of international bodies which pronounce on such things, Canada generally performs well. This is shown by respectable growth rates, sustained and impressive job creation, relatively stable prices, and high per capita income (Table 4.2). These indicators, of course, are based on aggregate figures and mask serious chronic structural problems.

Table 4.2
(continued)

	rate (%) by year					
	1979	1981	1983	1985	1987	1988
GROWTH IN CONSUMPTION PRICES						
United States	11.2	10.3	3.2	3.5	3.7	4.1
Japan	3.6	4.9	1.8	2.0	−0.2	0.5
Germany	4.2	6.4	3.3	2.2	0.3	1.2
France	10.6	13.3	9.5	5.9	3.3	2.7
United Kingdom	13.4	11.9	4.6	6.1	4.2	4.9
Italy	14.8	17.7	14.7	9.2	4.7	5.1
Canada	9.2	12.4	5.8	4.0	4.4	4.1
Average	8.8	9.4	4.1	3.8	2.8	3.2
PRODUCTIVITY GROWTH						
United States	−0.4	0.8	2.2	1.3	0.8	1.5
Japan	3.9	2.8	1.6	4.2	3.3	3.9
Germany	2.6	0.7	3.4	1.2	1.0	3.1
France	3.2	1.9	1.0	1.8	2.2	3.1
United Kingdom	1.4	2.3	3.9	2.1	2.2	2.0
Italy	3.9	0.7	0.4	2.0	2.9	2.9
Canada	−0.2	0.9	2.4	1.7	2.1	0.7
Average	1.2	1.3	2.1	2.0	1.6	2.3

SOURCE: OECD, *Economic Perspectives*, data tape, June 1989; Department of Finance, *Revue économique trimestrielle: Tableaux de référence annuels* (juin 1989), Table 90.
* Growth rate in real terms: GNP for the United States, Japan and Germany; GDP for France, United Kingdom, Canada and Italy.
† Unemployment rates are calculated according to national definitions.

The way in which economic problems are identified and given priority is a political issue which has significant impact on policy initiatives. The government of Canada and business interests, when arguing for free trade, have identified comparatively low levels of labour productivity and problems with economies of scale as the two primary problems Canada must solve. The easiest solution to economic restructuring, it is argued, would be to gain greater access to export markets, through trade liberalization primarily with the United States. It is assumed that greater competition would force a more rational restructuring of the economy through the mechanism of economies of scale and increased productivity levels.

From another political perspective, one which examines the effect of economic activity on people within the country, the problems are categorized differently.[9] These can be identified as: gross regional inequalities; high rates of unemployment (particularly outside central Canada); a highly skewed distribution of income; and relatively poor provision of social services.[10] While all these chronic problems can be linked to the nature of export-led growth in Canada, the focus here will be on regional inequalities and unemployment.

Existing trade patterns are fairly clear and consistent. Canada maintains substantial trade surpluses in merchandise arising from the primary sector. We tend to maintain a surplus with the United States, our major trading partner, in live animals, food, crude materials, and fabricated materials. In manufactured products and in services we consistently have a trade deficit with the United States, although there are some notable exceptions to the general trend within each sector. For example, in the manufactured category Ontario has generated a healthy surplus in transportation equipment, although this has dropped rather alarmingly recently.

Natural resources account for about one-half the value of all exports.[11] Canada tends to import more than it exports of items that are labour-intensive; over 90 per cent of our labour force is concentrated in the services and manufacturing sectors, areas where Canada has a substantial trade deficit. So while Canada maintains an overall trade surplus with the United States, the way in which this surplus has been generated has had an impact on the structural nature of unemployment. The heavy reliance on trade in primary products and semi-fabricated materials is responsible for high rates of unemployment in regions of the country which are most dependent on resource exports. It also results in a poor integration of sectors, a volatile economy, poor distribution of income, and particularly high regional inequalities. The pursuit of an export-led growth policy which will make the country even more dependent on trade will not induce a restructuring of the economy so that exports of diverse manufactured products and services can flourish.

Given the structure of export activity and the present ability of industries to pursue competitive advantages, free trade is likely to increase the overall volume of trade between Canada and the United States. But, as Mel Watkins has pointed out, enhanced trade will occur in precisely the industries where Canada already performs well.[12] The result will be greater economic interdependence between the two nations, but in particular, even greater Canadian dependence on American markets, which now account for between 75 and 80 per cent of all exports. It is also likely that the structure of trade between the two countries will remain relatively stable. Both the United States and Canada are likely to export more of the types of goods and services they do already, and as a result the existing trade patterns will intensify. For Canada this means the sectors where we have a trade surplus may continue to be strong, whereas sectors where we have trade deficits will probably not experience dramatic changes in their export abilities. What is more, these

Table 4.3
Provincial Share of Gross Domestic Product, 1961, 1971, 1981, 1988 (in %)

Province or Territory	1961	1971	1981	1988
Newfoundland	1.3	1.4	1.3	1.3
Prince Edward Island	0.3	0.3	0.3	0.3
Nova Scotia	2.6	2.5	2.1	2.4
New Brunswick	2.0	1.9	1.7	1.9
Quebec	26.1	25.1	22.9	24.0
Ontario	41.1	42.1	37.1	41.4
Manitoba	4.6	4.1	3.7	3.6
Saskatchewan	4.0	3.6	4.0	3.1
Alberta	7.9	8.1	14.0	10.5
British Columbia	10.0	10.7	12.6	11.2
Yukon and NWT	0.2	0.3	0.3	0.4

SOURCE: Department of Finance, *Revue économique trimestrielle: Tableaux de référence annuels,* June 1989,
     Table 7.2.

sectors are likely to face increasing competition in the domestic market. The results, in short, will be increased exports of resources in a raw, or semi-processed state, accentuating the structural difficulties of the country.

Regional Disparities

Canada has had little success with improving the economic position of poor regions of the country.[13] More specifically, past trade liberalization has not improved the relative position of the poorest provinces which are heavily dependent on resource exports.

During the last thirty years the Atlantic provinces' share of the national income has actually decreased. These four provinces together account for less than 6 per cent of Canada's GDP (see Table 4.3). Alberta, one of the three wealthiest provinces, has experienced the most improvement, while the share contributed by Nova Scotia, Quebec, Manitoba, and Saskatchewan have decreased.

The most telling indicator of relative strength and productivity of provincial economies is the earned income of the people in the province. The disparity between the Atlantic provinces and the rest of Canada are particularly large (see Table 4.4). In 1971 Newfoundland's per capita income was only slightly more than one-half the national average and remained constant over a ten-year period. During this time, Newfoundland's exports accounted for about one-half the provincial income. New Brunswick also experienced a decrease in its per capita income during this period, at the same time that exports as a proportion of provincial

Table 4.4
Disparities in Regional Income, 1971, 1981, and 1988: Market Income* per capita
by Province (national average = 100)

Province	1971	1981	1988
Newfoundland	56.0	56.0	58.2
Prince Edward Island	51.5	56.4	58.4
Nova Scotia	67.6	59.3	69.7
New Brunswick	64.3	58.5	69.0
Quebec	90.1	86.7	93.8
Ontario	117.8	104.6	113.7
Manitoba	89.1	87.8	86.2
Saskatchewan	83.3	101.4	78.1
Alberta	107.0	152.8	114.1
British Columbia	106.0	111.5	97.0
Yukon and NWT	118.6	122.1	134.0

SOURCE: Department of Finance, *Revue économique trimestrielle: Tableaux de référence annuels*, June 1989,
    Table 8.2.
* Market income is defined as wages and supplementary income, net unincorporated business income,
  net farm income, and interest, dividend and miscellaneous investment income. It does not include
  transfers to individuals.

income increased significantly: in the early 1970s exports accounted for
about one-quarter of New Brunswick's provincial income and rose dramatically to over one-half in 1980 (see Table 4.5).

In contrast, the provinces with per capita income over the national
average (Ontario, Alberta, and British Columbia) either did not increase
their reliance on exports, or increasingly relied on exporting end products, rather than raw or semi-processed resources. British Columbia's
exports as a proportion of gross provincial product have decreased substantially from about one-third in the early 1970s to less than one-
quarter in 1986, although this province's exports are still concentrated
almost entirely in crude and fabricated materials. Alberta's exports as a
proportion of total income have remained relatively constant, with crude
and fabricated materials accounting for most of its exports, while
Ontario's exports have increased significantly. This growth has primarily been in the exports of end products.[14]

Employment

The five provinces east of Ontario have consistently high rates of unemployment. While the economic difficulties associated with the crisis of
the early 1980s resulted in large increases in unemployment rates for all
provinces, those which experienced the most volatility were British
Columbia, Alberta, and Newfoundland. These are provinces whose

Table 4.5
Exports as a Proportion of Gross Provincial Product:
Totals and by Major Commodity Groups for Selected Provinces
1973, 1981, 1986

Commodity Group	1973	1981	1986
BRITISH COLUMBIA			
Total Exports	32.7	28.7	23.0
Food★	6.4	6.1	1.6
Crude materials	7.2	6.7	5.6
Fabricated materials	18.1	14.6	14.4
End products	1.0	1.1	1.4
ALBERTA			
Total Exports	17.8	19.0	18.0
Food	0.5	0.3	1.9
Crude materials	14.9	13.2	11.4
Fabricated materials	1.9	3.3	3.7
End products	0.3	1.2	0.7
ONTARIO			
Total Exports	20.3	24.8	29.6
Food	1.0	1.1	0.8
Crude materials	1.8	1.0	0.7
Fabricated materials	4.1	8.4	7.0
End products	13.2	14.1	21.0
NEW BRUNSWICK			
Total Exports	24.3	43.6	26.5
Food	4.7	6.7	4.1
Crude materials	2.7	3.1	1.4
Fabricated materials	15.0	32.0	20.3
End products	1.6	1.5	0.6
QUEBEC			
Total Exports	16.0	22.2	16.6
Food	3.2	4.1	0.9
Crude materials	2.9	3.3	1.8
Fabricated materials	6.6	8.8	7.7
End products	3.2	5.8	6.1

SOURCE: Calculated from Statistics Canada Catalogue 65-001 for each year and Catalogue 13-213 S.
★ The drop in food as a proportion of total BC exports reflects a decrease in shipping of prairie grain.

exports are particularly reliant on resources and which have a relatively
high proportion of their labour force employed in resource-exporting
industries (see Table 4.6). All provinces have experienced lower unemployment rates in 1987 and 1988, although the recovery has been slower
for the poorest provinces.[15]

The structure of employment in the provinces with the most volatile
employment record during the economic crisis is significant: a relatively
higher proportion of the labour force was concentrated in resource-

Table 4.6
Umemployment Rate by Province, 1981-86 (percentages)

Province	1981	1982	1983	1984	1985	1986
Newfoundland	13.9	16.8	18.8	20.5	21.3	20.0
Prince Edward Island	11.2	12.9	12.2	12.8	13.2	13.4
Nova Scotia	10.2	13.2	13.2	13.1	13.8	13.4
New Brunswick	11.5	14.0	14.8	14.9	15.2	14.4
Quebec	10.3	13.8	13.9	12.8	11.8	11.0
Ontario	6.6	9.8	10.4	9.1	8.0	7.0
Manitoba	5.9	8.5	9.4	8.3	8.1	7.7
Saskatchewan	4.7	6.2	7.4	8.0	8.1	7.7
Alberta	3.8	7.7	10.8	11.2	10.1	9.8
British Columbia	6.7	12.1	13.8	14.7	14.2	12.6
Canada	7.5	11.0	11.8	11.2	10.5	9.5

SOURCE: Statistics Canada, *Historical Labour Force Statistics* (Ottawa 1988), Catalogue 71201.

extracting industries and services and a smaller proportion in manufacturing. In 1981 Alberta, for example, had 14 per cent of its labour force in the primary sector and only 9 per cent in manufacturing; Newfoundland, about 11 per cent in primary industries and 14 per cent in manufacturing; and British Columbia, 7 per cent in primary industries and 14 per cent in manufacturing. The contrast with Ontario is striking, with less than 6 per cent in the primary sector (largely agriculture), but 25 per cent in manufacturing. The recovery occurred quickest in provinces where goods produced were sold mainly within Canada. The exception to this was Saskatchewan, which has a high proportion of goods exported with only 6 per cent of its labour force in the manufacturing sector. About 23 per cent of its labour force is in the primary sector, with a heavy concentration in agricultural production. The difference in the performance of this province is accounted for by the fact that agricultural exports were not affected in the same way that other resource sectors were by the economic crisis.

The conditions which favoured the exports of resources and semi-processed materials in the early periods of Canadian development have persisted. Increased trade liberalization has done little to change the nature of exports outside the central regions of the country and there is little indication that further trade liberalization, through the Canada–US free trade agreement, will encourage more diversity in the nature of exports or more integration between the resource industries and other sectors of the economy. This means that the regions of the country which are dependent on resource exports will continue to experience extremely unstable economic conditions in the future.

The persistence of income inequalities and differing unemployment rates between regions cannot be explained with traditional economic theories. Under the assumptions of traditional growth models, there should, ultimately, be equalization of factor returns within a nation, unless artificial barriers to both internal and international trade exist. While there are still barriers to trade within the nation, it is not clear that their removal would be of significant benefit to the poorest regions of the country. And, as has been shown, the reduction of international barriers to trade has done little to enhance the position of poorer regions.

The result of the export-led growth strategy, rather, has been to reduce the interdependence of regions within the country, as trade with United States becomes dominant. This is best illustrated by the decline in manufacturing trade between the two provinces with the most significant interprovincial trade, Quebec and Ontario. Both provinces increasingly rely on the United States for trade. In the late 1960s Quebec exported about 15 per cent of its manufacturing shipments and Ontario about 14 per cent. The proportion Ontario has exported has increased dramatically, growing from about 23 per cent in 1979 to 31 per cent in 1984. Quebec's manufacturing exports have also risen, although not as much, from about 19 per cent in 1979 to 21 per cent in 1984. So while each province was the other's largest trading partner twenty years ago, this is no longer the case. Now Quebec sends 17 per cent of its manufactured items to Ontario and Ontario sends 8 per cent to Quebec.[16] It is clear that for both provinces there has been a trend for manufacturing trade with the United States to become increasingly more significant than trade with each other.

DISCUSSION OF THEORETICAL ISSUES

The New Trade Theory

The public policy decisions which pursue export-led growth and free trade are based on traditional notions of the benefit of comparative advantage for all trading nations. These benefits will accrue if the assumptions of the theory hold, namely that markets are efficient because they are perfectly competitive and returns to scale are constant. Trade will take place between nations under these conditions because of underlying differences in factor endowments, technology, or tastes. Free trade, then, becomes essential in order to maximize the benefits of trade and promote efficiency in nations.

The real world experience, however, has not conformed to the assumptions of traditional trade theory. It has become obvious that under certain circumstances strategic trade policies, in which governments actively supported home industries, proved to be beneficial. This was most notable in the case of Japanese industrial targeting, American defence procurement, and subsidies to high-technology industries in various countries.[17] The possibility of retaliation by trading partners was always present, but in practice the threat invariably did not materialize. Therefore the assumption that free trade would emerge as the best possible outcome for all countries (because of the potential of retaliation in response to protectionist measures) became less plausible. Some countries which were particularly well positioned to support industries in imperfectly competitive international markets got away with special measures to enhance the position of home industries.

It took a long time for formal trade theory to catch up with reality. While empirical evidence clearly demonstrated the existence of non-competitive industries, this fact could not be accommodated in economic models. The absence of formal models which could explain firms' behaviour under imperfectly competitive conditions tended to undermine what was intuitively obvious: that if a government could provide special help which would enable an industry to capture a larger share of the world market, benefits would accrue to that country. The move towards free trade through the intermediate step of managed trade continued to be based on the theoretical assumptions of competitive markets.

During the past ten years economists have paid increasing attention to the development of models of imperfect competition.[18] However, the "new trade theory" is far from being a unified approach which gives clear signals for public policy, although in general the results of the models indicate that the benefits to be derived from free trade are questionable and that trade is not necessarily mutually advantageous to nations.[19]

The findings of the new trade theory are not startling. They state in formal general or partial equilibrium terms what some economists have long recognized, namely that increasing returns (which leads to imperfect competition) can give rise to international trade. That is, differences in tastes, factor endowment, and technology are not the only reasons trade occurs. Under imperfectly competitive conditions excess returns are possible and this can increase national income if a country is able to provide policies which will shift the advantage from competitors to the home firm. This can occur in a variety of ways, such as by providing substantial initial subsidies so that barriers to entry are sufficiently large that excess returns are permanent. Other subsidies – tax policies to lower costs to penetrate export markets, and import restrictions in the form of tariffs or quotas – can also be effective.

Generally the focus of the imperfect competition models is on the ability of strategic trade policies to enhance national welfare. However, there is no consistency in the findings which give a clear signal to policy-makers. This is because there are serious empirical difficulties in creating models of imperfect markets. Economists still do not really know how oligopolists behave and cannot predict with certainty the results of different policy initiatives under different market conditions. The lack of uniformity in results regarding net welfare points more to the technical difficulties of dealing with a great many variables and assumptions used in analysing the behaviour of firms under specific conditions than it does to the validity of questioning the assumptions of comparative advantage. For example, each model has to make assumptions about the degree of price competition, the relative easy of entry into the industry, and the extent of collusion. When the assumptions differ, so do the conclusions about the effect of strategic trade initiatives of net welfare.

This confusion over results indicates to many economists that the new trade theory gives little insight into the advantages of strategic trade initiatives over free trade.

However, the focus of government policy on net welfare ignores what may be the most significant benefit from strategic trade policies. There is some evidence that the most important benefit is the redistributive effect, rather than the net welfare effect.[20] This could have particularly critical implications for Canada if policy objectives were to focus on regional development and the net welfare of particular groups. The new trade theory may not provide policy-makers with guarantees for improving national welfare (at least when compared with the ideal of the perfect competition model and benefits to be derived from comparative advantage). But if policy objectives were to shift the emphasis from aggregate growth towards regional development and more equitable distribution of national income, the new trade theory would provide justification for interventionist policy.

Despite the willingness of economists to recognize the possibility that government policy can influence the terms of imperfect competition in favour of domestic firms, there continues to be a reluctance to deviate from support for the free trade ideal.[21] In part the argument focuses on the spectre of massive trade retaliation which would leave countries much worse off than if non-interventionist policies were pursued. Strategic trade policies are considered aggressive and predatory, where national income is raised at the expense of other countries. But more significant is the problem of deciding which type of government intervention in targeted industries will be most appropriate. Since the imperfect competition models themselves are far from unanimous in recognition of large welfare benefits to be derived from intervention, the risks inherent in the possibility of picking loosers rather than winners appear greater than letting the market take its course. For some, such as Krugman, the entire decision-making process is open to such manipulation and extreme pressure from interest groups, that the best interests of the country may not be served. So while free trade may have lost the glamour it once had, and no longer even has its theoretical security, it still has more credibility with most trade economists than any alternative.

Efficiency and Welfare

Whether free trade policies are preferable to strategic initiatives simply because the latter require planning, which is too difficult and uncertain, is not a minor issue. No economic policies provide a comfortable degree of certainty, and the risks inherent in making wrong choices are great. But the problem is a political one which relates to the objectives of a nation and the issue raised earlier in this paper – how economic problems are defined. Policies that rely for their justification on economic efficiency will be inadequate if a nation wants to protect resources, prevent environmental damage, provide a more equitable distribution of wealth between regions and groups, and ensure that everyone who wants to work is employed. For economists, efficiency and welfare have specific meanings related to the allocation of total resources. Other objectives, particularly those that deal with quality of life and those that are difficult to quantify, simply cannot be taken into account.

The faith in free trade rests on the efficiency of the market – on the ability of prices to provide the correct signals to guide production and distribution. The aggregate economic decisions of individual economic units, then, become the hegemonic force in development prospects for the nation. My point is that the direction of growth will be distorted under these conditions because the economic planning by firms exploits a perceived advantage that already exists, not a potential one in the future. The ad hoc planning of individual firms responds to current market conditions and what can be anticipated for each specific industry in the near future. For either a nation or a region, the possibilities of realizing dynamic efficiencies are virtually non-existent. The major distinction here is between what we recognize as efficiencies in the classical sense, and those in the Schumpeterian sense. Schumpeter recognized that economic success cannot be understood by examining activity at a given point in time.[22] Performance, as it unfolds over decades and even centuries, is what counts: "A system – any system, economic or other – that at *every* given point of time fully utilizes its possibilities to the best advantage may yet in the long run be inferior to a system that does so at *no* given point of time, because the latter's failure to do so may be a condition for the level or speed of long-run performance."[23]

The achievement of the Schumpeterian analysis of capitalism was the recognition that monopolistic concentration was a strength rather than a weakness of the system. The traditional critique of capitalism, from both classical and marxist theory, focused on the failure of markets to be perfectly competitive. Schumpeter recognized that competition could not be considered only in terms of price competition – that is, in the static sense of dealing with the problematic of the optimal allocation of existing resources – but that dynamic efficiencies can be pursued when price competition alone is not the guiding principle of market activity. This recognition led to the assertion that non-competitive activity, while resulting in higher prices and distortions in resource allocation at any given point in time, may actually increase overall efficiencies over a long period. This reasoning was based on the assumption that higher returns of monopolies were able to finance higher rates of investment, more research and development, and sustain firms over periods of economic crisis to such an extent that downturns in the economy are less pronounced than would be the case under perfect competition.[24] That is, long-term planning would be more feasible when corporate entities were able to be protected from the volatile nature of the market through the "insurance" of higher prices and returns than would have existed under competitive conditions.

Competition under monopoly conditions is not thwarted simply because price competition in the static sense is circumvented. Rather, competition takes a new and more potent form: competition which is truly revolutionary comes from "the new commodity, the new technology, the new source of supply, the new type of organization"; this is the competition which "strikes not at the margins of the profits and the outputs of the existing firms but at their foundations and their very lives."[25] This type of competition, according to Schumpeter, is the real engine of growth and change over time.

The traditional economic signals (prices – even good price and market forecasting) are inadequate guides for the future and can only lead to short-sighted restructuring based on short-term needs of individual firms within specific industries. The Schumpeterian concept of dynamic efficiencies is important for understanding how factors other than prices can influence economic decision-making. It also gives insight into the concept of time over a very long period and different ways to evaluate economic success. However, this is not an argument for allowing monopoly interests to dominate policy decisions. The realization of the dynamic benefits of non-competitive activity within a nation is far from certain, given the international scope of corporate organization. International corporations do not need to plan for the future within the confines of the nation. There is no need to use higher returns to plan for future development within a specific nation or to pursue research to develop new ideas and technologies if these corporations can count on freely moving production whenever domestic resources become scarce.

In Canada the commitment to free trade is somewhat deceptive. The Canada–US free trade agreement is not a move towards greater competitiveness in the classic sense, but one which permits greater concentration and control by monopoly interests. This agreement is a strategy to foster the objectives of the most powerful interests of exporting industries. What has become clear, even in the short time since the agreement has been in effect, is that government intervention on behalf of corporate interests is accelerating. Corporate concentration in Canada is much more pronounced than in the United States. According to a study done for the Macdonald Commission, while nearly four-fifths of American economic activity is essentially competitive; the estimate for Canada is substantially lower, with only two-fifths of economic activity classified as competitive.[26] Canada is notoriously permissive in its control over corporate concentration and the recent spate of mergers and acquisitions, particularly in the resource sector, indicate the attractiveness of current policy to business.

While the free trade agreement will certainly limit the ability of government to intervene in the economy in ways which would permit the greater integration of the resource sector with the manufacturing sector, the government can, nonetheless, design programs to improve the performance of the exporting sector which will have negative consequences elsewhere. The redesign of the tax system, for example, is dramatically shifting the burden of taxation away from industry to households. Free trade will not mean less government support of industry; but that support will take a different form. It will virtually prohibit action in certain areas (such as requirements that a certain proportion of resources be processed in Canada) but promote those in others. In addition to tax policy, the government can pursue other avenues, such as promoting mega-projects in the energy-exporting sector and maintaining policies which provide cheap access to public property in the forestry industry.

The move towards free trade has simplified the government's task of picking which industries to support. This was done in response to corporate pressure, rather than a plan designed to meet the nation's needs. While the new trade theory indicates that government policy designed to promote the ability of domestically located firms to gain larger shares of international markets can improve national welfare, it is unlikely to achieve this effect in Canada because of the nature of the industries which have been targeted for expansion under the free trade agreement. The industries most likely to benefit are those in the resource sector, industries which generate relatively few benefits within the country. Government support of these industries, then, essentially subsidizes foreign consumers (as the old trade theory tells us) and corporations whose interests are not nation-bound.

The pursuit of export-led growth through free trade prevents the pursuit of policies that will promote dynamic efficiencies for Canada in the Schumpeterian sense. Rather, a different dynamic occurs, one that is in the interest of corporate entities which are not nation-bound. There is a real conflict in policies which promote export industries based on competitive advantages that currently exist and those which could realize the potential of long-term dynamic efficiency. Decisions for the future must be planned collectively within a nation on the basis of information that not only anticipates future demand for exports, but also takes into account the structural problem of the economy and the goals of the population. The new trade theory gives an important theoretical rationale for government intervention in influencing the direction of trade for a nation. However, the strategy being used by Canada continues to operate as though expansion of trade alone will solve Canada's economic problems. Strategic trade policies need to be pursued, for trade will continue to be a major feature of economic activity. But these strategic policies cannot be initiated solely on the basis of what is good for specific corporations at a given point in time.

CONCLUSION

In the debate on whether Canada should enter a free trade arrangement with the United States, the anti-free trade forces (particularly the opposition parties) tended to focus on how this agreement would prevent the state from successfully targeting export industries. Whenever alternatives to free trade were discussed, it was in terms of increasing exports with nations other than the United States and how winning export industries could be more successfully identified. Vulnerability as a result of even closer ties to the United States was the issue, not the whole issue of trade itself and the extent to which the structure of Canada's international trade and the focus on export-led growth perpetuated the chronic economic problems of the country.

Trade liberalization in the past has not produced a restructuring of the economy to encourage a better integration between the resource-producing sectors and the manufacturing and services sectors. The consequences of this have been an accentuation of the problems which Canada has continually faced: regional disparities have not lessened and employment in resource-exporting regions continues to be highly volatile.

I have argued that the pursuit of export-led growth through the Canada–US free trade agreement will produce more of the same, but at an accelerated rate. Economic decision-making will be based on the short-term interests of the exporting industries responding primarly to immediate or near-future price conditions. The ability to pursue dynamic efficiencies, in the Schumpeterian sense, requires a concerted national plan which does not focus on exports, but which places trade policy within the context of a larger strategy for economic development. In Canada now, trade strategy is the economic strategy for the country.

NOTES

1 Exports as a percentage of national income for other countries are as follows: United States, 10%; Japan, 15%; France, 22%; Italy, 24%; United Kingdom, 27%; and Germany, 32%. Canada, *How to Secure and Enhance Canadian Access to Export Markets* (Ottawa 1985).

2 Irma Adelman, "Beyond Export-Led Growth," *World Development* 12, no. 9 (1984): 937–49.

3 J.S.L. McCombie, "Economic growth, the Harrod Foreign Trade Multiplier and the Hicks' Super-multiplier," *Applied Economics* 17 (1985): 55–72.

4 J. Verdoorn, "Fattori che regolano lo sviluppo della produttivita del lavoro," *L'Industria* 1 (1949).

5 Nicholas Kaldor, *Strategic Factors in Economic Development* (Ithaca: Cornell University 1967), lecture on "The Role of Increasing Returns in Industry."

6 Raymond Lubitz "Export-led Growth in Industrial Economies," *Kyklos* 26, no. 2 (1973): 307–21.

7 The development of this perspective was pioneered by Harold Innis. See, for example, *The Fur Trade in Canada: An Introduction to Canadian Economic History* (Toronto: University of Toronto Press 1956). His work has had an enormous impact on subsequent scholars in Canada. See, for example, Wallace Clement and Glen Williams, eds., *The New Canadian Political Economy* (Montreal: McGill-Queen University Press 1989).

8 Royal Commission on the Economic Union and Development Prospects for Canada, *Report* (Ottawa 1985), Vol. II, 199.

9 See, for example, Daniel Drache and Duncan Cameron, eds., *The Other Macdonald Report* (Toronto: Lorimer 1985).

10 Canada has a fairly miserable record for spending on social programs. According to the statistics of the Organization for Economic Co-operation and Development (OECD), Canada is ranked ninth out of the twelve leading industrial nations. We spend less of our national resources than most

on pensions, about average on health and education, but more than average on unemployment benefits. We spend more on unemployment payments not because our benefits are more generous than that of other countries, but because our rate of unemployment is so high. (Report, Royal Commission on the Economic Union and Development Prospects for Canada, *Report*, II.)

11 This figure for resources as a proportion of total exports has dropped from over 80% in the 1950s as a result of the sharp increase in shipments of auto parts. Ibid., II: 406–7.

12 Mel Watkins, "Feeding the Hand that Bilks Us," *This Magazine* 22, no. 1 (March/April 1988).

13 For a discussion of the static nature of disparities in unemployment rates and average weekly earnings over the past twenty-five years, see Kathleen Day, *Regional Disparities in Wage and Unemployment Rates in Canada: A Review of Some Issues* (Ottawa: Bank of Canada, April 1989), Technical Report No. 51.

14 Statistics Canada, *Summary of Canadian International Trade, 1973–87*.

15 These are the official unemployment figures which count the unemployed only as those actively looking for work. Actual unemployment rates in all regions were considerably higher.

16 Statistics Canada, *Destination of Shipments of Manufacturers* (Ottawa 1979, 1984), Cat. 31–530; Bureau de la Statistique du Québec, *Les échanges de produits manufacturés entre le Québec et les provinces canadiennes, 1967–1984* (Québec 1987).

17 Richard G. Harris, "New Protectionism Revisited," the 1989 Innis Lecture, Canadian Economic Association meetings, Quebec City, June 1989.

18 The theoretical literature on imperfect competition is extensive. See, for example, Elhanan Helpman and Paul Krugman, *Market Structure and Foreign Trade: Increasing Returns, Imperfect Competition, and the International Economy* (Cambridge: MIT Press 1985); Paul Krugman, *Strategic Trade Policy and the New International Economics* (Cambridge: MIT Press 1986); James A. Bradner and Barbara Spencer, "Export Subsidies and International Market Share Rivalry," *Journal of International Economics* 18 (1985): 83–100; A.K. Dixit, "International Trade Policy for Oligopolistic Industries," *Economic Journal* 94 (1984): 1–16; Anthony J. Venables and M. Alasdair Smith, "Trade and Industrial Policy under Imperfect Competition," *Economic Policy* 3 (1986): 621–72.

19 In some instances, such as the debate over free trade in Canada, the models of imperfect competition have been used even to explain the merits of free trade. The contradictory outcomes of the models is a result of differing assumptions on which they were built.

20 See, for example, Richard Baldwin and Paul Krugman, "Industrial Policy and International Competition in Wide-bodied Jet Aircraft," in R. Bald-

win, ed., *Trade Policy Issues and Empirical Analysis* (Chicago: University of Chicago Press 1988).

21 See especially Paul R. Krugman, "Is Free Trade Passé?" *Economic Perspectives* 1, no. 2 (Fall 1987): 131–44; Richard Harris, "New Protectionism Revisited."

22 For an interesting discussion of Japan's ability to pursue dynamic efficiencies through targeting of technology intensive industries, see Giovanni Dosi, Laura D'Andrea Tyson, and John Zysman, *Politics and Productivity*, forthcoming.

23 Joseph Schumpeter, *Capitalism, Socialism and Democracy*, 3rd ed. (New York: Harper and Row 1950), 83 (emphasis in original).

24 Ibid., ch. 8.

25 Ibid., 84.

26 R.S. Khemani, "Extent and Evolution of Competition in the Canadian Economy" in D.G. McFetridge, ed., *Canadian Industry in Transition*. Vol. 2 of Background Studies for the Macdonald Royal Commission (Toronto: University of Toronto Press 1986), 135–76.

5 Disjunctions:
Free Trade and the Paradox
of Canadian Development

STEPHEN CLARKSON

Students of Canadian political economy have a question to answer. Why is it that, having vacillated between rebuffing and responding to the seductive charms of the United States throughout its history, Canada succumbed to the siren call of continental integration under American dominance at the very moment when United States' power was ebbing and when the institutions of the Canadian state had reached their most advanced stage of development? In seeking and negotiating the Canada–us free trade agreement of 1988, the Conservative government of Canada initiated a process which led it voluntarily to give up broad powers to intervene in its economy, maintain its social fabric, and promote its culture without gaining equivalent supranational power at the continental level.[1] The FTA opened up a generally less efficient private sector to takeover by stronger American competitors, even giving them unique access to Canada's services sector, a concession with potentially devastating implications for the integrity of Canada's social and economic structure.[2] Canada's signing the FTA was like performing a deliberate act of self-mutilation, an extraordinary political feat considering that it had secured few benefits, least of all any guarantee of increased powers to determine policies for the new continental market which it so blithely entered.

As recently as the spring of 1984 few academic experts would have had the temerity to suggest that Canada was poised to abdicate the bulk of its economic and cultural sovereignty. Conservative political scientists were describing how Canada as a "principal power" had followed a path towards greater autonomy on the world stage.[3] Neo-marxist political economists were documenting how Canada's once dependent capitalist class had grown in strength over a quarter of a century to become a normal and mature, if continentally oriented national bourgeoisie.[4]

Canadian politics at the end of the Trudeau era gave no indication that the political system was poised to self-destruct. In his successful campaign to become leader of the Progressive Conservative party and so leader of the opposition, Brian Mulroney had rejected out of hand the idea of free trade with the United States.[5] The governing Liberal party was going through its leadership renewal process to find a successor to Pierre Trudeau, having just abandoned discussions with Washington to negotiate some modest sectoral free trade deals with the United States.[6]

Four brief years later Canada had fundamentally realigned its basic relationship with the outside world by adopting an institutionally fragile, market-led regime confined geographically to the area north of the Rio Grande. In order to understand what appears to be an extraordinary historical reversal, we will apply and extend notions developed by the "Régulation school" in Paris to explain the evolution of postwar capitalist economies.[7] To do this we need first to re-examine the nature of the system the FTA was designed to replace.

CANADA'S MODE OF REGULATION UNDER AMERICAN HEGEMONY

The United States emerged from World War Two as leader of the capitalist part of a new bipolar global balance of power. In the first two postwar decades Canada participated actively in establishing and operating the new international economic and political institutions set up to manage this system. In response to the needs of an economy that had been industrialized by the war effort, the Canadian state developed a *mode of regulation** at the federal and provincial levels of government that was a combination of Keynesian macro-economic management, labour-management relations that accepted workers sharing in the prosperity they produced, and a broad, if modest, social welfare system.

At the same time the Canadian state was actively involved in fostering a *regime of accumulation*† that was continental rather than national in its

---

* The *mode of regulation* refers to the formal and informal rules established within a political system. It includes the way institutions pattern the relationship between labour and capital and regulate societal forces within the boundaries of the state. See Alain Lipietz, "The Globalization of the General Crisis of Fordism," paper presented at Queen's University, Kingston, Ontario, May 10–13, 1984: 4, 5.

† The *regime of accumulation* refers to the way the dominant economic forces operate in a given mode of production, including their trade strategies, their patterns of raising and deploying capital, and the conditions relating their processes of production to their patterns of consumption.

scope. In 1947 Great Britain proved unable to resume its traditional role as an imperial market for Canadian staple products sufficiently large to finance Canada's chronic deficits in manufactured goods with the United States. As a consequence, the country's accumulation strategy became explicity oriented towards increasing its integration in the American economy.[8] Since before the turn of the century Canadian élites had encouraged American direct investment to accelerate the exploitation of Canada's natural resources needed by US industry. American capital had also been sought to promote import substitution in a tariff-protected manufacturing sector that was increasingly dominated by the subsidiaries of US transnational corporations.

In some sectors, formal continental integration was pursued as official policy. Canada's attempt to retain its independent technological and production capacity in military aviation was aborted in 1959.[9] This caused the government to sign a defence production-sharing agreement with Washington in 1959 and so create a managed trade zone in military procurement, the Canadian sector largely made up of branch plants of the American military-industrial complex.[10] In 1965 another economic sector was continentalized when the Canada–US Auto Pact created a managed free trade zone for the "big four" American car companies and their Canadian assembly plants. In the same period the Canadian government was pressing Washington to allow the expansion of a continental market for the country's hydro-carbon and hydro-electric surpluses.

Canada's *system of legitimation*[*11] was in tension throughout this period, reflecting the way that Canada was pulled between the rival forces of a falling and a rising imperial power and internal pressures for autonomy. At one level, the generation that had fought in World War Two for "king and country" remained pro British at heart, resisting as late as the mid-1960s the adoption of a national flag distinct from the Union Jack. On another level, the continental reach of Hollywood and Madison Avenue meant that Canadians' consciousness was constantly being formed by the products of the American magazine, film, radio, and TV entertainment industries. To resist total cultural absorption and to accommodate the view that Canada should become autonomous, the Canadian state undertook moderate efforts to encourage national cultural expression via various state-supported institutions, in particular the CBC, a binational radio and television broadcasting network. However, the forces of Quebec nationalism threatened the integrity of the federal political system and so added a further strain to the country's system of legitimation.

---

* The *system of legitimation* involves the generation and communication of social norms, values, and identities that govern individual and group behaviour within a mode of regulation and regime of accumulation.

As a result of these developments, the relationship between Canada and its overpowering neighbour became intimate and clientelistic in the postwar decades. The two states chose to define their interests as complementary, not conflictual. The doctrine of quiet diplomacy, enunciated in 1965 by leading ambassadors of each country, expressed the willing support by Canada for United States' world leadership.[12] In exchange for the privileged access it gave the United States to its resources and markets, Ottawa received conditional exemptions from Washington's economic measures that threatened to damage Canadian interests.

A Keynesian mode of regulation and a continentalist regime of accumulation brought Canada great prosperity for twenty-five years, although a conflict-riven system of legitimation left Canadians disoriented and uncertain in the wake of the country's centennial celebrations in 1967. This was an arrangement that Canadian politicians would not willingly have altered had not change been thrust upon them.

CANADA'S MODE OF REGULATION UNDER AMERICAN DECLINE

It was not the arrival of Pierre Trudeau to power in 1968 that nudged Canada towards establishing a more self-consciously national mode of regulation. Trudeau was as committed an anti-nationalist in federal affairs as he was a dogmatic anti-separatist in Quebec politics.[13] What pushed Canada off the continentalist course on which it had been sailing for twenty years was change in the global power system whose reverberations in North America gave Ottawa no choice but to look for salvation to its own initiative rather than to its new imperial master's benevolence.

By the late 1960s the components of the postwar global balance of power had begun to change. The United States' financially extravagant and strategically fruitless military operation in Southeast Asia was perceptibly accelerating the decline of its hegemonic position. Washington's response to the shift in its international stature and its concomitant economic crisis had drastic implications for Canada. When President Richard Nixon unveiled his program of devaluation and protectionism on 15 August 1971 Canadian political leaders were shocked to discover that the United States had unilaterally changed the implicit rules that had governed the Canadian-American relationship. The United States was declaring Canada to be independent, a statement the president made in so many words in the Canadian House of Commons in 1972.[14]

Unable to secure an exemption from the economic body blow of Nixonomics, the Trudeau government found itself forced to shift towards a more national approach in its accumulation strategy. Canada's position as a dependent continental partner of what had been assumed would be an ever more prosperous United States was now in jeopardy. If Canadian oil was no longer to have privileged access to the US market; if US branch plants were to be discriminated against by their parents through the DISC program;[15] if, in short, the Americans were making their own mode of regulation more national and less continental, then the Trudeau government was forced to start thinking in terms of a national rather than a continental framework for its own regime of accumulation.

Internal strains within the federation were already forcing Canadian politicians to consider how to revamp their state structures. Provoked since the early 1960s by the demands of Quebec's nationalist movement for greater autonomy, a prolonged struggle over the constitution was pitting a defensive federal government against aggressive provincial regimes pressing for increased jurisdiction. Enriched by the quadrupling of oil prices resulting from the first OPEC crisis in 1973, Alberta led the resource-rich provinces into the constitutional fray to bolster their control over their staple-led economies and beat off the federal government, which had become increasingly interested in appropriating part of their economic rents to resolve its own fiscal problems.

With the country's oil and natural gas reserves fast depleting, with its imports of off-shore petroleum threatened, and with world market costs escalating, Ottawa found itself pressured by nationalist sentiments to adjust its mode of regulation. When Prime Minister Trudeau announced the National Oil Policy with its proposal for a new state-owned Petro-Canada in December 1973 he was signalling only one facet of the Liberals' new nation-building approach to economic policy in the 1970s.[16] A state-financed holding company, the Canada Development Corporation, was set up to channel national capital into indigenously owned enterprises and reduce the proportion of the economy controlled by foreign corporations.[17] Supporting the same trend to increased national control of the economy the government created a Foreign Investment Review Agency (FIRA) to reduce the costs and increase the benefits accruing from foreign direct investment in Canada.[18]

Doctrinal coherence was given to this newly national, supply-side approach by the policy paper published in October 1972 by Mitchell Sharp, the minister for external affairs.[19] Known as the "third option," the government declared that Canada was seeking to become less economically vulnerable to the United States and more diversified in its trading relations. To achieve this objective, it acknowledged, a comprehensive industrial strategy would be needed. Talk of industrial policies implied a more interventionist role, especially in the manufacturing and high technology sectors of the economy, than Ottawa had been prepared to play since wartime mobilization. It was more than many politicians and bureaucrats felt appropriate in an export-led capitalist economy heavily centred on the exploitation of staple resources, particularly when the Canadian state was experiencing severe fiscal strains.

By the mid-1970s Canada was experiencing strains resulting from an escalating inflation rate, accompanied by growing unemployment. The postwar consensus between capital and labour based on a Keynesian approach to macro-economic management, along with the institution of a broad set of social security programs, was now breaking down. In an open economy no longer pulled along by American prosperity, Keynesianism was no longer working. Labour unions were becoming increasingly militant as they tried to defend their real wages gains of the 1960s. Ottawa was also trying to reduce the drain on its budget by capping open-ended social programs whose costs escalated with the rise in levels of social distress and the advance of medical technology.[20] As the liberalization of world trade following the Kennedy Round forced down tariffs, the import substitution premises of Canada's postwar accumulation strategy came into question. Increasing trade deficits, growing unemployment, and rising interest rates were among the indicators of an economy in trouble. In recognition of its problems, the Trudeau government moved to the right. The Bank of Canada embraced monetarism. The government instituted wage and price controls. Having shifted the tax burden from business to the public it found its revenues shrinking. At the same time its subsidization of the domestic prices of oil added to rising deficits.

Though it abandoned its social-democratic dream of introducing a guaranteed annual income, the Trudeau government did not give up on the essentially national thrust of its system of legitimation. On the cultural front, for instance, new legislation and new funding of existing bodies such as the Canada Council had encouraged the development of cultural production at both the élite and mass levels with Canadian content on television, in music, in books achieving higher levels both in quality and in quantity. American films and American television continued to dominate Canadian screens, but Canadian culture by the end of the 1970s was more vibrant than it had ever been.

Despite the economic blows it had received, Canada seemed to be standing securely on the world stage by the end of the 1970s. Its significance in the community of capitalist economies had been recognized by its admission with Italy to the annual Economic Summit in 1976. It had used its foreign aid program as a means to project its bilingual personality abroad and it had continued its active involvement in multilateral institutions as a means to increase its influence in Washington with whose policies it tended quite often to disagree. The Canadian-American relationship had become less satellitic; the two countries' interests were now perceived as competitive. Conflicts were expressed more openly as differences between two friendly neighbours that nevertheless pursued sometimes divergent objectives.

The year 1979 represented barely a blip in this story of Canada's political development. A minority victory for Joe Clark in the May election produced a short-lived Progressive Conservative government that, having promised a redirection of policy, actually signalled that it would not deviate significantly from the national path that Trudeau had followed.

What did mark a significant change was the election of February 1980. Though headed by Pierre Trudeau and staffed by the same players who had run his governments in the 1970s, the team that swept into power seemed completely new. Freshly energized after their nine-month sabbatical in opposition the Trudeau Liberals acted as if inspired with a mission to finish in the 1980s the work they had left so incomplete at the end of the 1970s. They were going to complete the construction of the pan-Canadian state, which meant establishing a more centralist mode of regulation.

Trudeau led the political battle to defeat the Parti Québécois referendum of 20 May 1980 on sovereignty-association and check the momentum of Quebec indépendantisme. This victory enabled the federal government to seize the initiative in constitutional reform. By November 1981 Trudeau had battled the provincial premiers to a stalemate, concluding a constitutional compromise that, apart from an enhancement of provincial control over resource policies, conceded to the provinces no significant increase in powers. The federal system of legitimation was further strengthened by the constitution's new charter of rights and freedoms which gave a powerful boost to the sense of citizenship felt by the "third force" Canadians, those ethnic groups who had felt their status inferior to the two founding blocks of British and French Canadians.[21]

Simultaneously the government moved to transform the structure of the country's petroleum industry. In the shadow of the second OPEC price doubling during 1979 and in the expectation of continuing price rises by the Arab-dominated oil cartel, Ottawa introduced a National Energy Program to redistribute economic rents from oil-rich Alberta to the federal government, which wanted to use these windfall funds for a still undefined national industrial strategy. It toyed with the notion of a Swedish-style, high-tech industrial policy but settled for a more traditional, but still ambitious strategy aimed at building massive projects to develop new energy resources for export.[22] Heartened by this anticipated new source of mega-money, the government promised it would expand the Canada pension plan and so complete the network of social programs that cushioned the public from hardship.

HOW CANADA WAS PUSHED OFF
ITS NATIONAL MODE

These nation-building dreams only lasted as long as the global balance of power allowed Canada to maintain a more autonomous role. When the world market moved in the opposite direction from what Ottawa had expected and when the United States reacted aggressively to the decline of its global position, the Canadian government was forced to reorient its whole approach to governing.

Once the world price of petroleum started to lose its upward momentum, the economic foundations of the Liberals' centralist accumulation strategy were shattered. The levelling off and then decline of the world market price of oil had two direct consequences for the Canadian government. First, it made the main provisions of the National Energy Program unworkable. The petroleum industry, which was meant to enrich the federal government's coffers, now had to be given tax relief. Ottawa started what became a three-year process of unpicking the complex fabric of its interventionist and centralist energy policy.

The second direct impact of the world petroleum price's failure to keep on rising was to abort the government's staple-based industrial strategy, as articulated in its 1981 budget. The hope of constructing a series of energy mega-projects across the country to foster regional development and forge backward linkages with the industrial capacity of central Canada hinged on energy prices rising enough to justify highly capital-intensive investments. The scheme to enhance Canada's traditional export of resources by linking staple development with a more balanced industrial development had come to naught.

Responding to the workings of the international market was a relatively easy problem for Ottawa compared to the trouble it had in dealing with the political pressures emanating from the new Reagan administration. While the Carter administration in the late 1970s had been taking steps to reverse the perceived decline of American power, it had been well inclined towards its northern neighbour. President Jimmy Carter had taken a liking to Prime Minister Trudeau whose judgment on international affairs he respected. For his part Trudeau greatly appreciated Carter's overt support for his federalist position against the separatist project of Premier René Lévesque's Parti Québécois government in Quebec City. As a result the two countries handled their bilateral problems with a considerable measure of mutual understanding. The basis for this goodwill vanished when the California Republicans rode onto Capitol Hill early in 1981.

President Ronald Reagan's team of radical rightists came to power with no instinctive sympathy for the Liberal Pierre Trudeau and little basic knowledge of Canadian-American relationship. They showed no sensitivity to the special conditions that generated the more state-centred approaches taken by Canadian governments to resolving their problems. So when American oil entrepreneurs, who had helped finance the Republican party campaign, started complaining about the NEP, claiming that the "socialist" government in Ottawa was confiscating the assets of their Canadian operations, the Reaganites got angry. They felt they had been elected not just to get government off the backs of business in America, but to bring their message to the world. If Canada was erring by increasing its levels of state interference with the free flow of capital, they thought it should be made to mend its ways.

The Canadian-American relationship changed once more. Suddenly the Canadian government found itself the target of strong American pressure to intervene in its affairs and change its laws. No matter how many times Canadian officials and politicians explained the rationale for their policies, the representatives of Ronald Reagan demanded they be altered. Regulations that were perfectly acceptable to Washington in the oilfields of Norway or Indonesia were not tolerable on continental terrain. Even the innocuous FIRA came under heavy attack from Washington.

If Reagan's America was to "stand tall in the saddle again," it had to reverse its economic decline. To achieve this it was bent on building up its protectionist defences at home while pressing for the liberalization of its partners' allegedly unfair government-sponsored programs abroad. Canada became a test case for Reaganomics' international program. Threats of retaliation emanated from the White House, from the US Department of Commerce, and from the American embassy while protectionist bills crowded the congressional order papers.[23]

Although the Trudeau government dug in its heels to defend the NEP from the first onslaught of the Reagan administration's offensive during 1981, Washington's pressure reinforced the resistance within Canada to the Trudeau government's policies. The resource-rich provincial governments, the corporate-controlled media, the business lobbies, and significant sections within the federal bureaucracy were themselves bridling at the strengthened pan-Canadian mode of regulation that the Trudeau Liberals were trying to achieve. The fear of American retaliation against specific Canadian industries helped these élite groups in their struggle to push the federal government off its course. But fear alone was not enough. What finally brought the Trudeau group to a full stop was political blundering of its own making and further misfortune at the hands of the international economy.

The 1981 budget which was brought down in November was a bold attempt at radical reform, a comprehensive scheme to achieve equity in the tax system by closing the myriad loopholes that had been created to satisfy dozens of special interests over the years. In one sweeping act the minister of finance thought he could achieve what his predecessors had been unable to manage. The outcry of indignation that greeted the 1981 budget indicated just how all-embracing was the reform's scope. Governments need allies to achieve their goals. Unfortunately for Allan MacEachen, the minister of finance, so many sectors of the Canadian public lost tax concessions of one kind or another that not even the spokesmen for the labour movement rose to his defence. He had to beat a humiliating defeat.

The second blow Ottawa received at this time came through the international market place. Provoked by the irrationality of Reaganomics, world interest rates were driven up to the highest levels since Jesus Christ, as Germany's chancellor, Helmut Schmidt, put it. The global depression this induced had a worse impact on Canada than on any other country in the OECD, driving interest rates up over 20 per cent, pushing businesses into bankruptcy, and forcing people onto the unemployment rolls. While citizens demanded relief, the government aggravated their distress by maintaining its tight money policy.

When the alienation caused by the government's 1981 budget disaster was combined with the rage generated by the economic recession, the governing Liberal party was brought to its knees. In the deepest recession since the 1930s, government itself became the obvious scapegoat. Interventionism was discredited. Big government was blamed. The Trudeau government's pan-Canadian project came to a standstill. With only its constitutional goal achieved, the cabinet had to abandon its liberal, nationalist, and social-democratic agenda. Its very legitimacy in shreds, its popularity lost, it had no option but to look for an alternative strategy, wherever it might be. The Canadian left – whether the New Democratic party or the trade union movement – had no agenda that seemed credible for hard times: Keynesianism and big-spending government were recipes that had already been discredited. In contrast to Canada's disorganized, defensive left, the Canadian business community had developed a co-ordinated, coherent position and knew exactly what was good for it.

THE CONTINENTAL REGIME OF ACCUMULATION

While a pan-Canadian state structure had been solidifying during the Trudeau years, another phenomenon had been developing in the economic sphere. Canadian capital had been consolidating and continentalizing. Large sectors of the economy, such as the automobile industry, had been continental in scope all along with Canadian branch plants developing specialized niches in their transnational parents' corporate global strategies. While American capital retained a prominent place in high-tech manufacturing and resource exploitation, Canadian capital had shown growing dynamism through the 1960s and into the 1970s. Canadian banks had emerged from their protected oligopoly to expand at increasing rates in the United States and abroad.[24] Canadian real estate developers, who had amassed their first fortunes through cultivating special relations with government clients, had set their sights on still larger markets in American cities. Canadian media corporations, which had come of age in an economy where foreign ownership of newspaper, broadcasting, and cable companies was prevented by law, expanded their operations in the United States to the point where their foreign earnings started to dwarf their Canadian revenues. The Canadian defence industry had become a growth sector bloated by the orders of the Pentagon's rearmament program.[25] Companies in less-protected sectors were also drawing the conclusion forced on them by successive rounds of tariff reduction resulting from world trade liberalization. Facing American protectionism without the benefit of a secure home market, they started establishing branch operations south of the international border. Canadian direct investment in the United States grew sevenfold from 1975 to 1985, at a rate of 20 per cent per annum.[26] In effect Canadian capitalism had evolved its own continent-wide regime of accumulation. Having matured in this way, it was bridling against a nationally oriented mode of regulation that now stood in its way.

Canada's infant industries had grown up. Unlike the beneficiaries of infant-industry policies in other countries, Canadian corporations were telling Daddy he was no longer needed. Even if they didn't entirely move away from home, they wanted to live in Canada by different rules, rules that would help them network abroad in the big wide world. The paternalist Canadian state had become too restricting, too interfering, too demanding. If Daddy was to be tolerated, he had to be put in his place. But first he had an important job to do. He was needed to negotiate a new arrangement so the fully grown offspring could play in the neighbour's bigger yard if and when they wanted. He was to produce a new, more continental and more permissive mode of regulation better adapted to the needs of the regime of accumulation they had evolved.

The Canadian business élite was not a group of cavil compradors trying silently to surrender to the Yankees. It constituted a new Canadian-based capitalist class for whom the continent was its oyster. Whatever interests divided the various fractions of Canadian capital, the cumulative effect of their deep-felt hatred of Pierre Trudeau's government, of their realization that further trade liberalization was unavoidable, of their concern about getting better access to the American market had built up an extraordinary consensus that crossed previously insuperable barriers to political co-operation. The less competitive manufacturing sector was ready to practise survival of the fittest. Branch plants threatened by the end of tariffs were told by their head offices to toe the line of continentalism. The more aggressive resource exporters wanted reduced US tariff barriers to hurdle. Canadian finance capital hoped for exemption from US protectionist restraints. Small business dreamed of competing in the big league by expanding operations across the border.

As articulated by the Business Council on National Issues, the umbrella organization representing 150 of Canada's largest Canadian and foreign-controlled corporations, the business agenda for the Trudeau government had two parts. First the BCNI wanted a Canadian-American agreement that would secure commercial access for Canadian exporters to the US market and guarantee their freedom to locate in any state. Secondly, on the home front they wanted the replacement of the social-democratic interventionist state by a regime that responded to the norms of the neo-conservative ideology which had recently become the conventional wisdom among the élites of the OECD countries.

TOWARDS A NEW CONTINENTAL MODE OF REGULATION

Canadian business might have preferred to be dealing with an appropriately conservative government, but it co-operated with the Trudeau Liberals, helping them work out a way to bring in wage controls without price restraints in the 1982 budget, and encouraging them to re-examine their trade options with the United States. When Trudeau shuffled his cabinet in September 1982 it was clear that a giant step had been made towards achieving the business agenda. The nationalist Herb Gray had been replaced as minister for industry, trade and commerce by the continentalist Ed Lumley; Trudeau put his most able minister, Marc Lalonde, into Finance, where he proceeded to restore the department that is the traditional exponent of business interests to its primacy in the government structure. Though few Canadians realized it at the time, the decisive watershed had been crossed. The federal government was engaged in a project that few understood, a project that would ultimately change the country's mode of regulation. For the remaining years of the Trudeau era, the BCNI told the government directly what it wanted. It provided complete and detailed draft legislation for a new competition act that would accelerate, in the name of economic rationalization, Canada's already high level of corporate concentration. It weighed in heavily on the government's pension reform thinking, steering it away from what it considered to be a dangerously Swedish approach to a state-run, comprehensive system in favour of maintaining a less generous system controlled by the private sector.

By the time Pierre Trudeau had retired as prime minister the process of defanging the interventionist federal state had come a long way. This made the election in September 1984 of a majority Progressive Conservative government a less important date than it might appear. While the business community had more confidence in the Conservatives, particularly since their rhetoric extolled the market rather than the state, the new prime minister, Brian Mulroney, was intellectually and psychically too weak for comfort. A man of no fixed principles, he would turn in whatever direction the political wind blew him.

This uncertain quality of the new political leadership made the publication, in September 1985, of the report of the Macdonald Commission on the Economic Union and Development Prospects of Canada a far more significant occasion. Appointed by Trudeau in 1982 to help the Liberal party redefine its agenda for the 1990s, the commission, headed by the former minister of finance turned corporate lawyer, Donald Macdonald, had become a spokesman for business. Formally the product of a massive social science research effort, the commission became the mouthpiece of the Canadian business community's new neoconservative consensus. Claiming Canada to be threatened equally by American protectionism on the outside and market-inhibiting government policies on the inside, the Macdonald report recommended that Canada should sue for free trade with the United States and that the Canadian welfare state should be cut back to size.

Prime Minister Brian Mulroney was politically shrewd enough to see that a comprehensive and authoritative pro-business program articulated by a highly regarded former Liberal cabinet minister could meet his government's desperate need for a coherent policy agenda. No matter that the Macdonald report's analysis grossly exaggerated the "crisis" that American protectionism allegedly posed for Canadian exports. No matter that the Reagan administration had become far more mellow in its second term and, as a result, less of a threat to Canada's national mode of regulation. No matter that the economic gains that could be expected from abolishing tariffs between the two countries were minor compared to the impact of other factors, such as fluctuations in the exchange rate. Despite these analytical flaws the prime minister adopted the Macdonald report's economic recommendations almost immediately and announced he was requesting that the White House start negotiations for a new economic relationship with Canada.

Mulroney justified his historic move to the Canadian public in dramatic terms, painting the Canadian economy's problems in lurid tones. In so doing he put Canada in the weakest possible bargaining situation for the two years of negotiations that were to ensue. As *demandeur* in the negotiations, Canada laid its cards on the table, trusting that friendly noises between the president and the prime minister would encourage a generous American response. The United States made no concessions but sat back and waited. When the bargaining crunch came, the Canadian negotiators were under instructions to do anything to get a deal. The ultimate document represented an astonishing gain for American trade diplomacy while surrendering virtually no American sovereignty. For the first time the United States had gained access to another country's service sector. Both sides had granted national treatment for each other's investments, but the Americans had refused to agree to a definition of subsidy which might give Canadian exporters some security against harassment by American business competitors using US trade remedy legislation. The United States had won important precedents for its global trade liberalization strategy. Canada had made enormous concessions that limited the federal and provincial governments' capacity to make industrial policies to promote their exports, to husband their energy reserves, or to foster their cultural industries. In return Ottawa had won few concessions, apart from an elaborate dispute settlement mechanism of highly questionable effectiveness. Since the negotiating officials were advised by groups representing big business, the FTA incorporated business objectives: the private sector basically got what it wanted in the final text. Canadian-American "free trade" can thus be seen less as an expression of an export-led economy than as an arrangement assuring mobility for their capital to American and Canadian transnational corporations. The FTA established a mode of regulation to suit the continent's giant corporations.

The last stage on the route to Canada's new economic constitution was the 1988 federal election which served as a referendum to ratify the FTA. The campaign brought into full view the extent to which the provincial governments outside Ontario see their future in increasing continental integration of their resource industries. It was the resource-exporting provinces that had been most seriously hurt by recent US protectionist actions against softwood lumber and Atlantic groundfish exports.[27] Their support for a treaty that reduced the power of the federal state confirmed the proposition that increasing continental integration on a region-by-region basis produces increasing disintegration of the federal state.[28]

Quebec was a special case in which opportunistic alliances combined to produce a near-unanimous support for the FTA. The Liberal government of Robert Bourassa (who, as a student of the European Community, had opposed the idea of Canadian free trade with the United States) supported the federal government's FTA in gratitude for Prime Minister Mulroney's support of Quebec's constitutional demands. The Parti Québécois supported free trade on the grounds that the FTA would aggravate the disintegration of the federal system and so accelerate the province's achievement of independence. Paradoxically, "la belle province," which prizes its government's autonomy, was supporting a treaty that will constrain provincial powers and give the federal government disciplinary authority to enforce compliance with the FTA's provisions.

As for the Canadian voters, they remained deeply worried about free trade, a majority expressing opposition to the deal right up to the election.[29] In a development as unique as the pro-free-trade solidarity of the whole Canadian business community, a Pro-Canada coalition of trade unions, farmers, church, women's, environmental, elderly, native, cultural, and ethnic groups generated an unprecedented social cohesion in opposition to the FTA. A misguided campaign by the NDP and an ill-starred campaign by the Liberals allowed the Conservatives to become the Bolsheviks of Canadian politics – the party which received a minority of votes but formed a majority government and so was able finally to ratify the FTA.[30]

In the immediate aftermath of the agreement's ratification, shutdowns, layoffs, and mergers started to accelerate. Major transformations of the Canadian state are to be expected if only because both supporters and opponents of the FTA consider it to be a turning point in Canada's history. Since they agree on little else, there is no consensus on what the FTA will mean for Canada in the long term.

CANADA AS A POST-NATIONAL STATE

If Canada's fate is unusually dependent on external forces, both economic and political, what the new continental mode of regulation turns out to be will depend to a large extent on developments beyond its borders.

The decline of American hegemony may be irreversible, as Paul Kennedy implies.[31] Continuing failure to overcome ideological shibboleths about free enterprise and continuing incapacity to direct its energies from wasteful military projects to productive economic investment may doom the United States to continued indebtedness and the whims of foreign lenders. In this case the North American market of which Canada has become an integral part would be dependent on economic trends elsewhere in the globe. The extent to which Japan manages to keep its markets closed to North American exports will be important. So, too, will the autarchy of the European Community which may expand to include the former people's democracies but exclude North America. If the American economy continues to lose ground, there would be little prospect for Canada to do much more than follow suit. Canadian business people might continue to feel that they need to be in the US system and be ready to pay any price to continue to rent the attic. On the other hand, a depressed United States would spread unemployment throughout Canada and so discredit the FTA. Whether an abrogation movement could then generate a substantial head of steam would depend on the appearance of charismatic leadership, the access of the public to information not sanctioned by a continentally controlled media system, and the survival of memories of an independent Canada among the population. Even high levels of politicization might not prevail against an overriding sense that the free trade eggs could not be unscrambled short of driving Canadians to the brink of economic ruin.

America's decline may have been exaggerated and the United States' relative power may have stabilized, as Samuel Huntington riposts.[32] Thanks to the global dominance of the English language, the popularity of American culture as the embodiment of modernity and the superiority of the US service industry, the American economy may correct its imbalances and recover its leading international position. A prosperous America would provide demand for Canadian exports and legitimize the value of the FTA, silencing critics by raising employment rates and the standard of living. Whether the United States declines or stabilizes, actual US behaviour can be benign or malignant as far as its northern partner is concerned. A declining America can be cautious or a bully; a resurgent United States can be generous or imperious. Canada's fate will continue to be tied to the quality of leadership that finds its way to Washington.

A crucial problem would remain. If for the continental regime of accumulation there is no satisfactory mode of regulation with sufficiently articulated institutions to give the component parts adequate weight in decision-making for the Canadian region as a whole, then the whole system is bound to remain in a continual condition of instability. As it stands, the FTA has neutered the Canadian state of much of its economic-management and cultural-development capabilities. Apart from tariffs, federal and provincial governments are forbidden to pass laws controlling foreign investment or regulate banking, energy, or services to the advantage of Canadian-owned corporations. At the same time the American government's sovereign capacity to legislate in the economy is barely affected. The asymmetry of this arrangement promises to cause trouble, particularly since it is the Canadian public that will be sensitive to injuries and injustices arising from the FTA. A population conditioned to a continual involvement in federal and provincial electoral politics would be unlikely to take kindly to the proposition that, because of the (mixed) blessings of the FTA, their governments can no longer deal with acute economic problems.

It is true that a continental institution, the Canada–United States Trade Commission (CUSTER), has been established to oversee the enforcement of the FTA's provisions. It is also true that the agreement lays down in elaborate detail the procedures and time delays to govern dispute panels set up to verify the findings of national trade courts. If the panels perform as their proponents prophesy, then trade harmony will prevail in North America. If countervail actions escalate when uncompetitive American firms resort to countervail and anti-dumping suits to harass their Canadian competitors, as some insiders predict, Canadian business may find that the FTA has delivered less security of access than they were led to expect.[33] While it is conceivable that the reaction of business to this realization could be a nationalist call to abrogate the treaty, it is much more likely that entrepreneurs would simply decide to emigrate, taking their capital into Fortress America with them.

As federal and provincial governments lose the capacity to formulate micro-economic policies, their economic well-being will depend on the impact in the Canadian regions of policies made in Washington. CUSTER itself is not much of an institution when it comes to continental policy-making. Its members have no supranational independence; they are civil servants from the two member countries. It has no secretariat, no fixed address, and no collective policy-making capability. Since its decisions must be made by consensus, each party to the FTA has maintained a veto over its operations.[34] The instability heralded by this weak institutional set-up implies that, should the FTA survive its initial decade, some structural consolidation would need to occur to meet the continental system's managerial needs.

As it stands, each party can try to use CUSTER to discipline the other and enforce observance of the gains it made in the agreement. If the United States continues to take the offensive in extracting the benefits it won from Canada's concessions and if the Canadian government continues to adopt a supine attitude in the face of American bullying, then Canada's standard of living would be likely to degenerate. If this decline were palpable enough, that very deterioration could spark a nationalist response that could work to undo the agreement by reinstating a more national mode of regulation.

Other American factors will affect the impact of free trade on the Canadian political system. Much hangs on the evolution of American society. If the American political system can respond effectively to the serious forces causing internal instability and reverse current trends towards the polarization of class and race, it could again become a positive model as attractive to Canadian eyes as was the liberal America of Franklin Roosevelt. But if it does not manage to achieve a social consensus and fails to achieve a harmonious society based on a more equitable sharing of wealth, then Canadians, to the extent that they manage to maintain a sense of themselves as a distinct society, are likely to resist cultural integration into a system they find abhorrent.

The FTA is so comprehensive a document, its reach is so long, that there is no aspect of Canadian society that will not be touched by it. A degeneration of agriculture following the disintegration of Canada's marketing boards, already under strong US pressure, is already happening. Government reluctance to protect Canadian firms in the cultural industries – already noticeable in the violation of the "Baie-Comeau" policy which was designed to expand the sphere of Canadian-owned publishing houses – could become a sensitive issue among the cultural and intellectual sectors of the Canadian élite. A cutting back of social spending in response to the small-government agenda of the business coalition cannot be distinguished from the new continental mode of regulation. Prohibitive housing costs resulting from foreign capital pouring in to buy up cheap Canadian real estate can be linked to the "Canada for sale" attitude generated by the FTA proponents. A Canadian dollar pushed up above 85 US cents by inflowing foreign investment will gravely restrict exports even by the efficient steel and forest industries. While Canadian capitalists may show they no longer have a nationality, unemployed Canadian workers would have no such luxury. As a consequence, Canadian union leaders are moving to more national forms of organization. Those interested in Ottawa's responsible middle-power role in the world could have reason to grow disillusioned if Canada continues to behave vis-à-vis the United States in the UN Security Council the way the Ukraine used to behave vis-à-vis the Soviet Union in the UN General Assembly. Sounding more American than apple pie, it clung to Cold War rhetoric long after Reagan's Washington embraced perestroika. If the FTA means that the weak eddies of Canadian cultural creativity are swamped by an uncontrollable torrent of American "entertainment," then the identity needs of the Canadian community are unlikely to be met.

The FTA as the new economic constitution for North America is likely to be as effective as any constitution. If it fails to meet its constituent members' needs, it will come under pressure for change, whether or not it has the status of a treaty. The system of legitimation that was made possible by a national mode of regulation could produce pressures that demand a return to the status quo ante FTA. However much the regime of accumulation may be continental, Canadians' identity needs will require some satisfaction. It is quite possible that, as Naomi Black argued almost two decades ago, integration is impossible. An excessive degree of economic integration that failed to meet the public's identity needs could well trigger a nationalist movement aimed at differentiating the two systems and returning power to the federal and provincial governments.[35]

If this renewed cycle of differentiation were to gather momentum one could expect to hear the call for an interventionist, internationalist and social-democratic state as the core institutional framework for the revivified Canada. The economics of small markets and niche-finding might then come back into vogue. The value of communitarian consciousness and the energy of society's popular forces would be advocated. Canada might return to the international stage as a self-conscious middle power building coalitions with other medium-sized states. A national commitment to global policy-making on issues that transcend national frontiers, such as the depletion of the ozone layer, the homeless, pollution, third world debt, would have world federalist overtones but a new seriousness. Speculations of this kind presuppose the survival of a sense of national community and the continuation of an emotional commitment to the state even after Canada's state structure has been undermined.

Even laying out the elements for making a forecast of Canada's future under the FTA shows how perilous is the attempt at prediction. In essence Canada can be seen to be exposed to two somewhat contradictory trends. On the one hand the powerful force of globalization has obliterated market boundaries and disrupted whole societies. On the other hand the spirit of nationhood has shown its head all over the globe from Iran to Nicaragua, from Lithuania to Quebec. This contradiction poses a specific question for Canada. Will there be sufficient demands for the system of legitimation in the 1990s to modify the unstable mode of regulation that the FTA has introduced as a way to satisfy the continental regime of accumulation? The answer will depend on the persistence of a Canadian consciousness that differentiates itself from the American. Canada's survival within the FTA will depend on those north of the forty-ninth parallel retaining a sufficient sense of their nationality to insist that their state's mode of regulation respond not just to the demands of capital but to the needs of nationhood, not just to the regime of accumulation but to the system of legitimation.

The adjustment problems of middle powers faced by world upheaval do not often provide the stuff of large-scale history. Nor is there anything new in the spectacle of a vulnerable state facing a loss of its sovereignty. But as Europe prepares itself for 1992, the Canadian example could take on considerable relevance. This country has had a long experience in dealing with dependent integration in an external market, with the pressures of cultural assimilation, and with the centrifugal forces of regionalism. Understanding Canada's problems with continentalism may provide some insights into understanding challenges faced by smaller European countries in 1992. Understanding Canada's problems in the perspective of Europe may help distinguish what is genuinely unique to the Canadian experience from what are common problems of middle-sized states on the cusp of the post-national era.

NOTES

1 The debate about the virtues and vices of the FTA has produced three collections of value. Duncan Cameron, ed., *The Free Trade Deal* (Toronto: Lorimer 1988) argues against the FTA, while John Crispo, ed., *Free Trade: The Real Story* (Toronto: Gage 1988) provides the case in favour. A more balanced compendium presenting the two sides' positions can be found in Mark Gold and David Leyton-Brown, eds., *Trade-Offs on Free Trade: The Canada–U.S. Free Trade Agreement* (Toronto: Carswell 1988).

2 Robert Young, "The Canada–U.S. Agreement and its Inernational Context," in Gold and Leyton-Brown, *Trade-Offs on Free Trade*, ch. 1, points out how little academics know about services; Marjorie Griffin Cohen's *Free Trade and the Future of Women's Work: Manufacturing and Service Industries* (Toronto: Garamond 1987) examines the impact on women's employment of free trade in services.

3 "Bilateral relations with the United States resemble those between any two sovereign states ... Within Canada itself, the corresponding value of an autonomous society prompts a reliance on strategies that prohibit outright further American penetration and actively reduce the existing American prescnce." John Kirton and David Dewitt, *Canada as a Principal Power* (Toronto: John Wiley and Sons 1983), 43.

4 Jorge Niosi concluded in 1985 that Canadians had "increased control over their own economy, a process that began in 1970 and has accelerated since then." *Canadian Multinationals* (Toronto: Garamond Press 1985), 49. In the same vein William Carroll stated: "[I]n an era of rising and then declining

American hegemony, the dominant fraction of Canadian capital has consolidated control over circuits of finance capital at home and abroad ... the
American Challenge of the 1940's–60's has been beaten back ... the harvest of lengthening dependency that [Kari] Levitt foresaw has not been
reaped." William K. Carroll, *Corporate Power and Canadian Capitalism* (Vancouver: University of British Columbia Press 1986), 211.

5 In a speech in Thunder Bay during the 1983 Tory leadership campaign,
Mulroney sarcastically attacked John Crosbie's suggestion that Canada
should look at the possibility of free trade with the United States:
"There's a real beauty for you ... There's a real honey. Free trade with the
United States is like sleeping with an elephant. It's terrific until the elephant twitches, and if the elephant rolls over you are a dead man." (Lawrence Martin, "Tories take the gloves off," *Globe and Mail*, 3 June 1983: 8).
In the same speech, Mulroney went on to note: "And I'll tell you when
he's going to roll over – he's going to roll over in times of economic
depression and they're going to crank up those plants in Georgia and
North Carolina and Ohio and they're going to be shutting them down up
here ... That's why free trade was decided on in an election in 1911. It
affects Canadian sovereignty and we will have none of it, not during leadership campaigns, or at any other time." (Leslie Shepherd, "Tories touting
free trade split with party tradition," *Toronto Star*, 3 June 1983: A23).

6 Stephen Clarkson, *Canada and the Reagan Challenge*, 2nd ed. (Toronto:
James Lorimer 1985), ch. 14.

7 These have already been applied to the Canadian condition by Jane Jenson,
"'Different' but not 'Exceptional': Canada's Permeable Fordism," *Canadian
Review of Sociology and Anthropology* 26, no. 1, (1989): 69–94, and by
Rianne Mahon, "Post-Fordism, Canada and the FTA: Is there Room for the
Left to Manoeuvre?" paper presented at the University of Pisa, 21 April
1989, 29 pp. mimeo.

8 J.L. Granatstein, *How Britain's Weakness Forced Canada into the Arms of the
United States*, 1988 Joanne Goodman Lectures (Toronto: University of
Toronto Press 1989).

9 The legacy of the controversial cancellation of the Avro Arrow is a contin-
uing debate about the wisdom of the decision and its consequences: James
Dow, *The Arrow* (Toronto: James Lorimer 1979); Jon B. McLin, *Canada's
Changing Defence Policy, 1957–1963* (Baltimore: Johns Hopkins Press 1967);
Murray Peden, *Fall of an Arrow* (Stittsville, Canada: Canada's Wings
1978).

10 Danford W. Middlemiss, "Economic Defence Co-operation with the
United States 1940–63" in Kim Richard Nossal, ed., *An Acceptance of Para-
dox: Essays in Honour of John W. Holmes* (Toronto: Canadian Institute of
International Affairs 1982), 86–109; R.P. Byers, "Canadian Defence and
Defence Procurement: Implications for Economic Policy" in Denis Stairs

and Gilbert R. Winham, eds., *Selected Problems in Formulating Economic Policy* (Toronto: University of Toronto Press 1985); John J. Kirton, "The Consequences of Integration: The Case of the Defence Production Sharing Agreements" in W. Andrew Axline *et al.*, *Continental Community? Independence and Integration in North America* (Toronto: McClelland and Stewart 1974), 116–36.

11 Jenson develops a similar, though broader, concept with her notion of 'paradigm.' See Jenson, "'Different' but not 'Exceptional.'"

12 Livingston T. Merchant and A.D.P. Heeney, "Canada and the United States – Principles for Partnership," *Department of State Bulletin*, 2 August 1965.

13 Christina McCall-Newman, *Grits: An Intimate Portrait of the Liberal Party* (Toronto: Macmillan of Canada 1982), part II.

14 President Nixon's declaration of Canadian independence was given in the Canadian House of Commons where he said, "the fact of our mutual interdependence and our mutual desire for independence need not be inconsistent traits. No self-respecting nation can or should accept the proposition that it should always be economically dependent upon any other nation." *Hansard*, 14 April 1972: 1328.

15 Under the Nixon program, American firms which established a Domestic International Sales Corporation would receive a tax deferment on half the profits earned from exports. See Jim Cutt, "The National Economy" in John Saywell, ed., *Canadian Annual Review of Politics and Public Affairs* (Toronto: University of Toronto Press 1972).

16 Fred Lazar, "The National Economy" in John Saywell, ed., *Canadian Annual Review of Politics and Public affairs* (Toronto: University of Toronto Press 1974), 329.

17 Robert Couzin, "The Canada Development Corporation: A Comparative Appraisal," *McGill Law Journal* 17, no. 2 (1971): 405–36.

18 Jim Cutt, "The National Economy" in Saywell, ed., *Canadian Annual Review* (1974), 363–64. Also Michael Bliss, "Founding FIRA: The Historical Background" in James M. Spence and William P. Rosenfeld, eds., *Foreign Investment Review Law in Canada* (Toronto: Butterworths 1984), 1–11.

19 Mitchell Sharp, "Canada–U.S. Relations: Options for the Future," *International Perspectives*, Special issue (Autumn 1972).

20 R.J. Van Loon, "From Shared Cost to Block Funding and Beyond: The Politics of Health Insurance in Canada," *Journal of Health Politics, Policy and Law* 2, no. 4 (1978): 454–78.

21 Alan Cairns and Cynthia Williams, "Constitutionalism, Citizenship and Society in Canada: An Overview" in Alan Cairns and Cynthia Williams, eds., *Constitutionalism, Citizenship and Society in Canada*, vol. 33, prepared for the Royal Commission on the Economic Union and Development Prospects for Canada (Toronto: University of Toronto Press 1985).

22 G. Bruce Doern, "The Mega-Project Episode and the Formulation of Canadian Economic Development Policy," *Canadian Public Administration* 26, no. 2 (Summer 1983): 219–38.

23 For a detailed discussion of the American intervention in 1981 see Stephen Clarkson, *Canada and the Reagan Challenge: Crisis and Adjustment, 1981–85*, 2nd ed. (Toronto: Lorimer 1985), ch. 2.

24 Louis W. Pauly, "Setting the Ground Rules for Foreign Participation in Canadian Finance: The Case of the Banking Industry in Retrospect and Prospect," unpublished manuscript (1987). Louis Pauly, *Opening Financial Markets: Banking Politics on the Pacific Rim* (Ithaca: Cornell University Press 1988).

25 "With the Reagan rearmament program providing nearly ninety percent of demand, defence exports to the US nearly quadrupled within the first five years of the 80s." Howard Peter Langille, "Towards a Political Economy of Canadian Defence Regulation" (master's thesis, Norman Paterson School of International Affairs, Carleton University 1988), 37.

26 Alan Rugman, *Trade Liberalization and International Investment* Economic Council of Canada, discussion paper #347 (Ottawa, April 1988), 1.13.

27 In the end neither won exemption from American retaliation in the FTA.

28 Garth Stevenson, "Continental Integration and Canadian Unity," in W. Andrew Axline, et al., *Continental Community? Independence and Integration in North America* (Toronto: McClelland and Stewart 1974), 194–217.

29 Two weeks before the election an Environics poll confirmed that 51 per cent opposed the FTA, 29 per cent favoured it, and 11 per cent indicated no opinion. Michael Adams, "Election Report/1988," *Focus Canada Report*, 1988: 4.

30 For a discussion of the 1988 federal election, see Alan Frizzell, Jon H. Pammett, and Anthony Westell, eds., *The Canadian General Election of 1988* (Ottawa: Carleton University Press 1989).

31 Paul Kennedy, *The Rise and Fall of the Great Powers: Economic Change and Military Conflict from 1500 to 2000* (New York: Random House 1987).

32 Samuel P. Huntington, "The U.S. – Decline or Renewal?" *Foreign Affairs* (Winter 1988/89): 76–96. In 1982 80 per cent of all Eurocurrency liabilities were still issued in US dollars, compared to 81 per cent in 1970. R.O. Keohane, *After Hegemony: Co-operation and Discord in the World Political Economy* (Princeton: Princeton University Press 1984), 196–200.

33 Philip Slayton, a Toronto trade lawyer, expects US protectionist actions against Canadian exporters to increase *because of* free trade. "With other protectionist devices eliminated or restricted by the FTA, one can safely predict, as part of a U.S. defensive strategy, a dramatic upsurge in U.S. AD [antidumping] and CV [countervail] duty cases directed against Canada." "Developing a Free Trade Strategy," *Blakes Report* 5, no. 2 (March/April 1989), 2.

34 Stephen Clarkson, "A Bureaucratic Monstrosity" in Ed Finn, ed., *The Facts on Free Trade* (Toronto: James Lorimer 1988), 54–56.

35 A similar phenomenon helps account for Quebec's Quiet Revolution: French-Canadian society had become so integrated in North America that the Quebec state had to bolster the *system of legitimation* by instituting strong language laws. See William D. Coleman, *The Independence Movement in Quebec, 1945–1980* (Toronto: University of Toronto Press 1984).

6 Rights, Freedoms, and Market Power: Canada's Charter of Rights and the New Era of Global Competition

MICHAEL MANDEL

At first glance, the Canadian Charter of Rights and Freedoms seems rather out of place in the new era of global competition. The other phenomena of the new era, such as the Canada–US free trade agreement, subject us to the despotism of radically unequal market power, while the Charter seems to protect us from such things by guaranteeing democracy, equality, and our basic human rights. So the Charter is usually regarded as a kind of exception to the conservative trend of the times. But the Charter and the free trade movement have a lot more in common than is generally understood. I want to argue that they are both aspects of the same historical development: the contraction of the state in favour of the market place and the substitution of economic imperatives for more democratic ones. They each represent the triumph of the regulatory principle of "one dollar, one vote" over that of "one person, one vote." In other words, the "freedom" in free trade and the Canadian Charter of Rights and Freedoms is precisely the same: subjection to the unequal power of the market place.

Any brief treatment of this enormous and complicated subject must be very selective and to some extent schematic.[1] I will try to develop my thesis by examining: the contribution the Charter made to the victory of the free trade forces in the general federal election of 1988; the link between North American integration and the reception of this American-style legalization of government into Canada; the essential similarity between the politico-economic causes of the deregulation movement and the Charter; and finally, the contributions made by the Charter to the quest by business for freedom from popular control. I will then consider several possible counter-examples to the thesis, namely the "due process" limitations the Charter imposes on state repression and the Charter's egalitarian provisions, to show that what appear as exceptions are actually instances of the essential sameness of the deregulation movement and the Charter.

THE CHARTER AND THE FREE TRADE ELECTION

Canada's free trade election of 1988 was unprecedented, both for the coalescence of business around only one of the major parties and for the enormous amount of money spent in pursuit of victory. The Liberal party had betrayed business as a whole and turned the election into a general free trade referendum with no certain outcome, so business invested in the Tories: "In the largest lobbying and public relations effort in history, the pro-free-trade forces spent about six-and-a-half million dollars during the last three weeks of the election campaign. The anti-free traders could raise less than one million dollars."[2] Fully two million dollars was spent by just one big business coalition, the Canadian Alliance for Trade and Job Opportunities, in the final three weeks of the campaign (after the Liberals had nosed out in front in the opinion polls) to sell the Tories and villify the opposition through every conceivable medium of communication.

But the most valuable contribution to the campaign was unquestionably that of another group, the National Citizens' Coalition. It had already spent more than $400,000 on free trade propaganda before the tide-turning leaders' debates. However, its service to the cause went far beyond that. In fact, without the National Citizens' Coalition all the expenditure by business would have been illegal under the Canada Elections Act. This is where the Charter comes in.

The National Citizens' Coalition is a right-wing lobby group founded by an insurance executive from London, Ontario, and run by a small board made up of representatives of some of the biggest corporations in Canada. The group supports all of the expected right-wing causes: cuts in social spending, the abolition of medicare, extra-billing by doctors, a white-only immigration policy, traditional roles for women, sexual discrimination in wages, lower taxes for the rich, and so on. Its specialty is the full-page newspaper advertisement, such as those it bought during the free trade election. Since the entrenchment of the Charter, it has added litigation to its arsenal.

The Coalition's most important judicial victory to date was its unique contribution to the free trade election. In 1984 it persuaded an Alberta judge to strike down new federal restrictions on non-party campaign expenditures as an interference with "freedom of expression." The 1983 restrictions had been designed to limit the growing influence of wealthy groups, such as the Coalition, who, following the example of the right-wing political action committees in the United States, had started to spend great amounts on election campaigns. This was tending to render the already weak spending limits and disclosure rules in the law meaningless. Here we had one of the most direct ways in which the one-person-one-vote principle of democracy in government was undermined by the one-dollar-one-vote principle of marketplace despotism. The parliamentary parties had unanimously agreed to make it an offence to spend money for or against a party or candidate without authorization; with authorization, such expenditure would have to be included in tabulating the total expenditures limited by the act. The National Citizen's Coalition claimed that this interfered with freedom of expression; but government lawyers answered that these spending restrictions would actually *enhance* freedom of expression by not allowing the voices of the many to be drowned out by those of the few with money. Justice Medhurst of the Alberta Supreme Court followed the American precedents and ignored the question of inequality of economic power. The provisions were struck down in time for the Coalition to spend several hundreds of thousands of dollars on the 1984 election which followed a few months later, and which saw the election of the first Conservative majority government in thirty years. Four years later the Alberta judgment still ruled the land and permitted the unregulated spending spree of 1988.

THE QUEBEC INDEPENDENCE MOVEMENT AND THE AMERICAN CONNECTION

It is impossible to determine how much the Charter helped business in the 1988 election. But even if its contribution was substantial, this would not mean that we had the Charter to thank for the free trade agreement; the causes of the current trend to trade liberalization are naturally much deeper. So are the causes of the growing political importance of judicial forms of government – the "legalization of politics" – represented by the Charter.

The Charter's primary political purpose in Canada was to defeat the nationalist-independentist tendencies which had developed in Quebec during the so-called Quiet Revolution that followed the death of Duplessis. To counter this, a federalist strategy of Canada-wide bilingualism was developed, meant to ensure a continued English presence in Quebec and to enhance French Quebeckers' allegiance to Canada. This strategy, however doubtful, could not hope to succeed if limited to the sphere allocated to the federal government by Canada's original constitution, the British North America Act of 1867. Under it, the provinces maintained control over education and large parts of the economy. And, because of the increasing concentration of French-speaking Canadians in Quebec and of English-speaking Canadians outside Quebec, the movement in the 1960s within the provinces was all in the direction of unilingualism. This became most apparent when the independentist Parti Québécois was elected the government of Quebec in 1976, threatening the entire federalist strategy. From the federalist point of view, a constitutional rearrangement was urgent. But this rearrangement could not overtly or simply transfer provincial constitutional jurisdiction to the federal government, especially as this was the era of the resource boom and increasing clout for Western provinces.

The solution offered by the Liberal party headed by Pierre Trudeau was a Charter of Rights which would take certain language questions out of provincial jurisdiction by allowing a federally appointed judiciary to protect minority (French or English) language rights across the country. To get as much support for this as possible, both within and without Quebec, these linguistic rights had to be wrapped in a general Charter of Rights whose appeal would have to transcend the language issue. However, it is impossible to mistake for one minute which was means and which was end. Trudeau's own writings going as far back as 1965 make this clear, as does the fact that the first draft of the Charter was put on the table as a direct response to the disastrous (from a federalist point of view) Quebec election of 1976 and the new provincial government's centre-piece, Bill 101, the Charter of the French Language, which sought to make French the language of public life in Quebec. To this can be added other unmistakable clues: that almost all of the Charter of Rights was made subject to a government opt-out clause (section 33, the "notwithstanding" clause) *except* minority language education rights and interprovincial mobility rights, obviously the most crucial clauses to guarantee the English presence in Quebec; and that these two clauses were the most detailed and "un-charterlike" in the Charter, leaving no room for judicial discretion or any doubt that they were intended to overrule a provincial law already in existence. No wonder the government of Quebec would not sign. However, as a prelude to the new era, the federal government was able to rely on its own Supreme Court to legitimate the first non-unanimous constitutional amendment in Canada's history.[3]

What has trade liberalization got do do with all of this? It is important to see that the Charter of Rights represented an entirely different form of government from the received tradition of representative democracy through parliamentary sovereignty. Its central feature was the granting to the courts of supreme authority over government, not in the sense of merely ensuring that the government obeyed its own laws (the traditional function of the courts), but in the sense of having the unlimited right to veto those laws, indeed the right to final approval of the legitimacy of all government action. We are easily apt to confuse documents like the Charter with anti–discrimination laws that do *not* contradict this tradition of parliamentary sovereignty, such as domestic human rights codes that prohibit certain forms of discrimination in the market place, or international declarations of human rights that commit governments to certain policies but that do not carry with them any legal consequences. Such institutions preserve the supremacy of the legislature, even if they may create institutions which can be powerful influences on government.

This British tradition was of no use to the federal government in its struggle with the government of Quebec because it left ultimate control with the provincial governments. The federalists had to *legalize* a certain sector of the political system to wrench it altogether from the control of popular majorities and representative government. They had to treat certain matters as beyond politics, in order to get them into the courts. The Trudeau Liberals did not invent this strategy out of thin air; there was, in fact, a ready-made model to hand with which to replace the British one.

The reason the legalization strategy was a plausible, indeed powerful one, was that the model it relied upon was an American–patented device that had already made a great impression on Canadians. In fact, it was often lamented in the 1960s that many Canadians were misled by watching American television into believing that the constitutional rights the police read to suspects were the same as our own. The lament was not for the influence of American television but for the lack of the same constitutional rights. The ready acceptability of the legal form of politics in fact signalled the postwar transfer of Canadian allegiance from Britain to the United States, which only mirrored the shift which had already taken place in foreign ownership of the Canadian economy. The British approach had always been absolute parliamentary sovereignty, a proposition established by the English Revolution in the seventeenth century, and developed, conveniently enough, when Parliament represented the tiny proportion of the English population with property. When the Americans made their republican revolution a century later, they rejected parliamentary sovereignty in favour of government limited by a judicially enforceable bill of rights. The reasons were complicated, and included the familiar democratic claims against despotic government which explain the wide appeal of bills of rights even to this day. But there were also narrower concerns: with wider, though by no means universal suffrage; and with the protection of powerful interests represented by the wealthy framers of the constitution, who wanted guarantees for their property as much as for their political liberty. So the American constitution and its Bill of Rights put interferences with property beyond state and congressional reach with explicit clauses prohibiting the impairment of contracts or the issuing of paper money by the states, and entrusted the enforcement of these clauses to a federally appointed judiciary. And, as is well known, the judicial defence of property did not stop there. As America industrialized in the nineteenth century and the pressures of an enfranchised urban working class led to the regulation of the economy, the judges soon came to discover other *implicit* powers in the Bill of Rights. In the first third of the twentieth century, they increasingly interpreted the constitution to decree laissez-faire capitalism. This led to the famous confrontation with President Roosevelt in the thirties over the New Deal program. Though Roosevelt was able to wring submission from the Supreme Court on economic and political policy, the idea of judicial review had triumphed and was used to consolidate the New Deal consensus of the fifties and sixties.

Within a decade of the Roosevelt-Court confrontation, Canada had its own movement for a Bill of Rights. By 1950 the idea was basically accepted among most of the political actors, at least outside of Quebec. In Quebec it was only the racist, ultra-conservative elements of the Union Nationale under Duplessis who resisted it on principle as too permissive and cosmopolitan. Otherwise, the only obstacles were the lack of a formula for amending the constitution and a consensus on Quebec's place in it. The idea of a Bill of Rights appealed to different factions for radically different reasons. To the left it meant what it seems to mean to most people now: opposition to racial, sexual, and political discrimination. But to the centre-right it was seen as a way of keeping control, through judicial veto, of a government that had grown dangerously large during the war, and of the large mass of untrustworthy immigrants from lands unschooled in British traditions and full of dangerous ideologies. It was also seen as a way of emulating the world's leading power, the one which had come to dominate our economy and our culture. Indeed, it was a way of showing loyalty to the American side in the ideological struggle of the Cold War.

Judicial review was, in fact, part of an explicit strategy – a kind of legal Marshall Plan – of the American neo-colonialists to ensure postwar stability in Europe under US hegemony. Under American tutelage judicial review found its way into postwar constitutions from Western Europe to Japan. As American prestige grew in Canada so did the desirability of a bill of rights. Though the most Diefenbaker could achieve was a bill of rights applicable only to the federal government, by the time Trudeau entered federal politics the idea of a charter had acquired motherhood status and could be used as a Trojan horse for his Quebec policy.

So the reception of the Charter into Canada was quite clearly a function of our increasing integration into the growing American empire and our separation from the declining British one. Since 1982 us influence has grown rapidly through the conduit of the entrenched Charter. We have already mentioned the election spending laws case. To this can be added many more, including strikingly similar decisions in the realm of school prayer, the rights of criminal suspects, the rights of business and the rights of women, for example to abortion. The American way of thinking is becoming habitual to Canadian lawyers and judges. There is nothing surprising about this: try as politically sensitive Canadian judges might to go their own way, the Americans are the patent holders and major producers in the field of legal politics; it is only natural that they would be the experts in its logic.

THE CHARTER AND THE REGULATORY STATE

There are deeper reasons for the increasing reliance on judicial review both here and in the United States. The Trudeau strategy depended not only on the prestige of the American model of legal politics but on its general fit with current conditions. It is possible to see legal politics as a kind of defence mechanism developed to preserve the status quo of social power from the threats posed to it by three interconnected contemporaneous phenomena: the expansion of the suffrage, the deep involvement of the state in the economy, and the crisis tendencies of Western industrial economies.

The process of state involvement in the economy has reached enormous proportions approaching 50 per cent of Gross National Expenditure. This has been an increasing source of annoyance and concern to the most powerful – that is to say the wealthiest – sectors in society. Not only does the prominence of the public sector constitute an immediate interference with profit-making, but it also poses the long-term threat of popular control of the economy. In response business has mounted a campaign against government involvement in the economy, except where it is of direct benefit to business. The result has been a general contraction of the public sphere through the wholesale privatization of government-owned enterprise and, especially, the drive to end all purely political barriers to the free movement of capital throughout the North American continent, while protecting the rights of business to receive government subsidies so long as these subsidies do not "discriminate" on merely national grounds.

Central to business's case against government interference is an ideology that deems the economy a "private" sphere, despite the enormous social power that is wielded there. Increasing government involvement in the economy tends to break down the distinction between public and private spheres, politicizing the economy and making genuine democracy very dangerous for private business power. The idea is that great stretches of private power and privilege cannot coexist with heavy government involvement in the economy, universal citizenship (suffrage), and genuinely popular and participatory institutions. The more people participate in a regulatory government, the less likely they are to tolerate private power. One of the popular chords struck by Charter advocates was the general dissatisfaction Canadians felt with their experience of democracy. The kind of politics represented, for example, by the election of 1988, is not something people are going to stand up to defend, especially when the politics intended to replace it is only dimly understood. As a solution to the failings of democracy, the Charter seems a strange device. However, if the idea is not to *enhance* real democracy, but rather to *avoid* enhancement by giving merely a *sense* of enhancement with a formal substitute, the Charter makes perfect sense. In response to our frustration at the lack of democracy in our representative institutions we have been offered what is in essence a spectator democracy even further removed from genuine democracy and guaranteed not to behave radically.

How guaranteed? By personnel, because the government retains the power to appoint the judiciary, and also by nature. The Canadian Charter, like the American one, and all of the Western charters, applies only to *government* (section 32). Furthermore, it creates only negative obligations on the part of the government and no positive ones. There is a hortatory section which commits government to "promoting equal opportunities for the well-being of Canadians" (section 36), but it is conspicuous by its explicit unenforceability. Thus, the Charter is designed to leave the vast power of business untouched. Not only this, but it is even capable, in difficult moments, of weighing in on the side of a threatened status quo, against radical change by a "transient majority."

There is also an ideological fit between the Charter and the increasing crisis tendencies of Western industrialized economies. An economy in decline, as far as most people are concerned, cannot justify its increasing inequality in materialist, utilitarian terms. It must rely on abstract, classless, homogeneous "rights" issues. These have consequently come to replace the materialist emphasis in Western propaganda of the early postwar era of booming Western economies. In Canada, the constitution itself, patriation, the Charter of Rights, and the plea for "*national* unity" all had a part to play in taking our minds off Canada's mediocre economic performance and in unifying a country riven by enormous disparities in material well-being and life chances. When winning the lottery has replaced prospecting for gold and making a better mousetrap as the ideal ways to get rich, distributional rights will be increasingly emphasized at the expense of generalized improved benefits. And the increasing insecurity of a volatile job market, concession bargaining and plant closures mean people care at least as much about hanging on to what they have as they do about improving their condition. The Charter fits perfectly here, because the stock-in-trade of the legal profession is abstract right. Its inherently conservative form of legitimation eschews all concrete policy goals. In the philosophy of judicial propriety, "policy" is for the legislature, to be judged by its results; "principle" is for the judiciary, to be judged by its inherent, quasi-eternal rightness. Thus the increasing substitution of abstract principles for concrete policies represented by the Charter seems to have its source in the legitimation problems of an economic system less and less able to deliver the goods and forced to serve up rights as a substitute.

THE SUCCESS OF BUSINESS WITH THE CHARTER

In restricting itself to imposing negative constraints on government, the Charter is perfectly consistent with the free market ideology which declares that the only real danger to freedom comes from government and not from private power. But the Charter is not only ideology; business has made definite gains from it. Quebec itself is a particularly vivid example of this.

We are by now used to thinking of the language question in Quebec as a question of abstract right, having nothing to do with social power. That was the strategy of the federalists: to treat the issue as one of a beleaguered minority versus a tyrannical majority. But this required a major conceptual overhaul of the real social situation. The appeal of the nationalist program was based on the second-class citizenship of the mass of French Quebeckers, rooted in economic relations which at the outbreak of the Quiet Revolution had French Quebeckers, 80 per cent of the population, earning an average of 60 per cent of what English Quebeckers earned – with unilingual English speakers even better paid than bilinguals. The French-English struggle was also a class struggle: the language of capital was English and the language of labour was

French. This issued in massive popular support for Bill 101's attempts to restrict the use of English in public life to the bare minimum. The nationalists were forced to use an interventionist state because of the English stranglehold on private power. "Freedom of choice" in education and commerce is an attractive slogan, except that when all it means is freedom from government coercion it leaves everything to the despotism of private power, in this case unequally distributed between the majority and minority national groups. The role that the Charter played in fighting on the side of the English minority and the powerful interests it represented is a fascinating one, exhibiting exceptional crudity among lawyers and politicians alike, but it cannot be retold here. On the other hand, its most recent development is instructive for present purposes.

This is the decision of the Supreme Court of Canada on the provisions of Bill 101 having to do with business signs.[4] Bill 101 was rather mutilated after the Supreme Court of Canada had dealt with the provisions dealing with the language of the courts and the legislature and the language of education. What remained included a provision that all public commercial signs would have to be in French. An important aspect of this case, but one usually ignored by critics of the law, was that the law only applied to *commercial* signs. The precise text was as follows:

58. Public signs and posters and commercial advertising shall be solely in the official language.
59. Section 58 does not apply to advertising carried in news media that publish in a language other than French, or to messages of a religious, political, ideological or humanitarian nature, if not for a profit.

On the prompting of some English businesses, the Supreme Court of Canada decided unanimously that this violated "freedom of expression" under the Canadian Charter (and the Quebec Charter as well). But in order to come to this conclusion, the Court had to equate commercial advertising with all other forms of personal, political, and artistic expression; it had to treat the element of unequal economic power the same way it had been treated in the election expenses case discussed earlier – as irrelevant. How else could it be said that the government's intervention on a one-person-one-vote basis to overcome a minority monopoly was an interference with freedom of expression as opposed to an enhancement of it? The subsequent moral uproar in English Canada when the premier of Quebec invoked the Charter's override clause to introduce a compromise law illustrates how potent a symbol the Charter is in transforming business rights into moral rights.

Apart altogether from the national unity aspects of the case, it established, together with the 1987 *Irwin Toy Ltd. v. Québec (A.G.)* case, that as far as the Supreme Court is concerned, business advertising comes within the protection of the Charter as a fundamental freedom. Henceforth a heavy onus lies upon government to justify *any* regulation of it. According to a bare majority of the Court, this onus was met in *Irwin Toy* (advertising aimed at children), but the decision has nevertheless been very heartening to the business community. It has lent some legitimacy to the tobacco industry's last ditch attempts to protect their rights to advertise the most profitable commodity ever sold. In fact, the rise of French-Canadian big business undermines the national unity aspect of the Charter's defence of business rights: deregulation only helps those who have market power, and English market power is in severe decline in Quebec.

The position of the Supreme Court on the right to advertise, remarkable enough on its own, stands in stark contrast to the Court's 1987 decision that the right to strike is not constitutionally protected by the "freedom of association" clause.

The Charter has also helped business considerably in its fight against Sunday closing laws and it has helped professionals limit government regulation, as in British Columbia where physicians have been able to thwart government attempts to allocate them to under-served areas of the province. There has also been a general assault on union rights, financed by the National Citizens' Coalition among others, though its initial successes have been rolled back recently. However, the defence of union rights against the Charter has entailed major expenditures of energy and money.

The general result of all this is that business has been given some substantial help by the Charter in its quest for the minimal state. Only with the utmost effort has it been possible to make the courts sometimes resist the Charter's own logic and remain neutral in the class struggle. And all efforts to enlist the courts against business power (as in the right to strike cases) have failed.

HAS ANYTHING GOOD COME FROM THE CHARTER?

Though the basic thrust of the legalized politics of the Charter is, like free trade, anti-government, it is still theoretically possible that it could enhance human freedom otherwise than in a perverse way – that is, otherwise than by restoring the full despotism of unregulated market power. Governments have typically not only done things *for* people, but also *to* them. A great part of the appeal of the Charter lay in the many examples of oppressive government behaviour, including racial, sexual, and political discrimination. Charter defenders would point to the government-ordered internment of Japanese Canadians during the Second World War, the inequality of women and aboriginal peoples, and the suppression of left-wingers during the Cold War, most notably by the government of Quebec. Since 1982 there have been a fair number of cases that defenders have claimed vindicate the Charter's democratic pretensions. These must be carefully examined to appreciate fully just what can and cannot be expected from the Charter.

Procedural Rights

The busiest realm of Charter activity has been in the field of criminal procedure. With well over a million criminal or quasi-criminal prosecutions launched each year, and the detailed procedural guarantees outlined in the Charter, it was inevitable that some judges would take matters seriously. The Supreme Court of Canada encouraged this by a series of very activist judgments early in the life of the Charter. By now there is no question that the courts have used the Charter to expand the procedural rights of accused persons, prisoners, and immigrants. They have fulfilled the fondest hopes of Charter advocates in a realm of extremely high visibility, throwing out convictions even where warranted by the facts on the grounds of oppressive police behaviour, such as the denial of the right to counsel or the illegal obtaining of evidence. Laws which made convictions easier have been overturned for violating the "presumption of innocence" and stiff minimum penalties have also been thrown out as "cruel and unusual punishment." Contrary to the cases we have so far referred to, the most direct and obvious beneficiaries of these procedural rights are groups without social power. This is because people without social power are the main objects of the kind of law to which the courts have been busiest attaching procedural guarantees. In general, criminal suspects are made up of the most marginal social classes in Canadian society, characterized by the lowest levels of occupational status and the highest levels of unemployment. The unemployment rate of prisoners (at the time of arrest) is two to four times that of non-prisoners. Native peoples are notoriously over-represented. Prisons swell during periods of high unemployment. Refugee applicants are by definition either persecuted or forced to use the refugee process because they cannot meet the criteria – heavily weighted in favour of those with economic assets – for ordinary immigration. These facts have been underlined by those who seek to defend the Charter from the charge that it is only there to protect powerful people and power in general.

However, it is not surprising that the constitutional procedural requirements imposed by Canadian courts, like those imposed by courts in the United States, have not limited the level of punishment. Despite their formally "civilizing" effects, such rights as the right to legal representation pose no serious obstacles to law enforcement objectives. While police must change their form of behaviour towards suspects and the occasional conviction must be sacrificed to ensure that they do so, nothing in the decisions of the courts weakens their effectiveness once these forms are complied with. There is ample evidence from the United States and some from Canada that even the short-term effects on conviction rates are tiny or non-existent. They are more than compensated for by changes in police tactics and increases in efficiency, some of which are probably due in part to the constitutional rules themselves.

Furthermore, the constitutionalization of criminal procedure has not merely not been accompanied by *less* repression; it has gone hand-in-hand with *greatly expanded repression*. Along with the legalization of politics, the postwar period has seen an enormous growth in the proportion of the population subject to criminal sanctions. In terms of prison populations alone, Canada's historical high-water mark of the Depression was already equalled by the early sixties (the time of the Canadian Bill of Rights). Although a lot of the slack was taken up afterwards by the growth of the use of alternatives to prison, such as probation, by the 1980s we were back to all-time highs in prison *in addition to* a probation and parole population never before seen in history, three times the size of the prison population. The average adult probation and parole population for fiscal 1986–87 was 87,965, while the custodial population was an estimated 28,864, for a total rate 462 adults per 100,000 under criminal sentence. This was about four times the rate during the most repressive year of the Depression, when probation and parole supervision were all but unknown. Furthermore, there has been a steady increase, since the mid-1970s in both the length of prison sentences (life sentences constituting a higher proportion of the prison population than ever) and the intensity of probation conditions, including "residence requirements" indistinguishable from prison terms. The first decade of the Charter's procedural guarantees was also the most repressive, in criminal law terms, in Canada's history.[5]

There is some considerable controversy over the cause of all this. Official crime rates have risen steadily, but this seems due only in part to increasing crime; a substantial proportion seems due merely to increased policing. On the other hand, it has been shown that varia-

Table 6.1
Prison Population per 100,000 of Total Population

	Penitentiary*		All Adult Prisons	
Decade	Decade Average	Decade High	Decade Average	Decade High
1980–88	40	44.2 (1986)	106	114 (1987)
1970–79	38	41.3 (1973)	89	96 (1977)
1960–69	37	39.7 (1964)	100	106 (1963)
1950–59	34	36.0 (1959)	95	100 (1959)
1940–49	29	33.1 (1940)	84	97 (1940)
1930–39	35	43.1 (1933)	98	110 (1932)
1920–29	26	29.6 (1922)		
1910–19	24	26.6 (1910)		
1900–09	24	26.9 (1900)		
1890–99	26	27.9 (1898)		
1880–89	26	28.5 (1880)		
1870–79	22	28.7 (1879)		
1867–69	25	28.1 (1867)		

SOURCE: Statistics Canada, 1980-81 through 1987-88; Ontario, Ministry of Correctional Services
Annual Report, 1988; F.H. Leacy, Historic Statistics of Canada, 2nd ed. (Ottawa: Supply and
Services 1983), Tables A1-14, Z173–174, Z198–208, Z292–304; Janet B.L. Chan and Richard
V. Ericson, Decarceration and the Economy of Penal Reform (Toronto: University of Toronto
Centre of Criminology 1981), 77.
* Penitentiaries are prisons designated for sentences of two years or more in length.
The figures for adult prisons are all estimates recalculated to take into account changes that have
occurred in reporting and also, recently, the reclassification of some offenders as young offenders
under the Young Offenders Act.

tions in the level of punishment are not caused solely or even mostly
by variations in the crime rate but rather by economic conditions, and
more precisely by levels of social inequality. These, we know, have
increased steadily in the postwar period, and alarmingly in the last
decade.

Of course, whether the increase in punishment comes from increasing
crime or from increasing repression, neither alternative is very appealing: whether we are more repressed because we are more criminal or
more repressed without being more criminal, we are still more
repressed. The Charter cannot and was not intended to counteract these
trends. However, the simultaneous rise of legalization and repression
should dispel the notion put abroad by Charter advocates that the Charter is part of a general humanitarian or otherwise progressive trend in
Canadian society.

It could be simply a coincidence that the Charter appears in history
with an increasing rate of repression, but it is arguable that there is a
more organic link between the two. Punctilious attention to procedural

guarantees has a tendency to render acceptable levels of punishment that would not otherwise be tolerated. Indeed, exaggerated concern for the rights of the accused tends to coincide with more and not less repressive periods. By all agreement, the eighteenth century was one of the bloodiest in terms of legal repression. Yet it was the most solicitous to the accused when it came to criminal procedure. According to historians Douglas Hay and E. P. Thompson, this procedure was designed to legitimate both the system of criminal justice and the whole system of social power by the equal formal respect it paid to those it dispatched to the gallows for crimes against property.[6]

But there are more recent examples. When capital punishment was first restricted to only certain categories of murder in 1961, its retention for those categories was legitimated by guaranteeing appeals all the way to the Supreme Court of Canada. Attacks on the powers of the National Parole Board during the 1970s were neutralized by amendments in 1978 requiring the board to act in accordance with norms of procedural fairness; and when the new repressive powers given the board in 1986 were challenged on the grounds of retroactivity, the courts turned back the challenge by invoking the copious procedural rights under the new powers. In one Charter case which upheld the expanded "dangerous offender" legislation, the Supreme Court of Canada held that the difficulty of predicting dangerousness "does not appear to undermine the utility and fairness of the [dangerous offender] scheme so much as to fortify the conclusion that the procedural protections accorded to the offender, especially on review, ought to be very rigorous."[7]

In trying to understand the role of these procedural guarantees, it is worthwhile to consider the most enduring symbol of legality: blindfolded Justice. Why is she blindfolded? Naturally to encourage impartiality. She cannot favour one side if she is not acquainted with the parties before her. The usual implication is that this is to the advantage of the weak, who are shielded by impartiality from any undue influence of the strong on the course of justice. But putting a blindfold on Justice also forbids her from leaning *in favour* of the weak. "Thou shalt not wrest the judgement of thy poor in his cause" says the Old Testament, but it also says "neither shalt thou favour a poor man in his cause" (*Exodus* XXIII: 4–6). The commentator explains:

The Biblical view of justice is remarkable for its insistence on the strictest impartiality. If the matter in dispute is a question of money between a rich and a poor man, the judge is not to give a wrongful verdict in favour of the poor man on the plea that the rich man would not miss the sum involved. Sympathy and compassion are great virtues, but even these feelings must be silenced in the presence of Justice.[8]

Seen this way, blindfolded Justice is the perfect symbol for the free-contract ideology of trade liberalization. Treating each party as equal allows power no more but also no less than its due. The impartial state is the perfect non-interventionist state. It ratifies the status quo of social power by ignoring it: as if in a prize fight the referee ignored differences in the fighters' respective weights but only made sure that they did not rub resin in each other's eyes.

A vivid example of this effect can be found in the Supreme Court of Canada's very first decision on criminal procedure, *Hunter* v. *Southam*[9] where the Charter helped defeat charges of conspiracy to limit competition against Canada's two largest newspaper chains. The charges were thrown out for lack of evidence when the courts, ultimately the Supreme Court, ruled that the special powers of search under the Combines Investigation Act violated the Charter. The standard protections of common law and statute, fashioned for legitimating the punishment of the "ordinary" criminality of economic marginality and social weakness, were applied by this decision to the criminality of economic and social power. The rules designed for the puny individual involved in street crime were held constitutionally mandated to apply equally to the crimes of corporate power ("suite crime"). Justice was blind to Southam's assets of over one billion dollars and fifteen thousand employees. As far as she was concerned, Southam needed as much protection as any juvenile charged with "theft under."

The other side of the coin is the *Singh* case,[10] in which the Supreme Court of Canada decided in 1985 that the Charter required an oral hearing for every refugee claimant in place of the paper reviews then used. What followed was an unprecedented tangle, a rash of probably bogus claims leading to a backlog of over one hundred thousand claimants before a new law could be put in place for 1989. The government declared a partial amnesty for about fifteen thousand claimants in 1986 and it is now clear that most of the backlog claimants ultimately will be granted admission, if only because, by the time they finally get their hearings, they will have put down sufficient roots to be entitled to stay in Canada.

Singh was a decision whose immediate beneficiaries were people without social power. Not only that, the refugee claimant system allows people into the country who do not fit the economic logic and the foreign policy objectives that govern the ordinary immigration process. The crucial difference between the two systems of entry, from the government's point of view, is control. Ordinary immigration is within government control and can be subordinated to economic interest and foreign policy, but refugees are defined by treaty without reference to economic circumstances or politics.

Thus the Charter seems to have operated in this case as a perhaps substantial obstacle to the free play of market forces, if we construe market forces broadly to include the economic and foreign policy logic of the ordinary immigration process. However, even this putative success of the Charter is instructive. In the first place, *Singh* did not cause the refugee crisis. The causes are international, and they have to do with global integration of labour markets as well as economic and political volatility. With or without *Singh*, Canada would have had to deal with an enormous number of refugee applicants. Secondly, the benefits of *Singh* are only temporary. Almost all of the gains in access to Canada under it – those accruing to the claimants in the backlog – have come not from actually *granting* hearings but from the *inability* to grant them because of the costs involved. And the gains are not unambiguous. The government seems determined to punish the claimants by making them wait years for hearings that will be mostly pure formalities. One effect of this is that many of those in the backlog have had to endure years of uncertainty and family separation.

As for the new law, despite an initially high success rate for applicants, there is no reason to expect more generosity than prevailed in the absence of hearings. The criminal process is full of oral hearings and that has not prevented it from producing enough guilty verdicts to fill Canadian prisons to overflowing. Other things being equal, a system of oral hearings is unlikely to be more compliant than a system of paper reviews.

But other things are not equal. The new laws introduced by the government were not simply designed to comply with the court's due process requirements. Along with the hearings has come a determination to limit access to the system and a tightening up of the criteria intended to make it more difficult for claimants to succeed even when they gain access. The measures have already reduced the number of claimants dramatically. If *Singh* is an exception to the Charter's tendency to eliminate purely political obstacles to the free sway of social and economic power, it does not seem to be a large one. And, of course, it must be put in the context of the rising rate of overall repression of the 1980s: even including the large number of deportations of the 1930s, and given the reduction of deportations after *Singh*, our era is still between two-and-a-half and three times more repressive than the worst years of the Depression.

The Charter and Equality

From the beginning, the Charter has been seen as an anti-discrimination measure. The most popular successes of the American Bill of Rights in modern times, even surpassing the procedural rights of criminal suspects, have been the school desegregation decision of 1954 (*Brown* v. *Board of Education of Topeka*) and the decriminalization of abortion in 1973 (*Roe* v. *Wade*). During the Charter debate, these cases were cited as examples of how a Charter can intervene on behalf of the weaker side in unequal power relations. Defenders of the Charter never mentioned that the "separate but equal" doctrine struck down in *Brown* in 1954 had been erected by a prior Supreme Court in 1896 and had been sturdy enough to stand for fifty-eight years. Nor did they point out that the same clause used to desegregate public schooling in 1954 was used to strike down affirmative action programs passed by legislatures in 1978 (*Regents of the University of California* v. *Bakke*), or that the Supreme Court of the United States permitted Congress and the states to withhold medicare for abortions even where medically necessary, so long as they did not make it a crime (*Beal* v. *Doe* 1977; *Harris* v. *MacRae* 1980), a perfect example of Justice's blindfold in action. As for Japanese Canadians and communists, it also seems to have been forgotten that the American Bill of Rights had been no defence against either the program of internment of Japanese Americans by the US government or against McCarthyism.

Nevertheless, many hopes were raised among the "outs" by the Charter and they lobbied hard. The native peoples made a determined effort to "hijack" the Charter to pursue their claims for land and self-government, but they got nothing. This could teach us something, for the claims they made radically contradicted the logic of the market place. The native peoples did not ask merely for an end to discrimination by the state. They wanted something more in the nature of affirmative action – that is, government intervention on their side. But the Charter, a government-limiting document, could not grant that. The most it could do was try to exempt affirmative action from the reach of the Charter. Decisions under the Charter have cast some doubt on its success even in this regard. In one case, the government of Manitoba was prohibited by a court from granting preferential treatment to natives in wild rice growing licences on the grounds that this discriminated against non-natives (*Apsit* v. *Manitoba Human Rights Commission* 1987).

Women were most successful in their lobbying efforts, but the actual results achieved under the Charter have been at best double-edged. In the first place, since the Charter bids the government to respect sexual equality and puts on a big blindfold to history and social power, many claims for sexual equality have been made by men challenging legislative measures meant to overcome women's historical disadvantages. Men have even had some modest successes in the realm of sexual assault and welfare benefits. Even where women have been able to take advantage of the Charter, the results have been contradictory. The hockey player Justine Blainey was allowed to play boys' hockey over the protests of sports*women* who claimed the loss of their best players would ruin women and girls' hockey.

More typical and to the point of the current discussion was the successful claim of Toronto lawyer Beth Symes against the restrictions on childcare deductions under the Income Tax Act.[11] The act put a limit on the amount that could be deducted for child care, the way it puts a limit on most workers' deductions, but distinctly *unlike* the way it treats most business deductions, which are treated as fully deductible where "reasonable." Symes claimed that it was reasonable for her to have a full-time nanny (whose meagre wages were nevertheless about five times in excess of the act's allowed deductions) so she could make profits from her law practice. She claimed sex discrimination between businesswomen and businessmen. In effect, she was asking for the same preferential treatment over working-class women that businessmen had over working-class men. She did not appear in court on behalf of her sex; on the contrary, she was merely asking for full admission into her class. When the court agreed, day care advocates immediately pointed out that the decision would benefit only rich women. But the case was also an excellent example of the privatizing effects of the Charter. While day care advocates all over the world were calling for public, non-profit, low-cost day care, this decision harmonized with conservative governments' preferences for market solutions. The *Symes* decision funds private day care through tax deductions. And since the higher one's tax bracket, the more valuable one's deduction, it also exacerbates unequal access to day care.[12]

The Charter was nevertheless vindicated for many women by the *Morgentaler* case of 1988 in which the Supreme Court of Canada struck down the provisions of the Criminal Code regulating abortion. Canada had a more restrictive law than most industrialized countries and abortion had been a crime except when performed in certain limited circumstances. *Morgentaler* was at first regarded as a great victory for all women, because it appeared that Parliament was too divided or too afraid to bring in any new law, so that the choice would henceforth be left to each woman, free of government interference. Furthermore, since the law operated more harshly on poor women, if there was to be any differential impact of the decision, it would be the opposite of that in the *Symes* case. On the other hand, the court's reasoning was very limited and left a vacuum which was bound to be filled one way or another: first by some pro-life judges who granted injunctions during the summer of 1989 to men seeking to prevent their estranged but pregnant ex-fiancées from having abortions (this little brush fire was put out in 1989 by the Supreme Court in emergency session in the case of *Tremblay* v. *Daigle*); and then by Parliament, which introduced a bill to re-criminalize abortion, but in a much less restrictive manner, in the fall of the same year. Critics of that law say that it leaves women open to harassment by provincial governments and does nothing about the problem of access.

These events only serve to highlight the purely negative character of the *Morgentaler* ruling. This in turn has to do with the limits of legalized politics. The most the Court could be expected to do was to rule out making abortion a crime (though it has not even said that). It would have nothing to contribute to the other important aspects of abortion policy, including the central question of equal and adequate access to the now non-criminal operation. Immediately after *Morgentaler*, provincial governments stepped in to use their health-care jurisdiction to regulate abortion through restrictions on funding and public hospital policy. Most provinces cut off medicare for abortions they did not approve of on moral grounds. In this they were following the lead of the many states in the United States, which had, with the approval of the Supreme Court, trimmed *Roe* v. *Wade* to the bone through abortion funding restrictions. Recently, the Court carried this separation of public and private spheres to an almost unbelievable extreme by holding that while, for the time being, *Roe* v. *Wade*'s ruling that abortion could not be made a crime still stood, it was constitutionally permissible for a state (in this case Missouri) to prohibit all but life-threatening abortions from being performed using any public facility, defined as "any public institution, public facility, public equipment, or any physical asset owned, leased, or controlled by this state or any agency or political subdivision thereof."

Decisions like this – and developments like those in Canada after *Morgentaler* – show the "double impact" of legal politics on women. The effect is to remove the state and restore the market place. In Missouri the private clinics can perform whatever abortion a woman can afford. In Canada a woman can obtain whatever abortion she can afford. The result is that women benefit precisely according to their class. But the Charter is not otherwise indifferent to class power. If we combine the abortion decisions with the other deregulatory effects of the Charter, we can see that the result is to *enhance* class power. If some women win from this, most women lose. The FTA, for example, with its electoral debt to the Charter, will doubtless benefit some businesswomen (like the *Symes* tax case); but many women will see their jobs go south, their wages drop, and their social programs disintegrate, because they lack the market power that free trade is designed to unleash.[13]

The Charter and free trade are both on the same side. It is not the side of women any more than it is the side of linguistic or racial minorities. The Charter, when stripped of all the sentimentality surrounding it, is on the side of the free play of market forces, unhampered by any mere political interference, no less than free trade or the other elements of the new era of global competition.

CONCLUSION

The Canadian Charter of Rights and Freedoms is an example of how the very form of domestic government can be adapted to mirror and accommodate global movements such as trade liberalization and continental economic integration. The international proliferation of legal politics in our era can even be seen as the designated domestic counterpart of the new world order. If this is indeed the case, the strategy seems to be all the more effective for being disguised in a completely different ideological dress. In fact, the growing popularity of legal politics means it is increasingly chosen by opponents of the business world's agenda to protest the very developments which, on my thesis, they are designed to serve. Is this possible? Can a conservative form of politics be "hijacked" for progressive purposes? There is no shortage of theorists who argue that documents such as the Charter can actually be used to counter conservative forces, because such documents, or at least the institutions that administer them, are "relatively autonomous."[14]

In Canada we have the dismal example of the attempt by peace groups to use the Charter to oppose the successful integration of Canada into US nuclear weapons strategy (*Operation Dismantle* v. *The Queen* 1985). If this futile effort had any effect, it was to legitimate Cruise missile testing in Canada. A rather more complicated example is the Meech Lake Accord, which turned a large chunk of political debate in this country into pointless legal casuistry over the meaning of technically meaningless constitutional symbols, with each side (including the left) trying to achieve its hidden agenda through the pretext of constitutional text.

Political forms sometimes seem interchangeable. Clever constitutional arguments can indeed be made for socialism under the rule of the courts ("equal benefit of the law"), the way they were made in religious terms in the middle ages under the rule of the church ("the Poverty of Christ"). But the reason these arguments do not, in practice, succeed is that the institutions within which they are made are far more congenial to one kind of result than to the other. Let us not forget the historical anti-democratic sentiment behind legal politics. Its proponents, at least, believed that democratic claims were far more easily made through democratic institutions. Law was the solution to more democracy for those who stood to lose from it. De-legitmating government and fending off popular demands for more democracy is an important part of the current overall strategy of international business in its drive for the free exercise of economic power. Using constitutional rights as a form of politics – whether on the left or the right – contributes to the success of this strategy. Perhaps the effect cannot be observed in each case, but neither can the effect on the ozone layer each time you use the wrong kind of spray can.

NOTES

1 A complete account, so far as I am able to give it, can be found in my book *The Charter of Rights and the Legalization of Politics in Canada* (Toronto: Wall and Thompson 1989), where most of the points made here are argued more fully and where the many references supporting these points can also be found.

2 Nick Fillmore, "The Big Oink: How Business Won the Free Trade Battle," *This Magazine* 22, no. 8 (March/April 1989): 14.

3 *Re Constitution of Canada* (1981), 125 DLR (3d) 1 (Supreme Court of Canada); *Re Attorney General of Quebec and Attorney General of Canada* (1982), 140 DLR (3d) 385 (Supreme Court of Canada).

4 *Ford v. Quebec (A.G.)*, 50 NR 84 (Supreme Court of Canada 1988).

5 See *Regina v. Degan* (1985), 20 CCC (3d) 293 (Saskatchewan Court of Appeal 1982); Michael Mandel, "The Great Repression: Criminal Punishment in the Nineteen-Eighties" in L. Samuelson and B. Schissel, eds., *Criminal Justice: Sentencing and Reforms* (Toronto; Garamond Press 1990).

6 Douglas Hay, "Property, Authority and the Criminal Law" in Douglas Hay *et al.*, eds., *Albion's Fatal Tree: Crime and Society in Eighteenth Century England* (London: Allen Lane 1975); and Edward P. Thompson, *Whigs and Hunters: The Origin of the Black Act* (Harmondsworth: Penguin Books 1975).

7 *R. v. Lyons* (1987), 37 CCC (3d), 1,50 (Supreme Court of Canada).

8 J.H. Hertz, *The Pentateuch and Haftorahs; Hebrew Text, English Translation and Commentary*, 2nd ed. (London: Soncino Press 1937), 316.

9 *Hunter et al. v. Southam Inc* [1984] 2 SCR 145.

10 *Singh et al. v. Minister of Employment and Immigration* [1985] SCR 177.

11 *Symes v. The Queen*, Federal Court Trial Division, 11 May 1989.

12 Judy Fudge, "Comment of *Symes* – the Deduction of Nannies' Wages," seminar at Osgoode Hall Law School, 2 August 1989.

13 Marjorie Cohen, *Free Trade and the Future of Women's Work: Manufacturing and Service Industries* (Toronto: Garamond Press 1987).
14 See R.S. Ratner, John L. McMullan, and Brian E. Burtch, "The Problem of Relative Autonomy and Criminal Justice in the Canadian State" in R.S. Ratner and John L. McMullan, eds., *State Control: Criminal Justice Politics in Canada* (Vancouver: University of British Columbia Press 1987); and Amy Bartholomew and Susan Boyd, "Toward a Political Economy of Law" in Wallace Clement and Glen Williams, eds., *The New Canadian Political Economy* (Montreal: McGill-Queen's University Press 1989).

PART THREE

Restructuring Old Industries: The Anatomy of Industrial Change

7 The Globalization of Production and the Future of Canada's Mature Industries: The Case of the Automotive Industry

JOHN HOLMES

For more than half a century, from the 1920s to the late 1970s, the North American automobile industry served as a model of economic growth and technological change based on mass production, so much so that the manufacture of standardized products in large volumes using special-purpose machinery and unskilled labour came to be known as Fordist production. In the early 1970s the automobile industry was the epitome of the mature consumption good industry. But in the last decade and a half significant changes in international competitive conditions have forced North American–based auto makers to reassess their competitive strategies and to experiment with new models of production based on greater product diversity and more flexible methods of manufacturing. These changes have resulted in what some refer to as the dematurity of the auto industry and the 1980s have been characterized by extensive dislocation and restructuring within the industry.

By the end of the 1980s this restructuring had produced a very different set of outcomes for the auto industry in Canada from those that were being predicted at the beginning of the decade. Those predictions, generally based on some variant of the "world car" thesis (the extension of the Fordist model to the world scale via the internationalization of production and the development of the new international division of labour) were full of doom and gloom. For example, Ross Perry, a former auto policy adviser to the Ontario government, in a study prepared in 1982 for the Canadian Institute for Economic Policy predicted that the level of employment in the Canadian automotive industry would decline substantially over the 1980s and the Canadian trade deficit in automotive products, which had begun to grow rapidly in the late 1970s, would continue to deteriorate.[1] In a similar vein, but with more explicit reference to the world car thesis, Marc Van Ameringen argued:

... since the mid-1970s these firms [the American multinational vehicle and parts manufacturers which dominate the North American industry] have been rationalizing their North American operations as they establish a global system of vertical integration in automotive manufacturing. In Canada this has caused a number of firms either to close or scale down their operations and to relocate production facilities in low-wage areas outside the country. Although a recent upturn has spawned optimism that the deindustrialization process will be halted, the restructuring which continues to take place will result in a smaller automobile industry by the end of the decade and one that employs half as many workers as in the late 1970s.[2]

In the event, how different the 1980s turned out to be for the auto industry in Canada. The decade has seen significant absolute increases in both employment and output in the industry and Canada has increased its relative shares of North American production and employment. In 1984, 1985, and 1988 Canada set new records for the annual total number of motor vehicles assembled. This was in sharp contrast to the United States, where production in 1988 was still 13 per cent lower than in the record year of 1978. Total employment in the Canadian auto industry is now 17 per cent higher than the previous peak in 1978. Again this contrasts with the United States, where auto employment in 1988 was still 15 per cent lower than the peak year of 1979. Since 1980 new investments in the Canadian auto industry have exceeded $10 billion. There has been substantial new investment in auto assembly in Canada by both North American and Asian manufacturers, and Canada's share of North American vehicle production has increased from around 12 per cent in the late 1970s to 15 per cent in 1988 and is expected to increase still further to around 20 per cent by the early 1990s. Between 1980 and 1987 shipments for the Canadian auto parts industry rose from $4.0 billion to over $12.0 billion and the industry almost doubled its share of the North American parts market. Not only has the parts sector expanded in size, but it has become more Canadianized during the 1980s, with independent Canadian parts producers now accounting for over 15 per cent of production as compared with around 5 per cent in the mid-1970s. In 1988 Canada registered a surplus on its automotive trade with the United States under the Auto Pact for the seventh consecutive year. In just four years (1982 to 1985) the accumulated surplus amounted to $17 billion which eliminated the accumulated Canadian deficit for 1965–81 of $14.7 billion.

The turnaround in the fortunes and resurgence of the industry in Canada following the 1981–82 recession must be understood in the context of the broader and continuing rationalization and reorganization of the automobile industry both within North America and internationally. In the last two decades major structural changes in the world economy have created new competitive conditions, not just for the automobile industry but for virtually every manufacturing industry. In turn, the changed competitive conditions have triggered the rapid and widespread reorganization and restructuring of production in these industries. Manufacturing in general during this period has been affected by two broad developments. First, within the world economy there has been the further internationalization of all three circuits of capital (commodity, financial, and productive). This has led to a fundamental shift in the international competitive environment and the emergence in many industries of new geographical divisions of labour at the global, continental, and intra-national scales. More concretely, this process has been manifested in the globalization of production, the necessity for manufacturers to be not just nationally but globally competitive, and the crystallization of integrated regional continental markets in North America, Europe and the Western Pacific Rim (the so-called trilateral or triad markets).

Secondly, and particularly within North America and Western Europe, changes in technology, in forms of industrial organization, and in the organization of work have all been important elements of industrial restructuring. This has been true not only of the emergence and rise of new industries, but also of the transformation of a number of the formerly mature Fordist mass production industries such as automobiles and consumer electrical goods. A recurring theme in discussions of these changes is the need to increase the flexibility of methods of manufacturing and marketing. In fact, terms such as flexible specialization, flexible accumulation, flexible integration, and flexible production systems have been coined to describe what some commentators perceive to be an emerging post-Fordist model of industrialization.[3]

The auto industry in Canada is a particularly interesting sector to analyse with respect to questions of export-led growth and uneven development. First, the industry occupies a position of prime importance within the industrial structure of Canada and since the signing of the Canada–United States Automotive Products Trade Agreement (more commonly known as the Auto Pact) in 1965 it has also been a major contributor to Canada's export trade. Secondly, since the auto industry is highly concentrated geographically in southern Ontario and part of southern Quebec, it has been a major factor contributing to uneven regional growth and development within Canada, particularly during periods, such as the 1980s, when the auto industry has experienced substantial real growth.

One specific feature of the auto industry serves to differentiate it from other mature manufacturing sectors in Canada. After the signing of the Auto Pact, automobile production in Canada and the United States became fully rationalized and integrated into one continental-wide production system. Today over 80 per cent of all vehicles assembled in Canada are exported to the American market and about 70 per cent of the Canadian market for North American-built automobiles is supplied by vehicles assembled in the United States. Thus, since the mid-1960s the auto industry in Canada has been much more than a branch plant industry designed only to serve the protected Canadian domestic market.

The objective of this chapter is to describe and analyse the recent development of the auto industry in Canada, with particular emphasis on the changes that have occurred in the last decade as a result of restructuring in response to the globalization of production and intensified international competition. Within this broader context the chapter seeks to explain the strong resurgence of the auto industry in Canada during the 1980s. It will also try to assess the future prospects of the industry by drawing out the implications of the continuing process of restructuring, particularly in light of the implementation of the recently concluded free trade agreement between Canada and the United States and the establishment of a significant number of Japanese transplant auto production facilities in North America.

THE GLOBALIZATION OF PRODUCTION, NEW COMPETITIVE CONDITIONS, AND TECHNOLOGICAL CHANGE

Prior to the mid-1960s, production throughout the international automotive industry was organized on an essentially national basis. Most of the advanced industrial countries had an insulated domestic market supplied by locally based (although in many cases foreign-owned) producers. In Canada the long-standing existence of significant tariffs on imported automobile parts entering Canada and a 60 per cent Commonwealth content rule on automobiles made and sold in Canada resulted in the development of an inefficient, smaller replica of the US industry, dominated by the same three giant corporations, but designed solely to serve the domestic market. Major changes occurred in 1965, when the Auto Pact forced the rationalization of the Canadian auto industry and its integration with the US industry on a continental basis.[4]

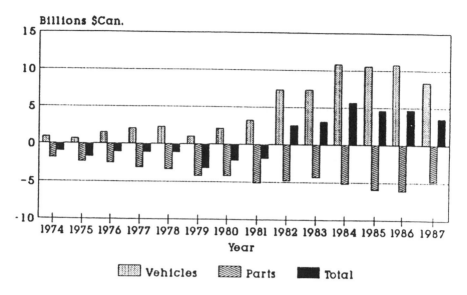

Billions $Can.

Chart 7.1.
Canada–US Trade Balances in Automotive Products, 1974–87
SOURCE: *Statistical Review of the Canadian Automotive Industry: 1987* (Ottawa: IST 1989).

Most importantly for Canada, the pact contained key safeguards to guarantee a minimum level of automobile production in Canada.[5]

By the early 1970s the North American auto industry was fully integrated, productivity in Canadian plants had caught up with, and in the case of assembly, surpassed that in US plants, and through the collective bargaining efforts of the UAW, Canadian auto workers had achieved nominal wage-rate parity with their American counterparts. With the Canadian dollar standing at slightly above par, the labour cost differential in Canada's favour that had existed in 1965 had been considerably narrowed. Throughout the 1970s Canada's share of the North American market, output, and employment remained relatively constant. Although there were normal year-to-year investments in new equipment, there was little by way of major new investments in either the assembly or parts sectors. In the 1970s Canada again began to accumulate deficits on its automotive trade with the United States, which although not large relative to the value of total trade under the Auto Pact, nevertheless involved substantial absolute figures (see Chart 7.1).

After 1979 the whole of the North American auto industry was thrown into a major crisis, at the heart of which lay "fundamental changes in the nature of world markets and in the basis of competition for these markets."[6] First, the industry was forced to adjust to changed competitive conditions brought about by the internationalization of production and the globalization of markets in the industry and, in particular, by the rise of Japan as a major world producer and exporter of automobiles. Secondly, the North American auto industry came under tremendous pressure to increase productivity and reduce costs. This pressure resulted not only from the intensification of international competition, but also from rapidly escalating unit labour costs resulting from the slowdown in productivity growth that had occurred during the 1970s in North American manufacturing, including the auto industry.[7] These two factors, which were not entirely unconnected, resulted in far-reaching changes in both process and product technologies in the North American auto industry. These changes have been felt from the shop floor right through to the broader regional and international organization of automobile production systems.

During the postwar period competitive strategies between auto makers within national markets (and this was particularly true of the North American market) focused on marketing and price competition, the latter being achieved primarily through auto makers seeking to obtain ever-increasing economies of scale in production. Throughout the 1950s and 1960s the use of Fordist production methods pushed minimum efficient scales of operation (MESS) in the industry ever higher.[8]

This process, coupled with a levelling off in world demand for cars, led to substantial overcapacity in the world industry by the mid-1970s. This, in turn, led to an intensification of competition at the international level among auto makers, both for the markets of the OECD and for markets in those developing countries which were perceived to offer the greatest potential future growth in demand for mass consumption products. Thus, in the 1970s the annual growth rate in demand for autos in the OECD fell to 1.6 per cent (from over 6 per cent in the previous decade) and imports as a percentage of new vehicle sales in the seven largest national markets, increased from 2 per cent in 1955, to 14 per cent in 1970, and to 24 per cent in 1981. Between 1978 and 1982 world demand for cars declined by 13 per cent, but world trade in automobiles increased by over 30 per cent.[9]

The most significant component in this increased trade in motor vehicles was the rapid growth of the Japanese auto industry, based on a strategy which combined production for a highly protected domestic market with production in Japan for export to North America and Western Europe. Of all the major auto-making nations, only Japan produced more cars in 1981 than in 1973, a period during which Japan's share of total world vehicle production rose from 18 per cent to 30 per cent.

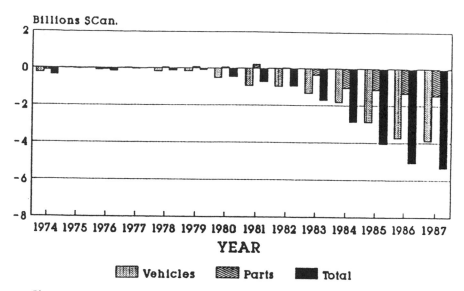

Chart 7.2.
Canada–Overseas Trade Balances in Automotive Products, 1974–87
SOURCE: Statistics Canada, cats. 65–202, 65–203.

Furthermore, during the same period Japan's exports of motor vehicles almost tripled, from 2.1 million units to nearly 6 million. If intra-European and US–Canada trade are factored out, Japan accounted for 71 per cent of total world automobile exports by 1981. In 1982 over a third of all Japanese vehicle exports were directed to North America, where they accounted for over 20 per cent of both the Canadian and US markets.[10] While Canada was experiencing a positive balance in its automotive trade with the United States, its annual overseas balance of trade was in deficit and this deficit rose from $119 million in 1977 to $1.62 billion in 1983, mainly as a result a flood of imported Japanese cars (see Chart 7.2).

Japan's auto export position was so strong by the early 1980s that it threatened both the long-established trade regime rules and the competitive position of North American and European-based auto makers.[11] The response was various quotas on Japanese imports into Western Europe and the voluntary restraint agreements (VRA) worked out between the governments of the United States and Canada and the Japanese auto makers. The quotas and VRAs, it was argued, were temporary measures designed to give North American and European auto makers a breathing space during which to fashion a response to the new competitive challenge presented by the Japanese.

The competitive position of North American-based auto makers was also being eroded by their own escalating production costs. Throughout the 1950s and 1960s the annual increases in base wage rates in the North American auto industry were financed out of sustained increases in labour productivity. However, the slowdown in labour productivity growth which began in the early 1970s and lasted for over a decade, coupled with the continuation of annual increases in base wage rates which had become such an entrenched feature of postwar pattern bargaining in the auto industry, was a major factor contributing to the increase in unit production costs and the decline in the profitability of North American auto makers.

The combination of escalating costs and Japanese competition, in conjunction with the rapid rise in gasoline prices through the 1970s and the slump in demand associated with the adoption of monetarist policies in North America and Western Europe, resulted in a collapse of what had been the stable postwar Fordist model of production in the automotive sector. Therefore, after 1979 the market and competitive conditions which had been associated with Fordism for almost half a century changed. "The types of automobile demanded across the developed world converged dramatically ... suddenly every world manufacturer was a threat to every other manufacturer in a largely integrated world market."[12]

This raised the possibility of dramatic shifts in the location of employment within the international auto industry, since national auto industries were very differentially positioned to deal with these new competitive conditions. Certainly, the issue that overrode all others for the North American automobile industry in the early 1980s was the productivity and cost differentials that existed between it and the Japanese automotive industry. For example, in 1981 it was estimated that the combination of lower hourly compensation and superior productivity of both direct and indirect labour yielded a landed cost advantage of C\$1,882 per vehicle in Japan's favour on Japanese-built cars imported into North America.[13]

In an effort to close this enormous cost gap, North American auto makers turned to a variety of strategies. These included direct attempts to cut costs, innovations in product technology, and the development of strategic alliances and joint ventures with Asian car makers to either build sub-compact cars offshore for sale in North America under Big Three badges (for example, GM importing from Suzuki, Isuzu, and Daewoo, Chrysler from Mitsubishi, and Ford from KIA) or to build compact cars in joint-venture assembly plants located in North America (for example, NUMMI (GM-Toyota), CAMI (GM-Suzuki), Mazda (Ford-Mazda) and Diamond-Star (Chrysler-Mitsubishi). The two principal strategies, however, have been the further internationalization of production in the industry and the development of new manufacturing technologies.

The Internationalization of Production

There is no doubt that production in the auto industry during the 1980s has become increasingly internationalized and global in extent. The form that this internationalization is taking, however, is complex, and space only allows us to stress the two most significant aspects of this process: the limited relocation of production in the automotive industry to the semi-industrialized countries, and the increasing integration of production within and between the auto industries in the OECD countries, including the development of transplant production facilities in North America (and Western Europe) by the Japanese auto makers.

Increasing internationalization in the auto industry differs from the process in industries such as clothing and consumer electronics, in which production has simply "moved south" to take advantage of lower wages. Although there has been some shift of automotive production to the semi-industrialized countries (the SICs, which accounted for virtually zero per cent of world auto production in 1950, progressively increased their share from 2.4 per cent in 1960 to 9.5 per cent in 1980), in 1979 they still accounted for only 2.7 per cent of car imports and 2.8 per cent of parts and components imports to the OECD.[14]

Instead, internationalization in the auto industry has taken the form of integration within and between the industrialized countries through an increasingly complex and multilateral network of foreign direct investment, joint ventures and sophisticated joint marketing strategies, technology licences, and the development of world-wide procurement of some original equipment parts and sub-assemblies such as engines, transaxles and wheels.[15] Given the relatively high capital intensity of the automotive industry (with the important exception of auto assembly activities), the wage differentials that exist between the less developed countries and the more industrialized countries appear to be relatively unimportant. Such factors as the ability to gain access to markets still partially protected by tariff and non-tariff barriers, or to obtain state subsidies to socialize the costs of fixed capital, have been much more important in shaping the internationalization of production in the automotive industry.

Not only have North American-based auto makers and parts producers had to contend with increased competition for their domestic markets from imported vehicles assembled in Japan and South Korea and from the internationalization of the auto component industry; since the early 1980s they have also been faced with a major competitive challenge in the shape of the establishment by the Asian producers of transplant assembly and component production facilities in North America.

By 1991 eight of the nine major Japanese vehicle producers will be assembling automobiles in North America. Japanese firms (and the Korean firm Hyundai) have either already opened or have under development thirteen automobile assembly plants in the United States and Canada, three of them as joint ventures with the Big Three, all of them with the exceptions of NUMMI and arguably Mazda on completely new green-field sites (Table 7.1). Total Asian investment in the assembly sector exceeds $5.5 billion and by 1991 Japanese-managed assembly plants in North America will employ thirty thousand workers and produce approximately two and a quarter million vehicles a year, including two million automobiles. By 1991 Honda alone will manufacture over half a million automobiles a year at three assembly plants in North America. There has also been a substantial wave of investment in the United States and Canada by Japanese-owned and Japanese joint venture component supplier firms with the establishment of over two hundred new plants by the end of 1988.[16]

There is no doubt that American insistence on the implementation by Japan of the VRAS on cars exported to North America in the early 1980s sent a strong signal to Japanese producers either to conform to the "access via investment" rule of the auto trade regime or face the possibility of more overt protectionist sanctions. Although clearly this was an important factor in the decision by the Japanese auto makers to establish production facilities in North America, there were other factors which should not be discounted. These include the Japanese companies' own long-term corporate strategies for growth in profits given the fiercely competitive nature of the Japanese domestic market; the revaluation of the yen against the other OECD currencies; and the evolution of a more general marketing and production strategy within the world auto industry which is predicated upon the recognition of the formation of a triad of world regional markets. This requires that any auto maker must be a major actor in each of these markets and there is a growing recognition that this goal cannot be met simply by exporting into one or another of the triad markets from an offshore production base, but requires the establishment of production facilities in each market.[17]

The Impact of Technological Change on the North American Auto Industry

The rationalization and restructuring of the domestically owned North American auto industry during the 1980s has seen a reduction of the Big Four to the Big Three (through the takeover of AMC by Chrysler, which itself came close to the brink of bankruptcy in 1979–80), and the

Table 7.1

Planned Japanese–Korean Vehicle Production in North America

Auto maker	Direct investment (C$ million)	Start-up date	Volume (000's) 1985	Volume (000's) 1990		Estimated direct employment
US PRODUCTION						
Honda Marysville, OH	600	1982	140	360		3500
Nissan Smyrna, TN	500	1983	110 40	120 120	(trks) (cars)	2100
NUMMI GM/Toyota Fremont, CA	250	1985	60	260		2500
Toyota Georgetown, KT	650	1988		200		2000
Mazda Flat Rock, MI	600	1987		260		2000
Diamond Star Mitsubishi/Chrysler Bloomington, IL	900	1988		240		1800
Subaru/Isuzu Lafayette, IN	670	1990		120		2000
Honda East Liberty, OH	380	1990		150		1800
Nissan/Ford Avon Lake, OH	900	1991		135		2000
TOTAL USA	5450		350	1,965		19,700
CANADIAN PRODUCTION						
Honda Alliston, ONT	200	1987		80		700
Toyota Cambridge, ONT	400	1988		50		1000
GM/Suzuki Ingersoll, ONT	500	1989		200		2000
Hyundai Bromont, QUE	300	1989		120		1200
TOTAL CANADA	1400		0	450		4900
TOTAL	6850		350	2415		24,600

SOURCE: Canada, DRIE, *Report on the Canadian Automotive Industry in 1985; Auto-in-Michigan Newsletter* 2, no. 2 (March 1987); *Automotive News*

closure of a number of assembly and parts plants by both the Big Three and the multinational parts producers. However, it has also entailed massive new injections of capital to re-equip existing plants and build new facilities.

This new investment has been tied to the introduction of new forms of automation and the reorganization of work and production both within the individual factory and across the wider production system.

As we noted earlier, these qualitatively significant changes in production technology have been driven by the need of the Big Three to reduce the competitive gap between themselves and Japanese auto makers. Thus they have been designed to increase productivity and quality, lower costs (not only labour costs but also, for example, inventory costs, reduction of lead times for new models, or the long-term costs of capital goods), and enable firms to respond rapidly to changing market and competitive conditions – particularly the need for a more differentiated range of products targeted at particular market niches.

What has been developing in North America during the 1980s is a new hybrid model of production which seeks to graft what are perceived to have been key elements of the highly successful Japanese system of production management (for example just-in-time methods, quality circles, team concepts of work organization, relational subcontracting) onto the use of advanced forms of computer process control equipment centred around flexible automation.[18] This new approach has placed demands on the industrial relations system to increase productivity, lower labour costs, permit increased flexibility in the deployment of workers, develop a "multi-skilled" and highly committed labour force, and to produce sustained labour-management co-operation on the shop floor. There has been mounting pressure to transform the traditional Fordist industrial relations system to produce a new industrial relations system involving the redesign and broadening of jobs, a dramatic reduction in the number of job classifications and lines of demarcation, the substitution of contingent compensation schemes for annual increases in base wage rates, and the introduction of forms of teamwork. However, the development of a new industrial relations system is proving very problematical and has been anything but straightforward.[19]

THE RESTRUCTURED CANADIAN AUTOMOTIVE INDUSTRY

The further internationalization of production, and the introduction of the new process technologies discussed in the last section have had a significant impact on the structure of both the assembly and component sectors of the auto industry in Canada.

The Vehicle Assembly Sector

Three developments within the Canadian assembly sector since 1980 deserve comment: the increased share of North American vehicle assembly accounted for by Canada, the new investments in assembly capacity

Table 7.2
Changes in Employment in the North American Auto Industry, 1979–82, 1982–84

| Year | Total Automotive Industry Employment | | Vehicle Assembly Employment | |
| | US | Canada | US (SIC 3711) | Canada (SIC 323) |
	(in thousands)			
1979	994.6	123.8	464.2	52.6
	(−29.1%)	(−20.3%)	(−29.9%)	(−18.8%)
1982	704.8	98.7	325.4	42.7
	(+23.0%)	(+25.4%)	(+19.6%)	(+15.9%)
1984	867.2	123.8	389.4	49.5
Change 1979–84	−127.4	0.0	−74.8	−3.1

SOURCE: Report on the Canadian Automotive Industry in 1985 DRIE, Tables 6.1, 6.2.

made by Asian auto makers, and the new investments made by North American auto makers.

As was noted earlier, the final assembly of vehicles, whether they be for local sale or export, is likely to remain highly concentrated within existing auto-producing regions of the world. This has important implications for Canada's future role within the broader North American auto industry, particularly when viewed in the context of the continental spatial division of labour which developed in the wake of the Auto Pact and the strong economic performance of both the Canadian assembly and parts industries during the 1980s. The deep recession of 1981–82 seems to have marked a watershed in the recent development of the auto industry in Canada. The data on output, employment, and plant capacity utilization rates all reveal that the Canadian portion of the North American automobile industry fared much better than its American counterpart in the period after 1978; the impact of the 1981–82 recession was more muted and the post-1982 recovery was far stronger in Canada (Tables 7.2, 7.3, 7.4).

Thus during the 1980s, although Canada's share of the total North American market has remained steady at around 8 to 9 per cent, its share of total North American vehicle production and auto industry employment have both risen to close to 15 per cent. During the same period Canada's production/sales ratio rose as high as 202 for automobiles and 272 for commercial vehicles, and Canadian CVA levels were substantially above the levels demanded by the Auto Pact. One consequence has been a significant increase in the relative importance of auto-

Table 7.3
Changes in Motor Vehicle Production, North America, 1978–82, 1982–84

| Year | Total Vehicle Production (cars, trucks and buses) (in thousands of units) | | Car Production | |
	US	Canada	US	Canada
1978	12,871	1,818	9,165	1,162
	(−39.7%)	(−32.0%)	(−44.9%)	(−32.0%)
1982	6,955	1,236	5,049	788
	(+53.8%)	(+48.5%)	(+50.9%)	(+29.8%)
1984	10,697	1,835	7,621	1,023
Change 1978–84	−2,174	+17	−1,544	−133

SOURCE: *Ward's Automotive Yearbook*, 1987

motive products in Canada–US trade. By 1985, for example, the automotive sector accounted for 43 per cent (up from 28 per cent in 1981) of all manufactured exports from Canada to the United States and 40 per cent (up from 29 per cent) of manufactured imports from the United States.

What factors explain this unevenness? Certainly is it true that it would have been difficult for either Ford or Chrysler to close a Canadian assembly plant and still meet the minimum levels of production in Canada to which they are committed under the provisions of the auto pact. It is also true that during the early 1980s, given the pattern of market demand in North America, there was a more favourable product mix of vehicles being built in Canada. But by far the most important factor underlying the stronger performance of the industry in Canada during the 1980s has been the real production cost differential (of which labour costs are the principal but not the only component) that has again developed between the Canadian and US segments of the auto industry since the late 1970s.

In part the labour cost differential, which is of the order of 30 per cent or $7.50 an hour in Canada's favour, is due to the lower value of the Canadian dollar against the US dollar. Although resistance by Canadian auto workers to concession bargaining in the early 1980s and the retention in Canadian labour contracts of the annual increases in base wage rates after they were abolished in the United States has meant that Canadian nominal base wage rates are now more than $2 an hour higher than in the United States, in real terms the hourly payroll cost in Canada is approximately 25 per cent lower than in the United States. Another

Table 7.4
Capacity Utilization Rates, North American Transportation Equipment Industries, 1978, 1982, 1984 (per cent)

Year	US	Canada
1978	74	84
1982	50	61
1984	64	84

SOURCES: DRIE *Rates of Capacity Utilization*, various years; US Bureau of Statistics, Capacity Utilization Rates for Selected Industry Groups

important component of the labour cost differential results from the lower cost to the employer of employee benefit packages (particularly health insurance) in Canada. In 1986 the hourly cost (in real terms) of employee benefits in the auto industry was approximately 55 per cent lower in Canada than in the United States. When it is considered that productivity and efficiency in Canadian assembly plants are generally judged to be on a par with or greater than those in the United States,[20] these savings are both substantial and significant.

After 1979 the unevenness of the process of restructuring and, in particular, the significant difference in the economic performance of the auto industry between the two countries placed considerable strains on the relationship between the Canadian and American wings of the international UAW. The extent and depth of the auto industry crisis in the United States, and specifically the scale of layoffs, considerably undermined and weakened the bargaining strength of the UAW and made issues such as job security and extended unemployment and retraining benefits of utmost importance to members in the 1984 and 1987 rounds of collective bargaining. In contrast, the relatively strong position of the Canadian industry and the significant production cost differential in Canada's favour enabled the Canadian region of the UAW to negotiate higher wage and pension settlements. After 1979 there was an increasing divergence in collective bargaining goals between the American and Canadian sections of the UAW. While the content of labour contracts in the United States has changed to reflect the new industrial relations, the union in Canada has clung tenaciously to the traditional Fordist pattern, particularly with respect to wage and work rules.[21] These tensions came to a head in the 1984 round of collective bargaining and resulted in the secession of the Canadian auto workers from the UAW to form their own autonomous union, the CAW.

No existing assembly plants closed during the 1980s; indeed, there has been new investment (which exceeded $4.2 billion in the Canadian assembly sector between 1985 and 1987 alone), in the form of both extensive modernizations of existing plants undertaken by the Big Three and construction of new assembly plants by both Asian auto makers and AMC/Chrysler.

Since 1984 Honda, Toyota, CAMI (a Japanese-managed joint-venture between Suzuki and GM), and Hyundai have constructed assembly plants in Canada to supply both the Canadian and American markets. In 1982 the federal minister of industry, trade and commerce established a joint industry–labour Task Force on the Automotive Industry which, in a recommendation that was clearly directed at the Japanese, urged that foreign producers who annually sold more than three thousand vehicles in Canada should be required to manufacture or buy parts in Canada with increasing levels of CVA as their sales volumes increased. Once annual sales exceeded twenty-eight thousand vehicles, importers would be expected to operate under virtually the same terms as those set out for qualified North American producers under the Auto Pact with regard to both the production/sales ratio and CVA levels. Although it is doubtful whether the recommendation would have been enforceable even if it had been adopted as government policy, the task force report sent a clear message to the Japanese producers who were already under strong pressure from both the federal and Ontario governments to establish production facilities in Canada.

By 1985 virtually every automotive importer (both Asian and European) had secured an individual special export duty remission order from the Canadian government which allowed them to earn a dollar of duty-free imports for every dollar of CVA they exported (initially exports to the United States were excluded but later this exclusion was removed). Through these orders the Canadian government provided an incentive for vehicle importers to buy parts in Canada from independent parts manufacturers. In addition, the four Asian companies listed above announced that they would build assembly facilities in Canada. While their decision to assemble vehicles in Canada was probably at least in part a response to the implied threats of protectionism in the task force report, the low value of the Canadian dollar made manufacturing in Canada attractive in comparison to the United States. In fact, by the end of 1987 Canada accounted for over 20 per cent of all investment, employment, and output to be generated by announced Asian built and owned North American assembly plants.

The fact that at least a proportion of their Canadian output would be exported to the United States was implicit in the decisions made by the Asian auto makers to build assembly production facilities in Canada. Even with the lower efficient scales of production allowed by new flexible production equipment, the Canadian market would still not be sufficient to absorb all their output. Moreover, each company stated that they eventually intended to meet the requirements set out in the auto pact for qualified producers. However, with the possible exception of CAMI, it would likely be some time before they would be able to meet the required auto pact CVA level, or even the 50 per cent North American content required for a vehicle to enter the United States duty free from Canada.[22]

At the time that they committed themselves at the urging of the Canadian government to building assembly plants in Canada to produce for both the Canadian and American markets (that is, before the negotiation of the Canada–US free trade agreement) the four Asian auto makers stood to benefit from three aspects of existing Canadian customs law:[23]

- the export remission orders allowed *importers* to earn a dollar of duty-free imports for each dollar of CVA exported (these are the so-called export-based duty remission orders);
- special individual Canadian automotive duty remission orders were offered to all companies setting up assembly plants in Canada and allowed the company to import an amount of products duty-free based on the CVA of the products it exported, with the amounts related to the company's progress toward meeting the criteria to qualify as an "Auto Pact Producer" (the so-called production-based duty remission orders);
- the general export drawback program under which the government remits the duty paid on the importation into Canada of materials and components which are made into products for subsequent export.

These duty remission/drawback schemes were an irritant to the United States, who viewed them as blatant subsidies to attract Asian auto makers to produce in Canada.[24] Under the FTA all three kinds of duty remission have either been cancelled or will be phased out during the 1990s.

The Big Three also made significant new investments in new technology and plant in their Canadian assembly operations during the 1980s as part of their overall strategy of rationalizing and restructuring their North American operations. Perhaps the most spectacular and certainly the largest of these new investments has been undertaken by GM in the development of the Autoplex project at its existing Oshawa, Ontario, location. When complete, this complex of three assembly plants, the first-ever heavy automotive stamping facility in Canada, and associated component manufacturing facilities (some in-house and some involving independent suppliers who have established nearby plants to feed components into the Autoplex on a just-in-time basis), which has involved at least $3.5 billion of new investment by GM alone, will be the largest automotive manufacturing complex in North America.

GM has also moved towards developing a more regionally integrated production system in southern Ontario built around their assembly facilities at Oshawa, Scarborough, and Ingersoll (the new CAMI plant), their drive-train plants at St Catharines and Windsor, and their trim plant and fabrication plants in Windsor and Oshawa. The development of this regional production complex in southern Ontario will allow GM to better align Canadian component parts manufacturing to Canadian assembly operations – a system abandoned at the time of the Auto Pact in favour of extensive plant and product rationalization on a continent-wide basis. The return to a more national alignment of assembly and parts manufacturing is felt necessary to reduce vulnerability to outside forces. One obvious source of such vulnerability is the split in the union, which has increased the potential for disruption in production in one country when the union in the other country may go on strike. Management feels that the return to the alignment of facilities domestically is no longer as uneconomic as was the case prior to 1965 because of the significant expansion in Canadian output over the past twenty years and the emergence of new technologies which allow smaller efficient production runs, faster tool and model changes, and flexible machinery enabling greater product variation on the same line.

The Automotive Components and Parts Sector in Canada

Two factors are key to understanding the changes that have occurred in both the structure and performance of the automotive parts industry in the 1980s: the internationalization of the component industry, and the significant qualitative changes that have occurred in the relationships between assemblers and their component suppliers. The combined result of these factors has been a significant restructuring of the parts sector, which is being progressively pushed towards the point where it can be globally competitive. There is some evidence to suggest that value-added per employee in the sector has increased rapidly as a result of both a move towards the production of higher-value parts in Canada and an increase in labour productivity. In addition, Canadian parts firms have been able to achieve high levels of quality. For example, DesRosiers reported that a quarter of all the parts plants receiving the top quality rating from GM were located in Canada, as are over 10 per cent of the 643 plants around the world which hold Ford's QI rating.[25]

What are the implications of the globalization of production in the auto components industry for Canada? One feature of the emerging new international pattern for component production is the making of parts in Canada which have a high energy content – for example, parts made from aluminum or plastics. This reflects Canada's relative international advantage in energy costs as well as its labour cost advantage within North America.

Some production of relatively labour-intensive parts, such as wiring harnesses and soft trim, has disappeared as a number of firms have closed plants in Canada and shifted to the cheaper labour areas along the Mexican border, the most recent and highly publicized being Allen Industries from Hamilton and Fleck Manufacturing from Huron Park. Some of the large plants of the multinational parts manufacturers were closed, particularly at the time of the 1981–82 recession. However, the parts sector as a whole has experienced significant growth, with employment rising from 47,300 in 1980 to 78,200 in 1987. In particular, a handful of independent Canadian parts manufacturers has emerged which have grown rapidly by taking full advantage of the changing nature of assembler-supplier relationships, their labour cost advantage, and their favourable location relative to the reconcentration of the North American assembly industry into the Great Lakes region. The most startling example is the now financially troubled Magna International which was transformed from being a relatively small dependent subcontractor in the late 1960s into the largest independent parts producer in Canada with all the characteristics of a major first-tier supplier. During the mid 1980s Magna was opening a new plant every three weeks and by 1988 operated over 120 facilities employing 15,000 workers in Canada and the US (compared with 60 plants and 5000 workers in 1984). Magna's phenomenal growth during that period was based on a combination of the capacity to develop innovative product technology and a non-union, low wage, labour relations strategy.[26]

However, it must be stressed that the success stories in the Canadian auto parts sector of firms such as A.G. Simpson, Tridon, Magna and the Woodbridge/Waterville group, have been aided in two ways by government policy and programs. First, the export-based duty remission programs provided a strong incentive for importers to buy Canadian-made auto parts. Secondly, these firms were among the prime beneficiaries of the $60 million in interest-free loans and grants made under the ILAP program in the early 1980s, and later federal and provincial government assistance programs. In fact, during the 1980s there has been a shift in emphasis in government policy from solely assembly to both assembly and parts production.

One consequence of the rise of these Canadian auto parts manufacturing firms and the disinvestment through plant closure or sellouts of some of the large multinational component producers is that the share of parts industry shipments accounted for by independent Canadian-owned firms has increased, from around 4 per cent in 1972 to over 16 per cent in 1985, while the share taken by the foreign-based multinational parts producers has fallen from 54 per cent to 38 per cent.

THE CANADA–UNITED STATES FREE TRADE AGREEMENT AND THE FUTURE PROSPECTS FOR THE AUTOMOBILE INDUSTRY IN CANADA

Besides removing the present duty of 9.2 per cent on automotive products in ten equal steps between 1989 and 1998, there are a number of other aspects of the FTA which may have a significant impact on the Canadian auto industry as it was set up and shaped under the Auto Pact. In addition, the FTA curtails the various Canadian duty remission/drawback programs which will directly affect the Asian producers who have established assembly facilities in Canada, in part, as a consequence of the existence of those remission programs.

The FTA includes a major change in the definition of what is to be counted as North American content in order for a vehicle to qualify for duty-free entry to either country, and there are also restrictions on which companies will be allowed to qualify under the terms of the Auto Pact. Costs which can count towards the attainment of the required 50 per cent North American content requirement are restricted to the value of materials originating in either country, plus the *direct* cost of assembling the product in the exporting country. The foreword to chapter 10 of the FTA, the chapter which deals with the auto industry, explicitly states that one of the virtues of the new and more stringent North American content definition is that it will be impossible for the new Asian vehicle assemblers in North America to reach the content level without manufacturing major components in North America or purchasing such components from North American suppliers. The FTA sets out three categories of participants in the Canadian automotive industry:

- those companies that are already recognized as qualified producers under the auto pact or who will qualify by the 1989 model year (the 1989 date leaves the door open for CAMI to possibly qualify). After the 1989 model year it will be impossible for any other producer to qualify for auto pact status. With respect to passenger vehicles, the companies in this group are GM, Ford, Chrysler (and AMC), Volvo, and possibly CAMI;
- those importers who previously qualified for export-based duty remission orders (thirteen companies are listed); and

- those vehicle manufacturers who were given special production-based duty remission orders allowing them to use the export of vehicles assembled in Canada (including exports to the United States) to earn CVA. The companies in this category are Honda, Hyundai, Toyota, and CAMI (if the latter doesn't meet the deadline for qualifying for auto pact status).

On the surface, this differentiation of producers into the three groups does not seem to be of much consequence. After 1998 the Canadian subsidiaries of the Big Three will no longer have to meet the production/sales ratio and percentage CVA requirements to which they were committed under the Auto Pact in order to import vehicles duty-free from their parent companies in the United States. The only requirement will be that the imported vehicles meet the 50 per cent North American content rule of the FTA. If the Asian producers meet this 50 per cent rule they, too, will be able to import and export vehicles between the United States and Canada duty-free.

So what advantage is there to belonging to the first group as opposed to the third, and what incentive is there for the Big Three to continue to meet their commitments under the Auto Pact after 1998? The answer to both these questions lies in the feature that in 1965 appeared to be simply an accidental by-product of the way Canada chose to implement its side of the Auto Pact. In order to avoid having to obtain a GATT waiver, Canada has always viewed the Auto Pact as a multilateral agreement which allowed qualified producers to import components or vehicles duty-free, not just from the United States but also from *anywhere in the world*, for direct sale in Canada or for assembly into a vehicle in Canada which was to be sold in Canada or exported to the United States. As long as the vehicle being shipped from Canada to the United States had the required North American content (easily obtained with US stampings and Canadian assembly) the foreign engine or transaxle which would have been dutiable going into the United States directly could enter duty-free in the vehicle coming from Canada.

Under the FTA the combined effect of the different membership categories and the abolition of the duty remission/drawback orders will be to produce within Canada what Macdonald has called a "two-tier automotive manufacturing industry." On the one hand, General Motors, Ford, Chrysler (and possibly CAMI), so long as they comply with the provisions of the Auto Pact, will be able to continue to bring parts and vehicles into Canada duty-free from any country (including such low-cost countries as Brazil, Korea, Mexico, Taiwan, and Thailand). On the other hand, Honda, Hyundai, Toyota and any future new producer, "operating in Canada in the same way as their commercial rivals, will have to pay duty on anything they import from countries other than the United States, no matter how large their production/sales ratio and CVA credits eventually turn out to be."[27]

Thus, with the duty on vehicles from the United States being phased out by 1998, only two incentives will remain for the Big Three to continue to produce significant quantities of assembled vehicles and components in Canada: the possible economic advantage of manufacturing in Canada because of significantly lower production costs (which, at least at the present time, depends on low energy costs, a weak Canadian dollar, and the lower cost of health care benefits); and the continuing advantage of being able to import vehicles and components duty-free from third countries as long as the auto maker continues to maintain its Auto Pact status. The latter incentive is gaining in importance with the progressive internationalization of automobile production, and particularly, with the growing importance of Mexico as a source for components and vehicles within North America.

CONCLUSION

We argued earlier that the North America continent is likely to remain the site for significant levels of vehicle assembly. What proportion of these vehicles will be assembled by US-owned as opposed to Asian-owned firms is more problematical. One effect of the new investments in North American assembly plants during the 1980s has been a substantial increase in total assembly capacity. Even though it may be argued that the vehicles assembled in the Japanese plants will at least in part be substituted for vehicles presently being imported from Japan, it is generally estimated that there will be an annual excess capacity of at least 2.5 million vehicles in North America by 1992, which will occasion further plant closings.[28] At the moment, most Canadian plants (with the possible exception of GM's van assembly plant at Scarborough, Ontario, and the old AMC/Chrysler Jeep plant in Brampton, Ontario) seem relatively secure; they have been recently modernized, are relatively efficient, and have product commitments for the foreseeable future. Of course, their major advantage over American plants remains the 30 per cent production cost differential in their favour. As long as this differential is not significantly eroded by a strengthening of the Canadian against the US dollar, it is expected that Canada will continue to increase its proportion of total North American vehicle production into the 1990s.

Although there have been signs in recent years that certain segments of the parts and components sector in Canada have become globally competitive, at present there are less than a handful of firms (outside of the in-house plants of the Big Three) which could be said to be fully developed first-tier suppliers. Therefore the future of the parts sector in Canada is still far from certain, particularly given the loss under the FTA of the duty remission orders which had begun to open up export markets to the parts sector in the mid-1980s.

In closing, it is worth repeating the caveat made in the introduction. While both the general competitive pressures generated by the globalization of production and the qualitative significance of technological change may well be important and common features of recent restructuring in a number, if not most, of Canada's mature industries, this chapter has restricted its analysis to developments in the automotive products industry. The experience of the automotive industry in Canada during the postwar period should not (and perhaps cannot) be generalized to other Canadian industries. Certain features of the auto industry make it unique among Canadian industries, not the least of which is the fact the industry has made the transition from a branch-plant industry, serving the limited domestic market and sheltered behind tariff walls, to an industry competing in a world economy characterized by the globalization of production in two stages. First, it was forced to restructure and become competitive at the continental scale in the mid-1960s. However, the Auto Pact which forced this restructuring guaranteed minimum levels of auto production in Canada. At the time, these guarantees were essential to maintaining an auto industry in Canada and are the reason why the repeated invocation of the Auto Pact by the proponents of the FTA during the 1988 election campaign, as the exemplar of how successful free trade would be, was so deceitful in failing to distinguish between "managed trade" and free trade. It is only during the present decade that the auto industry in Canada, and then as part of an already integrated North American auto industry, has been forced to respond to the changed competitive conditions brought on by the globalization of production and the unravelling of the postwar Fordist model of production.

At the moment, the short- to medium-term prospects for the auto industry in Canada seem reasonably positive. Such assessments, however, should be treated with great caution. The major restructuring of the world economy that commenced in the 1970s has still to run its full course. Even the question of whether a new stable model of production and trade will ever eventually emerge to rival the one that characterized the first three decades of the postwar period is an open one, let alone the precise contours that such a post-Fordist model might assume.

NOTES

Grateful acknowledgement is made of conference travel support provided by the Queen's University Advisory Research Committee. Thanks also to Hugh Holmes who helped prepare the tables and figures.

1 R. Perry, *The Future of Canada's Auto Industry* (Toronto: James Lorimer 1982), 77.
2 M. Van Ameringen, "The Restructuring of the Canadian Automobile Industry" in D. Cameron and F. Houle, eds., *Canada and the New International Division of Labour* (Ottawa: University of Ottawa Press 1985), 267.
3 See, for example, M. Piore and C. Sabel, *Second Industrial Divide* (New York: Basic Books 1984); A.J. Scott, "Flexible Production Systems and Regional Development: The Rise of New Industrial Spaces in North America and Western Europe," *International Journal of Urban and Regional Research* 12, no. 2 (1988): 171–87; S. Tolliday and J. Zeitlin, *The Automobile Industry and its Workers: Between Fordism and Flexibility* (Cambridge: Polity Press / Basil Blackwell 1986); P. Hirst and J. Zeitlin, *Reversing Industrial Decline: Industrial Structure and Policy in Britain and her Competitors* (Oxford: Berg 1988).
4 See my "Industrial Reorganization, Capital Restructuring and Locational Change: An Analysis of the Canadian Automobile Industry in the 1960s," *Economic Geography* 59, no. 3 (1983): 251–71, for a more detailed discussion of the impacts of the Auto Pact on the structure and geography of the auto industry in Canada; J.F. Keeley, "Cast in Concrete for All Time? The Negotiation of the Auto Pact," *Canadian Journal of Political Science* 16, no. 2 (1983): 282–98, for a good discussion of the politics surrounding the negotiation of the Auto Pact; and N.B. Macdonald, "Will the Free Trade Deal Drive a Gaping Hole Through the Auto Pact?" *Policy Options* (January/February 1989): 10–17, for a good summary of the provisions contained in the Auto Pact. Under the Auto Pact the continental integration of the industry was greatly facilitated by the existence of one international union representing auto workers in both countries and by a small number of common and economically powerful auto makers which already controlled production in both countries and whose economic interests would clearly be furthered by measures which would allow the rationalization of their existing Canadian operations.
5 The terms of the agreement itself specify that a qualified manufacturer may import vehicles and original equipment parts into Canada duty free provided that (a) the manufacturer maintains a ratio of production-to-sales greater than or equal to the ratio for the base model year (1964) or 0.75, whichever was greater, and (b) that the manufacturer maintains Canadian

value added (CVA) at least equal to CVA in the base model year. There are basically three ways of obtaining CVA in fulfillment of the pact requirements: through the assembly of vehicles or parts using Canadian labour and overhead; through the Canadian content of parts used in the vehicle assembly process; or through the Canadian content of parts purchased and exported by the manufacturer for assembly outside of Canada. In the letters of undertaking, the auto makers undertook to increase their CVA on passenger cars and original equipment parts at 60 per cent of the growth in the Canadian market and CVA on commercial vehicles at 50 per cent of the growth in the Canadian market. For cars the required production-to-sales ratios fall in the 95–100 range and the CVA in the 40 to 60 per cent range.

6 Canada, Federal Task Force, *A Strategy for the Canadian Automotive Industry* (Ottawa: Ministry of Supply and Services 1983), 45.

7 In my "The Crisis of Fordism and the Restructuring of the Canadian Auto Industry" in J. Holmes and C. Leys, eds., *Frontyard/Backyard: The Americas in the Global Crisis* (Toronto: Between the Lines Press 1987), I argued that this crisis was not only the manifestation in the auto industry of the more general breakdown of the Fordist model of accumulation but that, in a very real sense, the crisis was rooted in the very success of the Fordist model during the postwar boom.

8 Task Force, *Canadian Automotive Industry*, 51.

9 Canada, Department of Regional Industrial Expansion, *1981 Report on the Canadian Auto Industry* (Ottawa: DRIE 1984).

10 Canada, Department of Industry, Science and Technology, *Statistical Review of the Canadian Automotive Industry: 1987* (Ottawa: IST 1989).

11 For a description and analysis of these trade regime rules see J.A. Dunn, "Automobiles in International Trade: Regime Change or Persistence?" *International Organization* 41, no. 2 (1987): 225–52.

12 A. Altshuler et al., *The Future of the Automobile* (Cambridge, MA: MIT Press 1984).

13 Perry, *Canada's Auto Industry*, 32.

14 The main auto producers among the SICs are Brazil, Mexico, Spain, India, South Korea, and Argentina. The continued growth of assembly and parts production in Mexico during the 1980s should be noted since it is beginning to have important implications for the future of automobile manufacturing in North America. In fact, in 1986 Mexico became the second-largest supplier of automotive parts to Canada. Both Ford and Nissan have developed major assembly facilities in Mexico with the aim of supplying small cars into the North American market, a significant number of both North American and Japanese owned auto parts plants producing low-value parts figure among the maquiladoras of the free trade zones that line the US–Mexican border, and Mexico has become an important source

of engines and engine parts for the Big Three and for Nissan's plant in Tennessee.

15 See B. Dankbaar, "Maturity and Relocation in the Car Industry," *Development and Change* 15, no. 2 (1984): 223–50; and R. Jenkins, "Internationalization of Capital and the Semi-Industrialized Countries: The Case of the Motor Industry," *Review of Radical Political Economics* 17, no. 1–2 (1985): 59–82.

16 A. Mair, R. Florida, and M. Kenney, *The New Geography of Automobile Production: Japanese Transplants in North America* (Working paper, School of Urban and Public Affairs, Carnegie-Mellon University, Pittsburgh 1988), 18.

17 The Japanese auto-makers are building production facilities in Western Europe as well as in North America, in anticipation of the full economic integration of the European Community in 1992. Similarly, North American producers are expanding their production base in Western Europe and seeking to establish a secure footing in the Western Pacific Rim, largely through joint-ventures with Japanese, Korean, and Taiwanese auto-makers.

18 For a fuller description of this model, see D. Robertson and G. Wareham, *Technological Change in the Auto Industry* (Willowdale: CAW 1987); and my "Technical Change and the Restructuring of the North American Automobile Industry" in K. Chapman and G. Humphrys, eds., *Technical Change and Industrial Policy* (Oxford: Basil Blackwell 1987) and "Changing Buyer-Supplier Relations in the North American Automobile Industry: Towards a Post-Fordist Model?" paper presented in the Special Session on Post-Fordist Industrialization, Association of American Geographers annual meetings, Phoenix, Arizona, April 1988.

19 See, for example, H.C. Katz, "Recent Developments in US Auto Labour Relations" in S. Tolliday and J. Zeitlin, *The Automobile Industry and its Workers: Between Fordism and Flexibility* (Cambridge: Polity Press / Basil Blackwell 1986), 282–304; S. Wood, "The Cooperative Labour Strategy in the US Auto Industry," *Economic and Industrial Democracy* 7, no. 4 (1986): 415–47; and M. Parker and J. Slaughter *Choosing Sides: Unions and the Team Concept* (Boston: South End Press 1988).

20 H.C. Katz and N.M. Meltz, "Changing Work Practices and Productivity in the Auto Industry: A US–Canada Comparison," paper presented at the annual meeting of the Canadian Industrial Relations Association, Quebec City, June 1989.

21 For analyses of the divergence in auto industry collective bargaining strategies and outcomes between the United States and Canada see J. Holmes and A. Rusonik, *The Break-up of an International Union: Uneven Development in the North American Auto Industry and the Schism in the UAW* (Working paper 90–1, Industrial Relations Centre, Queen's University, Kingston 1990); R. White, "The Old and the New: Workplace Organization and

Labour Relations in the Auto Industry" in G.M. Olsen, ed., *Industrial Change and Labour Adjustment in Sweden and Canada* (Toronto: Garamond Press 1986), 222–27; and S. Gindin, "Breaking Away: The Formation of the Canadian Auto Workers," *Studies in Political Economy* 29 (Summer 1989); 63–89. Recently, however, cracks have begun to appear in the traditional and uniform Fordist industrial relations system in Canada. The collective agreement negotiated by the CAW with CAMI (GM–Suzuki) in many ways resembles the so-called world class NUMMI–UAW and GM Saturn–UAW collective agreements in the United States. In 1986 a new local agreement was accepted by the union under implied threat of closure for GM Ste Thérèse which was modelled on the concession agreement for GM Van Nuys.

22 Initially, the "transplant" assembly plants are limited to stamping and final assembly, with many of the high-value components being imported from Japan, hence the rapid increase in the overseas trade deficit in auto parts which has developed since 1984 (see Chart 7.2). However, the transplants are now increasing their North American content through, for example, the construction of engine plants by Honda, Nissan, and Toyota and the purchase of parts from the rapidly growing numbers of Japanese transplant auto parts producers in North America who have followed their assemblers to North America.

23 The discussion in this section draws heavily on Macdonald, "Will the Free Trade Deal Drive a Gaping Hole Through the Auto Pact?", 10–17.

24 It should be noted that the United States itself is not immune to such charges. Many of the Asian transplant assembly plants in the United States have received substantial direct subsidies from state and local governments in the form of worker training grants, site acquisition and servicing grants, and low interest loans (*Automotive News*, 31 July 1989) and have benefited from the US federal foreign trade sub-zone legislation.

25 D. DesRosiers, "The Size, Structure and Performance of the Canadian Automotive Parts Industry," paper for the First Policy Forum, International Motor Vehicle Program, MIT, Niagara-on-the-Lake, Ontario, May 1987.

26 For an analysis of Magna's spectacular growth see M. Anderson and J. Holmes, "New Forms of Industrial Organization in the Automobile Industry: The Case of Magna International," paper presented at the annual meetings of the Association of American Geographers, Baltimore, MD, March 1989.

27 Macdonald, "Will the Free Trade Deal Drive a Gaping Hole Through the Auto Pact?," 15.

28 One development which might partially offset the overcapacity problem would be the growth of *overseas* exports from North America, which during most of the postwar period have been virtually non-existent. There is now a very limited but growing export of some North American built

Japanese vehicles to Japan and plans for exports to Europe. While production capacity will be maintained in each of the triad markets, it is possible that there could be increased trade in vehicles between these markets to serve particular niches. The North American market, however, seems to be the triad market with the least potential for internal market expansion and hence the largest potential problem with over-capacity. The recent round of industry layoffs by the Big Three producers in the United States and Canada, beginning in December 1989 as the decade drew to a close, is perhaps an ominous sign that the problem is finally coming home to roost. Amid these layoffs, Toyota and Honda announced plans for expanded production in North America, while Nissan revealed plans to construct a second major assembly plant in the United States.

8 Structural Adjustment and Technological Change in the Canadian Steel Industry, 1970–1986

ANTHONY C. MASI

Over the last decade much attention has been focused on the future of manufacturing industries in the advanced market economies. While no universally accepted theoretical synthesis has emerged to explain the phenomena that have been observed, there is now general agreement that the decline in the manufacturing sectors is based on two general trends: the search to increase productivity, and the need to shed labour in sectors unable to compete in the international market place. Agreement over the types of empirical information needed to evaluate these industrial trends, however, has not made the interpretation of the statistical evidence unambiguous.

Case studies of industrial sectors in decline in the United States and Great Britain have drawn on the experiences of the protype smokestack industry, primary iron and steel production.[1] Most of those studies were inspired by a concern with de-industrialization. It now appears, however, that rather than de-industrialization, a massive restructuring of that sector was occurring. In that context, then, it is legitimate to ask to what extent other national steel industries have experienced industrial restructuring, and what role government industrial policies may have played in the process.

The classic characteristics of de-industrialization were never manifest in Canada's steel industry. Rather, it seems to be an example of successful industrial restructuring in a basic industry. By world standards the Canadian primary iron and steel industry is small, yet it has undergone sweeping changes that have dramatically improved its competitive position in the national economy as well as in export markets. As a result, Canada's steel industry has emerged as a stronger competitor owing largely to product specialization and the introduction of state-of-the-art technologies. And it is important to note that government policies have often helped, but sometimes hurt, Canada's steel industry in its quest to become more competitive.

This chapter will examine the performance and transformation of the Canadian steel industry in the period from 1970 to 1986, paying special attention to the role of government industrial policies, broadly defined. The experience of Canada's private steel sector working closely with state policy constitues an important primary source of information and a positive lesson for other industries undergoing radical changes. Primary iron and steel in Canada is an "infant" industry that has grown up. However, despite its remarkable success, the restructuring of Canada's steel production raises the disturbing question of who has borne the costs of the adjustments this industry has undergone. In industries in decline it is the productive workers who characteristically bear the brunt of the costs.[2] As the following case study points out, it is no less true for an industry that has successfully restructured.

The study of industrial restructuring focuses attention on the nature of changes in specific industrial sectors, using them to build a general case rather than simply as illustrations of aggregate patterns. This perspective sees the reorganization of activities as changing the nature of industrial production in the advanced economies, but not necessarily as a precursor to the eventual disappearance of those sectors. Rather, by restructuring, industries are supposed to emerge as stronger competitors on domestic and international markets.

According to a report on the steel industry in the United States done by the Office of Technology Assessment (OTA), "industrial restructuring refers to shifts in methods of production, nature of products, size of firms, rate of technological change, raw materials used, or types of markets served." The OTA further argued that such "structural changes in industries refer to permanent changes in the character and competitive positions of industry participants."[3] Such factors as the mix of technologies employed, the changing nature of the supply and demand curve, the geographical patterns of company locations, the costs of entry into the industry, and the raw materials used all play a role in industrial restructuring.[4] The industrial restructuring perspective sees increasing internationalization of markets emerging from product specialization; that is, both imports and exports are expected to rise in relation to gross domestic product. Industrial policies in the broad sense of the term have a bearing on the restructuring process in the steel industry. Such government policies may be either direct, such as subsidies, loan practices, export credits, or indirect, such as tax policies or tariffs.

A BRIEF DESCRIPTION OF THE CANADIAN IRON AND STEEL INDUSTRY

A convincing case can be made that the "Canadian steel industry is a vital link in the Canadian economy and provides the fundamental base for the continuing expansion of a competitive Canadian secondary manufacturing sector."[5] The steel industry purchases raw materials and equipment and also requires supplies and services from other sectors of Canada's industrial base. In addition, the industry provides secure, competitive supplies of steel products to the Canadian manufacturing sector for further processing (and increased value-added). The industry contains large, medium, and small producers, which, for the most part, operate in diverse and specialized market segments. There are five integrated producers, several of which have multi-plant operations, and a growing number of non-integrated mini-mills that operate in seven of Canada's ten provinces. The bulk of the industry is, however, located in Ontario where the three largest integrated producers have their headquarters and principal operating plants.

Canada's three private integrated steel producers are Stelco (Steel Company of Canada), Dofasco (Dominion Foundries and Steel Company), and the Algoma Steel Corporation.[6] The Sydney Steel Corporation (Sysco) on Cape Breton in Nova Scotia and Sidbec in Quebec are both owned by their respective provincial governments which purchased these oprations from Dosco at the end of the 1960s.[7]

As can be seen from Table 8.1, in 1986 Canada had fifty-eight establishments classified in the primary iron and steel industry (which covers most of Standard Industrial Classification 291, according to Statistics Canada).[8] Of these, twenty-six were located in Ontario and eighteen in Quebec. In Atlantic Canada only Sysco was in operation, while the remaining thirteen plants were in Western Canada. There are three major centres of steel production in central Canada: Hamilton, Ontario, where both Dofasco and Stelco have operating plants; Sault Ste Marie, Ontario, which houses Algoma; and along the St Lawrence River northeast of Montreal in Quebec where Sidbec, Stelco, and some mini-mills have located steel-making facilities in Sorel, Contrecoeur, and Tracy.

The only three plants in Canada with more than five thousand employees in 1986 were the integrated producers's establishments in Ontario. Of the five plants with between one thousand and twenty-five hundred employees, three were in Ontario, one in Quebec, and one in

Table 8.1
Employment Size of Establishments in the Primary Iron and Steel Industry by Region, Canada, 1986

Employees	Atlantic Canada	Quebec	Ontario	Prairies	British Columbia	Total Canada
Less than 50		1	6	1	2	10
50 to 99		2	4	2	1	9
100 to 199		4	3	2	1	10
200 to 499		9	6	1	1	17
500 to 999		1	1	2		4
1000 to 1499	1		2			3
1500 to 2499		1	1			2
2500 to 4999						
Over 5000			3			3
Total	1	18	26	8	5	58

SOURCE: Statistics Canada, Primary Metal Industries, Cat. No.41-250, 1985–86

Atlantic Canada. Quebec actually had more establishments in the two to five hundred range than Ontario, nine compared to six. It is clear, then, that the primary iron and steel industry is basically located in Central Canada, with most of it in Ontario. Since the major integrated producers are located in Ontario, that province accounts for just about 80 per cent of all the steel output of Canada. The mini-mills in the other areas are significant in local markets or with specific product lines, as is also the case with the two provincially owned integrated producers, Sidbec having a privileged status in the province of Quebec and Sysco specializing in steel rail. In 1970 there were only forty-five firms involved in the manufacture of primary iron and steel. More people were employed then, but the industry produced less crude steel. The reorganization of the industry and its restructuring of production seem evident in light of these changes alone. However, that restructuring has taken several forms and it is to those that attention must now be turned.

OUTPUT AND EMPLOYMENT

Average annual employment in the Canadian primary iron and steel industry peaked in 1980 at 61,238 individuals, with 47,854 of them being classified as production workers (see Graph 8.1).[9] Severe cuts in employment were experienced by the industry during the recession years between 1981 and 1983. Blyton et al. note that over twelve thousand lay-offs occurred as a result of that downturn, but significantly, the number of non-production workers has changed very little over this entire period.[10] In Canada it seems that production workers have

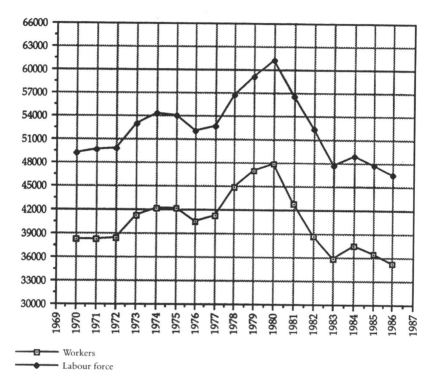

————□———— Workers
————◆———— Labour force

Graph 8.1.
Production Workers and Total Labour Force, Canadian Iron and Steel Mills, 1970–86
SOURCES: Statistics Canada, Primary Metal Industries, Cat. No. 41-250; Iron and Steel Mills, Cat.
No. 41-203; Iron, Steel and Pipe Mills, Cat. No. 41-231; various years

apparently borne the lion's share of adjustment costs in the iron and steel sector. The experience of Canada during the preceding period, however, was significantly different to that of other steel industries in the Western world. Rather than having had a contraction after 1974, now widely regarded as the starting point of a world-wide steel crisis, Canadian employment in primary iron and steel continued to rise until 1980. That 1981–82 recession hit the steel industry in Canada very hard indeed. Over the next three years, even after a mild recovery in employment levels in 1984, by 1986 total employment at 46,461 and production workers at 35,193 were still below 1970 levels. The third column of Table 8.2 shows the entire series of production worker employment for the Canadian primary iron and steel industry between 1970 and 1986.

Table 8.2
Productivity Statistics, Iron and Steel Mills, Canada, 1970-86

Year	000s tonnes of steel produced	No. of production workers	Workers per 0.00 tonnes	Value-added per paid man-hour			Ratio of value-added to wages	
				Current dollars	Constant 1981 dollars	Index with 1970 = 1.00	Ratio	Index with 1970 = 1.00
1970	11026	38317	3.48	10.49	19.01	1.00	2.70	1.00
1971	10854	38308	3.53	10.94	19.63	1.03	2.60	0.96
1972	11697	38378	3.28	11.25	19.87	1.05	2.46	0.91
1973	13199	41202	3.12	13.39	23.16	1.22	2.63	0.97
1974	13422	42091	3.14	15.08	23.90	1.26	2.70	1.00
1975	12808	42169	3.29	15.60	22.81	1.20	2.43	0.90
1976	13123	40573	3.09	17.44	24.29	1.28	2.40	0.89
1977	13482	41295	3.06	19.86	26.45	1.39	2.48	0.92
1978	14728	44791	3.04	21.47	27.24	1.43	2.48	0.92
1979	15854	46977	2.96	24.64	28.85	1.52	2.72	1.01
1980	15684	47854	3.05	25.21	27.08	1.42	2.51	0.93
1981	14637	42819	2.93	30.64	30.64	1.61	2.72	1.01
1982	11762	38735	3.29	27.08	25.57	1.35	2.02	0.75
1983	12728	35919	2.82	33.05	30.26	1.59	2.31	0.85
1984	14568	37482	2.57	36.22	32.52	1.72	2.34	0.87
1985	14532	36396	2.50	39.91	35.16	1.85	2.48	0.92
1986	13988	35193	2.52	39.35	33.29	1.75	2.38	0.88

SOURCES: Statistics Canada, Iron and Steel Mills, Cat. No. 41-203; Employment, Earnings and Hours, Cat. No. 72-002, various years

The proportion of the total labour force employed directly in production activities declined slightly from a peak of 79.4 per cent in 1979 to 75.8 per cent in 1986. Production workers were much more severely hit by the recession in 1982, during which year they represented only 73.9 per cent of total employment in Canada's primary iron and steel industry. A related feature of the decline in overall employment levels is the reduction in the average size of primary iron and steel establishments in Canada. From a high of 917 in 1975, average establishment size fell to 607 by 1986. Again, Table 8.1 shows the size distribution of these operating facilities in 1986 by region of the country.

There are two sources for these changes in the structure of the Canadian steel industry. First, the largest firms have been cutting back in terms of their total employment and some decentralization of their activities has also taken place. In a report (based on personal interviews with management) researchers found that Stelco was actively seeking to downsize both employment and basic capacity, and that Dofasco weighed the possibility of replacements for current employee vacancies "against the possibility of either doing without or of substituting with technology."[11] Secondly, barriers to entry into steel manufacture seem to have been lowered as opportunities to exploit new technologies, basically mini-mills utilizing electric-arc furnaces, allowed new firms to come on line over the period.

Production levels have been cyclical, but generally show an increasing trend over time. It is significant that the Canadian industry should actually have improved its output levels over a period when the entire world's steel industry was experiencing an unprecedented crisis. Crude steel production levels since 1970 have generally tended to rise (except in the recession years) even after the considerable labour-shedding of the early 1980s. In 1970 the Canadian steel industry produced just over 11 million tonnes of crude steel in ingot equivalents.[12] By 1979, the year with the highest reported production of any in the period under consideration, steel production in Canada had reached 15.8 million tonnes. Just under 14 million tonnes of ingot equivalent steel was manufactured by the Canadian primary iron and steel industry in 1986 (see column 2 of Table 8.2). The technology used to produce that steel has moved steadily in the direction of greater reliance on basic oxygen process in the integrated segment of the industry, coupled with a move to a greater proportion of output shifting to mini-mill production in ultra-high-power electric arc converters. In fact by 1984, Statistics Canada was no longer reporting open-hearth production separately from basic oxygen techniques, and industry sources report that with the exception of Sysco in Nova Scotia there was no open-hearth steel produced in Canada by 1988. In addition, electric-arc steel-making facilities moved from producing about 20 per cent of Canada's crude steel output in 1975 to just under 30 per cent by 1988.

It is generally recognized that the two most significant technological innovations in the processes used to manufacture steel have been the introduction of the basic oxygen process converter to replace the open hearth in integrated works, and the introduction of continuous casting to replace ingot production in both integrated facilities and in mini-mills. By 1988, in fact, over 70 per cent of Canadian steel was continuous cast rather than poured into ingots. However, two other features are also worth noting. First, the proportion of overall production carried out by electric-arc furnaces has also been steadily increasing. Small non-integrated producers can compete economically in regional markets and with special types of products and against imports, as the American experience has shown.[13] In fact, "recent history has made it evident that the small plant, specializing in a few basic products (e.g., reinforcing bar) or taking advantage of special circumstances, can successfully compete with the large blast furnace/primary steel producers." Their capital costs are substantially below those of integrated works and, given cheap electricity and abundant supplies of scrap metal, these mini-mills have become a force in the world's regional markets for steel.[14] Secondly, electric-arc furnace mini-mill production may still be economical in the absence of scrap if sufficient supplies of sponge iron can be manufactured. Sponge iron is a reduction of iron ore to a mix that, while still containing impurities, is 90 per cent metal and thus usable as scrap. Direct reduction technology is now used to provide sponge iron to several Canadian producers. The largest and most technologically advanced direct reduction facilities in Canada are the sponge iron shaft furnaces of Sidbec at the Contrecoeur works, thus making that establishment an integrated one without blast furnaces, since it uses the direct reduced sponge iron in electric furnaces. In other words, the contemporary structure of the Canadian steel industry has accommodated all four of these major changes in process technology.

MANUFACTURING PRODUCTIVITY

While drops in manufacturing employment may be reason for concern and policy intervention, they have not meant a reduction in industrial capacity. Even drops in overall output for a given industry within manufacturing may not be a manifestation of serious economic malaise if comparative advantages are to be found elsewhere in that sector. For example, overall tonnage of steel could drop, but the health of the industry could be improved if production shifted to lines with higher value-added. The link between employment and capacity is, obviously, productivity. Hourly productivity in manufacturing since 1973 has slowed down in all seven of the major industrial democracies. Canada's performance, however, was below average between 1973 and 1979, and 1979 and 1986 at just over 2 per cent per year.[15]

Over the same periods there were slowdowns in the average annual rates of manufacturing output, but for recent years this trend seems to have been reversed. During the years from 1960 to 1973 inclusive, Canada had an average annual percentage increase in manufacturing output of 6.5 per cent. The rate of increase in output fell to 2.2 per cent for Canada for the years between 1973 and 1986. The total aggregate hours of labour input in manufacturing in Canada did not change between 1973 and 1986.

In the steel industry, one way of measuring productivity is to examine the labour force required to produce one thousand tonnes of crude steel. This ratio went from 3.48 workers per thousand-tonne in 1970 to 2.52 by 1986, thus representing a reduction of about 28 per cent in the labour force needed to produce a tonne of crude steel in Canada. This is a relatively small number, and the fact that the ratio was more or less steadily decreasing shows the decline in labour inputs needed by the Canadian steel industry over the period under consideration (see column 4, Table 8.2). Indeed, the industry had become "leaner and meaner," largely at the expense of blue-collar workers.

Looking at another productivity measure, in current dollars there has been a nearly fourfold increase in value-added per hour of paid labour, having gone from $10.49 in 1970 to $39.35 by 1986. When corrected for inflation, the increase is still present but, naturally, much more modest. Using 1981 constant dollars, in 1970 each paid man-hour of labour contributed a value-added of $19.01, which by 1986 had grown to $33.29. Indexing those values with 1970 as the base year, that change represents a 75 per cent increase in value-added per paid man-hour of labour over the period under consideration (see Table 8.2, columns 5, 6, and 7). This made the productivity performance of Canada's steel industry one of the best in the country.

The performance of the Canadian steel industry can also be measured by the ratio of value-added to the wage bill. On this score, the industry's gains were more cyclical than was the case for the two other productivity measures discussed for which the Canadian steel industry had a clear pattern of increasing output per unit of input. In 1970 the ratio of value-added to the wage bill stood at 2.70, hitting a low of 2.02 in the recession year of 1982, and rising to 2.38 by 1980 (see Table 8.2, columns 8, 9). On the one hand, the observed pattern reflects differences in pricing structure, particularly raw materials, during the various phases of the business cycle.[16] Thus the relative vertical integration of the industry might play a role in the size of the ratio. On the other hand, that ratio might also be interpreted as an index of distributional outcomes. So a higher value indicates a larger share of the production surplus (above and beyond material input and energy costs) accruing to capital rather than labour. The fact that the ratio does not show a clear and unambiguous pattern of increasing productivity must be interpreted with caution. The principal reason probably has to do with the nature of investments in the Canadian primary iron and steel industry over the period under consideration. Smaller plants also mean smaller capital investments, thus reducing their impact on value-added. It also shows that the process of restructuring seems to have cost capital very little, allowing it to finance successfully investments in new technology.

In discussing the situation for the steel industry in the United States, Barnett and Schorsch argue convincingly that "insofar as relatively modern facilities are linked with older ones, the net benefit for product productivity is slight."[17] In other words, the productivity benefits associated with technological changes might not be realized if the patterns of reinvestment in plant and equipment are uneven and lead to bottle-necks. Further, steel is not without rivals as a preferred engineering material – aluminum, plastics, advanced ceramics have all made inroads into steel's traditional base. However, steel is still relatively inexpensive to produce and it has other features such as integrity at high temperatures and mechanical properties such as stiffness that make it likely to continue as "the staple engineering product for as far into the future as anyone can forecast."[18] Consequently, these two considerations have important implications for future investments and strategies in the Canadian primary iron and steel industry. Therefore, it is to such investments that attention must now be turned.

MANUFACTURING INVESTMENTS

According to Bradbury, "restructuring involves changes in the order and timing of investments in technology in plant and in the methods of production."[19] Canadian mills have been geared to Canadian demand, thus insulating themselves from the vagaries of the world market for steel. They have generally had relatively high capacity utilization rates, which is "crucial in a capital intensive industry."[20] The Canadian industry has traditionally upgraded and modernized its facilities to the best available technology. It has also given some attention to environmental controls, which the industry likes to refer to as "non-income generating capital investments," because they simply detract from industry revenues.[21]

A relatively common misperception of Canada's potential natural advantages in steel production is that the country does better than most of the larger industrial democracies because it has abundant supplies of the necessary raw materials. But Canada's iron ore deposits, while indeed plentiful, are not inexpensive to mine, nor are they rich in content, nor do transportation costs render them particularly attractive. In addition, metallurgical-grade coals (low in sulphur content) are imported from the eastern seaboard of the United States. Consequently, Canada's only real advantage lies in cheap electrical energy supplies based on hydro power plants in Quebec and Ontario.[22] Consequently, much of the relatively good international performance of the Canadian steel industry has been made possible by state investment in the energy sector. This has enabled the industry to innovate, adopt innovations from elsewhere, and to invest strategically with good returns.

Canada's steel industry generally receives high marks for its use of technology. According to Chandler, "much of Canada's steel technology – in place, on the drawing board, and being planned – is state of the art, the best available in the world."[23] The key is cost reduction based on getting more capacity out of existing facilities – higher productivity and quality at lower costs. Thus, even though the Canadian steel industry is small by world standards, it is widely regarded as one of the most efficient in the world. It places a strong emphasis on the development of new technology, and the early acquisition of the most up-to-date technologies.

In North America it was the Canadian, not American, steel industry that first introduced basic oxygen furnaces (at Dofasco), and first used continuous casting (at Atlas). In fact one could characterize the Canadian steel industry with the phrase "best available technology at the company level." This tradition of being at the cutting edge in terms of best available technology has given Canada a distinctive advantage in the troubled times the world steel industry has faced. Automation, computers, and statistical process controls are applied differently throughout the industry. Each company maintains a distinctive character in the way in which it approaches these technological innovations.[24]

This level of technological performance in research and development and the adoption of new techniques in steel production stand in sharp contrast to the negative picture one has of Canadian industry in this regard (see the chapter by Gertler in this volume). The steel industry has bucked this trend. The growth in mini-mill production illustrates the positive impact of new, small-scale technologies at the plant level. Quebec-based QIT-Fer et Titane has been for some years producing a high-quality pig iron in kilns as a by-product of its smelting process for extracting titanium dioxide (a whiting agent for paints and plastics) from selected iron ores. This pig iron used to be sold to the foundry sector for casting and wrought iron work, but the 1981–82 recession hurt those sectors more than it did the purchasers of the titanium pigment. Consequently, QIT had to do something with the excess pig iron. It entered the steel industry with one of Canada's most modern steelmaking shops and now sells the semi-finished steel to another minimill, Ivaco in Marietteville, Ontario, where it is turned into marketable products.[25] It is one of the genuine success stories of the Canadian steel industry, but it is not an isolated example.

TRADE BALANCE

The steel industry's performance on international markets runs counter to most other secors of Canada's manufacturing industries. Starting in 1976, Canada shifted from being a net importer to being a net exporter of steel products in tonnage terms (see Graph 8.2). This completely reversed the pattern of the early period. In Graph 8.3 one can see the cyclical, but diminishing, importance of steel imports as a percentage of apparent steel consumption in Canada. Graph 8.4 illustrates the steady rise in exports as percentage of mill shipments from the Canadian primary iron and steel industry over the period 1970 to 1986. Graph 8.5 shows how exports to the United States as a percentage of those mill shipments has increased over that same time period, going from under 55 per cent in 1966 to around 80 per cent by 1986.[26]

Some of the success of Canadian exports of steel to the United States in the early 1980s was based on Canada acting as a middleman in the resale of steel produced overseas in countries that signed Voluntary Restraint Agreements (VRAs) with the Americans. Canada did not sign a VRA with the United States on steel products, which helped to increase its share of imports into the American steel market even as the overall share of steel from those markets in the United States was shrinking. Now that the United States is monitoring more closely the import and export of steel by Canada, the total volume of Canadian steel shipped into the American market is unlikely to increase. Rather, the pattern of cycles in that market would actually lead to a prediction of decline. Even within the parameters of the Canada–US free trade agreement, the total volume of Canadian steel that will be shipped into the American market is likely to remain at present levels. Consequently, to obtain better economic results from their exports into the United States, Canadian producers may attempt to reposition themselves at the higher value-added end of the market.

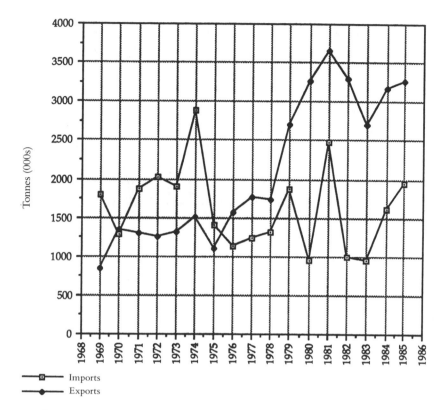

Graph 8.2.
Foreign Trade in Steel Products, Canada 1969–85
SOURCE: United Nations, Bulletin of Steel Statistics for Europe, Annual, various years

In an informative study on the effects of the VRAS on the steel industry in the United States, Canto argues that "even though the tonnage of steel imports was reduced, the overall value of imports remained approximately the same," and further that the "net effect of increased competition in higher priced steels, and less competition in lower priced steels was, if anything, to hurt the US steel industry." As a result, the voluntary import restraints program "did not stop the decline in the industry employment levels."[27]

For Canada this has immediate implications. "About 20 percent of total Canadian steel production is exported to the United States; this amounts to about three percent of US steel consumption. Canada is also

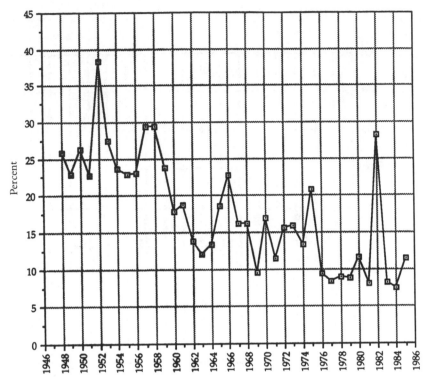

Graph 8.3.
Imports of Steel as a Percent of Apparent Consumption, Canada, 1948–85
SOURCE: United Nations, Bulletin of Steel Statistics for Europe, Annual, various years

the largest customer for US steel exports. Canada receives about 23 percent of total US exports, which represents 0.3 percent of US production and five to six percent of Canadian consumption." Therefore, "uninterrupted access to the US market is critical in light of the fact that other international markets will remain protected and that almost a quarter of Canadian steel is exported to the US."[28] Therefore the dependence on the American market for exports, combined with the fact that Canada receives the lion's share of the steel exported from the United States, might be reason for concern and certainly is worthy of additional research.

A complicating factor here is that Canadian firms traditionally trade in semi-finished outputs to overcome potential bottlenecks and are therefore able to run at higher operating rates. Some other trade also involves shipping semi-finished steel to automotive stamping shops in the United States, re-importing the parts for assembly and then re-

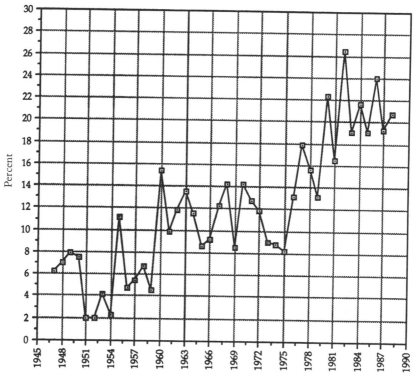

Graph 8.4.

Exports as a Percent of Mill Shipments of Rolled Steel Products, Canada 1947–88

SOURCE: Bulletin of Steel Statistics for Europe, Annual, various years

exporting the car. In fact, Hogan states that the "1965 treaty between Canada and the United States in respect to automobile imports and exports ... accounts for a significant percentage of steel exports" from Canada.[29]

The depreciation of the Canadian dollar has given the steel industry a shot in the arm and encouraged Stelco and Dofasco to expand. Crandall makes the case that "because of the depreciation of the Canadian dollar ... incremental expansion by Stelco and Dofasco ... may pose a grater threat to US firms located in the Great Lakes region than the newest mills in Latin America or Asia." However, along these lines, Barnett and Schorsch note that "present exchange rates have maintained and even increased the competitiveness of the Canadian steel industry ... but this masks the fact that the industry's prospects are now much gloomier than they had been only five years ago."[30] The rationale for such a statement is to be found in the debate on industrial policy.

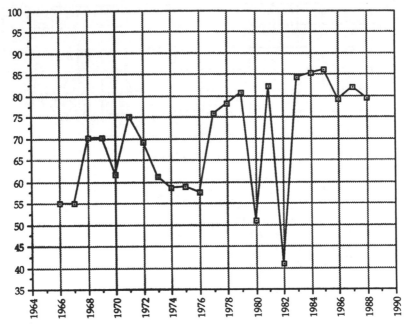

Graph 8.5.
Percentage of Net Shipments of Rolled Steel Products Exported to the US from Canadian Mills

SOURCE: Statistics Canada, Primary Metal Industries, Cat. No. 41-250, various years

THE INDUSTRIAL POLICY DIMENSION

According to Barnett and Schorsch, "successful industrial policies are based upon an industry-government consensus that realistically identifies the existing obstacles to superior economic performance and then establishes a policy environment in which these obstacles can be overcome by appropriate managerial strategies."[31] In fact, a large measure of the success of Canada's steel industry is due to informal arrangements between the privately owned Big Three steel producers and the federal government. These arrangements played a major role in transforming the industry from an inefficient one into a world-class competitor. In slightly different form others have made similar claims and "while no explicit steel policy was promulgated," what did emerge could be seen as a "policy/strategy consensus."[32]

The relationship between steel and the state in Canada has been characterized by at least five distinct factors. First, Stelco, Dofasco, and Algoma in the 1950s divided and allocated product markets, thus specializing to achieve scale economies. They were able to do this because the Canadian government seems to have been "flexible" in its application of anti-combines legislation.[33] The twofold result of this policy was greatly to reduce the risks associated with investments in the steel industry and to increase the international performance of Canadian steel makers.[34]

Second, and following from specialization, output targets were established for products which Canadian steel-makers were expected to dominate on the domestic market, while entire product lines for which there was no chance of competing on costs were left to imports. Very high capacity utilization rates were thereby achieved, thus minimizing the trauma associated with world competition. With this "tacit consensus" Canadian steel-makers were able to build sufficient capacity only for the markets in which they had or could obtain a comparative advantage, an advantage that was partially due to tariffs and transport costs. In fact, it appears that in boom times Canada traditionally imports steel and at slack times it is able to reduce imports considerably.

Third, Barnett and Schorsch argue that "in an effort to avoid becoming solely a source of raw materials for more developed economies, Canadian policy makers have traditionally sought to use high tariffs in manufactured goods to create a domestic manufacturing sector that could process indigenous raw materials." Canadian tariffs have always been higher than those of the United States.[35] In addition, subsidized transport (high relative to the cost of steel products) may have helped Canadian producers protect the domestic market. The natural "domestic" market for certain Canadian steel products was also redefined to include areas in the continental United States where, on the product lines in which Canadian producers specialize, there are no competitive American mills. Thus Canadian steel has successfully entered the United States' domestic market.

Fourth, the tax policies of the federal government, by allowing depreciation of capital expenses over only a two-year period made reinvestment, modernization, and new entry into the iron and steel industry relatively easy. By contrast, the equivalent us depreciation period at the beginning of the 1980s was eleven years, though Howell et al. claim it to be closer to fifteen.[36] Further, the tax codes in Canada have generally included an allowance for resource extraction and processing. Thus, the relatively high cost of capital in Canada, which has often been cited as a reason for retarded economic growth and slow technical progress, was short-circuited in the case of the primary iron and steel industry. This substantially reduced the costs of overhead and generally led to high capacity utilization rates.

Fifth, while other social, political, and economic factors certainly influenced these decisions, up until 1981 the implementation of government wage and price controls had tended to coincide with industry-wide contractual negotiations between firms and the unionized portion of steelworkers. The effects were to restrain costs by keeping the wages paid to steelworkers lower than in the United States. The wage premium for steelworkers relative to other manufacturing workers was also kept lower than in the United States. This, too, increased the competitiveness of Canadian steel producers.

In practical terms, all of the foregoing policy measures have combined to foster superior economic performance, based on high operating results and high rates of capacity utilization. The specialization of product lines by the Big Three was matched by the fact that "Canada's integrated mills did not seek to compete with mini-mill operations in bar-like products; instead they either surrendered these markets or built their own mini-mills."[37] The space afforded the mini-mill sector has indeed complemented the success obtained by the integrated producers in Canada. Canadian firms are considered leaders in mini-mill technology and operating procedures. While the mini-mill segment of the steel industry in the United States has recently been praised for helping that industry rise up from the ashes, it is interesting to note that at least four of the most successful mini-mills operating in the United States today are owned or controlled by the Canadian steel industry: Co-Steel International (Ferrco) owns Raritan, and Chapparral and Ivaco has interests in Atlantic and Laclede.

Since the tariffs on steel were not as high as on finished manufactured goods, and given the high cost of transportation relative to final market price for the products, it was less attractive a target to American investors. Consequently, the Canadian primary iron and steel industry is largely Canadian-owned. Despite this, United States' interests are dominant upstream from the primary iron and steel industry in Canada in terms of ownership of iron ore mines and the supply from the US east coast of metallurgical-grade coals. Furthermore, the United States is in a dominant position downstream in terms of user groups for Canadian steel products through its ownership of most of the automobile industry on the continent. This obviously clouds the waters with regard to the successful implementation of a strategy/policy consensus covering all industrial sectors in Canada.

However, not all outcomes from this strategy/policy consensus have been favourable. This is evident in the over-expansion of the Canadian steel industry in the late 1970s and the failure to modernize the old Dosco works in Nova Scotia (Sysco) and Quebec (Sidbec). An over-zealous federal program wished to exploit Canada's apparent (but practically non-existent) natural advantage in resources and to foster steel as an export industry. In national terms, overall public assistance to

Canada's steel industry has not been on a very high level. However, since the late 1960s in the case of Sysco and the mid-1970s at Sidbec, provincial governments have infused massive amounts of public funds to help those producers retire debts, purchase new equipment, and cover operating losses. After being allowed to divest itself of a disastrous share in an iron ore venture (at Fire Lake and Port Cartier), Sidbec has actually begun to turn a profit and will probably be able to become self-financing for future investments. Sysco, unfortunately, is an entirely different story.

In a complaint to the federal government, Algoma has estimated that its operations have been hurt by the massive subsidization of Sysco. Since they are the only two producers of rails, Algoma feels justified in pointing out that over the last twenty years or so, approximately $900,000 (current) have been spent for every job at the Sydney plant. The regional development dimension has apparently made delivery of national industrial policy more complicated indeed. In any case, notwithstanding the Canada–US free trade agreement, in July 1989 steel rail products from Canada were hit by countervailing duties because the provincial subsidies are considered unfair trading practices by both the United States International Trade Commission and GATT (the General Agreement on Tariffs and Trade).

Regional rivalries and public-private interests are not the only difficulties to be encountered in the policy area. Product market differentiation is another. "The auto industry is a particularly important market for Canadian steel ... To a large extent, the current health of the Canadian steel industry reflects the health of the automotive industry."[38] Notwithstanding the fact that automobiles use less steel today than in the past, over the last decade or so the Canadian steel industry has been able to increase the volume of its sales to the automotive sector (see the chapter by Holmes in this volume). This type of linkage, however, indicates the difficulties in designing and implementing sectorally specific industrial policies for the steel or any other Canadian industry.

Finally, the role of labour in these processes needs to be considered carefully. Tentatively, it seems to be the case that workers in the primary iron and steel industry in Canada have not represented a major impediment to the introduction of up-to-date technologies at the industry level. And the evidence given earlier in this chapter seems to indicate that management was successful in achieving quantitative flexibility in its labour inputs by technological substitution, task redefinition, and traditional lay-offs in downturns and rehirings in upturns. However, the available data only cover three years since the end of a serious recession. Labour's reaction to restructuring deserves continued consideration as a longer series becomes available. The fact that Dofasco is not unionized is also worthy of special analysis in the context of labour's reaction to shifts in managerial strategy (see the chapter by Morris in this volume).

CONCLUSIONS

Overall, the restructuring of Canada's primary iron and steel industry has already changed its prospects for future growth and development. It is well managed and technologically up to date, but it is not without potential problems on the horizon. The trends in the industry seem to indicate increased space for mini-mills and downsizing of large integrated producers, together with their relocation into markets that they wish to serve.

In Canada it is "clear and significant ... that both labour and capital were not subject to the identical and long-term crisis pressures that have been exerted on the USA, European and Japanese steel industries. Canadian steel producers were not forced into the massive over-production and restructuring crises which devastated so much of the international steel production system."[39] Yet there are some disturbing trends that must be followed much more closely.

The Canadian steel industry may be in the throes of the "American disease of the 1950s," that is, "overoptimism in regard to potential market growth and the permanence of existing comparative advantages."[40] All five of the policy dimensions which favoured the transformation of Canadian steel from a small, protected, inefficient industry into a world leader in technological implementation and operational performance may now be eroding. Large federal deficits have meant the cancellation of some tax incentives, such as the resource depletion allowance. While policy-makers of earlier times were sensitive to the necessity of maintaining high capacity utilization rates and operating margins, political interference and regional rivalries have seen the creation for the first time in the postwar period of significant excess capacity. The free trade agreement with the United States, while representing no direct threat to Canada's steel industry, may nevertheless threaten production and employment in other sectors that use Canadian steel. Cost advantages enjoyed by Canadian producers over their American counterparts are not as significant as they once were. The 1981 strike, coming at a time of serious economic downturn, saw the industry grant a 51 per cent increase in wages to the workforce over the three-year life of the negotiated settlement. Finally, with the gathering strength of the Canadian dollar, the increased cost of Canadian steel exports is likely to make them less competitive in the United States and elsewhere abroad.

It may be that the Canadian state and Canadian steel industry were willing and able to arrive at a policy/strategy consensus only because the prospects for growth overall in the economy and specifically for that sector were quite good until the beginning of the 1980s. It remains to be seen how both parties will react to slow growth or actual decline in this period following the 1981–82 recession. The realignment of major producers, including Dofasco's recent purchase of Algoma, might mean that the Canadian state is not willing to see the industrial policy for that sector degenerate, as it did in Great Britain, into the "state-sanctioned maintenance of an efficient status-quo."[41]

On balance, the evidence on the aggregate level as well as for the individual firms involved in the Canadian steel industry clearly documents a massive restucturing that is witnessing a labour-shedding accompanied by increases in the number of establishments and a more efficient mix of production technologies and products. As for the role of labour, the most striking aspect is the decrease in total employment in the industry since the recession of 1981–83. The role of state policies seems to have helped create a competitive industry that was able to hold off imports while increasing its presence on the world, or at least American, market for steel products. The way in which the primary iron and steel industry has modified itself in adjusting to changes in production conditions and to new market realities might serve as a lesson for the restructuring of other industrial sectors in Canada.

NOTES

Portions of this paper were presented at the Conference on Export-Led Growth and Uneven Development: The Cases of Canada and Italy, 19–22 April 1989, Università degli Studi di Pisa, Italy. I would like to thank the Faculty of Graduate Studies, McGill University, and the Cassa di Risparmio di Pisa for travel and sojourn grants. The research for this paper was made possible by a team research grant from the Fonds pour la Formation de Chercheurs et l'Aide à la Recherche (Quebec) and their support is gratefully acknowledged. I would also like to thank Christopher Green, Michael Smith, and the editors of this volume for their useful comments.

1 On the general topic of deindustrialization see F. Blackaby, ed., *De-Industrialization* (London: Heineman 1979); B. Bluestone and B. Harrison, *The Deindustrialization of America* (New York: Basic Books 1982); R. V. Ayres, *The Next Industrial Revolution* (Cambridge, Mass.: Ballinger 1984); M. Piore and C.F. Sabel, *The Second Industrial Divide* (New York: Basic Books 1984);

R.D. Norton, "Industrial Policy and American Renewal," *Journal of Economic Literature* 24 (March 1986); R.A. Matthews, *Structural Change and Industrial Policy* (Ottawa: Minister of Supply and Services and the Economic Council of Canada 1985). On the measurement controversies surrounding this debate see B. Bluestone, "Is Deindustrialization a Myth?" *Annals of the American Academy of Political and Social Sciences* 475 (September 1984); R.Z. Lawrence, "Is Trade Deindustrializing America?" *Brookings Papers on Economic Activity* 1 (1983), *Can America Compete?* (Washington, DC: Brookings Institution 1984), and "Myths and Realities on America's Need for an Industrial Policy" in S.A. Shull and J.E. Cohen, eds., *The Economics and Politics of Industrial Policy* (Boulder: Westview 1986); S.S. Cohen and J. Zysman, "The Myth of a Post-Industrial Economy," *Technology Review* (February/March 1987). Studies dealing specifically with the steel industry that are relevant to this topic include W. Adams, "The Steel Industry" in W. Adams, ed., *The Structure of American Industry* (New York: Macmillan 1974); H.G. Mueller, "The Steel Industry," *Annals of the American Academy of Political and Social Sciences* 460 (March 1982); S. Woolcock, "Iron and Steel" in S. Strange and R. Tooze, eds., *The International Politics of Surplus Capacity* (London: George Allen and Unwin 1981); I. Magaziner and R. Reich, *Minding America's Business* (New York: Harcourt Brace Jovanovich 1982); M. Borrus, "The Politics of Competitive Erosion in the U.S. Steel Industry" in J. Zysman and L. Tyson, eds., *American Industry in International Competition* (Ithaca: Cornell University Press 1983), A. Cockerill, "Steel" in P.S. Johnson, ed., *The Structure of British Industry* (London: Granada 1980); and finally, Y. Meny and V. Wright, eds., *The Politics of Steel* (New York: Walter de Gruyter 1987).

2 D. Massey and R. Meegan, *The Anatomy of Job Loss* (London: Methuen 1982); see also A.C. Masi, "The Bagnoli Steel Complex" in R. Nanetti and R. Catanzaro, eds., *Italian Politics: A Review*, Vol. 4 (Bologna: Il Mulino 1990).

3 Office of Technology Assessment, *Technology and Steel Industry Competitiveness* (Washington, D.C.: U.S. Government Printing Office 1980).

4 See W.H. Goldberg, *Ailing Steel* (New York: St Martin's Press 1986).

5 A.V. Orr, *A Report by the Sector Task Force on the Canadian Primary Iron and Steel Industry*, December 1978.

6 During 1988, Dofasco purchased Algoma, but for purposes of this chapter, which due to the availability of data at the time of this writing (August 1989) ends with 1986, they will be treated separately for most of the quantitative analysis. The implications of the government's response to the merger are discussed below.

7 W.M. Williams, "A Historical Sketch of the Canadian Steel Industry," *CIM Bulletin* (Canadian Institute of Mining and Metallurgy) 79, no. 893 (September 1986), provides an interesting and informative historical sketch of the Canadian steel industry.

8 All the data presented on the Canadian primary iron and steel industry come from Statistics Canada publications which are fully referenced in the graphs and tables themselves. The only exceptions are the figures on imports and exports of steel products (which are from the United Nations, Economic Commission for Europe).

9 For more detail on de-industrialization and the restructuring of Canada's manufacturing sectors see A.C. Masi and M. Del Balso, "Industrial Restructuring: The Experiences of Italy and Canada," paper presented to the Conference on Societies in Transition, Montreal, 9–11 June 1988. For steel sector specifics see W.T. Hogan, *World Steel in the 1980s* (Lexington, Mass.: Lexington Books 1983) and the Report of the Premier's Council, *Competing in the Global Economy*, Industry Studies, Vol. II (Toronto: Queen's Printer for Ontario 1988).

10 P. Blyton, *et al.*, *Human Resource Management in Canadian and U.K. Work Organizations*, Interim Report for the Canadian High Commission (London 1989), 143.

11 Ibid., 144.

12 There is less waste when steel is continuously cast as compared to when it is moulded into ingots. Consequently, the industry and statistical agencies that report data on steel production use coefficients to convert cast steel into ingot equivalents.

13 D.F. Barnett and R.W. Crandall, *Up from the Ashes: The Rise of the Steel Minimill in the United States* (Washington, D.C.: Brookings Institution 1986).

14 Williams, "Historical Sketch," 97. However, Williams goes on to argue that it is "too soon to say how important these smaller companies will become in the over-all pattern of Canadian steel production."

15 A. Neef and J. Thomas, "Trends in Manufacturing Productivity and Labor Costs in the U.S. and Abroad," *Monthly Labor Review* (December 1987).

16 See K. Stegemann, *Price Competition and Output Adjustment in the European Steel Market* (Tuebingen: Mohr 1977).

17 D.F. Barnett and L. Schorsch, *Steel* (Cambridge, Mass.: Ballinger 1983), 159.

18 Williams, "Historical Sketch," 97.

19 See also L.A. Sandberg and J.H. Bradbury, "Industrial Restructuring in the Canadian Steel Industry," *Antipode* 20, no. 2 (September 1988).

20 H.E. Chandler, "A Profile of Canada's Steel Technology," *Metal Progress* (April 1985), 85.

21 The evidence seems to indicate that firms operating in the United States have been somewhat harder hit by these costs than their Canadian counterparts.

22 Together with the location of the major manufacturing industries that utilize steel in their production processes in central Canada, cheap electric-

ity can help account for the concentration of small-scale producers in Ontario and especially Quebec. However, the Midrex sponge iron shaft furnaces used for direct reduction at Sidbec require large amounts of natural gas as a reducing agent, and the province of Quebec does not have abundant supplies of it.

23 Chandler, "A Profile," 55.

24 Blyton, *et al.*, *Human Resource Management*; H.E. Chandler, "A Profile." "Of all the major Canadian steel companies, Dofasco has weathered the recent economic squalls most successfully, a consequence of keeping up to date technologically, and having the right mix of steel products. There is also no doubt that good management has played an important part in this success story" (Williams, "Historical Sketch," 96). One reason may be that experience has taught management to be careful in basing decisions only on the advice of technicians since "engineering analyses usually overstate the economic benefits of new technology." R.W. Crandall, *The U.S. Steel Industry in Recurrent Crisis* (Washington, DC: Brookings Institution 1981), 84.

25 This story was told to me by Professor W.M. Williams, Birks Professor of Metallurgy, Department of Mining and Metallurgical Engineering, McGill University.

26 For an interesting, and now classic, analysis of the relation between industrial structure and the importation of steel products see W. Adams and J.B. Dirlam, "Steel Imports and Vertical Oligopoly Power," *American Economic Review* 54, no. 5 (September 1964).

27 V.A. Canto, "The Effect of Voluntary Restraint Agreements: A Case Study of the Steel Industry," *Applied Economics* 16 (1984): 186.

28 Report of Premier's Council, *Competing in the New Global Economy*, 60.

29 Hogan, *World Steel*, 142.

30 Crandall, *The U.S. Steel Industry*, 92; Barnett and Schorsch, *Steel*, 226.

31 Ibid., 227.

32 Ibid., passim; Hogan, *World Steel*, 138; Crandall, *The U.S. Steel Industry*, 92.

33 See in particular, T.R. Howell, *et al.*, *Steel and the State* (Boulder: Westview Press 1988), 455.

34 The claim for an "informal agreement" among the producers and between them and the federal government is often repeated in descriptions of the Canadian steel industry. The fact that the Big Three steel-makers were producing in a parallel fashion does not necessarily mean that they were in violation of the competition laws. In a small country, economic reasons alone, without the need for collusion, might have given rise to a similar outcome. For more details see I.A. Litvak and C.J. Maule, *Corporate Dualism and the Canadian Steel Industry* (Ottawa: Minister of Supply and Services 1977) and J. Singer, "Trade Liberalization and the Canadian Steel

Industry" in J. Singer and J.M. Munro, *The Impact of Trade Liberalization*, Vol. 2 (Toronto: University of Toronto Press and the Private Planning Association of Canada 1969).

35 Barnett and Schorsch, *Steel*, 216. D. Cameron, ed., *The Free Trade Papers* (Toronto: Lorimer 1986), Appendix 1: 210–11, cites the 1985 tariff on iron and steel products for Canada to be 5.6 per cent compared to 3.6 for the United States, while for 1987, P. Wonnacott, *The U.S. and Canada* (Washington, D.C.: Institute for International Economics 1987), Table 1.1, indicates the Canadian and American tariffs of these items as 5.1 and 2.7 per cent respectively after the Tokyo round of the General Agreement on Tariffs and Trade. For more details on the effects of tax structures see T. Zollo, *et al.*, *Tax Competitiveness of the Canadian Steel Industry* (Ottawa: Conference Board of Canada 1988).

36 Howell, *et al.*, *Steel and the State*, 455.

37 Barnett and Schorsch, *Steel*, 222; Barnett and Crandall, *Up from the Ashes*.

38 Report of the Premier's Council, *Competing in the New Global Economy*.

39 J.H. Bradbury, "Technical Change and the Restructuring of the North American Steel Industry" in K. Chapman and G. Humphrys, eds., *Technical Change and Industrial Policy* (Oxford: Basil Blackwell 1987), 166–67.

40 Barnett and Schorsch, *Steel*, 226.

41 Ibid., 227. The Bureau of Competitive Policy (Consumer and Corporate Affairs) extensively analysed the potential effects of the Dofasco takeover of Algoma on the structure and performance of the Canadian steel industry. It concluded that even though Dofasco and Algoma are respectively the second and third largest steel producers in Canada, "the two companies have concentrated a large portion of their production in separate product markets" (news release, 30 September 1988). The extent of present and potential future foreign competition in the Canadian market for hot rolled sheet and strip steel, as well as efficiency benefits (capital expansion and operating savings) played a major role in the decision of Corporate Affairs not to apply to the Competition Tribunal.

9 A Japanization of Canadian Industry?

JONATHAN MORRIS

Japanization describes a whole gamut of changes taking place in mass production industry world-wide that emulates the "best practice" found in Japanese manufacturing methods.[1] It is too early to say whether this process will diffuse to all Western economies in the same way. The industrial relations structure, the role of the state, the legislative framework, and cultures of work organization in different countries will all combine to produce distinctive outcomes in each location. Yet it is a process likely to continue to expand, particularly in certain sectors such as automobile, metal fabrication, and electronics which, in response to the last downturn in the economy, have looked for new ways to change their manufacturing methods.[2]

What then is this process of Japanization? The key element copied by foreign companies stems from a desire to improve and control product quality and production flexibility along the lines practised by Japanese companies. This includes a whole series of changes in the demands on labour, trade unions, and corporate sub-assembly suppliers. This gamut of Japanese corporate practices covers: manufacturing methods, including total quality control and just-in-time production; personnel policies involving employment contracts, recruitment and training, payment and reward systems; and finally, industrial relations practices and relations with subcontractors.

First, the Japanese give priority to creating a flexible system of production in the workplace and in production methods. Both total quality control and just-in-time systems depend upon a flexible form of work organization which is the antithesis of hierarchical mass production work methods known as Fordism. In the Japanese system, workers need to be able to switch jobs frequently at short notice and be "multi-skilled." Moreover, if subcontractors are to be able to supply components just-in-time to final assemblers they need to be in close proximity to the final assembler. Mair *et al.* estimate that for the automobile industry the maximum distance subcontractors can locate away from the final assembler is equivalent to three hours' driving time.[3] While such complexes are beginning to emerge both in North America and Western Europe, they are embryonic and unlikely to develop to the extent currently evident in Japan.[4]

A second broad area of Japanese industrial practice is found in the area of personnel practices. Included under this heading are employment contracts, recruitment and training procedures, payment/reward systems, and consultation and communication. Lifetime employment is perhaps one of the best-known features of Japanese personnel practices and is part of the wider notion of company-based welfare. However, while lifetime employment contracts would seem an idyll to employees, they constrain mobility and only apply to a limited number of workers. Those entitled to lifetime employment are only the core workers of large private sector organizations and, as we shall see later, this may only mean a small percentage of total workers inside and outside directly related to the organization. Given the system of lifetime employment for core workers, it is not surprising that great care is taken in selection, induction, and training of workers. However, this attention is also part of the wider ethos of total quality control and the notions of a culture of company loyalty and corporate paternalism.

The final category of Japanese industrial practice is that of the wider social and political and economic conditions. This broad area would include the nature of trade unionism, the dual economy, buyer–supplier relationships, the role of the state and the links between finance and manufacturing capital.[5]

Large Japanese corporations make extensive use of a dual economy both within and outside the workplace. This, of course, is not unique, as some sort of dual economy exists in all mixed economies; what is unique here is the extent of the dual economy. This is predicated by a number of factors; first, the extensive use of the dual economy *within* corporations and factories, with estimates of the total of core workers (i.e., those with lifetime employment) being between 40 to 60 per cent, the remainder being non-core workers, including large numbers of temporary and part-time workers, and many female workers.[6] Secondly, there is the far greater use of the subcontracting system; JAMA Canada estimate for example, that whereas in the North American automobile industry some 70 per cent of modular parts are produced in in-house, in Japan the comparable figure is nearer 30 per cent.[7] Ninety per cent of Japanese businesses are small ones (i.e. under five hundred people) and 80 per cent of Japanese workers are found in such enterprises.[8] Workers in such organizations do not generally have lifetime employment, and working conditions are characterized by low pay and lack of union representation. When these workers are added to the non-core workers in the large corporations, the number of workers *not* enjoying lifetime employment guarantees is estimated to be closer to 90 per cent.[9]

Buyer-supplier relations between large and small firms within this dual economy also tend to be radically different from those found in the West. Not only is the volume of work subcontracted out greater, but the nature of the relationship differs. First, it is closely linked with the ethos of total quality control and just-in-time manufacture. Basically the typical Japanese system is long-term and based on collaboration and trust ("relational" contracting) whereas the typical Western system is short-term and based upon confrontation and mistrust ("competitive" contracting). Japanese corporations maintain control either by subcontracting to other companies within the broader corporate group, by taking a shareholding in independent subcontractors or by their sheer market control power. Moreover, the subcontracting networks also tend to be far more hierarchical and structured.[10]

The final two areas of analysis are the role of the state and the financing of industry. The Japanese state has played a highly unusual role in its support of industry. While levels of financial assistance are low and akin to a laissez-faire approach, the *degree* of control has a far greater affinity to centrally planned economies, via the targeting of key industries and technologies through control over finance sources, over foreign exchange, export subsidies, public provision for research and development, and the more general use of bureaucratic hurdles.[11]

Much of the finance for manufacturing investment in Japan is raised from banks, in contrast to North America and Britain where finance is raised on the stockmarket.[12] Moreover, the manufacturing and financial organizations may be within the same conglomerate trading groups – the *zaibatsus* or *sogo shosha* – which results not only in cheap finance but in long-term finance. Thus, Japanese firms are allowed far longer payback periods in which to amortize investments than is true in American and British corporations.

This last point is exemplified by one case from the study of Morris.[13] Matsushita Industrial Canada were one of nine colour television producers in Canada in the mid 1970s, along with four American, one Dutch, one Canadian, and three other Japanese owned plants, when a mini recession struck the industry. The non-Japanese plants all closed with the result that only five producers are left in Canada in the late 1980s – Matsushita, Mitsubishi, Sanyo, Hitachi, and the French-owned

Thomson group. The future of Zenith, the last remaining US-owned colour TV producer, is at present in some doubt.[14]

The combination of industrial practices running through manufacturing methods, personnel practices, and wider structures are the backbone of Japanese industrial corporations. The replication of these practices in the West, and in Canada more specifically, can be termed Japanization, whether it be by Japanese transplants or Western firms attempting to emulate these practices. With Western social economic conditions so different from Japan's, it is doubtful that any liberal democratic country will fully Japanize production organization. Nonetheless, the far-reaching changes in production inspired by Japanese corporate leaders are a force to be reckoned with. One way to gauge the nature and extent of Japanization in a country such as Canada is to refine the concept by distinguishing between three types: direct, mediated, and full.[15]

Direct Japanization is covered in the next section of this paper. The second type of Japanization is further subdivided into "mediated Japanization I" which refers to the attempts of Western companies to emulate Japanese practice, while "mediated Japanization II" refers to the attempt by Western companies to legitimize measures that they were already trying to implement by equating them with Japanese companies' successes. The final type of Japanization is full (or permeated) Japanization. This would be evidenced by Canada (or other Western countries) developing strategies similar to those of Japanese in terms of investment strategies and methods and the role of the state – that is, the last two of the wider structures outlined earlier. Of the three levels, full Japanization is unlikely to be anywhere outside of Japan itself.

The remainder of this paper will be divided into three further sections. The first and second sections will provide evidence that a process of Japanization has begun to transform production methods, employment relations, and subcontracting in the Canadian economy. The former will draw on recent empirical evidence provided by the author from Japanese transplants in Canada.[16] The latter will concentrate on the extent to which Canadian firms have aped the practices of Japanese companies in a sometimes desperate attempt to negate the competitive advantages that these companies have. Finally, the last section will explore the major implications of these changes for Canadian labour.

JAPANIZATION: JAPANESE TRANSPLANTS IN CANADA

Japanese direct investment in Canada has been relatively small, and in its early days was concentrated in trading companies and resource based projects.[17] As late as 1980 there was little investment in manufacturing.

Table 9.1
Major Japanese Corporate Investments in Canada,
1965–84

Sector	1965–84
RESOURCES	
No. of projects	39
Total invested ($M)	972.9
% Japanese	26.1
Japanese investment ($M)	254.1
TRADING	
No. of projects	39
Total invested ($M)	162.1
% Japanese	90.1
Japanese investment ($M)	146.1
MANUFACTURING	
No. of projects	12
Total invested ($M)	76
% Japanese	47.5
Japanese investment ($M)	36.1
INVESTMENT	
No. of projects	13
Total invested ($M)	153.9
% Japanese	67.2
Japanese investment ($M)	103.4
TOTAL	
No. of projects	103
Total invested ($M)	1364.9
% Japanese	39.5
Japanese investment ($M)	539.7

SOURCE: R. Blain and G. Norcliffe, "Japanese Investment in
Canada and Canadian Exports to Japan, 1965–84,"
Canadian Geographer 32, no. 2 (1988), 141–50.

However, in 1981 there were record levels of Japanese investment, encouraged by the size and affluence of the Canadian market, the relative weakness of indigenous manufacturing, weaknesses in foreign investment reviews, and the fall in the value of the Canadian dollar (see Table 9.1).

Accurate contemporary data on Japanese investment in Canada is not available. However, Langley estimates that in 1985 such investments totalled US$1675 million, which represented some 2 per cent of the total Japanese foreign direct investment compared to 30.2 per cent in the United States.[18] Moreover, despite the relatively small amount of manufacturing investment in Canada, there was a considerable surge between 1984 and 1988. As Table 9.2 illustrates, this has been particularly concentrated in automotives, components, and related products.[19]

Table 9.2
Automobile and Auto Component Firms in Canada

Company	Parent/ partner	Full/joint venture	Location	Year operational	Product line
CAMI Automotive	G.M. Suzuki	J	Ingersoll, Ont.	1988	Automobiles
Captin	Toyota	F	Delta, B.C.	1985	Aluminium wheels
Copar Int.	Long Manuf. Toyo Radiator C. Itoh & Co.	J	Oakville, Ont.	1988	Automotive radiator
Daikyo Magna	Magna Int. Daiko Co.	J	Tillsonburg, Ont.	1988	Plastic trim
F & P Mfg. Inc.	Fukuda Press Press Giken	J	Tottenham, Ont.	1987	Stamping parts
Fujima Int. Inc.	Magna Int. Fuji Tool & Die	J	Ontario	1987	Stamping dies
General Seating of Canada	Lear Siegler NHK Spring Co.	J	Ontario	1989	Seating
Honda of Canada Mfg	Honda	F	Alliston, Ont.	1984	Automobiles
Mitsubishi Electronics Industry Canada	Mitsubishi	F	Waterloo, Ont.	1987	Car audio
Nichirin Rubber Ind.	Nichirin Inc.	F	Brantford, Ont.	1987	Hose and tube assemblies
NTN Bearing Mfg	NTN Toyo Bearing Co.	F	Mississauga, Ont.	1973	Bearings
Quality Safety Systems Co.	TRW Canada Ltd	J	Tecumseh, Ont.	1987	Seat belts
Rockwell International	Rockwell Int. Mitsubishi Steel Mitsubishi Canada	J	Milton, Ont.	1986	Suspension
Toyota Motor Mfg Canada	Toyota Motor	F	Cambridge, Ont.	1988	Automobiles
VDO Yazaki	Yazaki Corp. VDO Instrument	J	Barrie, Ont.	1987	Meters
Woodbridge Inoac	Woodbridge Group. Inoac MTP	J	St Jerome, Quebec St Mary's Ont.		Panels and trim

SOURCE: JAMA Canada, *Japanese Automobile Industry in Canada* (1986); author's survey.

At an extremely rough estimate – from provincial government sources, newspapers, trade magazines, and personal contacts – there were forty-two wholly or partly owned Japanese manufacturing plants operating in Canada in 1988. The majority, twenty-two, were in automotives and related industries; other major sectors were electronics and general metal fabrication.

Given the sectoral distribution of plants it is only to be expected that the bulk of plants (thirty-one) were located in southern Ontario, in the northern section of what has been termed the North American "transplant corridor."[20] This is compounded by many Japanese firms entering into joint ventures with auto component firms in southern Ontario. Quebec has six plants, both in electronics and auto components, and British Columbia two. The predominance of Ontario is likely to be strengthened by the size of some of the investments. While there are a number of small Japanese-owned plants in southern Ontario, it is also home to the three large automobile manufacturers – Honda, Toyota, and CAMI (GM/Suzuki) – which will have approximately $1120 million invested in them and which will employ 3700 at full production.

The main question is, how Japanized are these plants? That is, how many of the features outlined in the previous section have been transferred across the Pacific? In order to answer this question the paper will draw on a wider survey I conducted of Japanese manufacturing investment in Canada in 1988.[21] This survey included sixteen firms, with eleven face-to-face interviews with senior personnel and five questionnaire replies based upon the interview schedule. Ten of the firms were from the automobile sector, with the rest from a diverse array of sectors, including specialized furniture, sports equipment, metal manufacture, mechanical engineering, and consumer electronics. Twelve plants were located in southern Ontario, with three in British Columbia and one in Quebec.

In general the plants were relatively recent starters: eleven had located since 1983, including five in 1988 (see Table 9.3). While nine firms had chosen the 100 per cent owned subsidiary route, seven had entered the Canadian market through a joint venture, which has been a particularly attractive route for the smaller auto subcontracting firms (although Suzuki, one of the smaller Japanese auto producers, have also chosen this route).

The overwhelming considerations in transferring production from Japan to Canada were market-driven ones – that is, firms felt a necessity to produce close to the markets they were serving. Eight of the firms, of course, were subcontracting firms, largely tempted into transferring production in order to serve original equipment manufacturers who were similarly moving production from Japan. The increased value of

Table 9.3
Start-up Dates of Plants in Survey

Year	No. of starts
1966	2
1972	2
1975	1
1983	2
1984	1
1985	2
1987	1
1988	5
Total	16

the yen was not a significant factor, largely because ten of the plants had located before the "Plaza" agreement in 1985 which led in part to the massive revaluation of the yen.[22] While this did not play a big part in the initial location decision, eleven of the firms considered that it had a considerable influence on subsequent events, either in quickening expansion or in hastening the search for local content. While only two firms maintained that protectionism was a factor, the myriad of import quotas, tariffs, and voluntary trade restrictions must also have been as a considerable spur to relocation and must have acted as a hidden agenda.

While the main motives for production transfer were market-driven, the operations were clearly viewing the continental, rather than purely the Canadian, market place. Only four of the plants served the Canadian market exclusively; three were relatively small plants with American counterparts, while the fourth was a subcontractor located close to the CAMI plant and providing it with the bulk of its output. A substantial minority were export-based platforms exploiting the advantages of a Canadian location to serve the North American market, the vast majority of which is, of course, in the United States. A number of firms had well-integrated North American operations. Matsushita Industrial Canada, for example, imported chassis and receivers for colour televisions from two large plants in Mexico, other components from Atlanta, Georgia, finally assembled them at Toronto and then exported the finished product to the United States. The three large automobile producers are similarly well integrated into North American production and distribution networks.

Turning to more specific aspects of Japanization, the first issue to be considered is that of training and recruitment. The commitment to training and recruitment is part of the wider issues of total quality control and company loyalty. If production workers are to be responsible for quality, then clearly both the recruitment of "appropriate" workers and their subsequent training are crucial. Moreover, the notion of company loyalty and a long-term commitment to employees requires that employees with the "correct attitudes" be hired. A variety of methods were used to recruit direct production workers in the sample, including newspaper advertisements, word of mouth, the use of government agencies (for example, the Canada Employment Centre), private recruitment agencies, and direct recruiting from technical schools.

In Western Europe and United States Japanese plants have, in the vast majority of cases, had little difficulty in recruiting labour. In the case of the Nissan car plant in the northeast of England, for example, some 20,000 applications were received for an initial 500 jobs.[23] Similarly, at the Mazda plant in Flat Rock, Michigan, 130,000 written requests were received for application forms and 96,500 completed for 3,100 available jobs.[24]

This labour market situation, in Britain at least, has been used by indigenous industry in the automotive industry to claim, with some justification, that those Japanese transplants have a considerable competitive advantage in terms of recruitment and hence productivity and quality. Clearly, in a Canadian context, Japanese plants have not been able to achieve similar advantages, given the relatively low rates of unemployment in southern Ontario. Firms in southern Ontario, for example, reported extreme difficulties in recruiting labour, in contrast to the CAPTIN plant in British Columbia, which had three thousand applications for the initial seventy jobs. Nevertheless, all three of the major auto producers have carefully chosen locations which are closely linked to their subsequent ability to recruit "suitable" labour. Both CAMI and Honda chose semi-rural locations close to the heartland of the Canadian auto industry but sufficiently removed, with the former being described by the *Globe and Mail* as a "fertile cattle and corngrowing area."[25] Toyota have also chosen a site removed from the immediate auto production localities, as have all of the Japanese transplants in the United States, with the exception of Mazda.[26]

The explicit intention of such locations is to employ young, green labour with little industrial experience, let alone automobile industry experience. Honda, for example, at their Alliston plant recruited young workers, 85 per cent of whom lived within a thirty-minute drive from the plant, in an area which was mainly agricultural. The average age of workers in 1988 was twenty-seven, and the "good attitude" of workers was given as an important reason for Honda's decision to locate in the district.

In passing, it should be mentioned that few of the plants were unionized. Only five out of the sixteen had unionized labour forces and of these two were joint ventures in which the North American partner was already unionized, two more were takeovers of existing businesses and only one was a unionized greenfield site. Neither Honda nor Toyota were unionized and while the CAMI plant did recognise the Canadian Auto Workers, employees worked under a very different employment contract than would be found at the majority of the Big Three plants in Canada, especially in such features as team working. Moreover, it is surely no coincidence that the only auto plant to be unionized is a joint venture and that part of the quid pro quo for starting such a venture with flexible working arrangements would be union recognition. This, obviously, has important implications for organized labour, which will be discussed later.

"Attitude" was a key factor in the recruitment policies of a number of Japanese transplants. As CAMI's application information, as quoted in the *Toronto Star*, states, "The selection system is designed to produce a competitive and motivated workforce that shares CAMI's values and expectations."[27] The company has a rigorous recruitment procedure: the potential employee has to go through twenty-eight hours of aptitude tests, personal psychology, dexterity, problem-solving ability, and human relations skills testing. The company has sent over two hundred of its workers for training in Japan. The attributes required of these mainly young rural workers is positiveness and flexibility for multi-skilling.

Honda, meanwhile, place a similar emphasis on a good attitude and this, rather than written tests or dexterity skills, is the main criterion for selection. Nevertheless, 90 per cent of workers have grade twelve education or better and 40 per cent have a community college diploma or university degree. Potential recruits at Honda face three interviews, one with a large group, a small group interview which includes questioning by production workers, and finally individual interviews by management.[28]

The third automobile manufacturer, Toyota, is reported to be extremely choosy about recruitment; only high school graduates are recruited in Japan and the Canadian plant is following suit. Recruits then face two days of aptitude tests and a series of further tests to measure leadership qualities and the ability to work in teams.[29] At Toyota's second Canadian plant, the BC-based aluminum wheels producer CAPTIN, the management have sought a family-oriented team approach. Recruits' resumés are first screened by management before general interviews take place, followed by second interviews; only then do they receive a final application form. If recruited they then face a six-month probation period.

These examples illustrate clearly the overriding emphasis placed on recruitment and training. This needs to be placed within the context of the attention placed upon human resource management and the view that labour is a crucial determinant of success or failure in any venture.

The next issue of Japanization to be addressed is the use of core and peripheral workers. Do, for example, Japanese transplants make extensive use of a peripheral buffer workforce? The answer is both yes and no. Yes, in the sense that the assembly plants tend to be fairly vertically disintegrated compared to the big three producers and therefore make more extensive use of subcontractors. In terms of peripheral workers within factories, however, there was little evidence of extensive use of either temporary or part-time labour. While ten of the plants used such labour, in only a few cases was this extensive. And these cases only involved the hiring of students in summer production peaks, which included one of the auto assemblers.

A third aspect of Japanization is the question surrounding local content, buyer-supplier relations, and just-in-time (JIT) production.[30] Without going into too much detail, it was clear that in all but two cases, the survey firms went far beyond the screwdriver assembly plant characterization, despite considerable consternation that this would be the likely outcome. Local content levels (that is, North American) were relatively high and increasing. Moreover, the plants were often integrated into North American corporate production structures, as in the case of Matsushita Industrial Canada. But the main issues here are the *nature* of the buyer-supplier relations and the structures of the subcontracting system. Did they, for example, follow a typical Western, Fordist pattern, or were they more akin to the Japanese system? One way in which the local content issue does impinge upon the discussion is that, if Japanization is to be fully introduced, local content levels will have to be high. For JIT systems to operate fully, for example, suppliers will need to be close to the original equipment manufacturers (OEM's).

The firms in the survey were, of course, intimately linked in a number of cases, with Japanese-owned subcontractors supplying to Japanese OEM's and therefore boosting their local content (see Table 9.4). In Japan there is a complex interweaving of big firm–supplier relations. Japanese auto firms tend to subcontract out more of their production and there are signs of moves in this direction by North American producers; Chrysler, for example, is considering selling its Acustar parts division.[31] Japanese auto producers also rely heavily on a tiered structure of subcontractors, dealing with the tier 1 parts suppliers who assemble and supply modular parts, who are in turn supplied by tier 2, and so on

Table 9.4
Main Customers of Japanese Owned Subcontracting Firms

Firm	Activity	Major Customer
A	Automotive components (electronics)	General Motors (60%) Chrysler (40%)
B	Automotive components (metal)	Komatsu, Caterpillar
C	Automotive components (plastics related)	Ford (30%), Chrysler (30%) GM Toyota
D	Automotive components (metal)	Honda Canada (20%) Honda US (80%)
E	Automotive components (plastic)	CAMI (85%) Hyundai (15%)
F	Automotive plant (metal)	Toyota, Honda, CAMI
G	Automotive components (metal)	Toyota, Japan (70%) Toyota North America (30%)
H	CTV components	Matsushita (20%) Mitsubishi (40%) Hitachi (20%) RCA

SOURCE: J. Morris, *The Changing Industrial Structure of Canada in the 1980's: The Role of Japanese Foreign Direct Investors, Report Submitted to Canadian High Commission* (London 1989).

NOTE: Percentages of plant output in brackets where data available.

down to tier 7. Modular parts have been traditionally produced in-house in North American firms, while single components come from thousands of suppliers.

The differences between Japanese and Western firms in subcontracting relationships goes beyond quantities contracted out; there are also a number of fundamental *qualitative* differences. The Japanese system is formulated around a number of key principles. Contracts would be awarded to a relatively small number of key suppliers who would receive long-term, often open-ended, contracts which are single sourced. The system is geared towards the supply of small volumes of components frequently. The whole basis is trust and manifests itself in close collaboration, technical and otherwise. The traditional North American pattern has been vastly different, based upon a large number of suppliers, short-term contracts, lack of collaboration, large batch orders and bidding.[32]

The shift from one system to the other requires considerable organizational and cultural changes in Western subcontractors and OEM's, particularly with regard to the ability to supply components with virtually no defects on a JIT basis. This is one reason – but only one – why Japanese OEM's have been so eager to bring their own subcontractors to North America.[33] It has been estimated that in Canada less than ten subcontractors meet the criteria of tier 1 suppliers. Certain firms have adapted, notably the Magna Corporation and the Woodbridge Group, although both have entered into joint venture agreements with Japanese owned subcontractors.

How far, then, has Japanization been introduced in the area of buyer-supplier relations? JIT supply systems were operated by half of the firms, with one more saying that they planned its introduction. The firms who had implemented JIT were all automotive/auto component firms; with the exception of one CTV producer, only one auto firm did not use it. For those firms who had not used such a system there were clear reasons why it was inappropriate; four used large amounts of semi-finished products/raw materials as their main input (such as plastics, steel) in which JIT supply was not feasible, particularly given the volumes they required. An important wider issue is, of course, illustrated by this point, that JIT systems are to an extent industry-specific, as are a number of aspects of Japanization.

However, it is worth examining in more detail the JIT systems being operated by these firms. In the main, delivery was of the daily delivery, not multiple deliveries, type, although this was partly owing to the infancy of plants; the evidence from American plants is that it is far more extensive. The CAMI plant at Ingersoll is a good example of these tentative moves towards the system. They were introducing JIT deliveries on selected components; the majority of suppliers will be within a four-hour drive time, but subcontractors were being encouraged to open new capacity nearer than this. Daikyo Magna, for example, were to supply them with plastic-injected moulded parts from a factory at Tillsonburg, thirty minutes drive away from the main plant. They will supply CAMI just-in-time with four-hour windows. CAMI will give DDM orders of six months but on the Friday of each week will indicate the exact amounts that they need for the following week. Other plants, such as the Woodbridge plant at St Mary's, will operate on a similar basis.

A second facet is obtaining components from a single source; only six of the firms reported such a policy, although eight reported close links with suppliers, with the respondents again concentrated in the automobile sector. CAMI are one such firm; it was attempting to establish long-term relationships with suppliers and concentrating on a small number of big suppliers grouped into a first tier. The firm was also attempting to introduce quality-assured supplies, thus eliminating inward inspection and inefficiencies. CAMI carefully audited suppliers on quality, finance, production methods, industrial relations, and other factors. Only three of the eight Japanese-owned subcontractors supplied just-in-time, although two delivered daily. Four offered quality-assured supplies and all but one acted, at least to certain firms, as sole supplier. All reported long-term contracts and all but one reported close technical collaboration. Indeed, one maintained that a prerequisite for supplying to OEM's at the tier 1 level was being a "full service supplier" – including the provision of design, modelling, engineering, and service.

Given tentative moves to Japanese buyer-supplier relationships, how far did work organization follow this trend? Eight used quality circles, for example, and many displayed the more obvious signs such as single status. There was also evidence of greater flexibility at a shop-floor level. Honda workers, for example, were employed to carry out a range of functions without rigid job descriptions or pay classifications, as were those at CAMI, and all company employees have to spend some of their time "on the line." Japanese plants have also introduced the notion of team working; at Toyota, for example, functions were carried out by teams of between four and eight "multi-skilled" workers in which the team leader plays a crucial role. A great deal of responsibility for productivity and quality was placed at the team level. As Jim Cameron, CAMI's vice-president of personnel says: "We won't have a lot of time and motion engineers figuring out better ways to do the job ... We will have a well trained workforce that knows how to – on an organized basis – problem solve ... The system will allow for awesome speed to make changes in the work place immediately ... one of the keys to Suzuki's success, from what we've seen, is how quickly they are able to implement suggestions and how open they are to suggestions from the people who are the experts on the shop floor" (quoted in *Toronto Star*, 24 July 1988).

A similar attitude exists at Honda. The plant was still building up to full production slowly at the time of interview, whereas the Canadian plant manager contested that in a comparable Big Three plant they would have rushed as quickly as possible into production without worrying about quality.

JAPANIZATION: THE EMULATORS

Canadian based-industries and companies are trying to emulate aspects of Japanese practices. However, the problems of companies attempting to introduce such practices do not necessarily mean that such transfer is not feasible, but rather but that there may be initial problems or resistance to change. The focus here will be on two industries – steel and automotives. These industries have been chosen for two main reasons: they are, in many ways, the most amenable to many of the features outlined earlier, and they are the best documented.

The Canadian Steel Industry

The Canadian steel industry, like those in the majority of OECD countries, underwent a fundamental restructuring in the 1980s, following a fall in demand from consuming industries (particularly automobiles and construction), increased competition because of a growth in capacity in newly industrializing countries (NIC's), and the substitution of new materials (see the chapter by Masi in this volume).[35]

In 1988, 70 per cent of Canadian steel output was produced by three companies, Stelco, Dofasco and Algoma, with these three being reduced to two by the takeover of Algoma by Dofasco. In the 1980s all three companies streamlined their operations and cut their workforce. Despite this downsizing in the Canadian steel industry, the crisis was not of the magnitude of the industry in the United States or Western Europe, partly because the inherent conservatism of these companies in the two previous decades had led to far lower rates of expansion. Moreover, the end users themselves, particularly the auto industry, fared far better in Canada than industries in other countries, notably the United States. Finally, the restructuring process has not been so painful due to the technological proficiency, efficiency, and profitability of the Canadian steel industry.[36]

Blyton *et al.*'s 1989 study of the two largest, fully integrated producers and two minor provincially owned companies found a number of aspects of Japanization. A number of common strategies have been employed by the Canadian companies in response to the changed market demand situation in the 1980s: a streamlining of the workforce; a major increase in overtime; and major technological investments.

It is in the field of overtime worked that the effects of Japanization are most obviously felt. Blyton *et al.* argue that this reflects a management policy of meeting demand in-house rather than using outside contractors. However, they argue that it is also a reflection of the adoption by end users of JIT production systems which has led to reduced buffer stocks in, amongst others, automobile companies. Thus steel companies needed to smooth production planning and respond much quicker to changes in client demands.

While JIT systems require quicker lead times, total quality control programs of end users also impose demands. The interviewees in the Blyton et al. study clearly pointed to greater demands by customers to the quality produced and greater specificity of the product. In many respects this is in turn driven by market demands of customers; automobiles, for example, are increasingly being sold with guarantees on rust prevention as standard even on cheaper product ranges. The implication of this for the steel industry is an increased demand for special steels such as electro-plated and galvanized steels.

Blyton *et al.* also found new relations being formed between producer and clients; product design, for example, was often more collaborative or even client-led and customers were insisting on site-checks for quality standards. It is, therefore, evident that a policy of "getting metal out of the door" – first applied to Fordist production methods in the auto industry – is no longer sufficient. The Japanese auto producers, for example, have been relatively slow to turn to Canadian steel producers and have made it plain that quality standards must first be met; if not, they will continue to use imported steel from Japan despite the price differential.

Accompanying these features of Japanization was the concentration upon a core workforce, although ironically this led to a decline in casual labour in the steel industry. In line with the greater demands of quality from consumers, Blyton *et al.* reported moves to upgrade and/or retrain existing workers and, where possible, to recruit workers with higher educational standards. Moreover, in-process controls were being introduced, with measured and monitoring of production throughout the process, including systematic and formal attention given to the quality of work of each employee.

There were also moves to increase the numbers of engineers and scientists in management positions and these, inevitably, did not tend to be drawn from the shop floor as has traditionally been the case. Dofasco also sent hundreds of employees to study best practice in Germany and Japan and, since 1984, implemented Statistical Process Control (SPC) training and quality awareness seminars. Similarly Stelco devolved responsibility down to the shop-floor worker who was now responsible for a greater variety of tasks and skills, including SPC. They were attempting, in other words, to employ a smaller but more highly skilled workforce. This was reflected in their 1987 corporate reorganization program which decentralized responsibility and accountability to "strategic business units."

The steel industry, therefore, has undergone a partial transformation to Japanization. However, it is arguable that the moves towards Japanization are customer-driven, as opposed to the automobile industry where they are competitor-driven. Thus, while Canadian steel is still considerably cheaper than that produced in Japan or even in the United States, Canada's steel industry will increasingly have to compete on the basis of quality as well as price. This is likely to be the case as the free trade agreement comes into effect and Canada's previously protected steel industry comes into open competition with American steel producers, who have themselves been the subject of joint venture activity with Japanese steel producers eyeing the market created by Japanese auto transplants.[37]

The Canadian Automotive Industry

Canada has no indigenous motor industry, at least in terms of automobile manufacturers. So when discussing the Japanization of the Canadian auto industry what we are essentially looking at is changes in the operation of the Big Three branch plants in Canada, Ford, General Motors, and Chrysler, as well as the supply industry.

The Auto Pact in 1965 precipitated a period of rapid growth in the Canadian industry, but this began to slow in the 1970s after a combination of oil price shocks and penetration of markets by other international competitors, notably the Japanese. The Big Three producers have responded in a variety of ways to this crisis. General Motors alone has employed a vast array of different strategies at different plants. Many of these strategies, however, are closely akin to the Japanization concept and, indeed, this is seen in its most explicit form in Ford's After Japan (AJ) program.

Rutherford has summarized these responses:

- accelerated use of computerization
- joint ventures
- restructuring of parts delivery systems towards JIT systems
- improvements in product technology
- the forging of a "new deal" with labour to emphasize greater employee participation, fewer job classifications, increased flexibility in work arrangements, increased training and retraining, and a new emphasis on cooperation.[38]

Looking at the last item on Rutherford's list, there have been moves towards a greater emphasis placed upon recruitment and training in the Big Three auto companies, which is in itself a response to a number of changes within these organizations: greater shop-floor responsibility, task flexibility, and the use of in-process controls, to mention only three. The entry requirements for new production workers at the AMC/Renault Brampton plant (now owned by Chrysler), include a grade twelve diploma. All applicants were required to attend a three-day intensive assessment program, including aptitude test and psychological testing. Holmes notes the rise of cultural training as part of training and retraining programs, designed to strengthen commitment to production and the company. This is exemplified in a six-day retraining program at GM's Oshawa truck plant, 70 per cent of which is devoted to "cultural change training" and to induction in Statistical Process Control (SPC) methods.[39]

The search for greater flexibility has been introduced within workplaces agreed to by unions under the threat of subcontracting of, and reductions in, volume. In addition, a number of the auto producers have introduced quality circles and team working. Ironically, quality of working life programs were introduced in GM in 1970s but were abandoned. Since 1980 GM has introduced the team concept – essentially a shift of job responsibility to shop floor based teams – into all its new plants and some of its older ones.[40]

One final aspect of Japanization which the auto producers appear to be introducing is in the area of buyer-supplier relations. There are moves to try and localize component manufacture and introduce greater collaboration.[41] In the case of Chrysler, it is operating a strict JIT system at one of their plants, with a one-hour batch of part-finished goods acting as a buffer to production line interruptions. Seats, for example, are delivered to the plant four times a day from an adjacent supplier with five hours' notice of the number and style of seats required.[42] As a note of caution, however, whenever JIT systems are first implemented the auto producers often start with relatively easy components such as seats.

Perhaps the best illustration of an attempt at Japanization of a Canadian-based auto company is General Motors.[43] In 1984 General Motors of Canada was one of the largest manufacturing companies in Canada and the largest automotive manufacturer with 45 per cent of total vehicle production. Despite its relative success, the company faced a number of major difficulties in the early 1980s, represented in declining market share; their share of the passenger car market, for example, declined from 49 to 33 per cent between 1979 and 1985. The company therefore decided upon a major restructuring of its production and management systems involving the accelerated use of new technological and innovatory management practices and approaches.

Included in this strategy was a massive investment program of over $4 billion, half of which is to be spent on the GM "Autoplex" facility at Oshawa. Various new technologies in the Autoplex will encourage continuous employee involvement in production problems, with work groups of between eight and fifteen operators. The Autoplex will have a JIT inventory system which will be extended to parts suppliers who will have to meet the requisite quality standards and will be encouraged to collaborate in design at an early stage. Some 40 per cent of parts will be produced within four hours' time. Production of seats, at nearby Whitby, starts only two hours before they are installed on the production line. Interestingly, this represents a move towards vertical disintegration, as seats were previously produced in house. Indeed, this process is not confined to the OEM's, as Provost, a large component manufacturer, is now contracting out electrical components and fibreglass finishing.[44] Production will be carried out using new technologies which allow for smaller production runs, faster tool changes, and flexible machining. This new technology is being introduced with significant work reorganization, including a significant reduction of job classifications, job consolidations, the transfer of supervisory responsibility to production workers, increased training and retraining in new tasks, and continuous employee involvement and work group problem-solving.

The Autoplex, therefore, implies a significant shift by the company towards Japanization. However, there is a large gap between intention and successful implementation, which is contingent on the co-ordination of a number of constituent parts. Other of GM's revolutionary strategies, such as the Saturn plant in Tennessee, have yet to come to fruition. Nevertheless, it is clear that the company intends to take on board at least some aspects of the Japanese model.

THE IMPLICATIONS FOR CANADIAN LABOUR

This chapter has illustrated that the extent of Japanese investment is limited, albeit growing quickly in certain industries such as automobiles. It is now time to consider the important implications of these developments for organized labour in Canada, since these may ultimately be more far-reaching than the trends noted above.

The first implication is that the influx of Japanese plants into Canada and their non-unionized status will further erode the numbers of union members and hence union density.[45] This occurs at a time when union membership in Canada is considerably below levels in other OECD countries and is falling, though it is still above American levels. While these jobs would apparently seem to be new jobs, they are likely to lead to an absolute *and* relative decline in union levels (assuming these plants remain largely non-union), as they are likely to eventually replace jobs in North American owned unionized plants. Nowhere is this more apparent than in the automobile industry, where new Japanese-owned capacity is already leading the Big Three North American producers to revise downwards their capacity requirements for the 1990s, and is likely to foreshadow a considerable battle for market share during the coming decade.

The second, and wider, implication of Japanese investment is likely to be the demonstration effect of the new working practices being implemented in these plants. This is most apparent in the indigenous automobile industry which faces the most direct challenge. These patterns may also spread, however, to other industries; certainly there has been a fairly widespread diffusion of new working practices, such as flexibility deals, in Britain.

The absence of a union at a plant does not, of course, necessarily imply a weakening of the workforce or of lower wages. Indeed, non-unionized corporations such as IBM and Michelin have used a high-wage policy to discourage workers from organizing. All of the evidence, however, suggests that employees in non-union plants in general receive lower remuneration and the wage rates in the Japanese automobile transplants in Canada vis-à-vis the Big Three producers reflect this. For example, hourly wage rates in 1986 in the Big Three producers were estimated to be C$18.6; two years later in the Japanese transplants they varied between $15 and $18.[46] Moreover, terms and conditions of employment are far wider than simple remuneration; job gradings, descriptions, and other matters also come into the framework. Of course, the presence of a union does not necessarily imply a strong bargaining position.[47]

Organized labour in Canada is therefore likely to face considerable battles on a number of fronts in the coming years. The first battle will be for recognition in the new Japanese transplants. The second will be to negotiate conditions of work in non-Japanese plants which are aping the Japanese style. While the Canadian Auto Workers have been at the forefront of these battles for some time, other unions may soon have to follow.

NOTES

I appreciate the help given to me by Nick Oliver, Barry Wilkinson, Paul Blyton, Andrea Gorham, Steve Hill, Gill Ursell and Tod Rutherford. Funds were provided for the research in the second section by the Canadian High Commission in London and the Department of External Affairs in Ottawa via a Canadian Studies Research Award.

1 P.J. Turnbull, "The Japanisation of Production and Industrial Relations at Lucas Electrical," *Industrial Relations Journal* 17 (1986): 193–206.
2 N. Oliver and B. Wilkinson, *The Japanisation of British Industry* (Oxford: Basil Blackwell 1988).
3 A. Mair, R. Florida, and M. Kenney, "The New Geography of Automobile Production: Japanese Transplants in North America," *Economic Geography* 64 (1988): 352–75.
4 R. Child-Hill, M. Indergaard, and K. Fujika, "Flat Rock, Home and Mazda: The Social Impact of a Japanese Company on an American Com-

munity," paper presented to the Eighth Annual International Automotive Conference, University of Michigan, 1988. J. Morris and R. Imrie, *The End of Adversarialism: The Adaptation of Japanese-Style Buyer Supplier Relations in a Western Context* (London: Macmillan, forthcoming); J. Morris, "New Technologies, Flexible Working Practices and Socio-Spatial Differentiation: Some Observations from the U.K.," *Society and Space* 6 (1988): 301–19; J. Morris, "Japanese Inward Investment and the Importation of Subcontracting Complexes," *Area* 29, no. 3 (1989): 269–77.

5 M.A. Cusamano, *The Japanese Automobile Industry: Technology and Management at Nissan and Toyota* (Cambridge, Mass.: Council of East Asian Studies 1985); C. Littler, *The Development of the Labour Process in Capitalist Societies* (London: Heinemann 1982).

6 S. Sethi, N. Namiki, and C. Swanson, *The False Promise of the Japanese Miracle* (London: Pitman 1984).

7 JAMA Canada, *Japanese Automobile Industry in Canada* (Willowdale, Ontario: JAMA 1986).

8 JETRO, *Japanese Small Business Responds Big in an Era of Diversification and Sophistication* (Tokyo: JETRO 1987).

9 J. Kendall, "Why Japanese Workers Work," *Management Today* (January 1984): 72–75.

10 Y. Monden, *Toyota Production System* (Atlanta, Georgia: Industrial Engineering and Management Press 1983); M. Sako, "Buyer–Supplier Relationships in Britain: A Case of Japanisation," paper presented to the Japanisation of British Industry conference, Cardiff, 1987. P. Sheard, "Auto Production Systems in Japan: Organisation and Locational Features," *Australian Geographical Studies* 21 (1983): 44–68.

11 C. Johnson, *MITI and the Japanese Miracle: The Growth of Industrial Policy, 1925–1975* (Stanford, California: Stanford University Press 1982); I.C. Magaziner and T.M. Hout, *Japanese Industrial Policy* (London: Policy Studies Institute 1980).

12 J.C. Abbeglen and G. Stalk, *Kaisha: The Japanese Corporation* (New York: Basic Books 1985).

13 J. Morris, *The Changing Industrial Structure of Canada in the 1980's: The Role of Japanese Foreign Direct Investment, Report submitted to Canadian High Commission* (London 1989).

14 J. Buchan, "Take-over talk puts Zenith into play," *Financial Times*, 26 June 1988.

15 S. Ackroyd, G. Burrell, M. Hughes, and A. Whitaker, "The Japanisation of British Industry," *Industrial Relations Journal* 19, no. 2 (1988): 11–23.

16 Morris, *The Changing Industrial Structure of Canada*; J. Morris, "Japanese Manufacturing Investment in Canada: Regional Presence and Integration Strategies" in J. Morris, ed., *Japan and the Global Economy* (London: Routledge, forthcoming).

17 R. Blain and G. Norcliffe, "Japanese Investment in Canada and Canadian Exports to Japan, 1965–84," *Canadian Geographer* 32, no. 2 (1988): 141–50.
18 J. Langley, "Japanese Investment in North America: The New Wave," paper presented to the Conference Board of Canada's International Business Outlook Conference, Toronto 1987.
19 JAMA Canada, *Japanese Automobile Industry*.
20 Mair, Florida, and Kenney, "New Geography of Automobile Production."
21 Morris, "Japanese Manufacturing Investment"; Morris, *The Changing Industrial Structure of Canada*.
22 P. Dicken, "The Changing Geography of Japanese Foreign Direct Investment in Manufacturing Industry: A Global Perspective," *Environment and Planning A* 20 (1988): 633–54.
23 J. Morris, *Japanese Manufacturing in the EEC: Report to DG1* (Brussels 1987).
24 Child-Hill, Indergaard, and Fujika, "Flat Rock, Home and Mazda."
25 N. Hunter, "GM Canada, Suzuki, are set to build $500 million Auto plant in Ontario," *Globe and Mail*, 28 August 1986.
26 Mair, Florida, and Kenney, "New Geography of Automobile Production"; Child-Hill, Indergaard and Fujika, "Flat Rock, Home and Mazda."
27 J. Daw, "Japanese-style hiring hall knocks auto workers boots off," *Toronto Star*, 24 July 1988: F1.
28 J. Daw, "Honda settles in," ibid., 12 July 1987: F1.
29 J. Utting, "Team Toyota," ibid., 24 April 1988: F2.
30 United Auto Workers, "U.S. Auto Jobs: The Problem is Bigger than Japanese Imports," *U.A.W. Research Department* (Detroit, 1987).
31 D. Climenhaga, "U.A.W. will raise hell if Chrysler sells plants," *Globe and Mail*, 20 February 1988: 35.
32 R. Imrie and J. Morris, "Large Firm–Small Firm Links: The Changing Nature of Sub-Contracting in Wales," paper presented to Eleventh International Small Business Conference, Cardiff, 1988; Oliver and Wilkinson, *The Japanisation of British Industry*; Sako, "Buyer–Supplier Relations"; E. Schoenberger, "Technological and Organizational Change in Automobile Production: Spatial Implications," *Regional Studies* 21 (1987): 197–214.
33 Mair, Florida and Kenney, "New Geography of Automobile Production."
34 Ibid.
35 This section draws extensively from P. Blyton, G. Ursell, A. Gorham, and S. Hill, *Human Resource Management in Canadian and UK Work Organisations: Strategies for Workplace Flexibility*, Interim report to Canadian High Commission, 2 vols. (London 1989).
36 J. Bradbury, "Technical Change and the Restructuring of the North American Steel Industry" in K. Chapman and G. Humphrys, *Technical Change and Industrial Policy* (Oxford: Basil Blackwell 1987).
37 I. Rodger, "Kobe Steel to set up US venture," *Financial Times* 15 February 1989: 6.

38 T. Rutherford, "Work Reorganisation in the Canadian Automobile Industry," paper presented to the Employment and Economic Change in North America conference, Cardiff 1988, 11.

39 D. Robertson and J. Wareham, *Technological Change in the Auto Industry: Canadian Auto Workers Technology Project* (Willowdale, Ontario: CAW 1987); J. Holmes, "The Impact of New Production Technologies on the Organisation of Labour in the North American Automobile Industry," paper presented to the IGU Commission on Industrial Change, Krakow, Poland 1987.

40 Holmes, "Impact of New Production Technologies"; J. Slaughter, "The Team Concept in the US Auto Industry: Implications for Unions," paper presented to The Japanisation of British Industry Conference, Cardiff 1987.

41 P. Kumar, "Changing Labour Relations in the Auto Industry: A Case Study of General Motors" (School of Industrial Relations, Queen's University, Kingston, Ontario 1988).

42 Blyton, Ursell, Gorham and Hill, *Human Resource Management*.

43 Kumar, "Changing Labour Relations."

44 Robertson and Wareham, "Technological Change".

45 R. Adams, "Industrial Relations Systems: Canada in Comparative Perspective" in J. Anderson, M. Gunderson, and A. Ponak, eds., *Union Management Relations in Canada* (Toronto: Addison Wesley 1989).

46 J. Daw, "Union wages are unaffordable, auto part maker says," *Toronto Star*, 27 January 1987: D1; J. Daw, "World auto wages," ibid., 3 May 1987: F1; Author's survey.

47 S. Crowther and P. Garrahan, "Invitation to Sunderland: Corporate Power and the Local Economy," *Industrial Relations Journal* 19, no. 1 (1988): 51–59. N. Oliver and B. Wilkinson, "Japanese Inward Investment in Wales: The Trade Union Response," *Welsh Economic Review* 1, no. 1 (1988): 50–55.

10 New Staples and Mega-Projects: Reaching the Limits to Sustainable Development

PAUL PHILLIPS

The association of Canadian economic development with a small number of raw material exports (staples) has been at the heart of interpretations of Canadian economic history and growth since the early writings of Mackintosh and Innis in the 1920s.[1] Though a resource-based economy has been the generally accepted interpretation for the Canadian pattern of growth in the early period, a major change in the nature of the staples has developed in the twentieth century from that of earlier eras. Whereas the earlier staple trades demanded commercial capital and investment in infrastructure, particularly in transportation, the new staples of the twentieth century, namely mining, forest products, pulp and paper, hydro, oil and gas, but not wheat, required enormous investments in fixed capital without proportionate demands for development-supporting investments in infrastructure for forward and final demand linkages.[2] Large backward linkages did exist, but for the most part these were either captured by foreign manufacturers, leading to massive importation of capital goods and foreign investment, or were manifested in the initial construction boom. In this manner, Canada became addicted to the economic steroids of resource mega-projects for employment and foreign debt for capital. Canada's long-recognized reliance on exports has intensified existing problems of structural and regional imbalance.

The inflation of international commodity prices in the late 1960s and early 1970s masked the extent of the early symptoms of stagnation that followed the long postwar expansion and the degree to which the structure and pattern of Canadian trade was changing.

Table 10.1
Percentage of Canadian Exports to and Imports from the United States, 1946–87
(five-year averages)

Period	Exports	Exports excluding autos under Auto Pact	Imports
1946–50	35.0	49.1	67.3
1951–55	38.2	59.0	72.2
1956–60	55.5	59.2	69.4
1961–65	63.9	55.5	68.5
1966–70	68.5	59.4	72.3
1971–75	72.5	59.2	69.1
1976–80	75.6	61.7	70.4
1981–85	74.8	65.3	70.7
1986–87 (2 yr.)	76.5	68.3	68.5

SOURCE: Statistics Canada, *Summary of Canadian International Trade*, CS 65–001, various issues

RECENT PATTERNS IN CANADIAN TRADE: GOODS

Exports as a percentage of Gross Domestic Product (GDP) rose from 22 per cent in 1970–73 to 27 per cent in 1985–87, a formidable dependence on external trade for domestic aggregate demand. Moreover, the dependence on the American economy both for markets and as sources of imports has not only been excessive in the past, but for exports is also increasing (see Table 10.1). The statistics indicate that Canada's export trade is becoming less dependent on natural resources and diversifying more into manufactured end products, but this is an illusion because it is accounted for almost entirely by the growth of intra-firm transfers of autos and parts under the provisions of the Auto Pact. If we exclude trade under the Auto Pact, Table 10.2 indicates our meagre progress in developing exports of end product manufactures.

The concentration of Canadian exports in a small number of primary sector products reveals that almost two-thirds of our non-auto exports are accounted for by an excessive reliance on primary industry products. The forest products industry alone accounts for approximately the same amount of exports as the entire non-auto end-product manufacturing sector combined.

Moreover, there is every indication that we will not be able to rely on these traditional sectors for continued growth in the future. The reason is that existing, easily accessible (low-cost), non-renewable resources are being depleted, forcing industry to spend large amounts of capital in exploration and development of new properties, while renewable resources are reaching the limits of sustainable yields. The

Table 10.2
End-Product Exports as a Percentage of Total Exports Excluding Automotive Trade,
1946–87 (five-year averages)

Period	Total	USA	Rest of World★
1946–50	10.7	5.6	20.8
1951–55	7.5	7.2	16.3
1956–60	7.3	6.3	15.2
1961–65	10.3	11.2	14.9
1966–70	15.1	18.2	16.7
1971–75	16.1	18.1	17.8
1976–80	15.6	16.2	21.2
1981–85	18.7	18.9	19.7
1986–87 (2 yr.)	22.2	25.1	18.3

SOURCE: As Table 10.1.

★ includes non-Auto Pact trade in motor vehicles and parts with the rest of the world.

major non-renewable staple industries are mining, and oil and gas. In the base-metal mining industry known reserves have been declining since the early 1980s, despite recent high export prices. According to the chairman of the Mining Association of Canada, between 1982 and 1987 reserves of lead, zinc, copper, and nickel fell by between 20 and 35 per cent. At the same time, employment in the industry fell by 24 per cent.[3] While coal reserves are adequate, exports are plagued by high transport costs, poor quality (low thermal value), and stagnant prices.[4] In any case, given the recent environmental concern with acid rain, the future of the world coal market does not appear very bright.

Also, Canada is becoming a high-cost producer. Even if a major expansion in exploration does take place and is successful in augmenting mine reserves, the costs are enormous. The estimated average cost of opening a new mine is from around $25 million to $50 million – or from $500,000 to $1 million per job created. As one spokesman for the coal industry recently remarked, "the surface mines of the 1990s and beyond will be so computer-dependent that manpower will be reduced to one-third of current levels" – and with little in the way of backward or forward manufacturing linkages.[5] Therefore, even if in the short or medium run exports could be expanded significantly, labour income and employment gains would be small.

In the case of energy exports (oil and gas), the long-term prospects are equally dim. Production of relatively low-cost, conventional crude oil, according to the National Energy Board, is forecast to peak in the eighties and to decline by around 70 per cent by the end of the century. Replacing Western Canadian conventional crude by oilsands, heavy oil upgrading, or frontier sources would increase production costs by as

Table 10.3
Percentage of Exports by Major Commodity Groups, 1985–87

Commodity group	All exports	Non-Auto Pact exports
Meat, fish and cereals	6.3	8.8
Energy (petroleum, gas, coal, electricity)	9.3	13.0
Metals and ores (incl. iron and steel)	10.8	15.0
Wood and paper	15.0	20.9
Chemicals	4.8	6.7
Auto Pact trade	28.1	–
Total	74.3	64.4

SOURCE: As Table 10.1.

much as two hundred per cent. For natural gas, "projections made by the NEB in January 1982 suggested that there would be little exportable surplus (beyond licenses existing at that time) from 1990 onward and that 1997 would be the year when exports based on conventional supplies would have to cease." More recent projections are more optimistic but serve to extend the date by a few years.[6]

The export potential of renewable resources is likewise limited. The future of agricultural exports is clouded both by demand factors, particularly the massive subsidies currently offered by the United States and the European Economic Community, and by supply factors such as the declining availability of land owing to urban encroachment and the deterioration of soil quality because of salinization and soil erosion. This leads to the conclusion that a major commitment of resources to research and to new agricultural practices, including irrigation, is necessary to maintain existing levels of agricultural exports.[7] The declining state of fish stocks on both coasts is a cause of major concern and a sharp reminder that catches are currently in excess of sustainable yields. In the case of hydro, the NEB forecasts exports to peak in 1987.[8] Quebec, and to a lesser extent Manitoba, are the only provinces with significant undeveloped hydro resources. The long-run potential for nuclear power as an export commodity has virtually evaporated on grounds of both ecology and economy.

By far the most important resource export industry in Canada over the past century and a half has been forest products – particularly softwood-based wood and pulp and paper products. The potential for further growth in these industries is not great.

If realistic reserves are specified, then only Alberta has much scope for expanding softwood production using existing forest stands. For the nation as a whole, at a 2 per cent growth rate of harvesting, a deficit would exist by 1995 ...

In the longer term, even with some increase in utilization of hardwood forest reserves, Canada will face a major challenge in sustaining, let alone increasing, her forest harvests.[9]

Indeed, our failure to reforest will probably result in a reduction in our exportable surplus of forest products unless a major reforestation program is initiated. Already British Columbia sawmills have been forced to close because of a scarcity of logs.

To some extent, the relative scarcity of raw materials has served to cushion the effects of our tightening supplies by pushing up export prices and improving the terms of trade, the ratio of export prices to import prices. (When the terms of trade rise, Canadians can buy more imports with less exports.) However, these tightening supplies should also serve to warn us that, in the longer run, resource export-led growth is not sustainable.

A second consequence of this dependence on resource exports has been the underdevelopment of the capital goods sector in Canada. This is demonstrated by the reliance on imports for industrial machinery and other equipment, in particular computers and other electronic gear (see Table 10.4). Over a third of all non-auto trade is accounted for by machinery and equipment (not including aircraft and parts where Canadian exports and imports are roughly in balance). Even in agricultural machinery, where Canada once was an industry leader, imports exceeded exports by more than three to one in the most recent three-year period. It should be noted that these imports embody the new technologies where Canadian participation is notoriously weak.

RECENT PATTERNS OF CANADIAN TRADE: SERVICES

If the pattern of our trade in commodities is a cause of concern, the pattern and trends of our trade in services should be a cause for anxiety. Canada's deficit in the service sectors have been escalating rapidly in recent years. This is particularly the case for business services, the largest contributor to Canada's deficit in its balance of payments in services. (See the chapter by Gertler for a fuller discussion.) Perhaps more important, the deficit is particularly large in payments related to technology (research and development, royalties, patents and trade marks) and to management services, both a function of the degree of foreign ownership of the Canadian manufacturing sector. In the last three years business services accounted for almost 40 per cent of our international payments for services but almost 60 per cent of the net deficit in the balance of service payments.

Table 10.4
Percentage of Imports by Major Commodity Groups, 1985–87

Commodity group	All imports	Non-Auto Pact imports
Meat, fish, fruit and vegetables	3.1	4.4
Chemicals	5.3	7.5
Machinery (general purpose, industrial and agricultural)	9.6	13.6
Other equipment (mainly electronic including computers)	15.2	21.6
(computers alone)	4.0	5.6
Auto Pact trade	29.6	–
Total	62.8	47.1

SOURCE: As Table 10.1.

The second major area of business services within which Canada appears to be poorly situated to take advantage of strong growth in international transactions is in insurance and finance, where Canada's imports of services are almost 80 per cent higher than our exports, and account for an average of approximately 16 per cent of the net deficit in services in 1985–86.

The third major area where Canada has a large and growing deficit in service payments is in travel, a category also expected to grow relative to trade in goods because of its income elasticity and, not incidentally, the coldness of the Canadian winters.

Indeed, there is very little to create confidence in the potential returns to exports of services. The only categories in which Canada has had any consistent strength in recent years has been in consulting and professional services, commissions, and tooling and automotive, but they are dwarfed by the deficit in the other sectors. In the case of the latter, they are again primarily a reflection of the administrative arrangements under the North American auto pact.

Give these export-import structures and recent patterns of growth, what can be expected to be the effect on the future of Canadian economic and regional development?

TRADE, INVESTMENT, AND EMPLOYMENT

The patterns of trade in goods and services outlined above give little indication of any significant diminution in Canada's export dependence on natural resources in raw, crude, or fabricated form, the outputs of the primary industries and primary manufacturing. As employers, these are declining sectors. As Table 10.6 indicates, the goods-producing sectors generally are employing a smaller and smaller proportion of the

Table 10.5
International Transaction in Services, Selected Years, 1969–87
(balance of payments by category)

Category	1969	1981	1985	1986	1987
			(million dollars)		
Travel	−214	−1,116	−2,402	−1,166	−2,529
Shipping	− 60	440	208	− 16	− 107
Business services	−507	−2,277	−2,402	−3,599	−3,952
Consult & prof.	− 56	173	731	441	na
Manage & admin.	− 72	− 519	− 778	− 755	na
R&D	− 40	− 199	− 296	− 429	na
Commissions	46	86	156	157	na
Royalties, patents, trade marks	−132	− 655	− 997	−1,047	na
Insurance	− 30	− 113	− 268	− 401	na
Other finance	−	− 276	− 341	− 630	na
Communication	− 8	− 56	23	14	na
Tooling and auto	− 72	300	117	177	na
Gov't transactions	− 32	− 507	− 627	− 555	− 565
Other services	52	46	100	104	108
Total	−771	−3,414	−4,825	−5,231	−7,045

SOURCE: Statistics Canada, *Canada's International Transactions in Services*, CS 67–203, various issues

na: not available

labour force. It should be noted that in the case of agriculture and forestry absolute employment has fallen over this period by almost 40 per cent. While absolute employment growth did occur in mining, utilities, and manufacturing until 1981, it was very slow; and none of these had recovered to the pre-recession 1981 level of employment by 1987. All the other industries have either continued to expand employment steadily or with a slight interruption in the severe 1982–83 recession.

The pattern of investment and the distribution of the capital stock supporting recent economic growth, however, have been quite different. While services, broadly defined, have been responsible for the majority of new jobs, investment has been disproportionally concentrated in the goods-producing sectors, particularly in mining and utilities (see Table 10.7). As a result, these industries have become even more capital-intensive. This is dramatically illustrated in Table 10.8. The only staple export industry with a growth in capital-labour ratio of less than the all industry average was fishing (which reflects the uniqueness of that industry, particularly government protection of its labour-intensive organization).

What is also obvious is that the goods-producing export sector is highly capital-intensive relative to domestic-oriented end-product manufacturing or services-producing industries (see Table 10.9).

Table 10.6
Distribution of Employment by Industry, 1961–87

Year	Agriculture	Mining	Other primary	Manu-facturing	Const. trans/comm	Util.	Serv.
1961	11.3	1.3	1.7	24.0	14.3	1.2	46.3
1971	6.3	1.6	1.2	22.2	13.7	1.1	53.9
1981	4.4	1.9	1.0	19.4	13.0	1.2	59.2
1987	4.0	1.5	.9	17.1	12.3	1.0	63.2

SOURCE: Statistics Canada, *Labour Force*, CS 71–001, various issues

Table 10.7
Distribution of Investment for Selected Industries*, 1961–86

Year	Agriculture	Forest	Mining	Manu-facturing	Const. trans/comm	Utilities Services (ex.finance)	
1961	6.4	.6	6.1	11.6	12.5	7.2	27.2
1971	4.3	.4	8.1	13.2	10.9	8.7	25.4
1981	5.6	.3	10.9	14.4	11.0	9.1	19.2
1986	2.8	.2	6.9	13.4	8.2	6.4	23.5

SOURCE: Statistics Canada, *National Income and Expenditure Accounts; Annual Estimates*, CS 13–201, various issues

* Figures do not add up to 100% due to the exclusion of some industries, in particular finance.

One direct measure of this is the output per unit of labour. This is documented in Table 10.10, which gives both indexes of GDP per employee by industry, a measure of the relative rates of growth of labour productivity; and indexes of GDP per employee relative to the Canadian average, a measure of the relative labour productivities of the various industry sectors in Canada.

It is apparent that our export sectors generally have either a dramatically higher labour productivity (mining, utilities), or have a growth of productivity that is much faster than the domestic and service sectors in the last few decades (agriculture, forestry, mining, utilities), or both. The one exception to this pattern is fishing and trapping, which is of minor and declining importance in Canada's international trade though important to certain regions, particularly the Atlantic provinces. (It should be noted that forestry includes only primary forestry, not forest products, which are included under primary manufacturing. It is the processed and fabricated products, lumber, and pulp and paper, that comprise the vast majority of Canada's forest-based exports.)

Manufacturing productivity stands very close to the all-industry average in 1984: and similarly, its rate of growth since 1961 has approximated that of the economy as a whole. This, however, obscures

Table 10.8
Capital Stock per Employee by Industry*, 1961–87 (1971 $s per employee)

Year	All Industries	Agriculture	Forest	Fishing	Mining	Manuf.	Constr./Trans./Comm.	Utilities	Services
1961	16,820	10,970	6,940	10,830	69,050	12,200	21,280	255,860	12,030
1971	21,190	18,540	12,320	26,730	95,480	16,010	23,670	351,630	14,380
1981	24,870	30,060	15,490	13,330	120,200	19,660	26,790	409,500	15,420
1986	27,150	28,870	12,710	9,870	168,970	22,390	30,460	503,110	16,500
1987	27,030	27,990	11,910	9,740	171,940	22,660	29,500	515,790	16,650
% change 1961–87	60.7	155.2	71.6	−10.1	149.0	85.7	38.6	101.6	38.4

SOURCE: Calculated from Statistics Canada, *Fixed Capital Flows and Stocks, Historical, 1936–1983*, CS 13–568; Statistics Canada, *Fixed Capital Flows and Stocks*, CS 13–211, various issues; Statistics Canada, *Labour Force*, CS 71–001, various issues.

* Excluding residential housing.

Table 10.9
Capital Stock per Employee in Primary Manufacturing*, 1961–86
(1971 $s per employee)

Year	All manufacturing	Wood industry	Pulp & paper	Primary metals	Petroleum & coal
1961†	12,607	6,750	25,900	7,942	86,022
1971	16,832	11,266	39,548	34,118	100,660
1981	18,778	14,528	41,075	38,358	119,547
1986	20,948	15,609	49,580	44,580	139,669
% change 1961–86	66.2	131.2	90.7	630.3	62.4

SOURCE: Statistics Canada, *Census*, 1986, CS 93–152; and as Table 10.8

* NOTE: The labour force base is different from the previous table which is calculated from labour force survey data. This table is based on census data. This results in a slightly higher capital-to-labour ratio in 1961 and 1971 and a slightly lower ratio in subsequent years. The difference can be compared in the comparable columns. The results, however, should not affect the relative trends or relative ranking.

† 1961 Standard Industrial Classification.

divergent characteristics of primary (export) manufacturing and secondary (end-product) manufacturing. The former have on average significantly higher labour productivities than the latter and, in some cases, have more rapid increases in productivity growth over the recent period. This is also true of the transportation equipment subsector, which includes automobile manufacturing.

Given these trends in labour productivity (and the corollary, the high capital-labour ratios) in the export sectors, the employment gains from increased natural resource exports can be expected to be small and to be diminishing, at least in comparison with the industries oriented to the domestic market, particularly in services. At the same time, expanded natural-resource exports will require disproportionate amounts of capital investment which, given the high propensity to import capital equipment, will either exert downward pressure on the value of the Canadian dollar (which, given current Bank of Canada policy, means upward pressure on interest rates), or encourage foreign financing of that import through foreign ownership (itself encouraged by high domestic Canadian interest rates).

As we have demonstrated, resource-led economic development in Canada is heavily dependent of American demand. In the immediate postwar period, 52 per cent of Canada's exports of food and beverages, crude, and fabricated products went to the United States. In the period 1983 to 1987, the latest for which data are available, the proportion has risen to 69 per cent. While there has undoubtedly been a shift from

Table 10.10
Productivity Indexes: GDP per Employee, 1984

Industry	Index of productivity growth: 1961 = 100	Index of relative productivity: all industries = 100
Total	640	100
Agriculture	919	56
Forestry	718	86
Fishing and trapping	355	44
Mining	731	366
Manufacturing	631	101
Construction	584	111
Trans. & Comm.	642	106
Utilities	896	281
Trade	501	58
Finance	506	249
Service	531	31
Government	548	95

SOURCE: As Tables 10.7, 10.8

Europe as a destination of our exports to the Pacific Rim, in particular Japan, non-continental markets are still of limited importance to overall Canadian growth (though undeniably important in specific regions and industries – for example, grain and coal from Western Canada). Thus, in a very real and material sense, Canada has tied its economic development to that of the United States and to that country's demands for industrial raw materials and energy. This, of course, is even more accentuated by the implementation of the Canada–US trade agreement.

It is still too early in the trade agreement to discern in any detail its impact on restructuring the continental economy. However, from the limited evidence of plant closures, consolidations of operations, and multinational buy-outs of minority shareholders, the expected rationalization of multinational business on a continental basis has begun. This rationalization will not likely favour Canadian manufacturing. In a report to Ontario on the implications for American subsidiaries in Canada of a trade agreement, Baranson writes: "Under free market forces, where least-cost procurement rules would prevail, and with the retrenchment to automated, computer integrated manufacturing in the US, most Canadian satellite production facilities, along with any related RD&E facilities would dwindle and disappear."[10]

In a companion study prepared by the Ontario Ministry of Industry, Trade and Technology, manufacturers were classified by their sensitivity to removal of tariff and non-tariff barriers with the United States. Almost one-third of the manufacturing jobs were deemed "highly sensitive," mostly in labour-intensive secondary manufacturing. By contrast, only 12 per cent of manufacturing jobs were deemed secure ("less sensitive"), and were dominated by resource-related and primary manufacturing.[11] The implication of these analyses and projections is obvious: there is now increased reliance on resource-based industries. If realized, therefore, the potential for growth in goods production will depend on expansion of the resource industries and on their employment and income-generating capacity.

RESOURCES, RENTS, AND LABOUR INCOME

As shown above, Canada is reaching the limits of extensive growth in the resource industries. With capital intensification, this translates into stagnant or negative employment growth. What growth, then, can we expect in factor incomes? Income generated in the resource sectors accrues as labour income, rents, and returns to capital (interest, dividends, profits; management, licensing, and similar fees). The amount of income generated is also a function of international commodity prices, which are subject to wide fluctuations but which are not expected to show any consistent upward trend.[12]

Traditionally, the richness of the supply of many resources in Canada resulted in large resource rents, the income generated by the scarcity of the resource itself. In a competitive market, these rents should accrue to the owner of the resources, which means to the crown in Canada where the federal and provincial governments retained ownership of the majority of resources. However, Canadian governments have been manifestly unable, or unwilling, to collect these rents. In the forest products industry, it was the low level of stumpage rates (the taxes charged the lumber companies for cutting timber on crown land) relative to the prices paid by American companies for timber from privately held land, that led the US government to introduce the special softwood lumber duties on exports of lumber from Canada which have since been converted into an export tax. Similar undertaxing of resource rents has been documented for mining and oil and gas.[13] In the fisheries, where "common property" conditions exist, rents have been dissipated through over-capitalization, over-employment, and over-fishing. In agriculture, rents have been appropriated by the financial, transportation and food-handling sectors.[14]

In the mining and forest industries these unappropriated rents have been shared between capital and, after unionization, labour.[15] This has resulted in a high wage structure in these industries, a wage structure that has encouraged the employers, particularly in periods of lower prices and profits, to substitute capital for labour. This has been manifest in both industries in the 1980s and has contributed to the declining ability of the resource industries to employ labour. Additionally, the exhaustion of the most readily accessible reserves, the high cost of exploration, development, and research on new resource supplies, means that the amount of resource rents is falling. In any case, given the degree of foreign ownership, the increase in the capital intensity of production, and the low utilization of Canadian-produced capital goods, rents not collected by governments in Canada will accrue to capital, frequently foreign capital.

Because of the high degree of foreign ownership in the resource sector, a considerable portion of capital income generated in Canada accrues to foreigners. In addition, linkages to the capital-goods sector in Canada are weak and in decline.[16] Though there was a reversal in the trend to foreign control of Canadian industry during the 1970s and early 1980s, owing in part to government action in the establishment of the Foreign Investment Review Agency (FIRA) and of crown resource corporations (in particular Petrocan), recent moves by the Mulroney Conservative government to privatize crown corporations and to dismantle any barriers to foreign investment such as FIRA (as required by the Canada–US trade agreement) do not augur well for the future of Canadian ownership and control of resource income. The only barrier to increased US control is the declining competitiveness of American industry.

THE DECLINE OF AMERICAN HEGEMONY: THE NEW GLOBAL ECONOMY

In the immediate postwar period when Canada was tying its future to the American star, that star was undoubtedly the brightest in the sky. But in the subsequent decades, at least in relative terms, its brilliance has dimmed. In 1953 the United States accounted for 59 per cent of the GDP of OECD countries. By 1984 this had fallen to 37 per cent. American industrial production growth since 1970 has lagged behind all of the industrial seven except Great Britain (whose performance has been sad indeed), a reflection in part of the poor US productivity growth which has trailed even behind Britain. As a consequence, the American share of industrial output and of exports has fallen markedly in the postwar period, even though it remains the world's largest economy (though smaller that the EEC in total).

Bellon and Niosi credit the decline in the American economy to a number of factors:

Internally, the industrial decline of the United States can be explained by changes in the structure of overall demand, by the increasingly marginal position of industry, by the organization and strategy of American manufacturing corporations, and by the absence of a coherent industrial policy. Internationally, the decisive factors have been the rise of competitors, both industrialized and newly industrializing, and the impact of the American defence burden.[17]

However, the relative decline of the United States economy within the orbit of the major industrialized nations is only part of the story. The developed economies collectively are declining in relative importance to the rest of the world, the newly industrialized countries (NICS) in particular. As Hoogvelt has noted, while the NICS have increased their manufacturing sector to between a quarter and a third of their GDP, "the old industrial countries have over the past 20 years [1960–80] experienced 'deindustrialization', an average decline in manufacturing output relative to GDP of 5 per cent since 1960 and an even greater decline of labour employed in industry."[18] She also points out that, in response to protectionist development policies in developing countries, the migration of capital in the form of multinational corporations began to replace trade in goods and services so that by 1971 the value of international trade was less than the value of production by multinationals in foreign countries. In any case, an estimated two-fifths of foreign trade is not, in reality, "trade" in any classic sense, but rather intra-firm transfers within multinational corporations.[19]

In the face of its relative economic decline and subsequent change from a net exporter of goods to a net importer, and from a net creditor to a net debtor nation, the United States has increasingly turned towards "neo-protectionism" – quotas, "voluntary restraints," buy–American preferences, "fair competition" provisions, countervailing duties, and other non-tariff barriers. While for the most part not aimed at Canada, this neo-protectionism has had a powerful influence on Canadian policy and has been a major factor, if not the most important factor, in inducing Canadians to accept complete economic integration with the United States through the trade agreement.

As Bellon and Niosi conclude:

[Canadian] industry's loss of competitiveness, as a result of which it is losing foreign markets and must protect itself against new competitors, and the geographical, economic, political and cultural proximity of the United States are all making Canada move closer to the US in the commercial and industrial spheres.

Canada has been hurt more by the decline of American basic industry and by the obsolete technology it imports from the US than by the neoprotectionist movement in the United States. But the revival of protectionism over the past few years makes Canadian vulnerability clearer than ever, while at the same time giving new life to the free-trade forces. The protectionist threat is one of the main factors, in the short term at least, drawing Canada closer to the United States.[20]

To sum up the argument, therefore, America is becoming increasingly less competitive in the world economy as its industrial sector loses ground relatively to Europe, Japan, and the NICs. Canada, also suffering from declining competitiveness internationally, must turn increasingly to the continental market and to integration with the American economy to avoid being excluded from its most important market by US neo-protectionism and to get behind and benefit from such protection against the rest of the world. However, Canada's traditional exports to the United States, industrial raw materials, face a demand from an industry of declining competitiveness, and a competitive supply from third world countries desperate to export because of their need for foreign exchange to finance essential imports and their growing burden of international debt.

THE PROSPECTS

What are the prospects for export-led development in the future? On the basis of the above analysis, there are few grounds for optimism. Canadian exports are marked by two dominant characteristics – a concentration on crude and processed natural resources, and a concentration on the American market. We may take each in turn.

The concentration on crude and processed natural resources promises diminishing returns (in terms of Canadian development) for a number of reasons. In the first instance, extraction of non-renewable resources leads to the eventual using up of the most economical reserves and, therefore, a decline in resource rents (unless offset by a rise in prices, technological change, or new discoveries). Inevitably, it does mean more investment in exploration or in capital-intensive techniques of production or extraction. However, because of the high degree of foreign ownership, the high propensity to import capital equipment and finance capital, the low labour intensity (high capital intensity of production), the linkage effects and the employment opportunities tend to be low. As the reserves are used up and the extraction processes become more and more capital-intensive, the returns to Canada tend to diminish.

Secondly, the exploitation of renewable resources is reaching the limits of these resources. In conventional economic terms, with fixed land (natural resources), the increased application of capital and labour is bound, sooner or later, to produce diminishing returns except to the extent that these diminishing returns may be off set by technological change which increase the productivity of the factors and of the resource base itself. All of the evidence, however, suggests that rather than adding to the resource base, we have been eroding it and the environment that regenerates it (for example, through deforestation, soil erosion, exhaustion or depletion of fish and seafood stocks; acid rain, salinity of soils, water pollution, ozone depletion). Even if we manage our resource base wisely and ecologically, we are fast approaching the limits of sustainable yields. This means that we are reaching the limits of resource export-based economic growth. Future development, if there is to be any based on our resource industries, must therefore flow from diversification around the resource industries and from further processing and manufacturing of natural resources. Such a strategy is virtually precluded by a number of factors; the absence of a national economic strategy, the degree of foreign ownership of the resource and manufacturing industries, and the restrictive provisions of the Canada–US trade agreement.

The concentration of our export markets in the United States promises to bring diminishing returns for other reasons. The declining international competitiveness of American industry means that US demand for industrial raw materials will be restricted to the continental market, and, therefore, growth of demand is restricted to growth in the continental market within which we must compete with foreign end-products (to the extent they are not excluded or restricted by neo-protectionism) and with foreign sources of raw materials.

The major area within which the United States maintains international competitiveness is in the service, financial, and technology sectors. However, these are sectors that are labour and human capital intensive, and utilize minimal amounts of resource-based inputs. Thus, to the extent that the de-industrialization of the US economy continues to take place, the prospects for resource exports to our major market decline or, at best, stagnate.

The obvious alternative to the United States market are the NICs of Asia. Despite the recent growth of the NICs, Canada has been singularly unsuccessful in diversifying its exports away from dependence on the North American market. In any case, to the extent that Canada is reaching the sustainable limits of exploitation of its renewable resources and are running into diminishing returns in the exploitation of non-renewable resources, diversification will have limited growth or developmental impact.

Finally, the rising capital intensity, the high labour productivity, the degree of foreign ownership, the propensity to import necessary capital equipment, low rates of resource rent taxation, and the limited degree of resource processing before export, all serve to minimize the developmental potential, not only of export growth, but also of existing levels of resource exports. Thus, even from existing exports, we can expect diminishing returns.

NOTES

1 For an extensive bibliography of this literature, see Wallace Clement, "Resources and Staples" in Daniel Drache and Wallace Clement, eds., *The New Practical Guide to Canadian Political Economy* (Toronto: Lorimer 1985).

2 See Morris Altman, "A Revision of Canadian Economic Growth," *Canadian Journal of Economics* 20, no. 1 (1987) and Richard Caves and Richard Holton, *The Canadian Economy* (Boston: Harvard University Press 1961). For the "anti-staple" position, see K.A.H. Buckley, "The Role of Staple Industries in Canadian Development," *Journal of Economic History* 18, no. 4 (1950); E.J. Chambers and D.F. Gordon, "Primary Products and Economic Growth," *Journal of Political Economy* 74, no. 4 (1966); and Richard Pomfret, *The Economic Development of Canada* (Toronto: Methuen 1981).

3 *Globe and Mail*, 26 May 1988: B13; see also ibid., 23 February 1989: B1, for a report of a federal government study which confirms these figures.

4 Bruce Wilkinson, "Canada's Resource Industries: A Survey" in *Canada's Resource Industries and Water Export Policy*, John Whalley, research co-ordinator, study prepared for the Royal Commission on the Economic Union and Development Prospects for Canada (Toronto: University of Toronto Press 1986), 52.

5 *Globe and Mail*, 16 January 1989: B1, B3.

6 Wilkinson, "Resource Industries," 37–40, 46, 48.

7 Ibid., 15–16.

8 Ibid., 57.

9 Ibid., 84–85.

10 Jack Baranson, "Assessment of Likely Impact of a u.s.–Canadian Free Trade Agreement upon the Behaviour of u.s. Industrial Subsidiaries in Canada (Ontario)," Report to the Ontario Ministry of Industry, Trade and Technology, September 1985: 6–7.

11 Ontario Ministry of Industry, Trade and Technology, "Assessment of Direct Employment Effect of Freer Trade for Ontario's Manufacturing Industries," November 1985.

12 For a commodity-by-commodity review of expected supply, demand, and price conditions, see Wilkinson, "Resource Industries."

13 Eric Kierans, *Report on Natural Resource Policy in Manitoba* (Winnipeg: Government of Manitoba 1973), ch. 3; Caves and Holton, *Canadian Economy*, 206–15.

14 Paul Phillips, "Staples, Surplus and Exchange: The Commercial-Industrial Question in the National Policy Period" in Duncan Cameron, ed., *Explorations in Canadian Economic History* (Ottawa: University of Ottawa Press 1985).

15 Lawrence Copithorne, *Natural Resources and Regional Disparities*, study prepared for the Economic Council of Canada (Ottawa: Supply and Services 1979).

16 Wallace Clement, "Debates and Directions: A Political Economy of Resources" in Wallace Clement and Glen Williams, eds., *The New Canadian Political Economy* (Montreal: McGill-Queen's University Press 1989), 46–51.

17 Bertrand Bellon and Jorge Niosi, *The Decline of the American Economy* (Montreal: Black Rose 1988), 21–22 and 28–31.

18 Ankie Hoogvelt, "The New International Division of Labour" in Ray Bush, Gordon Johnston, and David Coates, eds., *The World Order: Socialist Perspectives* (Oxford: Polity 1987), 69.

19 Ibid., 75–76.

20 Bellon and Niosi, *Decline of the American Economy*, 163.

PART FOUR

The Social Costs of Adjustment

11 The Systematic Search for Flexibility: National Competitiveness and New Work Relations

DANIEL DRACHE

The ideological belief in trade as the most effective way to create jobs and a high standard of living poses new problems for the future of collective bargaining everywhere.[1] Market liberalism sees "little pain and a lot of gain" from specialization, increased efficiency, and deregulation. It presupposes that a country's factories have to be able to undersell the world whatever the costs. Therefore, to be in a position to exploit fully these short-lived but intense export booms, trade policy *has to lead economic development*.

That trade should be the central principle around which policy-making is organized is a radically new departure for most labour movements. The globalization of production and the search for larger and larger markets have created unparalleled conditions of change for employment conditions and for trade unions at the bargaining table. As workplace production is being redesigned by the introduction of an increasing array of new technologies, the strategic question is, what will be the essential features of the next socio-economic system? Will it be based on a modified Fordist model of mass production? Or will flexible systems of production be the new paradigm of workplace organization? Will manufacturing continue to be the source of wealth and a high standard of living for industrial countries? Or will the service economy be the motor of growth and development in the future?

Answers to these complex questions have, more often than not, eluded governments who fail to see that the search for flexibility has contradictory consequences for industrial society and labour in particular. Typically, employers want to establish new systems of work relations to ensure maximum flexibility and minimum worker resistance. While the reasons for challenging existing work and employment practices are varied, they have not infused industrial organization with a new level of dynamism. Despite all the talk about workplace reform, productivity continues to lag – evidence that technological innovation is not an adequate response to new competitive pressures. But management's determination to increase productivity is a sign that business is deadly earnst in its efforts to link the drive for international competitiveness to new workplace conditions. Its single-minded pursuit of this goal has taken the labour movement by surprise.

From one end of the country to the other employers no longer hesitate to question the legitimacy of existing labour and employment practices. For Canada, with one of the most open economies in the world, a highly fragmented system of collective bargaining and a particularly weak form of social Keynesianism, it has been relatively easy for business to erode the social net and the collective bargaining system (see, for example, the articles by Bakker and Myles in this volume). Moreover, business has been able to exploit the segmented labour market which has existed in Canada. The result is not only sharp increases in income inequality but a marked increase in power accruing to business. This will have marked political and economic consequences.

CANADIAN TRADE DEPENDENCY:
ORGANIZED LABOUR IN THE GLOBAL
ECONOMY

With over 30 per cent of Canada's gross national product accounted for by exports, the costs of being active in the international market place have been high. For large parts of the country, Canada's open economy has not sustained dramatic improvements in real income for many in the labour force. Rather, increased openness has made it easier for Canadian industries to compete on low labour costs and low wages in an increasingly competitive labour market.[2] In theory, the internationalization of economic competition is supposed to mean higher wages and social welfare. But in practice, Canadian wages have fallen not only in the import-sensitive industries but in collective bargaining units throughout the economy. Canadian workers have not been able to bargain for the wage premium they have "earned" from improvements in productivity.

The downward pressure on wages has been far-reaching and broad-based. Annual rates of wage increases in collective bargaining settlements reached their lowest point in twenty-five years in 1984–85.[3] Since 1977 real wages have been eroding.[4] During the ten-year period from

1977 to 1987 paid workers' real average labour income declined by 4.8 per cent and real wages and salaries declined in most provinces. The purchasing power of Canadian workers remains depressed. Wages adjusted for increases in the consumer price index were "actually lower in 1987 than in 1982, the depths of the Depression."[5] The Toronto-Dominion Bank estimates that "more than half of all employees experienced a decline in real wages" in recent times.[6] Labour income in Canada, after adjusting for inflation, has grown by less than 2 per cent per year, half the rate of the 1970s.

This points to a deeper problem: all too frequently Canada's unions have not been an effective buffer against trends in the global economy. In Canada, most certainly, labour costs have not been taken out of competition by pattern bargaining or by the spread of unionization. Quite the reverse. For more than a decade Canadian labour has been losing much of the security and welfare of Canada's postwar Keynesian policies as employers have sought to accommodate flexible working arrangements. The ability of Canadian workers to protect themselves from the new international order has been very limited. The dramatic changes in compensation and other benefits can be traced to the defects of the collective bargaining system in Canada.

WAGES AND PRODUCTIVITY: A TENUOUS RELATIONSHIP

Decentralized Wage Bargaining

Wage determination is highly decentralized, with each group of workers required to bargain at the factory gate with their individual employer. With fourteen thousand autonomous locals negotiating more than twenty thousand contracts with different employers, Canada's system of collective bargaining is based on notions which presume and reinforce a truly competitive market economy, the very antithesis of a Keynesian model of regulation.[7] The existing collective bargaining regime has kept employer-labour relations closely wedded to the pure model of competitive capitalism while at the same time allowing unionization something of a legitimate role.

In practice, sectoral and national bargaining of the kind which exists in Europe is the exception. The absence of centralized structures explains the poor fit between the collective bargaining regime and the larger economy. Collective bargaining Canadian-style has only allowed workers to flex their economic muscles in fragmented settings, if at all. But fragmented collective bargaining has enabled employers to reduce the pressure on labour costs and initiate a long-lasting downward process of adjustment on wages and fringe benefits. Precisely because the institutional link between wages and productivity is tenuous at best, it is not surprising that the collective bargaining scheme has proven unable to overcome the swings in the business cycle. In a system where productivity gains are not meant to be shared, even the well-positioned workers in the most highly competitive export-sensitive industries have not shared on a regular basis in the productivity gains.[8] There are too many rough edges in Canada's market economy to produce any other result.

Playing Catch-up, Canadian Style

Canadian wages have been locked in a losing battle with strong and persistent inflationary price movements.[9] More importantly, in a system so influenced by the international environment, the gap has persisted between wages and productivity growth in the 1970s and again in the 1980s. The only exception was late 1960s, a time of double-digit inflation, when by striking legally and illegally, permitted in the aggregate Canadian workers to do better. Since then real wages have lost ground to productivity (see Table 11.1).

The fact that there was such a pronounced gap between productivity and wages in this period does not mean, of course, that workers were not improving their position relative to their previous circumstance. Growth rates were so high that wage increases, even though they failed to match productivity growth, often led to real improvements in rates. In addition, social security programs were gradually being enriched. Transfer payments as a percentage of personal income increased steadily from 1.8 per cent of personal income in 1947 to 11.7 per cent in 1966. By 1986 it had reached 14.3 per cent.[10]

But the obvious failure of wage increases to keep pace with productivity gains can only provoke greater militancy and stubbornness at the bargaining table. In a system of localized economic warfare, success depends on striking while the iron is hot. In the absence of a national wage-setting mechanism to ensure that the profitability of employers will be passed on to the workers, workers will always be playing catch-up in order to reduce the inevitable gap between profits, prices, and wages.

In Canada's export-led growth economy this means that organized labour has to make its claim for a share of the profits just as the boom is ending. Since unions cannot afford to wait until the inevitable bust arrives, they must strike with increasing frequency. Strikes will be long and, often, illegal. Not unexpectedly, almost one-third of all workers

Table 11.1
Trends in Real Wages and Output, 1974–87

	1974–75	1976–81	1982–87
Annual growth rate of real wages and salaries per person employed	1.5	0.4	−0.2
Annual growth rate of real GDP per person employed	0.5	1.0	1.6
Growth in real wages less growth in real GDP per person employed	1.0	−0.6	−1.8

SOURCE: Statistics Canada, *National Income and Expenditure Accounts.*

involved in strikes in the period from 1970 to 1979 struck illegally, resorting to wildcats, slowdowns, work-to-rule campaigns and other kinds of illegal activity when a contract was still in force.

This increasing wave of industrial insurgency should not be interpreted as a sign of strength, but of weakness. In an open economy, friction between employers and employees is inevitable; there will be localized strikes when workers feel cheated. But Zohar found that these kinds of micro-eruptions have had surprisingly little macro-impact on productivity and wage growth.[11] With the strike power restricted to pursuing economic gains in localized settings, legal and illegal strike activity failed to narrow the gap between productivity and wage growth (see Table 11.2). The reason is clear. In a decentralized bargaining system, employers have a huge incentive to meet the challenges from the new international environment by pressing for more wage concessions wherever the opportunity presents itself.[12]

NEGOTIATING TECHNOLOGICAL CHANGE:
THE MAGNITUDE OF THE ADJUSTMENT
PROBLEM

The effects of these new competitive pressures will have a far-reaching impact on Canada's highly decentralized collective bargaining regime. In theory, workers are expected to negotiate changes in working conditions, hours, and pay. In fact, the introduction of new technologies is largely occurring without any major input from Canada's trade union movement. The recent CAW settlement at Ford may mark an important turning point for Canada's trade union movement. The union successfully negotiated a high degree of economic security to protect its members from future technological change or job loss. Ford agreed to set up a $100 million fund to pay for the adjustment costs due to techno-

Table 11.2
Average Annual Rates of Change in Real Labour Compensation and Output per Hour,
1961–73 and 1973–84 (percentages)

	1963–73		1973–84	
	Real compensation	*Output per hour*	*Real compensation*	*Output per hour*
Food	3.3	3.3	1.9	1.4
Beverage	3.6	5.6	2.7	−1.2
Tobacco	4.6	5.4	3.5	1.5
Rubber	2.7	4.3	1.8	3.9
Plastic	2.6	8.5	1.2	2.2
Leather	2.4	2.0	1.1	3.9
Textiles	2.9	6.9	1.8	5.9
Clothing	2.6	2.0	0.5	2.9
Wood	4.0	2.8	2.2	5.0
Furniture	2.7	4.4	1.1	−0.4
Paper	3.1	2.4	2.2	0.2
Printing & publishing	2.4	1.6	1.4	2.1
Primary metal	2.9	3.4	2.7	1.0
Fab. metal	2.6	3.8	1.1	1.0
Machinery	2.5	3.0	1.0	1.4
Trans. equip.	2.7	7.8	1.5	2.6
Elec. equip.	2.1	4.8	1.9	6.9
Non metallic mineral prod.	3.4	5.1	1.6	0.2
Petro. & coal	3.7	6.8	2.9	−0.2
Chemicals	2.6	5.4	1.8	3.1
Other mfg.	2.4	3.6	1.3	1.7
Total mfg.	3.5	4.5	1.8	3.0

SOURCE: Statistics Canada, *Aggregate Productivity Measures*, cat. 15–204, June 1988, and Department of Finance, *Quarterly Economic Review*, Annual Reference Tables, June 1988.

NOTE: Changes in real compensation calculated as changes in nominal compensation minus the CPI.

logical change. Whether other companies outside the auto industry will adopt the same approach remains to be seen. Canada's industrial unions are ill-equipped to enter the global trade sweepstakes.

Canada's unions have had minimal influence in affecting the redesign of the workplace. They have neither the political nor the economic muscle to negotiate new shop-floor regulations to accompany technological change. A major report done for the Economic Council of Canada found that most business enterprises assume that new work practices fall within management's prerogative. Thus better than 80 per cent of firms believed that the introduction of new technologies does not even require the creation of labour-management teams, let alone the need to give workers a say in redesigning the workplace.[13] Businesses' lack of interest is not surprising. They have put their efforts into union avoidance rather than the organization of innovative shop-floor schemes to empower labour.

Major anti-union Canadian employers such as Procter and Gamble, Union Carbide, Syncrude, Shell, General Foods, MacMillan Bloedel, Canadian General Electric, and Esso Resources have adopted new management techniques as a way to ensure a union-free environment.[14] Not surprisingly, where workers have no independent power base or there is no sharing of information with the union and the worker, Canada's union leaders have been highly critical of management's efforts to introduce new organizational systems. They are convinced that management is more interested in greater productivity than in worker input in any real sense of the term.[15]

Multinational as well as Canadian employers have overwhelmingly rejected the need for business and labour "to work together as equal partners on both the shop floor and at the planning and policy level."[16] Rather they have put their energies and influence into convincing governments to make Canada internationally competitive by adopting the same conditions which prevail in the United States with respect to unemployment insurance, workerman's compensation, the cost of government, the level of taxation.[17] This has led to unprecedented attacks on Canada's public sector unions. As part of this offensive, in recent years a majority of provincial and federal governments have passed wage restraint legislation, a measure clearly intended to discipline the workforce. These tough anti-labour policies have been reinforced by other ad hoc measures. For instance, Canadian governments have restricted the right to strike of their public sector workers, as well as employing emergency back-to-work legislation against select groups of private sector workers. Between 1950 and 1965 there were only six instances of back-to-work legislation throughout Canada; in the period from 1980 to 1987, forty-three such measures were used by governments to undermine labour's bargaining rights.[18]

A NEW COMPETITIVE LABOUR MARKET: CANADA'S UNEMPLOYMENT PICTURE

The process of globally-induced adjustment has presented other kinds of risks for workers. Full-time employment has become more difficult to find. Canada's unemployment rate has remained among the highest in the industrial world, and for nearly six out of every ten unemployed persons in 1987, there is no job of any kind. The job vacancy gap is determined by the total of vacancies minus the total number of Canadians seeking work. This index indicates that there are nowhere nearly enough jobs to meet the needs of the unemployed. The mismatch between new jobs and the unemployed can be explained by structural changes in the economy. Between 1981 and 1987 the growth of managerial and professional jobs accounted for over 85 per cent of the total growth in full-time employment. Only 14 per cent of the unemployed were in these occupations in 1987.[19] Regionally, this imbalance in the labour market is even more pronounced. Ontario had the strongest record of job creation in the same period but only 26 per cent of the unemployed.

This failure to produce sufficient employment opportunities, however, does not mean that new jobs have not been created. Quite the contrary. Many of the new jobs are part-time and the recovery in the employment rate is *entirely accounted for by an increase in part-time employment*.[20] This explains the improvement in Canada's employment picture. According to Osberg, of more significance is the fact that proportion of Canadians who were employed full-time still has not recovered to its 1981 level. In August 1981, 56.1 per cent of the Canadian paid workforce was employed on a full-time basis; by December 1987, the comparable figure was 50.4 per cent.[21] Clearly, full-time employment has become a rarer form of work in Canada during the 1980s.

The trend to lower employment levels in the resource-based industries has been marked in Atlantic Canada, northern Ontario/Quebec, the prairies, and British Columbia. Labour shedding has cut the workforce by almost a fifth. The impact of trade on labour market adjustment has been pronounced and persistent. Between 1981 and 1987, as foreign markets and sources of supply have become more important to the Canadian economy, Canada has imported more goods. The trend to international specialization has been accompanied by higher levels of import penetration and a smaller workforce in the mass production industries. During the same period agriculture, manufacturing, and Canada's resources industries all registered negative employment growth, despite a limited recovery.

Compared to many European countries, Canada's labour market track record is poor. Successive governments have failed to allocate enough resources to reduce unemployment levels. Only Toronto "has managed to achieve unemployment rates that normally entire nations achieve." In 1986, when Canadian unemployment averaged 9.5 per cent, other countries with small, open economies, such as Austria, had an unemployment rate of 3.1 per cent, Norway's was 1.9 per cent and Sweden's was 2.7 per cent.[22] Moreover employment is increasingly punctuated by spells of unemployment. The Forget Commission on

Unemployment Insurance reported that, in 1985, only 63 per cent of Canadians in the labour force were employed for the entire year and even some of those people changed their jobs. For the unemployed, it takes longer to find work; for older workers who lose their job it takes on average twenty-nine weeks to find a new situation. Many older workers who lose their jobs leave the workforce altogether. A study of job loss and plant closures done by the Ontario government in 1988 showed that many workers on remployment took major pay cuts. Comparing earnings with the job held to the first job obtained after displacement, men between 45 and 54 suffered a wage loss of almost 25 per cent. For older women, the figure was close to 30 per cent.[23] The instability of a highly volatile labour market has thus created many victims because the pressure for adjustment is being borne by those who are most vulnerable and have the least amount of resources to cope with workplace and workforce adjustment.[24]

THE POST-FORDIST REALITY

It is against this background that one must assess the post-Fordist reality, which is leading to dramatic changes in work and employment practices.

The switch from inert mechanical systems of production to programmatically, electronically based technologies has made possible an array of organizational structures not available before. Inevitably, these new information-based technologies are the foundation of a different socio-economic order. But the question is, what sort? Is the current shakeout of the labour market and changing employment practices simply a transition to a new economic order which is a leaner and meaner version of Fordism? If so, what are its principle features?

Flexible specialization offers an alternative to Fordism at a number of levels. The vision is superficially appealing: highly skilled workers, increased participation in the workplace, a better-educated workforce in an environment where the individual worker will be more like a self-motivated artisan rather than a classic proletarian. This image is misleading. It is difficult to judge whether the new work relations constitute a principle of organization, such as Fordism was, or are simply a management strategy for obtaining immediate cost advantages. The fact that the new production methods are aimed primarily at reducing the costs of production raise serious doubts as to whether they are a new paradigm of workplace relations. In fact, the new search for flexibility may be an obstacle to the more fundamental changes needed in the reorganization of production relations and labour relations.

For instance, many of the measures to eliminate so-called rigidities can have reverse effects. Wage cuts frequently are a disincentive to automation and modernization of production facilities. Employers will prefer to use their existing but cheaper workforce rather than modernizing production facilities. Under a regime of flexible specialization, there is no assurance that employers would treat their workers any differently than before. In Europe it is the high-wage economy that has been the stick to force employers to increase output by continually upgrading the work process. If wages are reduced, this discourages investment. Similarly, the demand to reduce job security is equally problematic. Frequently, employers with this new-found freedom to change the ground rules in their enterprise cut their workforce rather than create new jobs. This too underlines the fact that, far from being a universal cure-all, the obsession with flexibility produces quite contradictory results.

Theoretically, the link between a good economic performance and productivity flexibility is not as straightforward as it appears. This is because, in Boyer's words, "flexibility is a defensive reaction for coping with the crisis which does not necessarily provide a means for overcoming it."[25] The pursuit of flexibility is first and foremost about quantitative change in work organization; rarely does it address the crucial larger issue – namely, that measures to boost productivity are only one of the factors that affect national productivity. A better performance depends on many other more decisive non-economic factors.

All of this needs elaboration as it pertains to the workplace. At the enterprise level, flexible work arrangements refers to the ability of a firm to adjust readily the labour it employs: the way the labour is used, and the need to adjust wages to output and the price of its products. There are three kinds of flexibility: (1) financial – mainly cost-cutting by slimming down the workforce, widely used in smokestack industries in decline; (2) functional – making more efficient use of permanent full-time employees through quality control, working smarter, continuous production; and (3) numerical flexibility – closer tailoring the size of the workforce to a firm's use of part-time, contractual, and temporary personnel.

The basic aim of a management strategy based on these three methods is to control labour costs and thus increase efficiency. While there are other routes to cost-cutting, controlling labour costs remains a central preoccupation for the reasons Kalecki advanced: it is the principle way to maintain discipline in factories.[26] Not suprisingly, employers are using the rhetoric of flexibility to increase their control over their workforces. They are looking to find ways to change the basic rules in their favour. Essentially these mean reducing their contribution to social income programs, introducing new forms of payment such as bonus schemes to tie existing wages to the economic situation of each firm, and making the firing of workers easier. If this is the case, the picture is a dark one: mass production Fordist industries want to become like small competitive firms which can hire and fire their workforce with as few restraints as possible.

NEW AND LOWER STANDARDS OF WORK
AND EMPLOYMENT: THE MINIMUM WAGE

In Canada, the impact of these new circumstances can only be viewed as leading to irreversible changes in work and employment relations. Governments have allowed the minimum wage to decline in real terms. This has created a new and lower standard for work and employment in the labour market. Since 1975 minimum wages have been allowed to erode 20 per cent in relation to the average industrial wage.[27] Today close to one-fifth of Canada's employed work at or near minimum wage levels. In Ontario, for instance, in 1987, 15 per cent of the workforce earned less than $5 an hour and over one-quarter of a million of those are employed full-time.[28]

This wholesale erosion of the minimum wage structure has triggered a massive ripple effect by lowering wages, particularly for women, visible minorities, and immigrants. In Canada these three groups increasingly make up a large proportion of the labour market and because employers often discriminate against them they are important in the organization of the labour market in the future.[29] They are expected to find employment principally in the service industries where there are few jobs at good wages. Most jobs will be in the fast-growing sectors such as accommodation and food, and retail and personal services which are known as low-wage job ghettos.

It is often believed that subsistence wages are confined to fast-food industries and personal services. This vast army work in retail trade, transport and building industries, and in providing the labour for delivery of public health and education services. However, the dramatic fall in minimum wage levels is more extensive, pervasive, and immediate than could have been predicted. In the United States, for instance, close to 10 per cent of those who receive minimum wages work for the state. In Canada the state is also a major employer at minimum wages. In creating a downward pressure on the wage structure the state has sent a powerful message to employers: firms do not have to invest in their

Table 11.3
Provincial Minimum Wages as a Percentage of the Average Industrial Wage, 1975–85

	1975	1977	1979	1981	1983	1985
Quebec	56	51	49	46	43	40
Ontario	47	43	42	40	37	38
Manitoba	56	52	47	45	46	45
Saskatchewan	53	51	51	48	46	46
Alberta	48	46	39	39	36	34
British Columbia	48	42	37	36	35	34
Newfoundland	45	41	41	42	42	41
Prince Edward Island	61	56	52	43	48	46
New Brunswick	51	50	43	43	44	40
Nova Scotia	52	52	45	45	45	44

SOURCE: Canadian Council on Social Development, *Work and Income in the 1990s* (1986).

workforce particularly when there is a large reserve of cheap labour desperate to work.

In Canada cutting minimum wages has given the state an important way to outflank the union movement which is numerically stronger than its counterpart in the United States. In that country the minimum wage legislation has also been used with dramatic consequences to reshape the wage structure. So sharp has been this decline that according to the Joint Economic Committee of Congress, eight of the thirteen million jobs created during this decade pay less than $8000 a year and half of them keep families in poverty. By 1987 real wages were lower than for any year throughout the seventies.[30] Each year minimum wages have been worth less and less as the federal government's Fair Labour Standard Act has failed to keep pace with inflation.[31]

The creation of a continent-wide low-wage economy is both a response to and an effect of new global and national pressures. As employers actively look for new kinds of employees, the skills of the older workforce are no longer needed in industries open to international competition. They want to hire fewer people at top rates and, most importantly, they want a labour force that can be easily reorganized to better fit the new equipment or work processes. In part, the way employers are attempting to force changes in compensation is to institute new pay policies for part-time and casual workers that will let them restructure their workforce by overturning existing standards and earnings levels.

With women and immigrants already earning much less than the unionized workforce, employers have taken full advantage of this cheap labour force. The trend to poor-quality employment with markedly lower skill levels in the service side of the economy has a permanent flow-on effect on all sectors. Government policy is premised on the anticipation that the vast majority of new jobs will be in the low end of the employment market. In this vision of tomorrow's labour market needs, secretaries, bookkeepers, truck drivers, janitors, cashiers and tellers, general office clerks, waiters, guards and other security people, typists, receptionists head the list of occupations that are expected to contribute the most to Canada's future employment growth.[32] The next ten occupations consist of labourers, welders, nurses, industrial farm mechanics, sewing machine operators, bus drivers, chefs and cooks, nursery workers, policy officers, stock clerks, and commercial travellers. The only occupation that required new skills reflective of sophisticated production systems was electronic data processing equipment operators. It ranked twenty-fifth out of thirty so-called growth occupations.

Faced with the new orientation of the economy, the high-growth sectors of the economy do not need a skilled workforce. Rather, Canadian businesses are only committed to promote micro-changes in the skills market that reflect their "blueprint" for global economic growth. In their view, resources need to be shifted away from goods to services so that Canada will not be caught flat-footed in the race to secure a niche as an exporter of tradable services.

CANADIAN WAGE COMPETITIVENESS

The upending of Canada's wage structure has been the result of two developments. Initially, the process was triggered by job loss and plant shutdown that resulted from the widespread disinvestment in Canada's industrial capacity. In the early 1980s, the epidemic of plant closures flooded the labour market which gave business a powerful weapon to demand wage and other concessions from organized labour.[33]

The second thrust has come fron the enormous expansion of the service sector. In the words of the Economic Council of Canada, "employment in Canada is polarizing into good-job and bad-job sectors in terms of pay, job security and skill. Between 1981 and 1986, the service sector is generating almost all of Canada's new jobs but 50 per cent of the jobs created between 1980 and 1988 lasted less than 6 months."[34] The enormous growth of short-term, temporary-help agency work has grown more rapidly than almost any other category. By comparison growth of jobs in the upper middle range only increased by 21 per cent. As a result, jobs were bunched at the very bottom and in the middle range

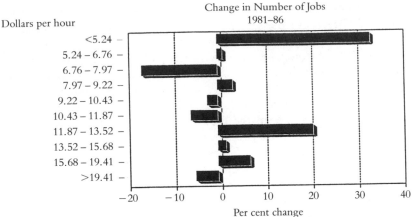

Chart 11.1.
Growing Wage Inequality
SOURCE: CLMPC Chart based on StateCan data

while, by contrast, the jobs lost due to de-industrialization simply were not replaced.

But while there are better paying jobs in services in a few areas, the service economy is first and foremost a low-wage economy. This is the main reason why job growth has changed the shape of the wage pyramid right across the face of the entire economy.[35] Canada's income ladder is being polarized between older and younger workers. New entrants, not adults, bear the brunt of the wage squeeze. In the meantime women, the young, and immigrants are being channelled into poorly paid sales and service occupations.

Faced with this kind of wage flexibility at the low end of the labour market, governments have increasingly come to rely on job ghettos and the gender gap to keep the lid on Canada's wage bill. By blaming the market, governments can attribute the decline in income levels to the "natural" forces of the market rather than to any anti-labour bias on their part.

THE ECONOMICS OF JOB GHETTOS AND THE GENDER GAP

While governments deny this unofficial policy by pointing to the recent passage of equal pay, pay equity, and fair employments standard legislation to end gender bias in the workplace, this array of legislative activity has produced little positive change. In Ontario, for instance, often seen as having the most comprehensive pay equity legislation in the country, 35 per cent of women workers are excluded from its provisions. Many are in all-female establishments or predominately female occupations. These women suffer this fate because under the government's legislation there are no male comparators. Technical loopholes and oversights like this have convinced many women that governments have bowed to pressure from employers and done the minimum to tackle pervasive gender-based income inequalities due to job ghettos.

Women have been most affected by the employment revolution but, despite this, they have not been able to use their collective strength to attack their poor employment situations. Women constitute the single most important supply of low-wage workers in Canada, as elsewhere. Not only have they entered the workforce in record numbers,[36] but employers have come to rely on the gender gap and job ghettos as entrenched institutions of the economy. In 1985 the average full-time full-year employed woman earned $13,027; the average comparable male earned $23,411, a gap of almost 45 per cent. In the service sector, the difference between men's and women's wages is more than 50 per cent. The average full-time salary of a woman working in a service occupation was $7,362 in 1985 compared to $16,028 for her male counterpart.[37]

The basic problem contributing to the wage gap is that women's work is undervalued. In most situations, the relative worth of women's work compared to men's show "a dual wage structure. Employers, whether consciously or unconsciously, have a double standard for wages."[38] The less well-known side of this story is that the state, one of the largest employers in the land, also relies on the undervaluation of women's work. It, too, is not prepared to implement tough pay equity provisions to pay its own workforce an adequate level of compensation. For instance, in Ontario virtually all childcare workers are female and half of the one hundred thousand daycare spaces are non-profit. Yet according to a recent report, "childcare workers tend to earn up to 30 per cent less than labourers or animal caregivers. Childcare workers averaged $267 a week while the average industrial wage was $404 a week in Ontario. In 1988 childcare workers topped the list of the 10 worst occupations in Canada."[39] What is equally disturbing is that less than 1 per cent are unionized and this group is presently excluded from redress under the act because of the lack of male comparators.

Similarly in health care, a huge sector employing over six hundred thousand people in Ontario, close to 80 per cent are female, including nurses, lab technicians, nurse's assistants, clerks, and the like. Most of the funding is public coming from the national system of health care and hence directly under the state's regulatory arm. Here, too, there are gender-based gaps in training, skill, stress, and the environmental factors that keep women's wages often below their comparable male counterparts. As the act is presently drafted, it is doubtful whether many health care female workers will benefit from the act's provisions.

A similar situation exists in the private sector. In textiles, manufacturing, tourism, and personal services, for instance, employers often rely on a predominately female workforce. Women's wages in these areas are in the $12,000 to $20,000 range. Given the government's unwillingness to attack gender-biased pay scales, it is not surprising that almost all small businesses of ten employees or less are excluded from pay equity redress. The most seriously affected are immigrant and visible minority women who are the most disadvantaged because they work in these sectors.

In creating few opportunities for women to end wage discrimination, the government has deliberately chosen the least effective route to tackle this pressing social issue. Since most jobs in the largest growing sector are those which pay around the minimum wage, doubling the minimum wage would do more to correct women's wage inequality than any existing measure. While a blunt instrument, by increasing the minimum wage this would be the most important adjustment to raise women's incomes and correct past practices.[40] Rather than following this course, the government is wedded to establishing quite different conditions for this kind of employment growth and remuneration, which reflects its broad commitment to maintaining the low-paying service economy as an essential component of its new international orientation.

TRADE POLICY AND FLEXIBILITY:
THE ECONOMIC AND SOCIAL AGENDA
OF BUSINESS AND GOVERNMENT

The kind of flexibility that governments here as elsewhere search for is particularly threatening because the new socio-economic order will require new skills, attitudes, forms of organization, new types of capital equipment and marketing strategies if Canada is to become competitive. What is involved in this prolonged process is, above all, to find ways to improve the existing compensation mechanism. Thus the state's role is crucial both in response to technological change and in the formation of a new set of macro-economic policies.

In Canada the state has had no difficulty in recognizing the interconnection between flexibility in work arrangements and corporate Canada's demand for higher profits. The key to instituting new structures of social flexibility does not rely only on the steps it has taken to alter labour market practices but also on measures that go to the heart of the

Keynesian welfare state system – namely, social security coverage. The most important new objective is to eliminate taxes and social transfers that, in the eyes of the business community, have an unfavourable effect on unemployment and compensation schemes.[41] That firms will be able to dispense with a significant part of their social contribution to Canada's universal programs is now a distinct possibility. They have been lobbying for this unparalled concession at the same time as many businesses are looking to change their industrial relations practices.

Compared to American and many European competitors, Canadian business is not disadvantaged. The direct cost of Canada's social wage is not paid to any great degree by employers. Key fringe benefits such as health insurance are funded nationally rather than negotiated at the firm level. By comparison, American firms pay higher health and related benefits which gives Canadian firms a strong competitive edge. Despite this, corporate Canada believes that access to social security coverage should be shifted onto the individual member of the workforce. No other issue has so galvanized the business community as the prospect of adopting new organizational forms to fully exploit, what it calls euphemistically, "human resources strategies and practices."

With the election of the Mulroney government in 1984, the distinct achievement of Canadian business has been to sell its leaner and meaner vision of Canada's social welfare system to governments. In the words of the president of the Canadian Manufacturers' Association, it has made "a thorough review of social programmes the number one priority of the government."[42] Just how important employment and income security provisions have become for business can be gleamed from its special relationship with the 1982 Macdonald Royal Commission appointed to make fundamental recommendations on the future of the Canadian economy. Its final report reflected a neo-conservative view of the world and it was not a coincidence that it reflected the social and economic agenda of the Business Council on National Issues, Canada's most powerful business lobby. The first recommendation called for cuts to unemployment insurance benefits – low by European standards though higher than those in the United States – and for sweeping changes to the entire system of social safety nets. Basically, this prestigious commission proposed a guaranteed annual income for those at the bottom of the income pyramid that was far below any established poverty guidelines. This attempt to rethink the delivery and the costing of income security programs was a crude political effort to establish new benchmarks for social assistance. To the extent that low wage-earners would find it more difficult to change jobs and look for better-paying work, it would ensure a downward pressure on the pay and employment practices.

The keynote to this drive to introduce flexibility "from above" is consistent with Ottawa's plan to cut spending by restructuring unemployment insurance benefits and other income security programs. The government intends to make individual workers pay more while, in the meantime, it is contemplating other changes to the rules.[43] The renewed calls for limiting benefits and tightening work search requirements shows the extent to which government as well as business now consciously link the need to restructure social programs to a strategy to facilitate a qualitatively different kind of trade-centred flexibility.

A FINAL WORD

The globalization of work and employment practices has an unmistakable character. Not only does it mean more low-paying work for large sections of the workforce but, increasingly, it relies on job ghettos, the gender gap and highly competitive labour markets. The return to the cruder assumptions of economic liberalism also presupposes greater freedom for employers to utilize labour only as the new technologies dictate. Thus the new standards of work are premised on a subsistence minimum that allows the labour market to function with less interference. The quest for flexibility via the state, through labour markets and, finally, by means of its trade policy, is indeed a grim reaper.

The question which needs to be asked of this new kind of trade-centred capitalism is the same that Marx posed to the first industrial revolution: in the words of André Gorz, "can [it] master the dynamics of the process it has set in motion? Will not the elimination of human labour raise problems that capitalism cannot solve on its own logic? Do not these problems, these contradictions present the socialist movement with the possibility of taking control of the process in order to turn it toward other goals, our goals?"[44]

Every indication is that trade unions urgently need to find new policies to counter the trend to earnings polarization as well as the downward drift in wages and conditions of employment. New techniques of organization are needed. Canada's theory of collective bargaining has been based on factory-by-factory bargaining, where each group of workers bargain at the factory gate with their individual employer. This scheme is ill-adapted to the global economy. In the nineties, the fastest-growing sectors are small service sector firms often employing less than twenty employees. With a highly decentralized and fragmented scheme of collective bargaining, it is too costly to organize these small units one by one. To be effective, unions need a radically different model, one which permits them to organize across sectors and take the focus away from the individual firm.

Unions must also develop non-traditional strategies with respect to women workers, the public sector, and groups not presently part of the trade union movement. This will require negotiating strategies which stress the need for secure, socially useful jobs at decent wages. In the 1990s the quality of employment has to be given top priority. To realize these kinds of objectives, unions will have to play a larger role at the local level in industrial restructuring policies. The control of pension funds will increasingly become a vital part of trade union activity. Measures like these will increasingly force trade unions to reshape their collective bargaining agenda. They will have to use their collective strength to improve social incomes as well as ensure that new programs, such as universal daycare, are adopted. The fact that these questions are on the agenda of many unions is grounds for optimism. The systemic search for flexibility has had the unintended consequences of forcing Canada's union movement to find ways to get out of the ditch that it is in. This in itself is no mean accomplishment, provided Canada's unions have the will and the vision to look at a range of alternatives to the pressures of globalization.

NOTES

Many thanks to Judy Fudge, Andrew Sharpe, Leon Muszynski, and Harry Glasbeek who gave me useful comments and criticism in preparing this article.

1 P. Armstrong, A. Glyn, J. Harrison, *Capitalism since World War II* (London: Fontana 1984).
2 Thomas Kochan, "Looking to the Year 2000: Challenges for Industrial Relations and Human Resource Management," prepared for the Economic Council of Canada (November 1988), 3.
3 Quoted in ibid., 9.
4 Fred Wong, "Trends in Labour Income," *Employment, Earnings and Hours* vol. 65, no. 7 (Ottawa: Statistics Canada 1988).
5 Arthur Donner, "Labour's Shrinking Share," *The Facts* 10, no. 3 (Fall 1988).
6 Toronto-Dominion Bank, *The Economy* 12, no. 1 (Summer 1989), 6.
7 This section draws on the study being completed by my colleague Harry Glasbeek and myself, *Work, Employment and Collective Bargaining Regimes, Canada 1960–1988*.
8 See Robert Boyer, *La flexibilité du travail en Europe* (Paris: Éditions La Découverte 1956), and Armstrong *et al.*, *Capitalism since World War II*. Interestingly, this is also true of mainstream labour economics which holds that the hourly wage equals the marginal revenue product of labour.

9 Ostry and Zaidi have written that since the early fifties "real wages per wage-earner-hour in Canadian manufacturing lagged behind the growth in output per wage-earner-hour, although the degree of lag varied from period to period." Sylvia Ostry and M.A. Zaidi, *Labour Economics in Canada*, 2nd ed. (Toronto: Macmillan 1972), 216.

10 Lars Osberg, "The Future of Work in Canada" (unpublished manuscript, Dalhousie University 1988), 24.

11 Uri Zohar, *Canadian Manufacturing A Study in Productivity and Technological Change* (Toronto: James Lorimer 1982).

12 Richard Freeman, "Canada in the World Labour Market to the Year 2000," a paper presented at Perspective 2000, Ottawa, 30 November 1988.

13 Kochan, "Looking to the Year 2000," 23.

14 Jacquie Mansell, *Workplace Innovation in Canada* (Ottawa: Economic Council of Canada 1986), 13.

15 Ibid., 37.

16 Quoted in ibid., 28.

17 Laurent Thibault, president of the Canadian Manufacturers' Association. During the November election, he said that he had changed his mind that the FTA would not require matching Canada's programs to the lower levels in the United States. Once the election was won, he has attacked the level of spending and the universality of these programs.

18 Leo Panitch and Donald Swartz, *The Assault on Trade Union Freedoms* (Toronto: Garamond Press 1988), 30.

19 "The Nature of Current Unemployment: Evidence from Job Vacancy Information," *Quarterly Labour Market Productivity Review* (Spring 1987), 34.

20 Ibid., p. 16 (emphasis added).

21 Osberg, "Future of Work," 16.

22 Ibid., 50.

23 Ontario, Ministry of Skills Development, *Adjusting to Change: An Overview of Labour Market Issues in Ontario* (Toronto: June 1988), 40.

24 Goran Therborn, *Why Some People Are More Employed than Others: The Strange Paradox of Growth and Unemployment* (London: Verso 1986), 26.

25 Robert Boyer, "Labour Flexibilities: Many Forms, Uncertain Effects," *Labour and Society* 12, no. 1 (January 1987).

26 M. Kalecki, "Political Aspects of Full Employment," *Political Quarterly* 14, no. 4 (1943).

27 Leon Muszynski, "Work and Welfare: A Guide to Income Security Reform in Canada," draft report prepared for the National Council of Welfare (March 1989), 27.

28 Social Planning Council of Metropolitan Toronto, *Social Infopac* 6 (1 April 1987).

29 Kochan, "Looking to the Year 2000." It is predicted that these three groups will constitute over 80 per cent of future workforce entrants in the US labour market between 1987 and 2000.

30 *New York Times*, 25 February 1989.

31 Ibid., 28 January 1988, reported that between 1981 and 1987, the US minimum wage as a percentage of the average hourly wage dropped from 46.2 to 37.3 per cent. Even this shift in the wage structure does not capture the magnitude of the change that has occurred. The minimum wage as measured as a percentage of the average service wage plummeted from 52.3 to 39.6 per cent in the same period. In real terms, wages at the bottom of the work pyramid are at their lowest level since 1955 and no longer keep a family of three above the poverty level.

32 Government of Canada, "Consultation Paper on Training, Department of Manpower and Employment" (1984), 29.

33 These events are examined in detail in D. Drache, "The De-industrialization of Canada and Its Implications for Labour" in G. Szell, Paul Blyton, and Chris Cornforth, *The State, Trade Unions and Self-Management* (New York: Walter De Gruyter 1989).

34 Economic Council of Canada, *Good Jobs, Bad Jobs* (Ottawa: 1990).

35 J. Myles, G. Picot and T. Wannell, "The Changing Wage Distribution of Jobs, 1981–1986," *The Labour Force*, StatCan., October 1988.

36 Between 1975 and 1986 the female labour force has grown by 56 per cent compared to 12.4 per cent for men.

37 L. Muszynski and M. Gunderson, *Women and Labour Market Poverty* (Ottawa: Canadian Advisory Council on the Status of Women 1990), 95. They add the following sentence on the origin of the wage gap. "Discrimination is a central factor that affects women's wages and employment opportunities" (91). Women are paid substantially less than men, even when hours of employment, eduction, and experience are taken into account.

38 Mary Cornish, "Equal Pay: Collective Bargaining and the Law" (Ottawa: Ministry of Labour 1986), 4.

39 "Report to the Minister of Labour by the Ontario Pay Equity Commission" (February 1989), 21.

40 This is one of the principal demands of the Equal Pay Coalition, which calls for an "integrated, broad-front approach" to end wage inequality for women. See its brief, "Bringing Pay Equity to Those Presently Excluded from Ontario's Pay Equity Act" (Toronto, 13 December 1988).

41 The question of flexibility is lucidly analysed in Boyer, "Labour Flexibilities," 108–15.

42 *Globe and Mail*, 1 March 1989.

43 The cuts to Canada's system of unemployment insurance are set forth in Ministry of Employment and Immigration policy paper, *Success in the Works: a Policy Paper* (Ottawa, 11 April 1989).

44 André Gorz, "The Socialism of Tomorrow," *Telos* 67 (Spring 1986), 201.

12 Canada's Social Wage in an Open Economy, 1970–1983

ISABELLA BAKKER

The free trade agreement (FTA) has been interpreted as a part of a larger neo-conservative effort to reduce the intervention of the state in the distribution of the social product, and to reduce the cost of social infrastructure and labour force support. As well, the agreement's promise to create a level playing field raises serious questions about the viability of different tax levels on different sides of the border. All these elements raise concerns about the linkages between Canada's social wage, the norms of trade regulation specified in the FTA, and the importance of the social wage for the living standards of workers in Canada.

This paper attempts to demonstrate that the redistributive role of the state envisioned by the Macdonald Commission and the Mulroney government cannot simply be assumed to benefit workers or harm the various branches of capital. Rather, state intervention in the distributive struggle must be quantified in order to ascertain whether and what kind of redistribution is occurring between capital and labour.

For the purposes of conducting such an empirical analysis national income is divided amongst three basic claimants: the working population, understood in a very broad sense as constituting all those who depend upon a wage or wage-earner for their subsistence[1]; capital, defined in terms of those whose income derives from property ownership (both individuals and corporations); and the state apparatus.[2] Given the complexity of modern-day state expenditure and taxation, it is difficult to ascertain which of these three claimants is "winning" or "losing."

In economics the net social wage can be defined as the net outcome after taking into account the taxes paid and benefits received by a worker or the working population at an aggregate level. The way it is derived here takes into account both government expenditures and taxes which are based on the traditional categories employed when estimating aggregate social spending levels.[3]

The conventional method divides the population into groups with different incomes and calculates the welfare type benefits received by each of these income categories. A progressive distribution of after-tax income (a positive social wage) is said to result if the lower income brackets receive relatively larger amounts of government benefits. Taxes are usually taken into account to show that higher income brackets pay more taxes.[4]

Another way of analysing the distributive impact of taxes and expenditures is in terms of social class. Classical political economists such as Smith, Ricardo, and Marx applied the concept of social classes (as opposed to income classes) in their attempts to distinguish income derived from labour as opposed to income derived from ownership of property in order to focus on isolating both the *social* costs and benefits of state intervention.

Such a distinction is valuable because it provides a number of analytical insights into key aspects of social reproduction and, in particular, the paramount importance of the wage relationship in ensuring labour discipline (see Appendix for a definition of social wage). For capitalists, the social wage is one of the fruits of working-class struggle and, as such, undermines market discipline by providing other sources of income (subsistence). This is what political economists call the "decommodification" of labour power. For instance, unemployment insurance, health care, and other social services reduce workers' dependence on wage labour as the sole means of subsistence.[5] In particular, the social wage comes under attack because it is thought to undermine both the move toward greater reliance on market forces and Canada's competitive advantage at the macro level.[6]

The following algebraic model demonstrates how to calculate a simplified net social wage where there is only capital and labour (the state imposes no overhead in this model and there is no debt or international flows):

R (revenue) $= T_w$ (taxes on workers), T_o (taxes on owners), T_c (taxes on corporations)

E (expenditure) $= B_w$ (benefits to workers), B_o (benefits to owners), B_c (benefits to corporations)

$$R = T_w + T_o + T_c$$
$$E = B_w + B_o + B_c$$

Net transfers to:

Workers $= B_w - T_w$ (social wage)

Owners $= B_o - T_o$ (state dividend)

Corporations $= B_c - T_c$ (net subsidies)

In this model it is possible to have a situation where overall social spending is falling but the social wage is stable or even climbing. It all hinges first of all on isolating a specific target population (in this instance the working class writ large and measured in terms of the working population) and then determining not only the specific incidence of spending but also of taxation. What is intriguing about this approach is that it provides a more dynamic picture of the distributive struggle. For instance, it is feasible in the context of this model that deficit financing because of insufficient tax revenue offers a win/win situation for both capital and labour. This "free ride" or positive social wage, even in the context of generally falling benefits (conventional measures of social spending), may help to explain the current hyper-active efforts of the Canadian government to trim the deficit. It is also possible in this model that the share of total social spending going to the working population is matched by equally high taxes. As a result, the social wage is equal to zero. The aim in this work is to examine the incidence of social spending and taxation on the basis of social class.

DERIVING THE SOCIAL WAGE

The concept of the social wage is part of what are still relatively underveloped attempts by political economists to provide a quantitative breakdown of public finance that distinguishes state activity on the basis of social class (see appendix for a brief discussion of the methodology). This section provides a brief review of one methodology for allocating various government expenditures and taxes to labour and then reports the net social wage findings for Canada for 1970–83. These results, using the same methodology, will then be compared with those from a United States study.[7]

In order to arrive at the net impact of both state expenditures and taxes on the standard of living of labour, taxes paid to the state are subtracted from the wages and benefits received by workers. This immediately presents a problem because conventional statistics make no distinction between those whose income comes from labour and those who derive their income from the ownership of property; hence, there is no distinction between workers and non-workers. Secondly, if all government spending is treated as a pure benefit, the very notion of social benefit loses all meaning since, for instance, defence spending is treated as equivalent to social welfare spending. As a result, a number of incidence assumptions are required in order to allocate benefits and burdens to labour.[8]

To determine the proportion of government spending directed towards labour, expenditures are classified according to three broad incidence categories: expenditures deemed to accrue exclusively to labour, those which partly accrue to labour, and those which do not benefit workers. The expenditures that are deemed to accrue exclusively to workers are: social services, labour and employment benefits, and housing assistance. The second group of state expenditures are treated as social consumption in general and the labour share in them is estimated by multiplying the total of the expenditure category by the share of total labour income in personal income (the ratio of wages and salaries to total personal income, the "labour share"). These include transportation, health, education, recreation and culture, and the environment. The "labour share" ratio represents an attempt to capture in empirical terms the proportion of certain state expenditures that benefit workers as opposed to those individuals who receive property income. For example, education was subdivided because of the strong evidence in the literature that the benefits of post-secondary education do not accrue in equal proportion to all social groups. A final category of state expenditures were excluded from labour income and consumption because they represent the expenses of reproducing and maintaining the system (the "faux frais" of capitalism as Marx referred to it). These include general government, protection of persons and property, foreign affairs, and international assistance. The appendix illustrates the derivation of the data for 1970.

In keeping with the effort in this paper to compare the Canadian social wage with American estimates of spending and taxation, tax incidence is also measured using the labour share methodology. Thus all income and sales taxes, with the exception of social security taxes, are allocated on the basis of labour's share in total personal income. Social security taxes (or insurance in Canada) are assumed to fall totally on workers since the payments are derived from labour income. Corporate taxes are assumed to fall entirely on capital.[9]

EMPIRICAL RESULTS

Figure 12.1 shows the annual average labour income, the annual average labour income plus the net social wage (both in current dollars) and then puts these results in perspective in terms of the social wage as a percentage of average annual wages. The results reveal that throughout the entire period, the social wage lifts the average annual income per worker. This is also revealed in Table 12.1 (column 1), which illustrates

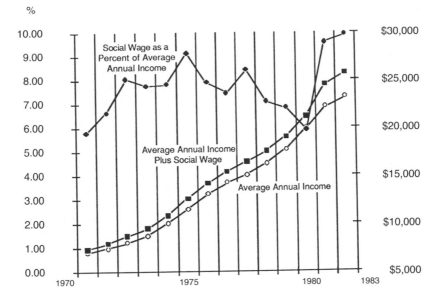

Figure 12.1.
Average Annual Income, with and without the Social Wage for Canada, 1970–83
SOURCE: Table 1.

the average annual value of the social wage per worker. The current dollar value of the social wage varies from a low of $429 in 1970 to a high of $2544 per worker in 1983.[10] A particularly pronounced jump in the social wage occurred in the recessionary period in the early 1980s. Figure 12.1 also shows the variation in the social wage as a percentage of average annual income. From a low of 5.79 per cent in 1970 to a high of 9.89 per cent in 1983, these figures again reveal a sharp jump in the recessionary period, from 5.92 per cent in 1981 to 9.59 per cent in 1982, reflecting the sharp increase in government social spending, particularly in the unemployment insurance category.

Figure 12.2 shows the difference between annual income with and without the social wage (what is referred to as the net transfer rate) for the United States. The results indicate that the true wage of workers (income plus social wage) is almost always below their apparent wage. For Shaikh and Tonak, this implies that, "it is the workers who generally end up transferring a net portion of their wages to the state."[11] Their results and those for Canada may not be conclusive but do point to the importance of developing a "net" empirical analysis for the overall assessment of distributive struggles.

Table 12.1
Social Wage Data, 1970–83

	Total wages and salaries (A)	Labour taxes (B)*	Labour benefits (C)†	Net social wage (D)	Net benefits as a % of wages (E)	Total workforce (thousands) (F)	Average annual income (G)	Average annual income plus social wage (H)	Average annual value of the social wage per worker (I)	Social wage as a % of average annual income (J)
1983	221,800	50,796.58	75,132.85	24,336.27	10.97	9565	$23,188.71	$25,733.01	$2,544.30	9.89
1982	211,604	46,872.22	69,309.22	22,437.00	10.60	9550	$22,157.49	$24,506.91	$2,349.42	9.59
1981	197,910	42,846.50	55,299.52	12,453.02	6.29	9926	$19,938.55	$21,193.13	$1,254.59	5.92
1980	171,424	35,893.24	48,435.06	12,541.82	7.32	9651	$17,762.30	$19,061.84	$1,299.54	6.82
1979	151,736	31,676.18	43,249.24	11,573.06	7.63	9321	$16,278.94	$17,520.55	$1,241.61	7.09
1978	134,933	28,529.65	40,921.86	12,392.21	9.18	8948	$15,079.68	$16,464.60	$1,384.91	8.41
1977	124,021	27,114.81	37,119.94	10,005.13	8.07	8681	$14,286.49	$15,439.02	$1,152.53	7.47
1976	111,884	24,332.69	33,915.45	9582.76	8.56	8543	$13,096.47	$14,218.28	$1,121.71	7.89
1975	96,623	20,137.64	29,830.60	9692.96	10.03	8375	$11,537.07	$12,694.44	$1,157.37	9.12
1974	82,867	17,758.63	24,795.94	7037.31	8.49	8224	$10,076.24	$10,931.94	855.70	7.83
1973	69,521	14,583.45	20,441.75	5858.30	8.43	7890	$8,811.28	$9,553.78	$742.50	7.77
1972	60,341	12,786.24	18,062.72	5276.48	8.74	7451	$8,098.38	$8,806.53	$708.16	8.04
1971	53,758	11,669.37	15,486.90	3817.53	7.10	7181	$7,486.14	$8,017.76	$531.61	6.63
1970	48,952	10,554.93	13,562.18	3007.25	6.14	7004	$6,989.15	$7,418.51	$429.36	5.79

SOURCE: National Income and Expenditure Accounts (Cat. #13–531), Consolidated Government Finance (Cat. #68–202), Historical Labour Force Statistics (Cat. #71–201A), Dept. of Finance Economic Review (selected years).

* Derived by looking at total government spending, and allocating a labour share for each expenditure category.

† All income and sales taxes, with the exception of social security taxes, are allocated on the basis of labour share in total personal income.

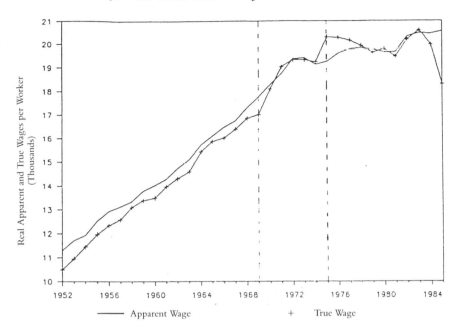

Figure 12.2.
Apparent and True Wages per Worker, United States 1952–85
SOURCE: Anwar Shaikh and Ahmet Tonak, "The Welfare State and the Myth of Social Wage" in
      Robert Cherry *et al.*, eds., *The Imperilled Economy* (New York: Monthly Review Press 1987).

Earlier social wage studies, which either ignored the taxes paid by
the recipients of social wage expenditures or underestimated them, provided important preliminary insights into the social wage but fell short
of providing a net analysis of social reproduction.[12] The impact of the
social wage, defined exclusively in terms of the benefits accruing to
every citizen, will differ significantly from the impact of the social wage
understood as the net result of subtracting the burdens (taxes) paid from
the benefits (services and transfers) received by the working population
as a whole.

Figure 12.3 presents the total social wage as a percentage of total
wages in Canada and the United States. According to the Shaikh and
Tonak study, the American social wage is generally negative, indicating
a net transfer from workers to the state and/or capital over most of the
period. By contrast, the Canadian social wage as a percentage of total
wages remains positive throughout the period. These findings have significant implications for the Canadian social wage in the context of trade
liberalization. Although a negative social wage does not necessarily
imply that capital is a net beneficiary (state overhead could absorb the

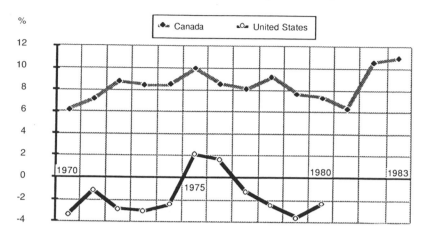

Figure 12.3.
Social Wages as a Percentage of Total Wages: Canada and the United States
SOURCE: Compiled using data from Stuart McGill, *The Australian Net Social Wage*, Ph.D. diss., New
York School for Social Research, 1989.

redistributed income), it does provide initial grounds for expecting that
US capital (in total) is in a more advantageous position than Canadian
capital. This can be illustrated recalling the algebraic model introduced
at the beginning of the chapter:

Revenue (R) = taxes paid by workers (T_w) + taxes paid by capital
(T_c)

Expenditure (E) = benefits to workers (B_w) + benefits to capital (B_c).
Net transfers are:

Social wage (SW) = (B_w − T_w)

Social dividend (SD) = (B_c − T_c).

United States

$R = 100$, $T_w = 85$, $T_c = 15$

$E = 100$, $B_w = 80$, $B_c = 20$

$SW = -5$, $SD = +5$

Canada

$R = 100$, $T_w = 80$, $T_c = 20$

$E = 100$, $B_w = 85$, $B_c = 15$

$SW = +5$, $SD = -5$

This hypothetical model, which does not take into account the share
of expenditure going to the state apparatus nor the revenue which the
state raises through debt financing, shows the potential implications for
capital of differences in the social wage between the two countries. In

this model American workers lose 5 and capital gains 5, whereas for Canada the outcome is reversed. Certainly the picture is more complicated in the real world: not only are there more claimants of government expenditures, with capital being divided into property owners and corporations, but there are also deficit financing and government bureaucracies (which take income from both classes).

Without data for all of the different components of the model it is impossible to ascertain whether capital is indeed a net beneficiary. For now, the limited evidence points to the differences in the social wage. At a minimum, the Canadian case indicates that capital cannot be receiving a subsidy from workers, while the American evidence offers the opposite possibility. Thus, an empirical political economy-based analysis reveals that the state is in a distinctly different *distributive* position in the two countries.[13]

In sum, the evidence presented here shows that the Canadian social wage has tended towards the positive, with workers receiving more benefits than they pay in taxes. At the macro level, this net outcome has important implications for Canada's competitive position, especially since in the United States the social wage has been mostly negative. This implies that there is a greater opportunity for the US state to redistribute income from labour to capital (e.g., government subsidies to the military industrial complex). What accounts for the apparent divergence between the Canadian and American social wage?

The Canadian social wage and distributive outcomes in general are profoundly influenced by domestic policy as well as Canada's interdependent relationship with the United States. It is in this context that the FTA, by limiting public intervention in the market place, threatens to push the Canadian social wage downwards. The more extensive and intensive intervention by the Canadian public sector (especially in the area of social services) stands in market contrast to the United States, where the prevailing policy direction has been towards less intervention.

CANADIAN POSTWAR ACCUMULATION AND THE SOCIAL WAGE

In Canada, changes on both the spending and taxing side since the early 1970s can be attributed to a host of domestic political institutions and relations, closely aligned with the influences of federalism. In this sense, the FTA does not represent a completely new set of forces operating on the social wage. Rather, it accelerates the pressure on taxation and spending levels by extending the influence of market forces on allocative and distributive decisions, thereby signalling a limited flexibility for the state in a number of key policy-making areas. For instance, according to Bruce Wilkinson, the FTA differs from the current GATT agreement in its "inclusion of agricultural products and a wide range of services and investment in the liberalization process; stronger commitments on the sharing of energy and other resource products; modifications in rules regarding safeguards, and a new dispute settlement mechanism for antidumping and countervailing duty cases as well as other types of disputes."[14] For Wilkinson and others who opposed the FTA, this initiative calls into question Canada's economic, political, and social identity by significantly reinforcing Canada's postwar march toward an everstronger economic and cultural dependency on the United States.

Canadian economic growth in the postwar period can be situated in the context of a general Fordist development strategy which tied economic expansion to the extension of mass production and consumption. The postwar "golden age" of capitalist expansion in the advanced industrialized countries is associated with the dual strategy of Keynesian macro-economic policy and the expansion of the welfare state. The former relied on the management of aggregate demand through the state sector; an effort was made to co-ordinate the ups and downs of the business cycle with the flow of profits and investment which remained in private hands. The latter involved the regulation of social wages through the Keynesian welfare state and tax system. The social wage in part contributed to a de-politicization or muting of capital-labour conflicts. These two aspects of regulation contributed to the conditions which generated a relatively prosperous and harmonious period of growth. Politically, collective identities were constructed within the discourse of nation-building and the institutions of federalism rather than around explicit class-based collective identities.[15]

The Canadian postwar accord did share certain similarities with the ensemble of institutional forms and policies associated with Fordism elsewhere, such as a stabilized norm of social consumption that would buffer working-class consumption levels through periods of economic boom and bust (for a more detailed discussion, see chapters by Drache and Donner). At the same time, labour accepted the logic of profitability and markets as the guiding principles of resource allocation. However, the Keynesian development strategy of sustaining aggregate demand through state intervention was to be severely constrained by the openness of the Canadian economy. The consequences of pursuing elements of a Keynesian strategy with the traditional reliance on staple exports set Canada on a path of interdependence and continental integration. The result was a strong penetration of foreign capital in both the resource and manufacturing sectors, and an ever-increasing balance of trade deficit in manufacturing products.[16] Relying on relatively unprocessed natural resources and the importing of capital and goods meant that Canada was particularly sensitive to trends in the international economy. It also required a commitment to more open international trade relations through organizations such as the GATT.

The openness of the economy (reflected in exports as a percentage of GDP) has meant that the government has had to compensate those who suffer from Canada's deteriorating competitive position in the international economy. This has meant bailing out firms, subsidizing unprofitable sectors, and funding a variety of welfare programs, especially unemployment insurance, job retraining, and retirement. Cameron examines openness, unemployment rates, and the growth of government spending. He concludes that: "The well-being of the Canadian economy, including the rate of growth and the level of unemployment, depends to a considerable degree on the economic well-being of its major trading partner, the United States ... If that proposition holds, and if the performance of the Canadian economy, in turn, influences the scope of the public economy, then the logical conclusion is that a major source of growth of the Canadian public economy is the US economy, and, in particular, the pattern of "boom and bust" sporadic recovery and frequent recession that has characterized it for decades."[17] What is unique about Canada is not its high dependence on foreign markets in general, but its "openness in the sense of heavy dependence on one trading partner – the United States." This, combined with Canada's relatively low commitment to full employment, has contributed to relatively high unemployment rates compared to Europe. Indeed, cyclical increases and declines in the net social wage closely reflect the unemployment rate. This trend reflects the importance of the unemployment insurance component of the net social wage. There were especially pronounced jumps after the two recessions in the early seventies and eighties, largely due to the increases in social transfer payments (especially unemployment insurance) rather than a rise in civil consumption expenditures. For instance, the sharp rise in unemployment from 7.5 to 11.2 per cent in the period from 1981 to 1984 was accompanied by a 24 per cent increase in social transfer payments.[18]

The tensions inherent in this postwar accumulation strategy erupted in the mid–1970s. As Wolfe notes, "Cyclical fluctuations in the demand for staple products imported inflationary pressures into the Canadian economy, leading to more militant wage demands by trade unions. The onset of the global crisis and the spread of protectionism threatened the delicate balance that Canada had maintained in its external trade relations through its privileged access to the US market."[19] Recession, instability in international resource markets, increasing distributional conflict over the labour process, and the international mobility of goods and investment seriously undermind the Keynesian compromise in the late 1960s and early 1970s. Until then, the burden of the Keynesian welfare state had been acceptable in the context of workers' rising standard of living and sufficient profitability stimulated by the high level of demand for Canadian resource exports in the international economy. Succinctly, on the expenditure side of the social wage, the age of "they say cutback, we say fightback" had arrived.

On the tax side, pressure to reduce capital's burden of the tax share has been reinforced, not only by the domestic forces alluded to above, but also by trends emanating from the United States.[20] For instance, the tax incentives for US corporations introduced in 1971 put significant pressure on the Canadian government to match the American incentive package when it introduced its 1972 budget. Naturally the government justified such analogous actions on the grounds that future investment by American subsidiaries in Canada would otherwise be undermined. Similar pressures operated on the Tory government in the mid–1980s when the United States lowered its income tax rates. The Wilson tax reforms, introduced in June 1987, proposed to reform the system in two stages: the first stage involved the personal and corporate income tax; the second, the federal sales tax. Since the Conservatives came to power in 1984 corporate taxes increased by only 8 per cent, income taxes by 45 per cent, and the sales tax by 67 per cent. It remains to be seen if the extra revenue to fund the first stage rate reductions on income tax will come from heavier corporate taxes. But given the postwar trend of declining corporate taxes, a sustained reversal seems unlikely. In the second stage of tax reform, the trend towards a regressive tax on people's consumption as opposed to their income, will become even more pronounced. This will have implications for the social wage for the reasons offered by Brooks and McQuaig:

What is really at stake here, in the long run, is our ability to finance Canada's social programs. Once the second stage of Wilson's tax reform has been phased in, with its increased emphasis on sales taxes and decreased emphasis on income tax, the burden will be shifted from the rich and from corporations onto the middle and lower middle class. Quite apart from questions of fairness, this shift will limit Ottawa's ability to finance social programs. There just isn't that much more to be squeezed out of these middle-income groups, which have limited resources to begin with. This will narrow the boundaries within which future political struggles will be fought. The prospect of ever larger annual deficits will make some social welfare programs seem impractical. Under these circumstances, fiscal restraint won't appear nasty or mean. It will simply be the only choice open to responsible governments faced with the reality of limited resources.[21]

To sum up, in terms of Canadian taxes, the postwar trend has been similar to that of the United States, where taxes on capital have declined substantially while the individual's tax burden has also risen significantly. Besides the direct impact this has on the social wage, there is the additional effect on the political limits to the future capacity of Canadian state to raise revenue for social programs. Domestic pressure by corporations to keep taxes low and tax expenditures flowing will be countered by members of the middle- and working class who see themselves as increasingly shouldering the tax burden. These pressures will be underlined by the necessity to harmonize tax levels with those south of the border in order to ensure secure investment and circumvent capital flight.

On the spending side, the boom and bust nature of Canadian export-led growth with its uneven development, unemployment, and resulting capital-labour conflicts may have contributed to the state's higher spending on some social wage–related benefits such as social security and social assistance grants. Thus, the demands arising out of this growth process probably account for the tendency of the benefits flowing to workers to outweigh the taxes paid. The likelihood of the Canadian state sustaining this pattern of responding to the demands for social support are very slim when faced with the political limits of taxation and the harmonization to American economic conditions which are explicitly part of the FTA.

CONCLUSION

The introduction of the FTA signals a major effort on the part of Canadian capital to equalize the social wage with the United States. In this context, the social wage is seen as an impediment to investment and competition in an open economy. The FTA's promise to create a level playing field raises questions about the viability of differential tax and benefit levels on different sides of the border. In the face of competition with the United States for investment in production and jobs, Canadians will be told that they have little choice but to follow the American lead. The imperatives of the level playing field and competition with their American counterparts will likely mean that the tax burden will continue to be shifted away from corporations. In this scenario, the tax burden will either be forced upwards for the individual taxpayer or services will have to be cut back drastically. If, as the evidence seems to indicate, Canadian social wage levels in the 1970s and early 1980s were partly buoyed by state borrowing, then the current attack on deficit spending may signal increased pressure on labour to finance the social wage or accept cuts in it. Canadian workers in the 1990s may be paying more taxes for less government services and transfers – witness the move toward consumption taxes – while on the other side, capital struggles to win the subsidies or net social dividend needed to compete in Canada's more open economy.

All indicators point to a heightened period of class conflict compounded by regional tensions arising out of the historical legacy of regional uneven development. Constitutional and institutional crises signalled by the demise of the Meech Lake Accord and the Senate crisis around implementation of the GST legislation will have an impact on shaping the future dimensions of redistributive politics.

APPENDIX

This paper focuses only on one aspect of the state's role in the distributive struggle, the social wage. Other outcomes with respect to the specific burdens (taxes) and benefits (services/transfers) to capital are not covered here. Also excluded is a discussion of the other key institutions and relations contributing to the reproduction of labour – direct wages and domestic labour.

Under capitalism, the struggle for reproduction becomes fragmented into a struggle over wages, over the sexual division of labour within the family and resulting patriarchal relations, as well as a political struggle with the state. In addition, the present work does not account for the full revenue (including deficit financing) and expenditure position of the state apparatus. The aim here is to assess empirically if the working population is "winning" or "losing" with respect to the state and then consider what implications this might have for increased economic integration between Canada and the United States.

Despite the fact that there are many hurdles to be surmounted in order to derive quantitative estimates of the class-based variables these obstacles can be grouped into two general categories. First, there is the complex process of transforming and allocating the data found in the conventional national income and expenditure accounts (NIEA). Secondly, it is necessary to allocate the various NIEA categories according to a series of incidence assumptions. Even if the aim were to provide an analysis based on income deciles, these tasks are far from simple. There is considerable controversy within the conventional literature about the distributive implications of benefits from government expenditure. One example of many is the unequal distribution of the benefits of government expenditure on education. There is equivalent controversy with respect to dynamic tax incidence.

Political economists face the additional challenge of reinterpreting both the NIEA accounting categories and the existing studies of incidence into a class-based framework. The task is somewhat easier for mainstream economists, since NIEA data are collected on the basis of Keynesian conceptual categories. Regardless of the difficulties facing political economists, it is essential to move beyond

The Estimation Procedure of the Net Social Wage, 1970

	Total	Working population share‡
SOCIAL EXPENDITURES		
GROUP I		
Social services	5,807,591	3,980,076
Labour and employment benefits	145,189	145,189
Housing assistance	59,556	59,556
GROUP II*		
Transportation	2,417,508	1,186,291
Health	4,223,973	3,093,638
Education	5,992,979	4,389,258
Recreation and culture	584,157	427,837
Environment	556,608	407,660
Total benefits received by working population		1,368,503
		13,562
		(NIEA basis)
TAXES		
GROUP I		
Social security taxes	1,054	1,054
GROUP II		
Direct taxes – personal minus estate, pension	10,227	7,400
Other current transfers	1,077	789
– hospital and medical care premiums		
– motor vehicle licences		
Property taxes†	3,337	1,222
Total taxes paid by working population		10,555
NET SOCIAL WAGE 13562.18 − 10554.93 = 3007.25		

* Excludes postal services because of discontinuity of data. In the Canadian case, the different historical role of the state and the differences in expenditure typologies with the United States result in the exclusion of the American category "natural resources and energy." In Canada, these expenditures categorized in part under "resource conservation," are mainly a subsidy to capital with minor public goods exceptions like forestry expenditures.

† Because there is no breakdown of property taxes according to business and residential (which is the case in the United States), a 50 per cent split of business property and residential property tax is used following the results of Richard Bird, *Financing Canadian Government: A Quantitative Overview* (Toronto: Canadian Tax Foundation 1979).

‡ The share figure is determined by calculating the ratio of wage and salary income to personal income for all years.

speculative discussions of the outcomes of distributive struggles. Consequently, it is necessary to begin providing quantitative breakdowns of public finance which distinguish state activity on the basis of class. The accompanying estimation procedure of the net social wage is thus a modest contribution to such efforts.

NOTES

I wish to thank the editors for their comments. I am also deeply indebted to Riel Miller for the care with which he commented on earlier drafts.

1 The broad definition encompasses not only those who work for a wage or salary, but also all the dependants upon which the reproduction of the working population as a whole depends. From the perspective of social reproduction of the working population includes the young, the elderly and the infirm. However, as is well understood by those trying to defend the welfare state, the elements of the population not in the workforce or potentially in the workforce are viewed as an expensive social overhead – hence the efforts to squeeze old age pensions and disability benefits. In addition, the current round of cutbacks are part of an effort to force as large a proportion of the costs of social reproduction on to the wage-earning members of the working population and household labour.

2 In defining the share of income absorbed by the state it is important to recognize that a large share goes to state workers. These public employees are, from the perspective of gaining their subsistence, members of the working population. This paper does not attempt to provide an empirical estimate of the proportion of national income absorbed by the state. However, the value of the services which the state provides for the working population are in part measured by the cost of wages paid to state workers. Of course, other costs, elements of state expenditure, are included as well.

3 For an examination of spending levels based on more traditional categories, see Ken Battle, *Social Spending and the Next Budget* (Ottawa: National Council of Welfare April 1989).

4 See W. Irwin Gillespie, *The Redistribution of Income in Canada* (Ottawa: Gage Publishing in association with the Institute of Canadian Studies, Carleton University 1980).

5 See Andrew Martin, "Labour, Politics and the Changing International Political Economy," unpublished paper (Boston: MIT 1988).

6 A simplified version of the social wage fits into the "schemes of reproduction" in the following manner:

Recalling that $c + v + s =$ total value produced, where c is constant capital, v is variable capital, and s is surplus value, we can further subdivide variable capital (or the value of labour power) into two components, the private wage (P_w) and the social wage (S_w), so that the reproduction scheme is now: $c + (vP_w + vS_w) + s =$ total value produced.

The social wage is the net outcome, taking into account the taxes paid and benefits received by a worker or the working population at an aggregate level.

7 To the extent that comparison is possible, given the variation in methods of collecting national accounts data.

8 There is considerable latitude for different methods of assigning incidence. For a discussion of the larger methodological implications, see I. Bakker, "The Reproduction of the Working Population," Ph.D. dissertation (New School of Social Research, New York 1985), particularly, ch. 6.

9 See ibid. In this work, an alternative methodology has been adopted. However, even if workers assume a large proportion of corporate taxes, the Canadian case remains largely positive. For a more detailed treatment of net social wage analysis from a comparative perspective, see Isabella Bakker and Anwar Shaikh, eds., *The Welfare State and the Net Social Wage: An International Survey* (forthcoming 1991).

10 This figure covers only workers. From the perspective of reproduction, it is important to note that workers support a greater number of people who are part of the working population writ large (see note 1).

11 Anwar Shaikh and Ahmet Tonak. "The Welfare State and the Myth of the Social Wage" in *The Imperilled Economy*, vol. 1 (New York: Monthly Review Press 1987). This contrasts sharply with the findings of Bowles and Gintis who, in their study argue that "there has been a substantial redistribution from capital to labour" over the postwar period and that the supposed increased social wage is a key source of the current economic crisis. See "The Crisis of Liberal Democratic Capitalism," *Politics and Society* 11, no. 1 (1982).

12 For a discussion of comparative methodologies, see Shaikh and Tonak, "The Welfare State."

13 This analysis must be careful not to lose sight of the fact that even if labour is in a net loss position (i.e., has a lower social wage), workers may gain materially in terms of a higher quality of social services than would otherwise have been possible. For a discussion of entitlements in democratic welfare state regimes, see Gosta Esping-Andersen, "The Three Political Economies of the Welfare State," *Canadian Review of Sociology and Anthropology* 26, no. 1 (1989).

14 Bruce Wilkinson, "The Canada–United States Economic Integration Agreement and the GATT" in Marc Gold and David Leyton-Brown, eds., *Trade-Offs on Free Trade* (Toronto: Carswell, 1985), 55.

15 Jane Jenson, "Different but not 'Exceptional': Canada's Permeable Fordism," *Canadian Review of Sociology and Anthropology* 26, no. 1 (1989).

16 David Wolfe, "The Canadian State in Comparative Perspective," in ibid.

17 David Cameron, "The Growth of Government Spending" in Keith Banting ed., *State and Society* (Toronto: University of Toronto Press 1985), 43.

18 Julia O'Connor, "Welfare Expenditure and Policy Orientation in Canada in Comparative Perspective," *Canadian Review of Sociology and Anthropology* 26, no. 1 (1989), 39.

19 Wolfe, "The Canadian State," 96.
20 For a good discussion, see David Dodge and John Sargent, "Canada" in Joseph Pechman, ed., *World Tax Reform: A Progress Report* (Washington: Brookings Institute 1988).
21 Neil Brooks and Linda McQuaig, "Taxing Our Intelligence: Michael Wilson's Great Reforms," *This Magazine* 21, no. 6 (November 1987).

13 Shaping or Serving Markets? Public Ownership after Privatization

JEANNE KIRK LAUX

The challenge for the 1990s is a challenge of imagination: to create a new political economy able to promote sustainable economic development and social solidarity within a world economy marked by competition on a global scale. Should public ownership, and more specifically, state-owned enterprises, be considered part of this future? Privatization programs in Canada, as in Europe, have led to the sale of some major companies and put into question the utility of state ownership. We will confront the rhetoric and the practice of privatization to show how neo-liberal governments continue to shape markets and will argue that in a volatile global economy state enterprises must be part, but only a part, of progressive political economy.

Today any realistic assessment of public ownership will take into account three certainties. First, there has been a world-wide reorganization of production – a complex process of investment and divestment within and across national economies resulting in the pre-eminence of knowledge-intensive industries dominated by internationalized oligopolies. In the 1990s the very boundaries defining a firm or an industry are blurred, as the leading companies devise strategies of flexible specialization, negotiate inter-firm alliances in research and development, subcontract production, and form joint ventures to spread risks and share markets.

Secondly, there has been an ideological sea change to neo-liberalism. Neo-liberal discourse proclaims international competitiveness to be the overarching objective and to reach it governments must select market-driven policies, minimizing the direct intrusion of the state in the economy. Social programs are reconstrued as costs-of-production. Competitiveness becomes the new patriotism and citizens are exhorted to accept difficult adjustments now in the name of future market-driven prosperity. Like it or not, neo-liberalism is still hegemonic. It constitutes the reference point for the left – whether in a combative mode (the fight against free trade in Canada) or in a co-optive mode (the deference to international competitiveness on the part of the socialist government in Spain).

And thirdly, the experience of Thatcherism in Britain demonstrates that in a permissive political conjuncture the state can withdraw from its direct role in production, even in the production of services assumed to be essential infrastructure for capitalist accumulation. At the other extreme, the Mitterrand experience of the early 1980s demonstrates the political possibility of nationalizing the leading competitive multinational firms. This outer boundary of direct state intervention was of course quickly redrawn by the centre-right in France. Yet the point remains. Although there is no alternative to state intervention in the capitalist economy, the commercial public sector can no longer be taken for granted as a permanent feature of the postwar mixed economy. Rather it has become a subject of politics and thus continually subject to redefinition.

These observations about global political economy, hegemonic ideology, and state intervention are both the starting point for strategic thinking about a new political economy, and constitute the rocky grounding for *realpolitik* choices among immediate policy options. The specific question to consider is whether state enterprises are still appropriate instruments for national development. I propose to address this question in the present tense – after privatization – rather than turning backwards to reconsider the past performance of state enterprises or the original reasons for their nationalization.

PRIVATIZATION: WHAT HAPPENED HERE?

With the election of a Conservative government in Ottawa in September 1984, privatization became official policy. As part of a broad program to "secure economic renewal," the minister of finance announced in his first budget speech that "Crown corporations with a commercial value but no ongoing public policy purpose will be sold."[1] In this reconsideration of the role of the state in the economy, Canada obviously was not alone. The trend to privatization ballyhooed in the international press began with the election of the Thatcher government in Britain in 1979 when the Queen's speech introduced proposals to "reduce the extent of state ownership and increase competition by providing offers of sale."[2] In both Europe and Canada during the 1980s privatization programs had a threefold impact: on commercial public sectors; on ideology; and on the left agenda.

Commercial Public Sectors

Across the political spectrum we find that West European governments in the 1980s declared their intent to denationalize, privatize, or rationalize their corporate holdings. Some governments on the centre-right, like Canada, were motivated by neo-liberal ideology and emboldened by the success of Margaret Thatcher in Britain – for example West Germany, Holland, and France (under Jacques Chirac after 1986). Other governments, formed by socialist and social democratic parties, refused to embrace privatization as a principle but felt compelled by fiscal constraints to divest some of their corporate holdings – for example, Italy, Spain, Sweden, and later Austria. All European governments, regardless of ideological stripe, were seeking a way out of recession. In the face of budget restrictions and intense international competition, they scrutinized the purpose and costs of public enterprises. All proceeded to sell some state companies outright, to cede a portion of shares held in others, or to close down money-losers. Nowhere, however, do we find a replication of the British experience. Rather than wholesale privatization, other European governments restructured their commercial public sectors with a view to competition – competition for sales in world goods markets as well as competition for scarce funds in capital markets.

A few examples must suffice.[3] On the left, Spain's socialist government, after two years in power, instructed its holding company INI to get the state out of businesses such as shipbuilding or ball-bearings which were unlikely to make it in international competition. At the time INI was responsible for 17 per cent of industrial investment in Spain through its 253 wholly or majority-owned companies. In Italy a Social Democratic government appointed a tough new chairman in 1983 to head the giant holding company IRI and authorized some thirteen state companies to go to the stock market for new financing. Arguing that "the era of rescues is past," non-competitive steel plants were sold off and high-tech firms encouraged to enter into joint ventures with leading foreign firms.[4] To the right, when West Germany's Christian Democrats regained power in a coalition government in 1982 they vowed, on grounds of efficiency, to reduce the state's commercial holdings. In addition to the state banks, the federal government had a controlling interest (more than 25 per cent) in nearly one thousand enterprises, often through large conglomerates such as Saltzgitter. Some companies were sold – notably the chemicals and energy giant VEBA in 1987 – yet overall, Germany's privatization served symbolic purposes and brought in revenue through partial divestments.[5]

The net effect of privatization programs, left or right, has been to circumscribe commercial public sectors and to restructure state-owned enterprises with a view to competition. Everywhere but Britain, the reality rather than the rhetoric of privatization in Europe shows that governments did not fully dismantle but rather streamlined their corporate holdings, waving the banner of profitability and competitiveness. Employment goals and subsidized public services have been devalued in favour of efficiency and credit-worthiness. The streamlining process has involved both divestment and new investment, typically taking place through holding companies, joint ventures, and subsidiaries of multinational state enterprises. These are flexible corporate vehicles compared to the archetypal stand-alone public enterprise, able to attract outside financing and make investments with little political accountability. After a decade of privatization, governments in the industrial countries oversee modified but vital commercial public sectors officially guided by private sector norms.[6]

Ideology

Although privatization has by no means been the exclusive preserve of Conservative governments, it is Conservative ideologues who transmuted the sell-off of state enterprises into an essential element in the ideological debate over states and markets. A higher truth – market forces – transcends issues of power and overarchs any partisan agenda, or so we are led to believe. The debate over states and markets, far from remaining abstract, is part of the construction of a neo-liberal hegemony with its very real political consequences. Thus the Conservative approach to privatization is clearly demarcated from others by its axiomatic and messianic character. Axiomatic? State enterprises are seen to be symptomatic of the intrusive state and their privatization is therefore ipso facto good. As Canada's Conservative minister of industry put it, in announcing the sale of state-owned corporations valued at over $2 billion, the "discipline and vitality of the marketplace will replace the often suffocating effect of government ownership."[7] Messianic? Under Thatcher, the British government quickly turned a reactive concept, denationalization, into an open-ended strategy – privatization (including liberalization, contracting-out, user fees, and so on) was part of a broad thrust to recast the balance of public and private power. British experience was not regarded as a strictly national policy but vaunted as a universal model: "Though many features of the UK scene are unique, the reasons for privatisation are likely to be the same, whatever a country's experiences: the desire to increase competitiveness and efficiency; and the belief that the powers of the free market place can achieve this better than state control."[8]

When privatization is construed in grandiose terms as "the act of strengthening the market at the expense of the state,"[9] it advances a political project aimed not only at putting Keynesianism in the dustbin of history but also at eliminating any basis for renewed liberal–social democratic coalitions. Upon taking power, Canada's Conservatives put the blame for economic stagnation on the Liberals, because "they substituted the judgments of politicians and regulators for the judgments of those in the market place."[10] Today the exuberant privatizers of the right are vocally convinced that success in selling state companies has knocked down what was the main platform of socialist and social democratic programs – nationalization. Here we may quote the populist Conservative premier of Saskatchewan, when announcing his intention to sell shares in three important state enterprises. Calling the opposition NDP a "left-wing organization" which, unlike Mikhail Gorbachev, ignores the global trend to privatization, he crowed that "This is their Alamo, this is their Waterloo, this is the end of the line for them."[11]

The Left Agenda

If privatization programs on the right buttress neo-liberal hegemony and if state enterprise sectors restructured by left or right governments neglect social purposes in favour of competitiveness, these two developments in turn have utterly confused the left agenda in so far as public ownership is concerned. For socialists such as Robin Murray, the disillusion with nationalized industry in a capitalist mixed economy is long-standing. The equation "socialism = nationalization plus the party" wrongly substitutes formal ownership for real changes in social relations. In Britain, certainly, nationalized industries, even under Labour governments, were typically dealt with at arms' length. Experience with the National Enterprise Board in the 1970s showed that in an internationalized economy this tradition can only result in ineffective industrial policy and company managers who align themselves with private sector norms.[12]

For social democrats more concerned by electoral politics, the relative ease with which privatization programs have been implemented is cause for consternation. The spasmodic nature of opposition to privatization and, by contrast, the broad public acceptability of share offerings by major state enterprises – British Telcom, the French state banking group Paribas, or Air Canada – show how far the tide has shifted from an era when public interest or economic nationalism or nation-building under-pinned state investment. As one discouraged NDP member put it at a 1988 post-election rally in Ottawa: "The politics of Keynesianism and state socialism won't get us elected." James Laxer's critical report on NDP economic strategy argues that although the party formally includes nationalization in its programs, rarely has it called for nationalization in practice.[13] Indeed, despite the Conservative privatization program under way at the time, the NDP did not make support for public enterprise part of its 1988 campaign in the elections which saw the Tories returned to power.

The greater the ambivalence about public ownership on the left, the less surprising it became, in conditions of recession and competitive world markets in the 1980s, for managerial socialism to appear as the new wave. Spain is an eloquent case in point. Prime Minister Gonzalez, a socialist, saw no alternative to state capitalism and heralded the prin-ciples of efficiency and competitiveness governing Spain's post-privatization public sector. As Gonzalez explained in a interview: "I think I am still a socialist, but there's a certain propensity to confuse socialist positions with stupid positions ... I am absolutely repulsed by the ideological intransigence of the left, who stick to the old idea that nationalization equals progress, when reality has shown the reverse."[14] All in all, it is hard not to concur with David Heald that while there has been much objection to privatization, there has been no "principled defence of public ownership" and that commitment to public ownership as such by parties on the left is "now diluted if not abandoned."[15]

PRIVATIZATION, CANADIAN STYLE

"In essence, we are turning business back to business – where it belongs."[16] By the end of Conservatives' first term in office in 1988, they had sold eleven crown corporations or shares in companies directly held by government with an asset value of $6.4 billion (see Appendix, p. 306).[17] In so doing the Conservative government in Ottawa turned its back on a long-standing Canadian tradition of public ownership and nation-building, embracing instead a "free enterprise" ideology.[18] The Tory privatization program represents the most significant withdrawal of the state from production in Canada since British Columbia's populist privatizations in 1977.[19]

Some of the companies sold had been in the public sector since before the Second World War; some were associated with nation-building objectives thought sacrosanct (for example, Air Canada); virtually all were profitable at the time of sale (exceptions are Pêcheries and Cana-dair) and a few even paid dividends to government (for example, Teleglobe). They range across industries from aircraft manufacturing to fish processing. Before assessing the impact of privatization policy on both the state and the market in Canada, we need to know some whys and wherefores. What was the official rationale, and how were the Conservatives able to implement a program which went against the grain of national tradition?[20]

Ministers and officials advance three principal reasons to justify the government's claims that "privatization is an alternative whose time has come:" the pocketbook, politics, and competitiveness.

The pocketbook. After the 1984 elections, privatization was initially presented as just one among a series of initiatives to "realize further cost savings through more efficient management across the entire federal government."[21] The common thrust of these initiatives was to reduce the federal deficit, either by eliminating programs or bringing in revenues. Over time, as other objectives came to the fore, financial management was retained as the official first principle of the privatization program. Typically the minister of privatization's speechs begin by stating pompously: "The government must improve the management of its assets." Then the principle is restated in more popular fashion: "Crown Corporations tie up a lot of public money." Officials always deny, however, that deficit reduction is their main motivation for selling off public enterprises: "This is not a financially-driven but an opportunity-driven initiative."[22]

Politics. What is the opportunity offered? Moving towards their 1988 reelection campaign the Tories developed a popular capitalism concept to appeal to Canadians beyond the narrow circle of financial and business élites who had directly benefited from the first round of sales of corporate assets. After experimenting with public share issues in the privatization of Fisheries Products International (a mixed government enterprise), Ottawa announced the much more significant sale of shares in Air Canada (April 1988). The legislation to privatize this major crown corporation was put through under the evocative title of the "Air Canada Public Participation Act." The privatization minister explained: "Through privatization, we give managers and workers a chance to run their own company, free from the weight of bureaucratic review. We give Canadians opportunities to participate in companies which are central to our economy."[23] An employee share plan (but not representation on the board of directors) and restrictions against any individual holding more than 10 per cent of shares have been the policy expressions of participation which could more aptly be called voter co-optation.

Competitiveness. From the outset the neo-liberal buzzwords of competitiveness, efficiency, and markets have punctuated all Canadian government policy statements on privatization. The president of the Treasury Board, heading the first task force on privatization, argued for the need to "make room for private sector initiatives" so as to "improve market efficiency." As for the former state enterprises, their "corporate efficiency" would be best achieved through "market discipline."[24] The minister of transport insisted on competitiveness as the rationale for promoting Air Canada's privatization before a House of Commons committee: "What the airline needs to keep pace within today's competitive environment is the access to the equity capital markets its competitors enjoy." Flexibility must replace administrative constraints – "private ownership will give Air Canada the freedom it needs to respond quickly and effectively to the demands of the market."[25] Following the Conservatives' re-election in 1988, competitiveness moved to the top of the list of purposes for privatizing – after all, "true competition is difficult to achieve where a nationalized industry has a major stake."[26]

But Canadian privatization in theory and in practice has proven to be at once more and less than the issues captured in these thumbnail sketches of official rhetoric. More in that the overarching purpose has to do with ideology and entails an all too successful effort to substitute market logic for public policy. The Conservatives have adopted the market discourse usually articulated by business and have gone further than business in attempting to undermine traditional political culture values concerning the role of the state and public enterprise in Canada. Less in that the privatization program as implemented appears uncomplicated. Rather than changing market structures to enhance competitiveness, the pattern of sales and the post-privatization behaviour of enterprises suggests that the privatization program has increased corporate concentration in the Canadian economy and reinforced existing government-business élite networks. Let me review in turn the impact of privatization on political discourse and on market structures.

Political Discourse: Substituting Market Logic for Public Policy

"The Privatization program is a symbol of this government's confidence in the private sector."[27] The Mulroney government's immediate adoption of an ideologically charged privatization program should have come as no surprise. After all, the short-lived Conservative government under Joe Clark found time to create a Privatization Secretariat headed by Sinclair Stevens, an enthusiastic privatizer who posted a list of companies for sale: Canadair, de Havilland, Northern Transportation Company Ltd. (NTCL), and Eldorado Nuclear Ltd. The same list would be put forward by the same minister, now heading the industry portfolio, in 1984. Clark's principal advisor, Jim Gillies, a self-anointed "neo-conservative" was persuaded that it was time to reverse forty years of excess concentration of power in the hands of the state.[28] The conservatives' intent was clear: "We are determined to get the federal government out of ordinary business and commercial operations and hand them over to private enterprise where they belong."[29]

Public opinion, however, proved hostile to the Clark government's attempt to sell off the state-owned oil company, Petro-Canada, and time ran out after a no confidence vote and the subsequent re-election of the Liberals. Nonetheless, the Tories nurtured their privatization project during the early 1980s when recession drained voter support from the Trudeau Liberals and the failure of energy megaprojects led to disillusion with ostentatious government intervention. In 1983 the newly elected Conservative party leader, Brian Mulroney, set up a task force to consider the future of state enterprises. The problem was seen to be political only: how to reduce the size of the commercial public sector without raising popular objections. The answer was twofold. First, all state corporations should be subjected to market discipline by, for example, imposing return-on-investment as a performance criterion and thereby obliging managers to rationalize activities. Secondly, selected companies which did not have symbolic importance in the public eye, such as Canadair and Eldorado Nuclear, should be sold off immediately after the election before there was time for opposition to develop.[30]

Privatization instantly became a Conservative government priority and it found strong symbolic support from the business community following the September 1984 election. Early in 1985 the Chamber of Commerce submitted a brief to the responsible minister, arguing that only national defence or regulation of monopolies can justify creating crown corporations. Canada, as a market system respecting property rights, must correct the "market distortion" represented by its commercial state enterprises.[31] This market logic has been respected in official discourse, as we saw above, to the point where senior government officials proudly report that even where government companies are not yet privatized, "the very fact that we start to treat some of these companies as investments rather than as policy instruments is a good first step."[32]

But imitative market logic cannot suffice to win the hearts and minds of the people. The Conservative government had both to defend itself against over-identification with the harsh social policies associated with Thatcherism and to confront a political culture in Canada favourable to public enterprise. Beginning in 1987, Ottawa tried to distance its policies from those of Thatcher: "Let me state from the outset that there is an important distinction between the Canadian government's privatization program and that of other jurisdictions such as the United Kingdom," the minister of state for privatization began, and then underscored the Tory policy agenda for pensions, job creation, and child care.[33] Or, speaking at an international colloquium, the deputy minister devoted her entire speech to the distinctive features of the Canadian privatization "model," concluding that "The model has profited from the British experience ... but the model is a Canadian model. We have had to take our unique conditions and circumstances into account.[34]

Unique perhaps, but not immutable. The Conservative government next set out to close the historical book. Obeisance was first made to traditions: "We are mindful of the fact that many of our national Crown corporations have earned the respect of Canadians for the key roles they played in the industrial and regional development of our great country."[35] This positive role was, however, quickly relegated to ancient history. After recalling the Welland Canal, the CNR, and the CBC, official statements emphasize that times have changed. "In Canada's early years, state intervention was important – in fact essential ... Today, Canada has a developed and maturing social and economic infrastructure." Thus, "the private sector is recognized as being more appropriately the principal stimulant of economic growth and renewal." In the 1980s, "the emphasis on state ownership and big government ... has to be curtailed."[36]

In turning the historical page to begin rewriting from a neo-liberal perspective the federal Conservatives are not alone. Quebec's Liberal government under Robert Bourassa adopted an identical perspective. In the world according to the Quebec minister of privatization, we learn that: "Quebec is an integral part of the international movement toward economic reorganization, whose goal is greater efficiency through entrepreneurial vitality"; that Quebec now has businessmen who are "able to take up the challenge and openly ask the government to allow them the freedom to operate that is their due"; and that "the initial goals that led the way to the creation of Crown corporations have largely been achieved."[37]

In Ottawa the actual practice of privatization taking place under the umbrella of market logic has been fairly straightforward. All crown corporations and government shareholdings were considered for sale. The onus is on ministers to demonstrate a public policy purpose which might preclude privatization. Initially the maverick minister of industry simply pre-empted cabinet by proceeding to sell the companies held by the Canada Development Investment Corporation (CDIC) which, as a state holding company, had the authority to divest companies not subject to legislative statutes but incorporated under companies law. CDIC set up a special divestiture committee of seven, headed by a dollar-a-year private sector man, Paul Marshall, CEO of Westmin Resources and also president of Brascade Resources. He brought in six other private sector men, two of them, like himself, from companies affiliated with Brascan, the major investment group headed by the powerful Bronfman family which controls Brascade Resources.

In order to undertake privatization of the remaining forty or more crown corporations, machinery of government had to be put into place to expedite the process. After an initial six months of jockeying for power among ministers, a unique all-ministerial task force was set up to advise the prime minister. The four ministers (from Treasury Board, Industry, Energy, and Ministry of State for Finance) were served by a small secretariat headed by the former vice-chairman of Canada's multinational telecommunications giant, Northern Telecom. The normal submissions to Treasury Board were not required because the task force reported directly to the prime minister. Only in the summer of 1986 did Mulroney institutionalize privatization and give the program high public visibility by naming a minister of state (privatization), creating a skeletal department to serve her, and then revising the cabinet committee structure to include Privatization and Regulatory Affairs. In the lead-up to the 1988 election, a cabinet reshuffle placed a powerful minister, Don Mazankowski, in charge of privatization, thereby demonstrating its priority and making possible the oft-delayed decision to sell Canada's flagship crown corporation, Air Canada.[38] Since its re-election, although the Conservative government proceeded apace to prepare several divisions of Atomic Energy of Canada Ltd. for sale and complete the divestment of Air Canada, until the budget speech of February 1990 only rumours enlivened a dossier now headed by a junior minister. The "very last minute" announcement by the finance minister that Petro-Canada is to be privatized, when carried out, will dramatically narrow the contours of the state enterprise sector. Here we can only assess the impact of the program as realized during the 1980s.[39]

Shaping Markets to Serve Business Interests

To what extent did the implementation of the privatization program carry out the government's high purposes, validating the claims of neo-liberalism by enhancing the market at the expense of the state? When we look at the list of buyers displayed in the Appendix there does not appear to be any simple pattern. Instead we find the complexity of Canadian class and regional interests well mirrored in the heterogeneity of the buyers who have acquired crown assets during the privatization program. Buyers include small commodity producers; aboriginal peoples' organizations; international (US) capital; Canadian finance capital and industrial capital. There are also alliances between state and private capital. Thus the two investment groups which bought out Teleglobe were themselves then owned by the pension funds of state companies (CN, CBC, Air Canada), provincial state enterprises (Quebec's Caisse de dépôt and Société générale de financement as well as Ontario Hydro), and private capital (Bell Canada, the Laurentian Group).[40]

The net effect on market structures of these transfers of public assets to a diversity of buyers has been to increase concentration in the Canadian economy. According to Statistics Canada, the share of business assets owned by the top twenty-five conglomerate firms rose to 35 per cent in 1986, up from 30 per cent in 1976. The current rash of mergers and acquisitions has presumably increased the figure, as the federal bureau of competition reported an increase of 69 per cent in corporate acquisitions annually from 1984 to 1987.[41] The early sales of crown corporations, because they took place by way of asset sales, paralleled this private sector trend.

Looking at specific industries, we note that selling Canadian Arsenals to the SNC Group increased concentration in the munitions industry and placed SNC in an advantageous "market" position since Arsenals had normally sold over 90 per cent of its production to the state. Already a producer of small calibre arms, SNC thereby acquired the only Canadian producer of 33mm calibre and larger ammunition. Teleglobe, the state enterprise responsible for Canada's overseas telecommunications, was initially sold to a small data communications company, but after privatization Canada's second-ranking corporation, Bell Canada Enterprises, acquired enough shares on the market to achieve the largest ownership interest.[42] By negotiating the sale of de Havilland to Boeing, the government increased aircraft industry concentration within Canada and also enhanced the American aerospace giant's global market power by adding a regional carrier to the family of aircraft offered Boeing's customers.

Even where privatization took place through wide public share issues, as in the case of the CDC, the market allowed for reconcentration of holdings. When the government disposed of its shares in CDC, the affiliated companies of the Brascan group put together approximately 15 per cent of the voting shares despite legislation intended to ensure dispersal of ownership rights.[43] Following privatization, management of this $8 billion holding company sold off groups of companies. Among them, the renamed Polysar Energy and Chemical Corp was quickly taken over by NOVA, already Canada's forty-fourth largest company.

The second impact of privatization on the market place has been to give particular companies policy benefits which enhance their market power. Just as cronyism and regional politics are intrinsic to the process of awarding government contracts, so in selling crown corporations also the government proffered favours to a select group of well-established companies. A few examples will illustrate how Ottawa sought to make sure that "privatization works" in the transition period. In the case of Boeing, the Memorandum of Understanding with the federal government offered this exceptionally profitable American corporation grants for 35 per cent of the cost of modernizing the Ontario plant and also agreed to provide 50 per cent of the funds to development a new version of the Dash-8 plane, using in each instance the federal Defence Industry Productivity Program (DIPP).[44] Teleglobe, once privatized, had its rates of return subject to regulation like the telephone companies, but by assuring the company a monopoly position in international communications for five years the government sent the company off to an easy start in the "market place." Immediately after Bombardier purchased Canadair and created the Canadair Aerospace Group, the federal government awarded an important contract for repair and overhaul of its CF-18 fighter aircraft to the company, despite the lower bid submitted by a more experienced company, Bristol Aerospace, located in Manitoba. More recently, the government sanctified Canadair/Bombardier's future as a subcontractor for Airbus by signing a Canada-France agreement and contributing $37.3 million or 24 per cent of the start-up costs (as did the Quebec government) in ostensibly recoverable loans.[45]

The reality rather than the rhetoric of privatization belies the neoliberal credo of competition and market discipline and shows rather that sales of crown corporations have tended to increase concentration and to give a select set of corporate élites the benefit of state support. Nonetheless, even though the importance of the sales made should not be underestimated, and the effect of the program on the norms governing state intervention is critical, a substantial state enterprise sector still remains in place. In Canada at the end of the 1980s the federal government owned outright some forty-three commercial corporations which in turn controlled more than two hundred subsidiaries and associate companies, which directly employed 128,000 people and represented $49 billion in assets.[46] Once we bring in the corporate holdings of the ten provincial governments and the territories, direct state intervention in the production of goods and services for the market remains significant in Canada, as it does in Europe outside of Britain.[47]

AFTER PRIVATIZATION, WHAT?

The era of privatization is practically over. In Italy, despite a continuing fiscal crisis, the latest reform package to reduce public spending, billed as "the most ambitious attempt ever," proposed raising the pensionable age, increasing railway fares, and selling public land, but did not mention privatizing public enterprises.[48] Global competitiveness in the 1990s calls for strategic state investments, not laisser-faire. Thus the Italian state holding company, ENI, has negotiated a joint venture with the chemical giant Montedison (government is one shareholder) to merge most chemical activities in order to achieve "a company of sufficient size to compete in international markets."[49] In France the October 1987 stock market crash provoked enough uncertainty to put the right's privatization policy on hold; the delay allowed the left to regain power in 1988 and to freeze both nationalizations and privatizations until after Europe 1992. State-owned carmaker Renault announced record profits for 1988, including profits for all its subsidiaries, and the economics minister approved the cross-investment between the two state-owned banking groups, BNP and the Union des Assurances de Paris, agreeing as well to contribute more state capital so the new alliance can expand its European market share.[50] In Britain, of course, privatization continues to be a high priority, but there is little left to sell now that the water authorities are being privatized and the Central Electrical Generating Board is being restructured preparatory to sale. From time to time in Europe or Canada we can expect to see another sale of a government's shareholding, but national policy-makers' attention no longer centres on privatization now that state capitalism has been nicely adapted to the new conditions of global competition and the new imagery of fiscally responsible state management.

The (New) Invisible Hand

In devising a new political economy, the prerequisite task is to clear away some of the ideological underbrush by debunking the myth of markets versus the state which the privatizers perpetuate. Although privatization programs led to the sale of major companies in Europe and Canada, a substantial state enterprise sector remains and state-owned enterprises still figure among the key players in both national and world markets. Even those governments professing neo-liberal values are unwilling to leave well enough alone. In the first place, they keep a hand on the helm of those companies privatized, rather than allowing them to set sail in the free market seas. In the second place, they cannot resist using state investment as a discretionary instrument of policy.

After privatization, most companies remain subject to state-imposed restrictions on their freedom of action. Untrue to the neo-liberal claims that privatization will give the corporation unfettered flexibility, sales have typically been conditional. In the case of asset sales, restrictions have been imposed by the terms defining eligibility for tendering; in the case of public share issues, legislation has specified just who may acquire shares. In either case, a memorandum of understanding or a shareholders' agreement may set the limits of managerial freedom. In Canada such arrangements have stipulated headquarters location (Boeing/de Havilland) or employment levels (Fisheries Products International). In Europe and Canada restrictions on share ownership by foreigners usually apply. For example, no foreign telecommunications carrier can acquire shares in Canada's Teleglobe, while other non-residents are collectively limited to a ceiling of 20 per cent ownership; for Air Canada, "aggregate non-resident ownership cannot exceed 25 per cent."[51]

Even in Britain ways have been found to avoid the full consequences of market logic while privatizing. The use of the "golden share" – a non-voting government-held share in privatized firms – is well known. As officials explain: "To secure matters of essential national interest ... the Government has retained specific powers over the future ownership or control or conduct of a privatized company."[52] The articles of association for many privatized commercial companies preclude any one investor or group acquiring more than 15 per cent ownership. When privatized BP moved to take over privatized Britoil, the threat of invoking veto by way of its golden share enabled the government to set a list of conditions, from headquarters location to amount of exploration and development expenditures.[53]

In France, too, the centre-right government which initiated privatization in 1986 devised both legal and informal procedures to shape markets and avoid selling to unwanted buyers. Legislation placed a 20 per cent ceiling on foreign shareholders and the sale of a portion of shares was negotiated with investors friendly to the minister prior to going to a public offering. These "noyaux durs" or hard-core shareholders were usually established French financial conglomerates and they agreed to keep their shares for five years to stabilize ownership.[54] Imitating the British golden share, Prime Minister Chirac also legislated a special share or "action spécifique" to give government a veto over any shareholder acquiring more than 10 per cent interest in a company deemed strategic, for example the oil company Elf Aquitaine.[55] Many of these restrictions are time-bound and we can expect companies to bargain with governments, as Canada's Polysar Energy and Chemical Corporation has already done. On instruction from his board, the president of this former CDC subsidiary lobbied government to change the corporate charter, because "the board of directors believes that, following the sale by the Federal government of its remaining shares in the Corporation, the shareholders should have complete latitude to adopt whatever articles and by-laws they wish as is the case for almost all other public companies."[56]

Where traditional matters of state, such as defence industries, are at stake, or where matters of competitiveness make industrial restructuring appear to be in the national interest, governments on the right do not shy away from direct intervention. For example, the grandiloquent privatization discourse of Jacques Chirac did not prevent him from assiduously avoiding the sale of Aérospatiale. Indeed, his government authorized a further capital investment of 95 million francs to give the state-owned aerospace and armaments company controlling interst in Sfena, a navigational equipment company in deep financial trouble, but a company which did subcontracting work for Airbus 320, for the Ariane rocket, and for the new tactical missile Hades.[57] An example from Canada is instructive regarding the willingness of privatizing governments to use state enterprise to restructure a vital industry. In 1988 the merger of two crown corporations, federal Eldorado Nuclear and provincial Saskatchewan Mining Development Corporation, resulted in the creation of a supercompany, Cameco (Canadian Mining and Energy Corporation), which controls half of Canada's uranium production and all its refining. Cameco set about to lay off workers – miners in the West and refinery workers in Ontario – and temporarily close a mine ostensibly due to soft prices in world markets for uranium. In fact, spot markets account for barely 15 per cent of world trade. Cameco was actually engaged in rationalizing its operations, giving greater importance to the Key Lake mine, a joint venture with the German company Uranerz Exploration and Mining; modernizing the mill at Rabbit Lake to reduce the workforce; and undertaking new mine development at Eagle Point where the ore grade is higher. All of these decisions may make sense from the perspective of competitiveness, but none was the subject of public policy once the federal crown corporation (Eldorado) was folded into Cameco with its majority provincial government ownership and articles of incorporation allowing for divestment of state shares at any time.[58]

The fact that states continue to shape markets using both investment and conditional divestment should now be self-evident and yet it is not always obvious – hence our subtitle, the (new) invisible hand. Media acceptance of privatization hype tends to camouflage state capitalism. For example, the 1988 "privatization" of Air New Zealand Ltd. really involved a corporate reorganization to block a hostile takeover bid from British Airways. Although the New Zealand government was indeed selling it assets (to a consortium including the state-owned Australian airline Qantas with a 20 per cent interest), it retained a single share which gives government 65 per cent voting control![59] The presence of the state as partner in commercial enterprises is also obscured by partial shareholdings and new company names, so that government-controlled enterprises may appear to be just one of the boys in the business press accounts. Canada's major energy company NOVA ($8.2 billion assets) is an extreme case in point. To read either the press or the company's own annual report, NOVA appears a stellar example of entrepreneurial private capitalism. Yet the company, which was created as a public-private joint venture financed by Alberta government capital, still has articles of incorporation which limit any shareholder to a 15 per cent holding (the largest shareholder currently is the state investment agency, the Alberta Heritage Savings Trust Fund), and the government appoints four of the eighteen directors.[60] Once we know where to look, we need not inquire whether the corporate vehicle should be a policy instrument – it is. We need rather to ask, can it not be better used?

CONCLUSION: SHAPING MARKETS TO SERVE SOCIETY

The purpose of this chapter has been to make a principled critique of privatization. We have found that state capitalism is alive and well. Even governments on the right, despite incantations about the market, use conditional divestment and continued investment to shape markets in the interest of business. Is there a principled defence of public ownership to be made? The time for defending state enterprises as such is over. The time for advocacy is now – to promote those many forms of public ownership which are the best guarantors that production and exchange may serve society. Progressive political economy means non-dogmatic political economy, willing to seek out new strategies favouring sustainable development and social solidarity in a competitive global economy. Wholly-owned commercial state entreprises will be part of the strategy, but only a part. In particular regions and industries other forms of public ownership, from community investment funds and co-operatives to corporate joint ventures or state investments placed through holding companies, will be better suited to our purposes.

State enterprises, and state ownership interests in commercial corporations, nonetheless are and will remain a component of any national strategy. Regardless of ideology, as the venerable business economist Raymond Vernon observes, few governments "seem to be prepared to give up the option of maintaining a core of state-owned enterprises."[61] In a volatile world economy, state enterprises may serve to ensure a modicum of investment and production within the national economy. In a highly concentrated national economy, state enterprises may serve, as Hershel Hardin energetically argues, to provide another actor in markets dominated by a very few, often family-controlled, private companies.[62] In industries marked by research intensity and rapidly changing technologies, state enterprises and joint ventures may serve to set an appropriate agenda for research and development and to capture social benefits. But past experience warns us not to expect these benefits to flow from ownership alone. The uses and abuses of state enterprises are a matter of policy and politics. In a era when nationally based solutions to the challenges of global competitiveness seem elusive, there is a tendency for policy-makers to follow market norms set by international business. In Quebec, for example, which retains its state-owned industrial investment corporation, the SGF, the strategy for the 1990s is "to seize the opportunities which globalization of markets and the Canada–US free trade agreement offer." Thus the provincial state holding company has set out to extend its investment into the United States on the one hand, and promote joint ventures with foreign capital in Quebec on the other.[63]

In order to consider, in a realistic manner, how state enterprises fit within a progressive political economy, I suggest we listen carefully to the experience of both François Mitterrand and Robin Murray. Murray inspires us to go beyond narrow notions of nationalized industry to adapt to globalization, all the while ensuring democratic values in the management of the company at home. Mitterrand forewarns us that fitting into international markets can come at the cost of progressive industrial policy in the national economy. In his pivotal article in the *New Left Review*, Murray rightly argues that the project is one of "reclaiming the social economy" in which state enterprises are understood to be one, but only one, means to create "socially owned liberated zones." Existing public enterprises should be democratized and the policy guidelines for managers revised away from the cost-effective market orientation to emphasize the interests of workers and users. The simple notion of owning the means of production (by nationalization) must be revised to meet the realities of transnational industries, where flexible specialization, control over technology, and commercialization are keys to survival and success.[64]

The results of French nationalizations under the first Mitterrand government are a sober reminder, however, that even Socialist state managers may feel compelled to adopt the corporate logic of competitiveness in world markets. The French Socialists were in the first instance truly persuaded of the need to push for exports, given the vulnerability of the franc and the precarious balance of payments. They were then simply unable to impose industrial policies on the nationalized "grands groupes" which were already transnationalized oligopolies, some earning more than half of their revenues from overseas activities.

Forewarned is forearmed! Whatever the collective agenda for progressive political economy, we should be firm about the premise: states shape markets and markets must be shaped to serve society. To do so, many forms of public ownership are called for. Where government chooses to be the sole shareholder of a commercial corporation, these state enterprises need both policy direction and strong worker and user group representation on the boards of directors. All should be directed to reorient economic activity away from exclusive reliance on export markets and to set technological, environmental and workplace standards which allow for sustainable development and a quality of life inadequately captured by the bottom line.

APPENDIX: PRIVATIZATION FACT SHEET

($ *million*)
(Assets: Book value financial year-end preceding sale)
(Employment: 1986)
(Rank: *Financial Post 500*, summer 1988)

WHOLLY–OWNED CROWN CORPORATIONS

1. *Northern Transportation Company*
When: July 1985
Government owned since: 1944
Price: $27
Assets: $75.1
Activity: maritime freight transportation services, northern Canada and Arctic.
Employment: 324
Buyers: Inuvialuit Development Corporation (Inuvik) and Nunasi Corporation
    (Ottawa)

2. *De Havilland Aircraft of Canada Ltd.*
When: January 1986
Government owned since: 1974
Price: $90 (plus negotiable notes to $65 million maximum)
Assets: $345.8
Activity: aircraft manufacture
Employment: 5400
Buyer: The Boeing Company (Seattle)

3. *Pêcheries Canada Inc.*
When: April 1986
Government owned since: 1984
Price: $5
Assets: $15.9
Activity: fish processing
Employment: 460
Buyer: Purdel coopérative agro-alimentaire (Montreal)

4. *Canadian Arsenals Ltd.*
When: May 1986
Government owned since: 1945
Price: $92.2
Assets: $135.9
Activity: ammunition manufacture
Employment: 924
Buyer: The SNC Group (Montreal, rank #204)

5. *Canadair Ltd.*
When: December 1986
Government owned since: 1976
Price: $120 (plus future royalities on Challenger aircraft sales)
Assets: $478.2
Activity: aircraft manufacture
Employment: 5431
Buyer: Bombardier (Montreal, rank #69)

6. *Northern Canada Power Commission (Yukon/NWT)*
When: March 1987/May 1988
Government owned since: 1948
Price: $19.5 (plus notes worth $56 million)/$53 million
Assets: $146.3
Activity: electrical power generation, distribution
Employment: 317
Buyer: Yukon territorial government/NWT government

7. *Teleglobe Canada*
When: April 1987
Government owned since: 1949
Price: $488.3 (plus $16.6 million redeemable preferred shares)
Assets: $502.4
Activity: overseas telecommunications
Employment: 1110
Buyer: Memotec Data Inc. (Montreal, rank #247; key shareholder [27%] is now
  Bell Canada Enterprises (rank #2)

8. *Air Canada*
When: July 1989 (1st tranche, October 1988)
Government owned since: 1937 (subsidiary of Canadian National Railways; reorganization as crown corporation 1977; 57% ownership retained after 1st share offering.)
Price: $738 million (1st tranche, $8 per share; 2nd tranche, $12; 72.1 million shares issued)
Assets: $3099
Activity: air transport, passenger and cargo as well as airline related businesses (touring, credit card, leasing aircraft)
Employment: 22,200
Buyer: Public share offering

MIXED ENTERPRISES

9. *Nanisivik Mines Ltd.*
When: October 1986
Government owned since: 1975 (18%)
Price: $6
Assets: $64.8
Activity: lead and zinc mining
Employment: 195
Buyer: Mineral Resources International (Toronto)

10. *Fisheries Products International Ltd.*
When: April 1987
Government owned since: 1984 (62.6%)
Price: $177 (federal government proceeds $104.4)
Assets: $224.1
Activity: fish/seafood processing and marketing
Employment: 8,650
Buyer: public share offering (9% Bank of Nova Scotia)

11. *Canada Development Corporation*
When: October 1987 (1st tranche, September 1986; 2nd tranche, June 1987)
Government owned since: 1971 (41% government ownership 1984)
Price: $376.7
Assets: $7,259

Activity: Holding company (mining, synthetic rubber, data processing, copiers, biotechnology, industrial automation)
Employment: 11,387
Buyer: public share offering; August 1988 takeover by NOVA Corporation (Calgary, rank #44)

SIGNIFICANT SUBSIDIARIES SOLD

12. *CN Route* (division of *Canadian National*)
When: December 1986
Government owned since: 1984 (merger of CN Express and CN Trucking)
Price: $29
Assets: $40
Activity: trucking and distribution services
Employment: 2227
Buyer: Route Canada Holdings Inc.

13. *CN Hotels* (division of *Canadian National*)
When: March 1988
Government owned since: 1956
Price: $260 (plus working capital)
Assets: $136
Activity: tourist services – hotels, restaurants.
Employment: 3400
Buyer: Canadian Pacific Hotels (Montreal, subsidiary of Canadian Pacific, rank #4)

14. *Northwestel Inc.* (*CN* subsidiary)
When: December 1988
Price: $208
Buyer: Bell Canada Enterprises (rank #2)

15. *Terra Nova Telecommunications* (*CN* subsidiary)
When: December 1988
Price: $174
Buyer: Newfoundland Telephone Company Ltd.

MERGERS

16. *Eldorado Nuclear Ltd.*
When: February 1988
Following passage of Bill C-121 "An Act to authorize the reorganization and divestiture of Eldorado Nuclear Limited" (royal assent July 28, 1988), the governments of Canada and Saskatchewan announced the merger of Eldorado Nuclear Ltd. (uranium mining and refining) with provincially owned Saskatchewan Mining Development Corp. to create Cameco (61.5% provincial government ownership; remainder federal).

SOURCES: Minister of State (Privatization), Information Kit (1989); *Public Accounts of Canada 1987*, III; Canadian National *Annual Reports* 1987 and 1988; *Hansard.*

NOTES

In revising this paper, I greatly appreciated the trenchant comments by Frances Abele and our editors' diligence.

1 Department of Finance, "The Budget Speech," 23 May 1985: 10.
2 Great Britain, *House of Commons Debates* 967, col. 48–9, 15 May 1979.
3 Detailed assessments of privatization in Europe can be found in John Vickers and Vincent Wright, eds., "The Politics of Privatisation in Western Europe," special issue of *West European Politics* 11, no. 4 (October 1988), which contains articles on Britain, France, West Germany, Belgium, Italy, Austria, Holland, and Sweden. For the earlier policy intentions, see the special issue on "Privatization of Public Enterprise, A European Debate," *Annuals of Public and Co-operative Economy* 57 (April–June 1986).
4 Quoted in the *Globe and Mail*, 25 February 1985: IB4. Riccardo Parboni, IRI's chairman during the privatization period, explains his views on state enterprise in "La privatizzazione dell'economia italiana," *State e Mercato* 12 (December 1984): 385–430.
5 Josef Esser, "'Symbolic Privatisation': The Politics of Privatisation in West Germany," in Vickers and Wright, *West European Politics*, 61–73.
6 For a more complete rendition of this argument, see Jeanne Kirk Laux and Maureen Appel Molot, *State Capitalism: Public Enterprise in Canada* (Ithaca, NY: Cornell University Press 1988).
7 Quoted in the Toronto *Star*, 31 October 1985: 1.
8 HM Treasury, "Privatisation in the United Kingdom, background briefing," no. 18/1: 1.
9 Thomas Kierans (then of McLeod Young Weir), "Strenghtening the Market at the Expense of the State," *Choices* (April 1985).

10 Department of Finance, "A New Direction for Canada: An Agenda for Economic Renewal," 8 November 1984: 1–2.

11 Press conference remarks by Grant Devine quoted in *Globe and Mail*, "Saskatchewan selling firms worth $2 billion," 9 March 1989: Al.

12 Robin Murray, "Ownership, Control and the Market," *New Left Review* 164 (July/August 1987): 87–112.

13 James Laxer, *Rethinking the Economy* (Toronto: New Canada Publications 1983), especially chap. 11, "Public Sector Versus Private Sector: The NDP Dilemma."

14 *Ottawa Citizen*, "A Man with a Vision," 5 March 1989: E4.

15 David Heald, "The United Kingdom: Privatisation and its Political Context," in Vickers and Wright, *West European Politics*, 44.

16 Office of the Minister of State (Privatization), speaking notes for the Honourable Barbara McDougall to the Rotary Club, Calgary, 23 September 1986: 15.

17 Book value of assets may of course be rather more or less than the market value, but we use it in order to have a standard of comparison. The overall value of assets transferred to the private sector is not impressive when compared to the nearly $50 billion remaining in the public enterprise sector in 1989 (not including the Bank of Canada). Most of these assets are accounted for by the financial intermediaries which channel credit to the private sector for housing (CMHC), agriculture (FCC), small business (FBDB), and export financing (EDC).

18 Hershel Hardin, in *Nation Unaware: The Canadian Economic Culture* (Vancouver: J.J. Douglas 1974), most eloquently expounds this tradition.

19 J.M. Ohashi, "Privatization in Practice: The Story of the British Columbia Resources Investment Corporation," in I.M. Ohashi and T.P. Roth, *Privatization: Theory and Practice* (Vancouver: Fraser Institute 1980), 3–107. The symbolic value of the BC sales was high, but their dollar value was low – approximately $150 million (in 1978 dollars).

20 For a well-documented account which applauds the Tories' privatization program, see W.T. Stanbury, "Privatization and the Mulroney Government, 1984–1988," in Andrew B. Gollner and Daniel Salée, eds., *Canada under Mulroney* (Montreal: Véhicule Press 1988), 119–57.

21 The Nielson Task Force on Program Review was the most ambitious. This is not to say that the Conservatives lacked zest in introducing market-driven policies, e.g., deregulation in the airline industry or a new competition law. Privatization of crown corporations was simply not dynamically linked to these broader policies.

22 Office of the Minister of State (Privatization), speaking notes for the Honourable Barbara McDougall to the Ottawa chapter of (the) Institute of Public Administration of Canada, Ottawa, 23 March 1987.

23 Ibid.

24 President of the Treasury Board, *Annual Report to Parliament on Crown Corporations and Other Corporate Interests of Canada, 1983–84* (Ottawa: Supply and Services 1985), iv.

25 Canada, House of Commons, 2nd Session of the 33rd Parliament, *Minutes of Proceedings and Evidence of the Legislative Committee on Bill C-129*, 14 June 1988: 24.

26 The Honourable John McDermid, Minister of State (Privatization and Regulatory Affairs), "Privatization: The Purpose, the Process," *Canadian Business Review* (Winter 1989): 16–17.

27 Office of the Minister of State (Privatization), speech, 23 March 1987.

28 "Neoconservatism: some elderly political theories, attractively spruced up," *Globe and Mail*, 27 August 1979: 1.

29 Cited in "Crown firms for sale: Tories draw up list," *Toronto Sunday Star*, 12 August 1979: A10.

30 "Summary of the Task Force's Final Recommendations."

31 Canadian Chamber of Commerce, "Submission on the Commercialization of Crown Corporations" to the Honourable Robert de Cotret, President of the Treasury Board (May 1985): 7, 34. It should be noted that the chamber's Working Group on Crown Corporations which prepared this report was set up at the suggestion of the Liberal government (Comptroller General's Office) in February 1984.

32 "Privatization of Crown Corporations," notes for a speech by Dr. Janet Smith, deputy minister, Office of Privatization and Regulatory Affairs to the Society of Management Accountants, Ottawa, 25 November 1987.

33 Office of the Minister of State (Privatization), speech, 23 March 1987.

34 Office of Privatization and Regulatory Affairs, "Canada's Privatization Program: an Overview," Notes for a speech by Dr. Janet Smith, Deputy Minister, to the International Colloquium on Privatization, Scotland, 3 November 1987.

35 Office of the Minister of State (Privatization), speech, 23 September 1986.

36 "Excerpts from Statements Made by the Honourable Barbara McDougall on the Reasons for Privatization, 1 May 1987 (part of the government's privatization information kit).

37 "La privatisation des sociétés d'État au Québec," notes pour une allocution de M. Pierre Fortier, ministre délégué aux finances et à la privatisation, devant l'Institut d'Administration Publique du Canada, Groupe régional de la capitale nationale, Ottawa, 23 mars 1987.

38 The first tranche of Air Canada was sold on 13 October 1988. The announcement of the share offering for the remainder of Air Canada was made on 17 May 1989 and the sale was completed 19 July 1989. Office of Privatization and Regulatory Affairs, *News Release*, 1989–002. In the first

offering, the company had retained the proceeds; in the second offering funds went into the general government budget.

39 *Globe and Mail,* "Ottawa decides at very last minute to sell Petrocan," 21 February 1990: A1. The budget speech also made official Ottawa's plan to sell its 50 per cent interest in the telecommunications company, Telesat Canada.

40 "Memotec débourse $488 millions pour Téléglobe," *Le Devoir,* 12 February 1987: 1; "Win puts underdog Memotec in big league," *Globe and Mail,* 12 February 1987: B1.

41 Reports summarized in the *Globe and Mail,* 30 January 1989: A6.

42 During the bidding process, the government's initial policy guidelines aimed at avoiding giving control of international satellite communications to the established telephone companies or "common carriers" by limiting their share of any consortium to a one-third interest. Richard Schultz, "Teleglobe Canada," in Allan Tupper and G. Bruce Doern, eds., *Privatization, Public Policy and Public Corporations in Canada* (Halifax: Institute for Research on Public Policy 1988), 348–50. On the snc purchase, see "Privatized Munitions Firm Faces Tough Terrain," *Financial Post,* 14 December 1985: 4.

43 Although the legislation limited any group of individuals to a 10 per cent holding in the cdc, an anachronistic definition of what the legislation says constitutes a "group" allowed this outcome; Bill C-66. Canada Development Corporation Reorganization Act. See "CDC Takeover Charges Fly at mp's Committee," *Globe and Mail* 9 October 1985: B1 for the short story and Canada, House of Commons, *Minutes of Proceedings and Evidence of the Legislative Committee,* 15 October 1985 for the full story.

44 "Letter of Intent among Canada Development Investment Corporation, Her Majesty the Queen in Right of Canada and The Boeing Company." Later, intimidated by a Boeing lawsuit, Ottawa instructed its investment holding company cdic to pay out $100 million to help Boeing clean up health and safety problems at the Ontario plant and offered another $55 million in forgivable dipp loans to develop a new version of the Dash-8 aircraft. See *Globe and Mail,* 1 February 1990: A1.

45 "Canadair gets $1.4 billion job – jet repair contract stirs bitterness," *Globe and Mail,* 1 November 1986: 1; "Canadair signs new $1.2-billion contract to make Airbus parts," *Financial Post,* 24–26 September 1988: 9.

46 President of the Treasury Board, "Annual Report to Parliament on Crown Corporations and other Corporate Interests," in Government of Canada, *Public Accounts of Canada 1989* iii. These figures exclude the cultural crown corporations, such as the cbc, the Canadian Wheat Board (which together employ another twelve thousand persons), and the Bank of Canada.

47 Five provincial governments (British Columbia, Alberta, Saskatchewan, Ontario, and Quebec) had explicit privatization programs during the 1980s while others rationalized their corporate holdings without grandstanding (e.g., Manitoba). For a critical assessment, see Maureen Appel Molot, "The Provinces and Privatization: Are the Provinces Really Getting Out of Business?" in Tupper and Doern, eds., *Privatization*, 399–425.

48 "Italy takes a knife to public spending," *Financial Times* (London), 23 March 1989.

49 "Italian merger closer," *Globe and Mail*, 15 December 1988: B25.

50 "State-owned concerns prospering in France," *New York Times*, 9 May 1989: D1, D8; "Renault income doubles, confirming turnaround," *International Herald Tribune*, 22 March 1989: 14; and "French giants allowed to ally," *Globe and Mail* 21 March 1989: B17. The French state also invested another $2 billion (US) in Renault (by capitalizing loans owed), at year-end 1988.

51 Office of Privatization and Regulatory Affairs, *News Release*, 17 May 1989: 1.

52 HM Treasury, "Privatisation Achievements," speech by John Moore, financial secretary, 18 July 1984: 18.

53 "BP wins right to control Britoil," *Financial Times* (London), 24 February 1988: 23; "BP to buy back Kuwait stake," *Globe and Mail*, 4 January 1989: B1.

54 François Morin has analysed the patterns of concentration and privilege created by the negotiated share shares in "Les trois cercles des liaisons financières," *Le Monde*, 17 septembre 1987. The Socialist government has sought unsuccessfully to undo these arrangements. "France tries to pierce hard-core holdings," *Globe and Mail*, 20 February 1989: B14.

55 Both the foreign ownership and strategic industry regulations are stipulated in France, General Legislation, Law no. 86-912 of 6 August 1986, article 10.

56 Polysar, *First Quarter Report*, 19 April 1988, statement by president and CEO Bernard F. Isautier.

57 *Tribune de l'Économie*, 26 May 1986.

58 "Low prices for uranium costing jobs at Cameco," *Globe and Mail*, 29 March 1989: B1.

59 "Air New Zealand, Ltd," *Wall Street Journal*, 22 December 1988: A12.

60 NOVA, *Annual Report* (1989) and NOVA, "Notice of Annual and Special Meeting," 13 March 1989: 3.

61 Raymond Vernon, ed., *The Promise of Privatization* (New York: Council on Foreign Relations 1988), 17.

62 Hershel Hardin, *The Privatization Putsch* (Halifax: Institute for Research on Public Policy 1989), 5. Efficiency arguments are advanced to support state enterprises by the Canadian Labour Market and Productivity Centre, "In

Defence of Public Enterprise: A Critique of the Economic Efficiency Case for Privatization of Crown Corporations," *Labour Issue Papers* 1 (July 1988).

63 Notes pour une déclaration de M. Paul Berthiaume, Président du Conseil et chef de la direction de la Société générale de financement du Québec, Assemblée annuelle des actionnaires, 27 avril 1989.

64 Murray, "Ownership, Control and the Market."

14 Post–Fordism: Some Issues for Labour

RIANNE MAHON

One of the underlying assumptions of the Pro-Canada Network has been that the free trade agreement (FTA) represents something more than just another step down the road to continental integration. The qualitatively new element is that the FTA threatens to expose Canadian workers directly to neo-conservatism, American style. This argument is important in that it draws attention to important phenomena which began to spread across the border even before the FTA was signed: deregulation, privatization, contracting-out, and the growth of "voluntarism."[1] What the concept of neo-conservatism fails adequately to address, however, is the series of important changes that are reshaping the very organization of production.

In Canada, as elsewhere, capital is experimenting with new technology and new forms of work organization in an effort to compete in the new global economy. As the Canadian Auto Workers (CAW) have noted, this search is leading to the emergence of a new model of North American manufacturing. Our analyses need to make the connections between this emergent model of manufacturing and the macro dimensions caught by the concept of neo-conservatism. Although others have insights into this complex process, it is the French regulation school which has gone the furthest towards developing the necessary concepts.

This paper, then, attempts to situate the FTA as part of the broader process of restructuring. The first section outlines the basic perspective while the second section sketches the contours of post-Fordism, US style. It will be argued that the latter is generating growth but of the wrong kind: polarized growth. The FTA might thus result in Canada's incorporation into such a polarized regime, but this should not be regarded as a fait accompli. The Canadian labour movement, in alliance with other popular forces, has a good chance of pushing for an alternative, "red-green" variant of post-Fordism. It is precisely this prospect that is addressed in the last section.

A REGULATION PERSPECTIVE ON RESTRUCTURING

Three concepts are central to the regulation approach. The concept "model of industrialization" refers to the principles governing relations in production and thus the inner logic of productivity growth.[2] The concept "regime of accumulation" refers to the macro-economic logic governing the relations between production and consumption. Although in particular periods a given regime may be said to be operative in a number of social formations, the regulation school recognizes that significant cross-national differences in the mode of regulation – the complex of norms and institutions through which conformity to the logic of the regime is temporarily secured – are likely to exist.

The regulation school initially developed these concepts to analyse the dynamics of postwar growth in which a Fordist logic was dominant. Yet as the crisis of Fordism became more and more apparent, regulation theorists began to focus on the crisis and the search process it has unleashed. For Leborgne and Lipietz, the crisis is rooted in a contradiction which lies at the heart of Fordist relations of production:

The taylorist principle, while polarising this collective capacity between a mass of unqualified and unmotivated operators ... and the designers and technicians of the Operations and Methods Office ... gradually confined the struggle for innovation to the latter sector. Yet this can only contribute to a general rise in productivity by the ever more complex machines that it designs. The majority of the production team finds itself excluded in principle from the battle for productivity.[3]

The formal denial of the knowledge or know-how accumulated by the direct producers[4] meant that rises in productivity depended primarily on the development of ever more expensive machines and thus a rising capital-output ratio. It is the crisis of this model that is reflected in the poor productivity performance of Fordist industries over the last two decades.

The search for an economically viable solution to the crisis thus necessarily operates at a number of levels. Experiments with neo-conservatism constitute an important (and regressive) part of this search, but such experiments need to be seen in relation to experiments with different ways of combining various forms of labour and technology to yield new models of industrialization. Is is here that we encounter the phenomenon associated with Japanization (discussed by Morris in this volume) and the left's fascination with Scandinavian experiments in reorganizing work. Both dimensions need to be placed together if the full meaning of restructuring is to be grasped. Regulation theory, with its concept of regime of accumulation, enables us to do just this.

Departing from the Fordist juncture, two basic alternative models of industrialization appear to be possible. Super-Fordism continues along the same path as its predecessor, attempting to realize capital's dream of a workerless factory by using robots to replace people. As Fiat learned from its Robogate experiment, this is an expensive solution and it does not eliminate capital's dependence on labour. It does, however, sharpen the distinction between the technicians in command of the automated factory and the remaining production workers, stripped of their skills. Flexible automation breaks with Fordist assumptions, seeking productivity gains from the combination of programmable, general-purpose machines and workers possessing skills whose involved participation is essential for achieving productivity and quality improvements.[5] Super-Fordism seemed initially to be the track followed by most North American business, but the emergent "North American model of manufacturing" seems to be leaning in the post-Fordist direction of flexible automation.[6] However, flexible automation can be pursued in different ways, and each holds quite different consequences at the macro level.

One choice is Piore and Sabel's "craft revival," which would substitute economies of scope for Fordist economies of scale. Another is the strategy of "diversified quality production," advocated by Sorge and Streeck, in which economies of scope and scale are combined.[7] The difference between the two involves not only the model of industrialization but also the link between this and the structure of consumption. The rejuvenation of mass production (so-called diversified quality production) seems to call for the extension and deepening of Fordist mass consumption and with this the retention of the relatively progressive features associated with Fordism. That is, visible class differences in consumption were reduced and workers' wages could be high enough to allow them to consume the goods they produced. Workers' consumption, moreover, was considered to be good for the national economy: mass demand created its own mass supply. The craft revival model, however, makes no such demands, as Piore and Sabel admit. Flexible specialization could well flourish in a regime which resembles "the old Bourbon kingdom of Naples, where an island of craftsmen, producing for the court, was surrounded by a sub-proletarian sea of misery."[8]

Although Piore and Sabel can hardly be considered advocates of this historically regressive version of post-Fordism, they fail to think through the relationship between changes in production and the structure of consumption. The construction of post-Fordist scenarios requires more than an analysis of possible models of industrialization. One has also to consider the way in which the latter may be combined with different structures of income distribution (and hence structures of consumption) to produce different regimes of accumulation. Here the two critical variables may be the structure of the service sector and the strength and strategic orientation of the trade union movement. The service sector has received a large amount of attention from those attempting to probe the implications of the current wave of techno-economic change. The business service sector is likely to expand as large firms and small pursue flexibility, in part by contracting out services – from design through marketing to catering and security – once performed in-house. The new technology can also be used to dramatically improve productivity and quality not only in areas such as finance but also in the social services.[9]

These points, while useful, fail to grasp the central issue raised that there is a major difference between a service sector tilted towards the low-wage food service and entertainment branches and one focused on the provision of collective services, performed by skilled, high-wage workers. As Myles shows in his chapter in this volume, social services can be organized in different ways. In countries where the Fordist mode of regulation assigned a strong role to the public provision of welfare, there is a greater likelihood of establishing a regime based on maintaining a high standard of living for workers in core industries. There are two reasons for this: first, the higher wages paid to skilled, unionized public service sector workers create mass demand for quality goods; and secondly, the expansion of a high-quality public service sector (services by and for the people) leaves less room for the proliferation of low-wage private services catering to the wants of the rich. Conversely, in countries where the public system has focused primarily on the most disadvantaged, it generates the kind of income inequalities required to stimulate the growth of a two-tier economy. The public sector also remains particularly vulnerable to tax revolts of the kind seen in the United States and Denmark.

The strength and strategic orientation of the trade union movement are also important. Piore and Sabel recognize the relevance of this in developing their assessment of conditions favourable to restructuring in the direction of flexible specialization. Thus unions that have come to rely on detailed agreements to regulate what happens on the shop floor are often reluctant to accept organizational changes considered necessary to the successful implementation of flexible automation, whereas those which have accepted greater functional flexibility (deployment across a broad range of jobs within the plant or firm) encourage restructuring along these lines. Piore and Sable, however, ignore some of the more positive effects of unionization.

Thus where unions are relatively strong, they are in a position to counteract the trend towards *numerical* flexibility – the hiring and firing of 'just-in-time workers' – that also forms part of the new strategy. More broadly, where unions have generally managed to organize only the core workforce in the high-productivity Fordist industries, they will find it harder to prevent the proliferation of low-wage jobs in the expanding service sector and will find few allies in their struggle to resist concessions. Where unions have organized a relatively broad section of the workforce and have negotiated on the basis of wage solidarity, it will be easier to resist the kind of wage spread that constitutes the emergence of a dual economy.[10]

The emphasis on unions does not mean that other social forces are irrelevant to the outcome. As we shall see below, the new social movements also have an important part to play in shaping the structure and content of the new regime. Here the key question is whether the unions can form a broad-based alliance with such forces behind a progressive variant of post-Fordism or whether the new right manages to gain the ascendancy with its belief in market-driven policies.[11]

The shaping of post-Fordism, however, is unlikely to be left to national actors on their own, given the growing importance of formal economic ties between countries. For Canadians, it is especially important to consider the kind of regime that is taking shape in the United States, as the FTA will certainly intensify the pressures for harmonization. This does not mean that the FTA necessarily will lock the Canadian economy into a continental mode of regulation: there is still some room for manoeuvre. Yet, if we are to exploit this, we need to have a fairly accurate view of what it is we wish to avoid.

POST–FORDISM, US STYLE

The United States, home of Fredrick Taylor and Henry Ford, led the way in defining an organizational approach to production that came to typify the Fordish model of industrialization. Although the United States has always been a welfare laggard, it joined Sweden in making an early breakthrough towards the establishment of Fordist macro-economic regulation.[12] The United States can thus be said to constitute the paradigmatic exemplar of Fordism. Yet the mode of regulation through which Fordism was institutionalized was flawed in crucial respects. For Piore and Sabel, the fatal flaw lies in the industrial relations system which, while it supported a Fordist dynamic by linking wage increases to the rate of productivity growth, entailed a strategy for shop-floor control which enmeshed workers and managers in an ever-more-finely detailed set of job descriptions and work rules. A worker's income came to be pegged to his or her job classification which specified the limited bundle of tasks he or she was to perform. Advancement and job security, in turn, were linked to a series of narrowly defined job ladders and to seniority systems within these. According to Piore and Sabel, it is this rigid system of shop-floor control that constitutes a major barrier to flexible specialization. Thus, for them, the crisis of American industry is rooted in Fordist capital-labour relations.[13]

Yet the crisis of American Fordism and the relations shaping post-Fordism, US style, need to be seen as the result of a series of broader failures, not only to achieve more positive forms of shop-floor control but, more importantly, to build a strong labour movement uniting all sectors and regions of the economy and to secure a universalistic Keynesian-welfare state.

The first failure occurred in the immediate postwar years. The defeat of the United Auto Workers in the critical 1946 strike against GM was followed by other defeats, including the passage of the Taft-Hartley Act which sharply circumscribed union rights originally gained under the Wagner Act.[14] "Operation Dixie," a campaign to organize workers in the south, was abandoned in the face of state-backed employer intransigence and internal union divisions. These setbacks, in turn, paved the way for the expansion of a dualistic welfare system based on rudimentary public assistance for the poor and the luxuriant growth of the semi-private welfare fiefdoms so eloquently described by Rothschild.[15] Confined to their areas of strength in certain Fordist industries, located primarily in the north and mid-west, and constituting but one interest group among many within the Democratic Party, US unions turned their attention to securing rising wages and a package of fringe benefits designed to compensate for the limited character of public social services. The original version of American Fordist regulation was thus capable of sustaining but a limited form of mass consumption, one from which between one-quarter and one-third of the population was effectively excluded.

During the 1960s, it appeared that a new wave of reforms would succeed in incorporating blacks and women – hitherto largely confined to the low-wage, secondary labour market – into the Fordist dynamic.

The consolidation of organized labour via the formation of the AFL–CIO in the mid–1950s, the latter's increased concern about unemployment linked to the earlier wave of automation, and the entry of blacks and the modern women's movement into national politics, all opened up the possibility of such reforms for the Democratic Party.

The centrepiece of the Kennedy-Johnson reforms was a series of labour market programs that promised to bring the poor into the mainstream of society. Unfortunately, during the Kennedy years the effects of the failure of Operation Dixie – the continued domination of the Democrats' southern ranks by a racist right wing – prevented the consolidation of precisely such an alliance around an active labour market policy that would apply to both workers in the core and those on the periphery. Under Johnson the administration was able to make some sort of a breakthrough by maintaining such interesting programs as New Careers, designed simultaneously to expand the social service sector and to create good jobs for the under- and unemployed. Nevertheless, the great War on Poverty focused almost exclusively on "the disadvantaged" and this, on top of the disruption caused by busing, generated a backlash among white workers.[16]

This series of failures to mend the flaws in American Fordism left unions and other progressive forces in a vulnerable position when the global crisis of Fordism finally hit. Confined to a shrinking part of the population, the unions found it hard to resist capital's demands for concessions on wages and work rules, and this only served to further undermine conditions for mass consumption. The failure to extend the universalistic principles of Roosevelt's social security act to other parts of the social service sector, moreover, has opened the way to the proliferation of low-wage service sector jobs. Unable to overcome the political schism between workers in the primary and secondary labour markets, the Democratic Party has vacillated between a defence of the past and a neo-liberal strategy of Reaganism.[17]

By 1984 less than one-fifth of the civilian labour force in the United States was unionized, as compared to 34.7 per cent in 1955. The decline had set in before the crisis had really begun to make its effects felt; however, when the crisis hit, membership tumbled in core industries such as auto, steel, and rubber owing, in large part, to plant closures.[18] Pattern bargaining, which had helped to sustain Fordist consumption, at least among core workers, has also been eroded. For the first time since 1956, the United Steel Workers had to abandon industry-wide bargaining for firm-level negotiations. In steel, as in auto, core workers have accepted wage cuts and the scrapping of work rules.

If increased polarization of wages and working conditions is the likely outcome of the restructuring of production in the goods-producing sector, the jobs being generated in the service sector will only exacerbate this tendency. And it is here that we see the effects of the dualistic welfare structure that blossomed during the heyday of Fordism. The latter has continued to mushroom even during the crisis, producing "a welfare state for the well-to-do; a conglomerate of semi-private pension and insurance and medical schemes, clustered at the edges of the public sector and dependent for its survival on public regulation ... as well as on public investment, public tax subsidies and public payments."[19] And it is this sector, together with government employment, private services such as employment agencies, and retail trade that have provided 93 per cent of all new jobs between 1981 and 1986.

It is precisely this kind of service sector job growth that seems to be increasingly concentrated in three industries: private health care, business services, and fast food services. Each of these, in turn, tends to be characterized by "occupational/status expremes unmediated by substantial middle ranges."[20] Rothschild and others have added to the data on growing income polarization. Thus income differentials in high-growth areas such as finance, insurance and real estate (32.7 per cent in the bottom quintile) and retail trade (57.5 per cent in the bottom quintile) are higher than in the durable goods sector (27.7 per cent).[21] The growing disparity in wages is partly a result of skidding – out of higher-paid manufacturing jobs into the service sector – and partly owing to the fall in relative wages in the service sector itself.

What makes Davis's contribution to the debate on growing income inequality in the United States unique is that he links the growth of a "split-level economy" to the contours of post-Fordism, us style. For Davis, the growing wage and income polarization reveals the shape of an emergent regime of accumulation based on a middle-class luxury consumerism which

signifies both state-originated transfers to the middle class and the conditions of extra-economic coercion or menialisation which now nurture the luxuriant growth of super-exploitative small business geared to the "affluent" market. It also involves a politically constructed stratification of occupational categories in the tertiary sector that disqualifies and deskills the majority of workers to the advantage of a credentialed or managerial minority.[22]

Such a regime is only economically viable in a country as large as the United States. Even if only a small percentage of the total population is in a position to consume the goods and services produced in this dualistic economy, the market will be deep enough to call forth supply. The longer-run political viability of such a regime remains an open question.

American unions have begun to respond to capital's offensive in diverse ways. Some, such as the UAW and the Communications Workers, have turned to co-operation with capital on the basis of "mutually agreed principles." But this strategy has run into problems, in part because of the conservatism of a managerial strata too well-schooled in the lessons of Fordism. More importantly, the co-operativist line fails to take into account the sharp power imbalance between capital and labour in the United States. If this strategy prevails, flexible automation may become the operative principle in American manufacturing, but it will not overcome the old divide. In fact, the core workforce is likely to continue to shrink, swelling the size of a secondary labour market providing inputs "just in time" to the core or catering to the leisure requirements of the rich.

Yet the American labour movement has looked to be on the verge of extinction before: economists were predicting its demise in 1932, on the eve of the explosive birth of the CIO. And there are signs that a new generation of working-class activists is in the making. This group has begun to take some creative initiatives in industries as diverse as steel, oil refining, and agriculture. In Silicon Valley, threats to worker health and safety may be laying the basis for the new unionism too. While this group remains a minority, it does offer some grounds for optimism, especially if it manages not only to rejuvenate American unions but also to create a new political force, capable of bringing the majority of American workers into politics. This would be no mean feat in a country where only half the population votes in elections and two-thirds of the non-voters are working class.[23] Yet Jesse Jackson's two campaigns may prove to have been a crucial turning point.

FROM PERMEABLE FORDISM TO NORTH AMERICAN POST-FORDISM?

Canada's version of Fordism set in motion a process of continental integration. Thus it has indeed been "permeable" to American capital which came to control so much of the resource and manufacturing sector; permeable to the policies of the American state; and permeable to the American labour movement via the role played by the so-called international unions.[24] Yet Canadian Fordism was never a simple "miniature replica" of American Fordism and the differences grew in the 1960s and 1970s. Although Fordist institutions have been under assault in both countries, progressive forces in Canada have been more effective in holding the line. Moreover, the very conclusion of the FTA gave birth to the Pro-Canada Network – an alliance of unions, the women's and environmental movements, artists, farmers and native people, anti-poverty groups, the peace movement and the churches – which holds the potential for countering Canada's incorporation into a continent-wide segmented economy.

Canada's model Ford was both dependent on, and different from, American Fordism. Although mass consumption played a part in Canada's postwar economic expansion, the accelerator was not so much investment in the consumer durables industries but the inflow of foreign capital related to the extraction and export of Canada's staples resource industries, whose product was destined primarily for the American market. Canada's mass production industries were largely assembly operations, established by foreign (mainly American) corporations, which remained dependent on imported technology and key components. And, as the 1968 Watkins task force on foreign ownership warned, Canada's miniature replica branch plants were rarely able to achieve Fordist economies of scale. The exceptions to the rule were those industries, such as auto and agricultural machinery, which were able to rationalise their operations along continental lines as a result of special Canada–US agreements that contained safeguards for a guaranteed Canadian share of industry employment (see the article by Holmes in this volume).

Canada's goods-producing sector thus became particularly vulnerable to developments in the United States. Both the staples and the manufacturing sector were dependent on the flow of foreign capital and technology from American sources. The staples sector depended on secure access to the US market, and manufacturing (other than automotive, at least since the 1965 Auto Pact) depended on the continued existence of the tariff to entice branch plants to locate north of border.

The permeability of Canadian Fordism came in the form of trade and investment ties, and also via the dominance of US–based unions, both the craft-based Gomperist unions once organized under the TLC and the Fordist industrial unions of the CIO/Canadian Congress of Labour. From 1950 to 1965 approximately 70 per cent of unionized workers were organized by unions headquartered in the United States. Collective bargaining in Canada has also developed along lines closer to the decentralized American pattern than to that of certain Western European countries where national wage setting through bi- or trilateral mechanisms has been the rule (see the chapter by Drache in this volume). In this sense, Fordist regulation in both countries can be described as centred in the private sector, with the state playing only a supportive role.

Nevertheless, federal industrial relations legislation did set the basic framework for collective bargaining in Canada. Although this system permitted provincial variations in union rights, it did not allow the formation of the Canadian equivalent of the "right-to-work" states which flourish in the American sunbelt. Since the 1960s, moreover, the fortunes of the two trade union movements have increasingly diverged: "The number of union members in the United States has declined continually since the mid–1950s ... Canadian union membership trends diverged sharply from the 1960s onwards. Although membership fell from 34 per cent in 1954 to just under 30 per cent by 1963, it grew from that point on and reached 39 per cent by 1978."[25] By 1984 the difference had become marked in all sectors of the two economies. In manufacturing, 45 per cent of Canadian workers were unionized as against 26 per cent in the United States; in mining, 32.8 as against 17.7 per cent; in transport, 54.9 as against 37.3 per cent; in services, 38.1 as against 7.3 per cent; and in government, 66.6 as against 35.8 per cent. Even in areas like clerical (30.2 as against 14.0 per cent) and retail (12.4 as against 7.8 per cent) Canadian unions fared better.[26] The Quiet Revolution in Quebec, in which state sector workers played an important part, and the struggles of postal workers particularly in British Columbia and Quebec, are largely responsible for these divergent trends. Nor was their impact only quantitative. The militant public sector unions seemed to inspire their private sector counterparts and began to change the balance between national and international unions within the CLC.

The CCF–NDP has never managed to give class the partisan political salience that it enjoys in many western European polities. Yet it has maintained a presence in federal politics that has proved important, especially under minority governments, and in provinces such as Saskatchewan, Manitoba, and British Columbia it has been and remains a major political force. Its steady presence in Canadian politics stands in marked contrast to the situation in the United States where the interwar period saw the virtual elimination of all class-based parties but the Communist party, and the latter never recovered from the effects of the McCarthy period. The Liberal party in Canada, which dominated postwar politics at the federal level, certainly played the same brokerage politics game as the American Democrats. Yet the Liberals had to look to the left, and this had an impact on their policies.

The greater impact of the left on Canadian policy was particularly marked in the 1960s and early 1970s when federal initiatives in the sphere of health and education led to a dramatic increase in expenditures. This was also the period when the Canada pension plan and the Canada assistance plan were introduced and unemployment insurance was liberalized. The Canadian welfare state may pale by comparison with its Scandinavian counterparts, yet it cannot be reduced to a miniature replica of the American. As O'Connor notes, "Despite similarities in social transfer and residual consumption expenditure and the low level of commitment to active labor market policies, there are some significant differences between the Canadian and US systems ... In addition to the marked differences in the health systems and in public educational expenditure, unemployment insurance eligibility conditions and benefit levels are very different."[27] As a consequence, a much greater proportion of Canadian social services are in the public (or para-public) sector and these jobs have been filled primarily by unionized workers. This has enabled public service unions led by CUPE, CUPW and more recently the nurses to rally a broad coalition of forces increasingly critical of government policy.

The sustained "assault on trade union freedoms", the cuts in funds for social programs, matched by a turn towards "targeted programs" (in other words, away from universality), the failure to come to grips with the crisis in farming or with environmental problems – all of these had helped lay the basis for a revival of left opposition. The association of the United States with Reagan's brand of neo-conservatism has lent additional force to nationalist resistance.

The opposition lost the first battle when the Tories managed to win the 1988 election and implement the FTA. Yet the war is far from over. In fact, by accelerating the process of restructuring, the FTA is forcing both capital and the state to develop a strategy to guide the process. The report of the Prime Minister's Advisory Council on Adjustment in 1989 constitutes but one of a growing number of documents calling for government-industry co-operation in the areas of research and development, training, and the like. More importantly, the formation of an "adjustment policy" will take place in a highly politicized environment, for the opposition to the FTA has made it difficult to attribute plant closures, mergers, and the like to "objective market forces."

The Premier's Council of Ontario in 1988 outlined an agenda for competing in the new global economy on a different basis from comparative advantage and free trade. It has called for a turn towards high value added production.[28] The Premier's Council's version of diversified quality production, however, would do little to halt the slide into a two-tiered economy, for it has little to say about the service sector. The strategy, moreover, relies for its success on the kind of business-government partnership which leaves little room for the participation of the progressive social forces that rallied to form the Pro-Canada Network.

The Ontario Federation of Labour seems to have recognized some of these problems. In the economic policy document prepared for its 1988 convention, it called for moves to halt the turn to "just-in-time" workers – usually women, youth, and visible minorities – in large-scale manufacturing and in the public sector by obtaining employment security for these vulnerable workers. It also issued a renewed effort to organize the unorganized in the private service sector. It recognized, moreover, that the instruments recommended by the Premier's Council gave workers little say. The OFL would thus rely on a different set of policy instruments such as planning agreements, public ownership, regulation and development funds. Finally, training and retraining are given greater emphasis and are seen as a matter for co-determination, not something unilaterally to be decided by employers.

That the trade union movement is beginning to articulate its own version of post-Fordist restructuring is a promising development. Yet if this strategy is to become the basis for turning the coalition of forces brought together to fight the FTA into an organic alliance, more will have to be done. Potential divisions among the constituent groups must be overcome by working out an alternative which allows all to realize their interests. The development of such a program can only be the result of a genuine dialogue that engages the leadership and the rank-and-file of the constituent groups. Yet it is possible to indicate some elements that might be integrated into the OFL's strategy which might help overcome some of these potential contradictions.

Although the OFL document refers to the need for greater investment in the environment, it needs to add more substance to this commitment. In particular, it does not go far enough towards resolving potential tensions between the labour movement and environmentalists. A "red-green" variant of the high value-added strategy seems a better way to create an organic link between workers and environmentalists and would give both forces a leading role in the innovation process. Such a strategy would emphasize innovations designed to meet workers' demands for a safer and more stimulating working environment and environmentalists' demands for ecologically sustainable development.[29] Such a strategy would give us a cleaner environment in which to live and work and at the same time would develop Canada's comparative advantage and thus help to renew the goods-producing sector. Moreover, in contrast to the Premier's Council's version, which gives business the primary role, unions and environmental groups would become central. For it is they who would be involved in identifying the needs and helping to develop appropriate alternatives.

The second element is the relationship between the goods-producing and service sectors. Although it is important to emphasize that "manufacturing matters," it is dangerous to suggest that it (and that part of the private service sector that produces "tradables") matters above all else. The revitalization of the welfare state must form an integral part of any alternative economic program. Producer services which are directly linked to the goods-producing sector can generate some good jobs, especially if the unions succeed in organizing this sector. Yet a revitalized welfare state will be the surest means for generating good service sector jobs, ones that provide the kind of income required to sustain domestic demand for high-quality goods. The development of universal daycare, "after four" and summer programs, and the provision of quality care for the infirm and the aged is also essential if the impending shortage of labour is to be avoided: women can only meet the demand for full-time workers if they are thus released from their "double burden." Workers, moreover, will only accept the job losses restructuring may entail if there are good alternative sources of employment. More broadly, there are real possibilities to reassert the principle of universality and also to improve the terms of the equity-efficiency trade-off. In other words, the interests of clients and workers are simultaneously served if new technology, new forms of work organization, and new categories of para-professional workers are used to increase the supply of efficient and high-quality universal daycare, health care, and care for the aged.

CONCLUSION

The FTA has placed the issue of restructuring firmly on the agenda. In the first round, the pro-Canada forces managed to raise a number of important issues. Although the battle was lost, the campaign served to politicize the broader questions associated with restructuring. What this chapter has argued is that to win the next round, labour and its allies will have to be able to meet head-on the pro–FTA forces' claims – that the agreement will generate growth – by pointing to the kind of growth that market forces, unleashed on the continent, are likely to produce. They will also have to develop their own alternatives, perhaps along the lines of a red-green version of diversified quality production, if they are to become an effective counter-force.

The formation of such a strategy that combines a red-green version of diversified quality production with revitalization of the welfare state is not only necessary – it is possible.[30] Major private sector unions have become increasingly involved in a struggle to shape the impact of new technology on the world of work and the public sector unions have been working in creative ways with client groups to oppose the cutbacks. In the first round of the fight against Canada's incorporation into the US economy, there was little reflection on these positive initiatives. In the next stage, it should be possible to move from the defensive to the offensive, by developing the broader implications of these particular struggles. This chapter has attempted to show how this might be dome.

NOTES

I would like to thank Frances Abele, Jane Jenson, and Donald Swartz for their very helpful comments on the first draft of this article.

1 In this context, voluntarism refers to the increasing emphasis placed on private charities (*vs.* public welfare) – Bush's "one thousand points of light." In Canada, too, private charities have had to absorb a growing case load.

2 See the chapters by Drache and Gertler as well as by Clarkson and Holmes in this volume. The core concepts of the regulation school are "regime of accumulation" and "mode of regulation" to which various authors add other supplementary concepts. I follow A. Lipietz in including the concept of "model of industrialization" because it allows one to place more emphasis on a crucial dimension that is otherwise but one component of the regime of accumulation. See A. Lipietz, *Choisir L'Audace* (Paris: Éditions La Découverte 1989).

3 D. Leborgne and A. Lipietz, "New technologies, new modes of regulation: some spatial implications." Presented at Conference on Technology, Restructuring, and Urban/Regional Development, Dubrovnik, Yugoslavia, June 1987: 4.

4 As Leborgne and Lipietz correctly argue, even during the heyday of Fordism, workers were never reduced to mere appendages of the machine. Capital continued to rely on their knowledge gained through "learning by doing." Nevertheless, the formal separation of conception and execution within the modern corporation made it difficult systematically to tap and develop such practical knowledge.

5 Flexible automation is also associated with the reorganization of inter-corporate and inter-industry relations along the lines of the Japanese just-in-time system. See A. Sayer, "New Developments in Manufacturing: The JIT system," *Capital and Class* 30 (1986).

6 For Canadian examples see D. Robertson and J. Wareham, *Technological Change in the Auto Industry* (Toronto: CAW 1987), and J. Holmes in this volume. For American examples see M.J. Piore and C. Sabel, *The Second Industrial Divide; Prospects for Prosperity* (New York: Basic Books 1984), and S. Cohen and J. Zysman, *Manufacturing Matters* (New York: Basic Books 1987).

7 See A. Sorge and W. Streeck, "Industrial Relations and Technological Change: The Case for an Extended Perspective" in R. Hyman and W. Streeck, *New Technology and Industrial Relations* (Oxford: Basil Blackwell 1988).

8 Piore and Sabel, *The Second Industrial Divide*, 279.

9 M. Aglietta, "World Capitalism in the Eighties," *New Left Review* 136 (1982): 37.

10 Jacobi argues that union strength at the national level will have to be combined with union strength at the local level. O. Jacobi, "New Technological Paradigms, Long Waves and Trade Unions" in Hyman and Streeck, eds., *New Technology*.

11 See M. Davis, *Prisoners of the American Dream* (London: Verso 1986) for a good discussion of the rise of the new right in the United States.

12 See A. Gramsci, *Selections from the Prison Notebooks*, Q. Hoare and G. Nowell Smith, eds. and translators. (London: International Publishers 1971) for the first discussion of the rise of Fordism in the United States.

13 Piore and Sabel, *The Second Industrial Divide*.

14 See Davis, *Prisoners of the American Dream* for a good dissection of the forces behind the rise of the new right in the United States.

15 E. Rothschild, "The Real Reagan Economy," *New York Review* (30 June 1988), and "The Reagan Economic Legacy," ibid. (21 July 1988).

16 M. Weir, "The Federal Government and Unemployment: Frustrations of Policy Innovations from the New Deal to the Great Society" in M. Weir *et al.*, eds., *The Politics of Social Policy* (Princeton University Press 1988).

17 The Dukakis campaign for "good jobs for all" and a public health insurance system is interesting in this regard. The program held the promise of an alternative to Reaganism, but Dukakis himself symbolized the "Massachusetts Miracle" – re-industrialization tied to military expenditure and an increase in income polarization. The Dukakis victory within the Democratic Party, moreover, came at the expense of Jesse Jackson's defeat and the latter arguably stood for precisely the kind of political alliance needed to really turn the situation around.

18 Between 1973 and 1986, the total wage bill in the durable goods sector declined by 17.5 per cent, largely as a result of employment cuts, although concessions also played their part. See B. Bluestone and B. Harrison, "The Great U-Turn: An Inquiry into Recent u.s. Trends in Employment, Earnings and Family Income." Presented at the ALC Conference on Structural Change and Labour and Market Policy, Saltsjobaden, Sweden, June 1988.

19 Rothschild, "The Real Reagan Economy," 50.

20 M. Davis, "The Political Economy of Late Imperial America," *New Left Review* 123 (1984): 24.

21 Figures calculated from Table 27 in L. Mishel and J. Simon, *The State of Working America* (Washington, DC: Economic Policy Institute, 1988), 15.

22 Davis, "The Political Economy," 27.

23 K. Moody, *An Injury to All: The Decline of American Unions* (London: Verso 1988), 344–45.

24 J. Jenson, "'Different' but not 'Exceptional': Canada's Permeable Ford-ism," *Canadian Review of Sociology and Anthropology* 26, no. 1 (1989).

25 L. Panitch and D. Swartz, *The Assault on Trade Union Freedoms* (Toronto: Garamond Press 1988), 99.

26 Moody, *An Injury to All*, Table 7, 332.

27 J. O'Connor, "Welfare State Expenditure and Policy Orientation in Canada in Comparative Perspective," *Canadian Review of Sociology and Anthropology* 26, no. 1 (1989): 144.

28 The ideas contained in the report also inform a recent report to the National Advisory Council on Science and Technology, chaired by the prime minister. More broadly, although the 1988 report centres on what to do about the Ontario economy, in which Fordist industries are concentrated, the ideas are of potential relevance to more resource-dependent provinces in that the cass for the turn to the high value added end of the market applies also to the resource sector. This is recognized in the British Columbia Federation of Labour's study of tech change at Cominco. See British Columbia Federation of Labour, "The Cominco Case Study" (TIRF Project Report for Labour Canada 1987).

29 In the Canadian context, Loblaws' new "Green" product strategy provides an indication that such a strategy is feasible, but Loblaws has not bothered to develop domestic sources for its products nor, of course, has it been concerned to develop safe chemicals and machinery in the workplace. With regard to the latter, Greenpeace's hiring of occupational health and safety activist, Stan Gray, to "carry their campaign into the workplace" is seen as a clear signal that this important force within the ecology movement wants to establish more effective ties with unions. *Ottawa Citizen*, 16 September 1990.

30 Since the agreement went into effect at least two major reports that focus on questions of productivity, innovation, and training, have been released. In both, the call is not for less government but rather for new public measures to encourage the kind of restructuring required if Canada is to meet the challenge of global competition. See Advisory Council on Adjustment, *Adjusting to Win* (Ottawa 1989) and Canadian Labour Market and Productivity Centre, *Working Together to Manage Change*, Report of the Business/Labour Task force on Adjustment (Ottawa 1989). For a critical appraisal of *Adjusting to Win*, see R. Mahon, "Adjusting to Win: The New Tory Training Initiative" in K. Graham, ed. *How Canada Spends, 1990–91* (Ottawa: Carleton University Press 1990).

PART FIVE

New Policy Directions for the State

15 The Global Political Economy and Social Choice

ROBERT W. COX

In the late twentieth century a powerful globalizing economic trend thrusts towards the achievement of a market utopia on the world scale. At present, no counter-tendency effectively challenges the globalization thrust. The market appears to be bursting free from the bonds of national societies, subjecting a global society to its laws. Yet, as Karl Polanyi discerned of nineteenth-century Britain, the freeing of the market can in the longer run provoke an equally powerful reaction, as society seeks to curb its disintegrating and alienating consequences. Elements of opposition to the socially disruptive consequences of globalization are already visible. The question remains open as to what form these may take, as to when and how they may become more coherent and more powerful.

The answer hinges on changes in the power relationships among social groups on the world scale.[1] In particular, it implies a weakening of the arrangements for management of international economic relations put in place during the Pax Americana of the postwar world. But the taming and civilizing of the market presupposes a development of social and political forces that are global in their reach. Such social forces are emerging among women, environmentalists, peace activists, indigenous peoples, trade unions, and churches, to name but a few examples of popular sector movements that increasingly are opposed to the harmful consequences of globalization. These movements present a dramatically different range of social choices and have the potential, if they can merge their consciousness and concerns, for a new political discourse.

Unfortunately, the left has either remained mired in its Keynesian positions of the 1960s, even more than usually fragmented by polemical sectarianism, or else (as in the case of some social democrats) has seemingly accepted the neo-conservative rationale of globalization without being very clear about how this is to be reconciled with socialism's commitment to social equity. There is an intellectual vacuum to be filled – a challenge to critical thinking on the left.

At the heart of the challenge is the question of the motive force for change. One effect of the globalization of production is that one can no longer speak of the "working class" as a unified social force on the national, let alone world, level. The working class now has a fragmented objective existence and a very problematic common consciousness. In the new emerging social structure, categories defined solely in relation to production are complicated by the categories of gender, ethnicity, religion, and region, since these are often the basis for segmentation. These categories do not displace production as a primordial factor in the structuring of society. They have become intermediate factors, the basis for self-awareness of group identities, between production relations and social forces.

Thus, the political basis for social action to confront the emerging global trends has to be rethought and recomposed in relation to the strategies of the past. By analysing the dynamics of the restructuring of social relations on a world scale, it is possible to see how changes in production become the basis for social movements for change, and for new forms of state and of world order.

THE GLOBALIZATION THRUST

The analysis of globalization must begin with the internationalization of production. The internationalizing process results when capital considers the productive resources of the world as a whole and locates elements of complex globalized production systems at points of greatest cost advantage. The critical factor is information on how most profitably to combine components in the production process.

Multinational corporations have encouraged this kind of thinking and planning, but the component elements now include joint enterprises, industrial co-operation agreements between multinationals and socialist-country enterprises, and world-class cottage industries as well as huge corporations. Producing units take advantage of abundant, cheap, and malleable labour where it is to be found, and of robotization where it is not. Transnational production requires an environment in which capital, technology, and inputs to the production process (whether raw materials or component parts), as well as finished goods, can cross borders relatively freely.

A second major development is the internationalization of the state. Throughout most of this century the role of states has been conceived as a buffer protecting the national economy from disruptive external forces in order to encourage internal levels of economic activity sufficient to sustain adequate domestic employment and welfare. The state's priority was domestic welfare. In the past couple of decades the priority has shifted to one of adapting domestic economies to the perceived exigencies of the world economy.

This has had an impact within the structures of national governments. Central agencies that act as transmission belts for the world economy (and in the cases of North America and of Europe, the continental economy) have become pre-eminent within governments over those agencies that deal with primarily internal affairs. Ministries of industries and ministries of labour used to combine with their respective domestic constituencies to guide and implement national economic policies. These domestic-oriented agencies have been subordinated to ministries of finance and offices of presidents and prime ministers that provide the direct links between world-economy negotiations (through bodies such as the OECD, the IMF, and the economic summits) and the development of national policies that implement the international consensus reached in these negotiations. Domestic economic and social interests have as a result been diminished as policy influences. The domestic-oriented agencies of the state are now more and more to be seen as conduits between world-economy trends and the domestic economy – in other words, as agencies to promote the carrying out of tasks they had no part in deciding.

Thirdly, the new international division of labour is creating a new pattern of uneven development. The concept of a "third world" no longer has a clear meaning, since many of the countries once considered as belonging to it have either found some niche as producers of manufactures, or natural resources (especially energy), or else have been relegated to a "fourth world" sunken irretrievably in poverty. This fourth world has become a concern to the world system, not as a potential partner in future growth but as an object of poor relief and riot control.

The World Bank shifted its emphasis in the 1970s towards "absolute poverty" in the fourth world, which it perceived as threatening social and political turmoil that could spill over into zones more integrated with the world economy in the form of regional conflicts and internal warfare. Economic aid for these countries became geared towards keeping people employed in low-productivity jobs (the celebrated "informal economy"), towards enabling them to provide for their own basic needs through do-it-yourself welfare, and towards limiting population growth so as to reduce the future size of the problem. A central concern of world-economy institutions became to prevent poverty somewhere becoming disruptive of growth elsewhere. This was the "poor relief" component of multilateral world-system policy. The "riot control" aspect was taken care of by bilateral military aid to repressive regimes for counter-insurgency and support of "low intensity" conflict.

Fourthly, the world economic crisis of the mid–1970s which ended a long phase of economic expansion stimulated by Keynesian demand management and Fordist industrialism brought about a new economic conjuncture. The rise in oil prices in the 1970s, combined with recession in the advanced capitalist countries, vastly increased liquidities held by the transnational banks which became avid lenders. Corporations were big borrowers, financing the restructuring of production through debt. Governments of newly industrializing economies (NIES) also borrowed heavily, because borrowing from private banks involved less onerous public policy conditions than borrowing brom the IMF, and because they hoped to be able to service their debt by exporting the products of debt-financed industries.

The United States became the world's largest debtor nation, effectively internationalizing its public debt. The United States, however, escaped the fiscal pressures that bore more heavily on other countries because it was the source of the world's most widely used transaction and reserve currency. Americans could enjoy through debt a higher level of consumption than their production would otherwise have paid for because foreigners were ready to accept a flow of depreciating dollars. The longer-run consequence for Americans was growing foreign ownership of their economy, as depreciating dollars held by foreigners could best be used in buying US industries and real estate. The American economy lost its one-time lead in productivity, but its hour of reckoning was postponed by the dollar's hegemonic role in world finance.

As the debt problem for debtor countries other than the United States became critical during the 1980s, it accelerated all of the foregoing tendencies. Conditions for access to more borrowing and for roll-over of existing debt became more closely tied to integration with the global economy and to the adoption of economic policies conducive to world-economy interests. Governments' accountability to foreign creditors came to outweigh accountability to their own citizens. They became the reluctant agents of international finance, which required of them freedom for transnational movements of capital, facility for the development of international production, devaluation of national currencies, raising of domestic prices, and allowing increased unemployment. The onus of adjustment has thus been placed upon labour and the more vulnerable social groups through cuts in government services, price rises in basic consumption items, and unemployment or pressures to accept sub-standard employment as the means of existence.

Fifthly, a global migration from South to North has been under way for some decades and may now be accelerating. By and large, our mind-set has not adjusted to seeing this as a long-term trend; we prefer to think of it in terms of an apparently episodic "refugee problem." During the late nineteenth century (1870–1900), Europe's population grew by one hundred million. This increase was accommodated by Europe's shift from a predominantly rural to an increasingly urban civilization, and by the emigration of forty million persons in an era of imperialist expansionism. In the late twentieth century, a reverse movement of perhaps even larger proportions is in progress.

It would be more realistic to see migratory pressures as bound up with the other structural changes noted above. The internationalizing of production, as it penetrates into the peripheries of the world economy, benefits some social groups and disadvantages others. Peasants become marginalized as the more well-to-do farmers or cattle ranchers who produce cash crops for exports are able to take over land. Production of basic foods for local markets takes a low priority with governments strapped by debt and concerned above all with increasing export income. Export-oriented manufacturing provides low-income jobs for some of those displaced from rural life, especially women. The gap between loss of rural work opportunity and new industrial jobs is considerable, creating a migratory pressure directed, first, towards the nearby urban areas, and then outward towards other countries wherever access, legal or (more usually) illegal, is possible.

The typical form taken by the internationalizing of states in the third world was until recently the military-bureaucratic regime that sought to encourage export-oriented development together with the enforcement as necessary of domestic austerity upon the politically excluded elements of society. Physical repression, ranging from widespread violations of human rights to open civil wars generate the "refugee problem." In part, it may be explained by a political psychology of authoritarianism, but in its broadest terms, the refugee problem has to be understood as a systemic consequence of the globalization trend. Even where bureaucratic-authoritarianism has been succeeded by fragile elected regimes, the impersonal pressures of the market and fears of insecurity continually replenish the migratory flow.

The new migratory movements from third-world to first-world countries, combined with the downgrading of job opportunities in advanced capitalist countries (the McDonaldization of the workforce) constitute what has been called the "peripheralization of the core."[2] The new masses of low-paid, insecurely employed, unprotected workers are segmented into groups defined by gender, ethnicity, religion, and national origin.[3] They often perceive each other as enemies, rather than blaming the system which subordinates them all. Segmentation perpetuates their political and economic weakness.

Finally, the cumulative result of all these structural tendencies in global political economy has rendered invalid the intellectual framework within which the state managers of the advanced capitalist countries confronted, relatively successfully, the problems of the postwar world. The neo-classical synthesis in economics ran aground on the stagflation of the 1960s and 1970s. Monetarism and supply-side economics claim succession to its hegemonic aura.

The left has yet to retool intellectually and develop a new critical perspective on the relationship between global change and social power. Take, for example, the concept of a core/periphery structuring of the world economy. The terms "core" and "periphery" were originally given a geographical meaning, distinguishing the economic-political metropoles from their dependent countries and territories.[4] These terms increasingly have to be given a social meaning as territorial boundaries and the efficacy of state regulation recede before the advance of the global economy and the big continental economies.

In the newer meaning, a relatively small core personnel, closely integrated with capital in forms of enterprise corporatism, is to be distinguished from a segmented periphery of relatively disposable short-term, temporary, part-time, subcontracting, putting-out, and underground-economy producers, and also from the temporarily and permanently unemployed. Production organizations have shifted from the economies of scale of Fordist mass production to the economies of flexibility of post-Fordism. These new technologies maximize the use of segmented workforces. The new semi-skilled workforces of the NIES' export platforms are predominantly female; ethnic differentiation in employment opportunities among various sections of peripheral labour is a universal phenomenon; and regional disparities provide the rationale for the differential location of labour-intensive and technology-intensive kinds of economic activity.

ALTERNATIVES IN FORMS OF STATE: HYPER-LIBERALISM OR STATE CAPITALISM

The same tendencies as are bringing about the core/periphery restructuring of the production process also manifest themselves in mutations in the forms of states.[5]

It has become a commonplace on both left and right of the political spectrum to accept that the capitalist state has both to support capital in its drive to accumulate and to legitimate this accumulation in the minds of the public by moderating the negative effects of accumulation on welfare and employment. As growth stagnates, the contradiction between the two functions of accumulation and legitimation sharpens. The contradiction manifests itself internally in the advanced capitalist country as a fiscal crisis, whereas for the late-industrializing third world country it manifests itself as an exchange crisis. In the Soviet Union, socialist legitimacy underwritten by job security and equal access to basic needs is threatened by economic reform measures deemed necessary by the leadership to relaunch economic growth.

As growth stagnated in advanced capitalist countries, governments in effect denounced the social contract worked out with capital and labour during the postwar economic boom. Governments had to balance the fear of political unrest from rising unemployment and exhaustion of welfare reserves against the fear that business would refrain from leading a recovery that would both revive employment and enlarge the tax base. In this circumstance they bent before the interests of capital.

During the postwar years, a neo-liberal form of the state took shape in countries of advanced capitalism, based on a negotiated consensus among the major industrial interests, organized labour, and government. It was "neo" in the sense that classical liberalism was modified by Keynesian practice to make market behaviour consistent with social defence of the more disadvantaged groups. In the neo-liberal consensus it had become accepted wisdom that society would not tolerate high unemployment or any dismantling of the welfare state. If these things were to occur, it would, it was said, cost the state the loss of its legitimacy. The truth of this statement has not been demonstrated uniformly. Indeed, it would more generally seem to be the case that the legitimacy of state welfare and of labour movements has been undermined in public opinion, not the legitimacy of the state. Large-scale unemployment has produced fear and concern for personal survival rather than collective protest. The unions are in strategic retreat, losing members, and unable, in general, to appeal to public opinion for support.

The disintegration of the neo-liberal historic bloc was prepared by a collective effort of ideological revision undertaken through various unofficial agencies – the Trilateral Commission, the Bilderberg conferences, the Club of Rome, and other less prestigious forums – and then endorsed through more official consensus-making agencies such as the OECD. These agencies of latter-day neo-liberalism prepared its demise. A new doctrine defined the tasks of states in stimulating capitalist development out of the depression of the 1970s. There was, in the words of a blue-ribbon OECD committee, a "narrow path to growth," bounded on one side by the need to encourage private investment by increasing profit margins, and bounded on the other by the need to avoid rekindling inflation.[6]

The government-business alliance formed to advance along this narrow path ruled out such corporative-type solutions as negotiated wage and price policies and also the extension of public investment. It placed primary emphasis on restoring the confidence of business in government and acknowledged that welfare and employment commitments made in the framework of the postwar social contract would have to take second place.

The restructuring of production has accentuated segmentation and divisions within the working class, but this tendency has not been uniform. In many Western European countries a long history of ideological education has maintained a sense of solidarity. The force of this tradition is much weaker in North America, although it remains stronger in Canada than in the United States. In both Italy and France there have been instances where unions have maintained solidarity of action between migrant workers and local established workers, whereas in other instances these groups have been opposed to one another. Segmentation has, however, been the underlying trend that explains the weakness of labour in preventing the disintegration of the neo-liberal social consensus and in opposing the program put in its place by the government-business alliance.[7]

If the strains tending towards a disintegration of the neo-liberal historic bloc have been visible since the mid–1970s, it would be premature to define the outlines of a new historic bloc likely to achieve any durability as the foundation of a new form of state. Two principal directions of movement in political structures are visible in the erstwhile neo-liberal states: the confrontational tactics of Thatcherism in Britain and Reaganism in the United States towards removing internal obstacles to economic liberalism; and the more censensus-based adjustment process as in Japan, West Germany, and some of the smaller European countries.

HYPER-LIBERALISM

The Thatcher-Reagan model can be treated ideologically as the anticipation of a hyper-liberal form of state, in the sense that it seems to envisage a return to nineteenth-century economic liberalism and a rejection of the neo-liberal attempt to adapt economic liberalism to the sociopolitical reactions that classical liberalism produced. It takes the "neo" out of neo-liberalism. The whole paraphernalia of Keynesian demand-support and redistributionist tools of policy are regarded with the deepest suspicion in the hyper-liberal approach. Government-imposed regulations to protect the public with respect to industrial activities (anti-pollution, safety and health controls, and so on) are also to be weakened or dismantled. The market is to determine how much protection the public really wants.

The hyper-liberal tendency actively facilitates a restructuring, not only of the labour force, but also of the social relations of production. It renounces tripartite corporatism. It also weakens bipartism by its attack on unions in the state sector and its support and encouragement to employers to resist union demands in the oligopolistic sector. Indirectly, the state encourages the consolidation of enterprise corporatist relations for the scientific-technical-managerial workers in the oligopolistic sector, a practice for which the state itself provides a model in its treatment of its own permanent cadres. Finally, state policies are geared to an expansion of employment in short-term, low-skill, high turnover jobs that contribute to further labour-market segmentation.

The political implications are a complete reversal of the coalition that sustained the neo-liberal state. That state rested on its relationship with trade unions in the oligopolistic sector (the social contract), an expanding and increasingly unionized state sector, readiness to support major businesses in difficulty (from agricultural price supports to bail-outs of industrial giants), and transfer payments and services for a range of disadvantaged groups. The neo-liberal state played a hegemonic role by making capital accumulation on a world scale appear to be compatible with a wide range of interests of subordinate groups. It founded its legitimacy on consensual politics. The would-be hyper-liberal state confronts all those groups and interests with which the neo-liberal state came to terms. It does not shrink from open opposition to state sector employees, welfare recipients, and trade unions.

The government-business alliance that presides over the transformation of the neo-liberal into a would-be hyper-liberal form of state generates an imposing list of disadvantaged and excluded groups. State sector employees made great gains in collective bargaining and wages during the years of expansion and they have now become frontline targets for budgetary restraint. Welfare recipients and non-established workers, socially contiguous categories, are hit by reduced state expenditure and by unemployment. Farmers and small businessmen are angry with banks and with governments as affordable finance becomes unavailable to them. Established workers in industries confronting severe problems in a changing international division of labour – textiles, automobiles, steel, shipbuilding, for example – face unemployment or reduced real wages.

As long as the excluded groups lack strong organization and political cohesion, ideological mystification and an instinctive focus on personal survival rather than collective action suffice to maintain the momentum of the new policy orthodoxy. If a small majority, or even an articulate minority, of the population remains relatively satisfied, it can be politically mobilized to maintain these policies in place against the dissatisfaction of a large minority or a slim majority that is divided and incoherent.

STATE CAPITALISM

While the hyper-liberal model reasserts the separation of state and economy, the alternative state form that some see as capable of renewed capitalist development promotes a fusion of state and economy. This state-capitalist path may take several forms all according to different national positions within the world economy and different institutional structures and ideologies. The common thread lies in a recognition of the indispensible guiding role of the state in the development of the nation's productive forces. The advancement of these forces in the world economy can only be achieved through a conscious industrial policy, arrived at by a negotiated understanding among the principal social forces and through the mediation of the state in a corporative process. Such an understanding would have to produce agreement on the strategic goals of the economy and also on the sharing of burdens and benefits in the effort to reach those goals.

The state-capitalist approach is grounded in an acceptance of the world market as the ultimate determinant of development. No single national economy, not even the largest, can control the world market or determine its orientation. Furthermore, unlike the neo-liberal approach, the state-capitalist approach does not posit any consensual regulation of the world market as regards multilateral trade and financial practices. States are assumed to intervene not only to enhance the competitiveness of their nations' industries but also to negotiate or dictate advantages for their nations' exporters. The world market is the state of nature from which state-capitalist theory deduces specific policy.

The broad lines of this policy consist of, in the first place, development of the leading sectors of national production so as to give them a competitive edge in world markets, and in the second place, protection of the principal social groups so that their welfare can be perceived as linked to the success of the national productive effort.

The first aspect of this policy – industrial competitiveness – is to be achieved by a combination of opening these industrial sectors to the stimulus of world competition, together with state subsidization and orientation of innovation. Critical to the capacity for innovation is the condition of the knowledge industry; the state will have a major responsibility for funding technological research and development.

The second policy aspect – balancing the welfare of social groups – has to be linked to the pursuit of competitiveness. Protection of disadvantaged groups and sectors (industries or regions) would be envisaged as transitional assistance, with the eventual goal of their transfer to more profitable economic activities. Thus training, skill upgrading, and relocation assistance would have a pre-eminent place in social policy. The state would not indefinitely protect declining or inefficient industries but would provide incentives for the people concerned to become more efficient according to market criteria. The state would, however, intervene between the market pressures and the groups concerned so that the latter did not bear the full burden of adjustment. By contrast, the hyper-liberal model would exclude the state from this cushioning and incentive-creating function, letting the market impose the full costs of adjustment upon the disadvantaged.

Where internally generated savings were deemed to be essential to enhanced competitiveness, both investors and workers would have to be persuaded to accept an equitable sharing of sacrifice, in anticipation of a future equitable sharing of benefits. Thus incomes policy would become an indispensible counterpart to industrial policy. Similarly, the managerial initiative required to facilitate innovation and quick response to market changes might be balanced by forms of worker participation in the process of introducing technological changes. The effectiveness of such a state-capitalist approach would, accordingly, depend on the existence of corporative institutions and processes, not only at the level of enterprises and industries, but also of a more centralized kind capable of organizing interindustry, intersectoral and interregional shifts of resources for production and welfare.

The state-capitalist form involves a dualism between a competitively efficient world market oriented sector, and a protected welfare sector. The success of the former must provide the resources for the latter; the sense of solidarity implicit in the latter would provide the drive and legitimacy for the former. State capitalism thus proposes a means of reconciling the accumulation and legitimation functions brought into conflict by the economic and fiscal crises of the 1970s and by hyper-liberal politics.

In its most radical form, state capitalism beckons towards the prospect of an internal socialism sustained by capitalist success in world market competition. This would be a socialism dependent on capitalist development – that is, on success in the production of exchange values. But, so its proponents argue, it would be less vulnerable to external destabilization than were socialist strategies in economically weak countries (Allende's Chile or Portugal after the "carnation revolution"). The more radical form of state-capitalist strategy presents itself as an alternative to defensive, quasi-autarkic prescriptions for the construction of socialism which would aim to reduce dependency on the world economy and to emphasize the production of use values for internal consumption.[8]

Different countries are more or less well equipped by their historical experience to adopt the state-capitalist developmental path with or without the socialist colouration.[9] Those best equipped are the late-industrializing countries (from France and Japan in the late nineteenth century to Brazil and South Korea in the late twentieth), in which the state (or a centralized but autonomous financial system as in the German case) has played a major role in mobilizing capital for industrial development. Institutions and ideology in these countries have facilitated a close coordination of state and private capital in the pursuit of common goals. Those least well equipped are the erstwhile industrial leaders, Britain and the United States, countries in which hegemonic institutions and ideology kept the state by and large out of specific economic initiatives, confining its role to guaranteeing and enforcing market rules and to macroeconomic management of market conditions. The lagging effects of past hegemonic leadership may thus be a deterrent to the adoption of state-capitalist strategies.

The corporatist process underpinning state-capitalist development, which would include business and labour in the world market oriented sector and workers in the tertiary welfare services sector, would at the same time exclude certain marginal groups. These groups frequently have a passive relationship to the welfare services and lack influence in the making of policy. They are disproportionately to be found among the young, women, immigrant or minority groups, and the unemployed. The restructuring of production tends to increase their numbers. Since these groups are fragmented and relatively powerless, their exclusion has generally passed unchallenged. It does, however, contain a latent threat to corporatist processes. Part of this threat is the risk of anomic explosions of violence, particularly on the part of the young male unemployed element. Such explosions often strengthen the established authority by reinforcing the demand for law and order.

The other part of the threat is the risk of political mobilization of the marginals, which would pit democratic legitimacy against corporatist economic efficiency. These dangers are foreshadowed in the writings of neo-liberal ideologues about the "ungovernability" problem of modern democracies.[10] The implication is that the corporatist processes required to make state-capitalist development succeed may have to be insulated from democratic pressures. To the extent this becomes true, the prospects of internal socialism sustained by world market state capitalism would be an illusion.

In short, the state–capitalist alternative has some potential for reconstructing national hegemonies and overcoming the impasse that hyperliberalism tends to rigidify. The narrowing basis of corporatism (particularly as regards its labour component) on which state capitalism must rest does, however, contain a latent contradiction to democratic legitimacy. Its historic bloc would be thin. The excluded groups available for mobilization into a counter–hegemony would be considerable, though the fragmentation and powerlessness of these groups would make the task formidable. In the medium term, state-capitalist structures of some kind seem a feasible alternative to the hyper-liberal impasse. The long-term viability of these forms is a more open question.

SOCIAL FORCES COUNTERACTING GLOBALIZATION

Hyper liberalism is the ideology of the globalization thrust in its most extreme form. State capitalism is an adaptation to globalization that responds at least in part to society's reaction. We must ask ourselves whether there are longer-term prospects that might come to fruition following a medium-term experiment with state capitalism.

This is best approached dialectically: by inquiring how the conditions created by the globalizing thrust could generate a response from a *prise de conscience* among those elements of societies that are made more vulnerable or are more exploited by it. Beginning with the constraints placed by globalization on national policies, we can proceed to popular responses.

The main external constraint on national policy is the international financial network. The very hint of a threat by a government to control capital movements or foreign exchange can lead to an investment strike and capital flight, precipitating thereby an exchange crisis that will require foreign borrowing and possibly devaluation of the national currency. Reluctance to follow a policy of openness to global economic movements makes foreign or domestic borrowing by the state difficult, as does a perception in the financial markets that the state is not managing its expenditures in relation to its revenues. The British Labour government was forced in 1976 to reduce state expenditures as a proportion of GNP by a combination of IMF pressures and the high cost of borrowing in the domestic finance market. The alternative to borrowing would have been to print more money and provoke a run on the pound.[11]

The French Socialist government under President François Mitterrand introduced during its first year a number of new social measures and carried out nationalizations of banks and industrial groups. In its second year, however, the government had to face deficits in the social services and unemployment insurance, in public enterprises, and in the balance of payments of the country, which resulted in an alignment of state policies to those of the other advanced capitalist countries: priority to anti-inflation measures, imposition of a wage freeze and abandonment of wage indexation, and cutbacks in government spending in general and in social expenditures in particular.

A combination of internal pressures from the more powerful domestic social forces and external constraints operating through financial markets and institutions of the world economy sets practical limits to the options of governments. If a government were determined not to heed the external forces, it would have to be prepared to rely exclusively on internal means of stimulating and co-ordinating the productive forces in its society. In the extreme case, this would mean mass mobilization, collective and egalitarian austerity, and the organization of production geared to use (or the basic needs of society) rather than exchange (or the possibility of profits on world markets). This would imply a shift towards what Polanyi called a redistributive society.

There is no indication that public opinion in advanced capitalist countries is psychologically prepared for such an alternative. The ethic of personal choice that nourishes the hope of a personal salvation on earth, as well as in heaven, is too widespread to succumb to a collectivist solution except perhaps under conditions of social and economic catastrophe.

Nor is there much prospect that governments in less developed or newly industrializing countries would be prepared for such a choice. A return to right-wing authoritarianism which reimposed an austerity intended to revive confidence among foreign creditors would risk popular explosions. The food riots of 1989 in Venezuela, Brazil, and Argentina were a warning. A left-wing nationalism that would turn its back on foreign credits and try to compensate for them by inward-turning autarkic mobilization of human resources lacks credibility. Elected governments in third-world countries have neither the will nor the authority to pursue either course.

The situation in the countries formerly self-designated as socialist is equally contradictory. Pressures are coming from the top for economic restructuring of a kind that would reduce the complexity of central planning by giving more scope to domestic markets and to incorporation into the global market economy. The hope of the economic reformers is that this will raise productivity and allocate resources more efficiently. At the same time, democratic movements from below challenge all forms of central direction and are likely to rise against the adverse consequences of economic reforms. They welcome markets as a means of overthrowing the autocracy and the shortage economy of planning; but they will surely protest when the consequences of liberalizing the economy brings about the typical hazards of capitalism, inflation and unemployment.

Three outcomes seem possible. One is a return to political repression, either as a means of continuing economic liberalization or of reviving Stalinist-type central planning. Another outcome could be a birth of corporatist politics in which particular groups try to take advantage of their strategic positions in industries or in regions to get as much as they can from the state. The notion of the state's commitment to the general interest of society as a whole thus risks becoming eroded in a *sauve qui peut* among rival claimants for whatever returns may be gained from economic reform. This outcome may be consistent with current trends in Poland and Hungary and conceivably even in the Soviet Union. A third possibility could be found within the democratization movement. It would lead towards a more participatory kind of economic management and planning inspired by the egalitarian idea innate in socialism.

In all of these cases, the prospect of turning around the segmenting, socially disintegrating, and polarizing effects of the globalization thrust rests upon the possibility of the emergence of an alternative political culture that would give greater scope to collective action and place a greater value on collective goods. For this to come about, whole segments of societies would have to become attached, through active participation and developed loyalties, to social institutions engaged in collective activities. They would have to be prepared to defend these institutions in times of adversity.

The condition for a restructuring of society and polity in this sense would be to build a new historic bloc capable of sustaining a long war of position until it is strong enough to become an alternative basis of polity. This effort would have to be grounded in the popular strata. The activities that comprise it will not likely be directed to the state because of the degree of depoliticization and alienation from the state among these strata. They will more likely be directed to local authorities and to collective self-help. They will in many cases be local responses to global problems – to problems of the environment, of organizing production, of providing welfare, of migration. If they are ultimately to result in new forms of state, these forms will arise from the practice of non-state popular collective action rather than from extensions of existing types of administrative control.

To the extent that such popular responses to the existing thrust of globalization come to fruition, they will change the meaning and the form of the polity. Such a long-term result could hardly be achieved in one national society alone; it would have to move forward simultaneously in several countries, and draw sufficient support in the world system to protect its various national bases. The existing globalization thrust grounded in the economic logic of markets would have to be countered by a new globalization embedded in society.

NOTES

1 I have discussed this in *Production, Power, and World Order: Social Forces in the Making of History* (New York: Columbia University Press 1987).

2 See, for example, Robert Ross and Kent Trachte, "Global Cities and Global Classes: The Peripheralization of Labor in New York City," *Review* 6, no. 3 (1983): 393–431.

3 Jeffrey Harrod, *Power, Production, and the Unprotected Worker* (New York: Columbia University Press 1987).

4 See, for example, Immanuel Wallerstein, *The Modern World-System* (New York: Academic Press 1974).

5 This section is based on parts of ch. 8 of my *Production, Power, and World Order*.

6 The McCraken Report, *Towards Full Employment and Price Stability* (Paris: OECD 1977).

7 On the segmentation trend, see, inter alia, Frank Wilkinson, ed., *The Dynamics of Labour Market Segmentation* (London: Academic Press 1981).

8 Some French writers have probed these questions, for example, Christian Stoffäes, *La grande menace industrielle* (Paris: Calmann-Levy 1978), and Serge-Christolphe Kolm, *La transition socialiste: La politique économique de gauche* (Paris: Éditions du cerf 1977).

9 Some recent US studies that have compared the institutional characteristics of leading capitalist countries include Peter Katzenstein, ed., *Between Power and Plenty: Foreign Economic Policies of Advanced Industrial States* (Madison: University of Wisconsin Press 1978), and John Zysman, *Governments, Markets, and Growth* (Ithaca: Cornell University Press 1983).

10 Michel Crozier, Samuel P. Huntingdon, and Joji Watanuki, *The Crisis of Democracy. Report on the Governability of Democracies to the Trilateral Commission* (New York: New York University Press 1975).

11 Laurence Harris, "The State and the Economy: Some Theoretical Problems," *The Socialist Register* (London: Merlin Press 1980).

16 Post-Industrialism and the Service Economy

JOHN MYLES

Throughout this century, Canada has led the way in the shift to a service economy where 70 per cent of the Canadian labour force is now employed. The implications of this transition with respect to the future of work and wages have been a topic of considerable attention and debate. Most recently, it has been associated with the thesis of the "declining middle" – the claim that the shift of employment to services is creating a more polarized wage and skill structure than in the recent past. The empirics of Canada's service economy with respect to wages and job skills are now fairly well understood. These is indeed evidence of growing dualization in the Canadian labour market, but this is not a result of the shift to services as such. Rather it is an economy-wide trend that represents one of several "branching points" in the transition to a post-industrial economy.

The transition to post-industrialism is a product of the enormous growth in productivity that has characterized most industrialized capitalist economies in this century. Productivity growth brings the opportunity to either increase the amount of goods and services available or to produce the current amount of output with less labour. Changes in the mix of employment (the service economy), changes in employment levels and in patterns of paid work time are outcomes of this process. But the precise nature and mix of these outcomes are highly indeterminate. Not all things are possible but there is already ample evidence for a variety of alternative national strategies for resolving these issues. The reason for this variation is politics: politics in the sense of strategic choices that are made (or not made) *and* politics in the sense of institutionalized power relations – between classes, between men and women – inherited from the past and embedded in our social, political, and economic institutions that condition the everyday common sense of élites and publics concerning what is both possible and desirable.

My objective here is to highlight the alternatives to the North American variant of the transition. From a distributive point of view, some of these alternatives are clearly more desirable than others. The risk, however, is that democratic socialists, labour, and the social movements will focus largely on the distributive implications of these alternatives. This would be a mistake. A necessary condition for any alternative economic strategy is that it promises an equal or better solution to the production problem as well – in other words, that it identifies a virtuous circle between employment, wages, inflation, and productivity to take us through the transition. Fortunately there is good reason to think that dualism and flexible labour markets are a less than optimal solution to the productivity problem in a post-industrial economy.

WHAT IS POST-INDUSTRIALISM?

The concept of post-industrialism[1] was introduced to make sense of emergent trends and patterns that were inconsistent with the conventional concepts of what has been called "industrialization theory" – explanatory models built around contrasts with non-industrial, usually agricultural, economies. If emergent trends could not be adequately understood with a theory derived from "the logic of industrialism," then presumably a theory based on "the logic of post-industrialism" was necessary.[2]

My use of the tern is less ambitious. As Block observes, the concept of post-industrialism (like post-Keynesian or post-Fordist) is a negative one.[3] It does not designate the kind of economy or society we are moving towards, but only the kind of economy and society we are leaving behind. It simply means that societies have moved beyond industrialism and are in the process of forging new types of social and economic arrangements, the parameters of which are still being created.

The key insight of the post-industrial metaphor is that "most labour in developed societies ... is now employed in the provision of services and advanced technologies that release labour from direct production."[4] The implication is that we now face a transition analogous to the transition from an agricultural to an industrial economy. Traditionally, 50 to 70 per cent of the adult labour force was required to produce the food needed for survival. Today 3 to 4 per cent of the labour force in Canada and the United States are directly engaged in agricultural production and are producing food surpluses.

The trend in manufacturing employment has been similar. In Canada less than 20 per cent of the labour force is now directly engaged in manufacturing and less than 30 per cent in the entire goods sector (manufacturing, resource extraction, construction, and agriculture). In the brief period between 1981 and 1986, the percentage of full-time equivalent jobs in processing, fabricating, and machining occupations declined from 17.7 per cent of all jobs to 14.9 per cent.[5]

Historically this trend can be dated back to the 1920s and reflects rising productivity in goods production. Post-industrialism does not mean that our economic well-being is any less dependent on goods production than it was in the past. Manufacturing matters, both as a generator of wealth and of employment. The point is rather that manufacturing has changed. It generates more information and data-based occupations (engineers, lawyers, accountants, designers) and the "direct producers" – craft workers, factory operatives, construction workers – continue to decline.

First, then, post-industrialism means a transformation in the way goods are produced. The results include a change in *mix* of labour used in goods production, and a change in the *share* of labour required for goods production. The first change is manifested in the growth of managerial, professional, and technical occupations and the shift of employment into producer services (engineering, legal, financial, and so on). The second change is manifested to varying degrees in a decline in total labour time, and a shift in employment towards consumer services.

Post-industrialism, then, also means a change in the *composition* of the labour force and in the *amount* of labour required to produce a fixed level of goods and services. Here I will deal mainly with the changing composition of employment (the service economy), returning briefly to the question of employment levels in the conclusion. It is important to bear in mind, however, that the two are connected. Rather than develop a service economy, for example, some countries (for example, West Germany) seem to be heading towards a "post-employment" economy. Surplus labour released by rising productivity simply "exits" from the labour market. In West Germany, for example, the labour force participation rate of older males (aged fifty-five to sixty-four) fell from 82 per cent in 1970 to 58 per cent in 1985.

WHAT IS THE SERVICE ECONOMY?

The growth of the service sector has brought forth some heavy rhetoric from both left and right, rhetoric that ranges from the Pollyannish (we have moved to the "knowledge society") to the apocalyptic (the "McJobs" scenarios). What we globally label as "services" is a mixture

Table 16.1
Non-agricultural Labour Force by Industry Sector

Industry	Canada (1982/83) %	United States (1980) %	Sweden (1980) %	Norway (1982) %	Finland (1981) %
Goods	30.4	32.0	36.5	31.8	41.3
Distributive services	11.9	10.7	11.1	14.3	11.8
Consumer services	21.0	22.5	12.0	17.5	14.9
Business services	10.9	11.2	4.3	6.2	4.7
Health, education, and welfare	18.7	17.3	30.5	23.4	21.3
Public administration	7.1	6.4	5.6	6.9	6.0
Total	100.0	100.0	100.0	100.0	100.0
(N)	(1982)	(1407)	(1148)	(1609)	(967)

SOURCE: Comparative Class Structure Project.

of industries employing skilled, well-paid labour, and industries that employ unskilled, poorly paid labour. This is most evident in consumer services. They include:

1 *Social services* (the "welfare state" industries, including health, education, and welfare) and public administration provide jobs with high skill requirements and high wages relative to jobs in goods production.[6]
2 *Personal services* including the "servant" industries (cleaning, food, accommodation services) and retail trade have very low skill requirements and low wages.

Producer services also provide a mixed picture:

3 *Business services* (financial, legal, engineering) provide high-wage, high-skill jobs, especially for men. Women tend to be in the middle to lower end of the industries in this sector. In part this reflects a classification problem: many women, such as bank tellers, are in the retail or consumer end of industries usually classified among producer services. This is the most polarized sector of the economy and the one where the gender gap in wages is most pronounced.
4 Wage and skill patterns in *distributive services* (transportation, communication, utilities, wholesale trade) are similar to those in goods production. Historically, these industries developed alongside industrial manufacturing and are often considered synonymous with the industrial revolution (for example, railways).

Table 16.1 shows the mix of these industries for North America (Canada, the United States) and three Nordic countries (Finland, Norway,

Table 16.2
Non-agricultural Labour Force by Industry Sector and Sex

	Canada (1982/83) %	United States (1980) %	Sweden (1980) %	Norway (1982) %	Finland (1981) %
MALES					
Goods	42.9	41.8	51.9	42.9	53.0
Distributive services	15.1	14.2	15.2	18.6	16.0
Consumer services	15.7	18.2	8.3	14.4	11.5
Business services	8.1	8.7	4.8	6.1	5.5
Health, education, and welfare	10.2	9.9	15.0	12.5	9.0
Public administration	8.1	7.3	4.8	7.5	5.5
Total	100.0	100.0	100.0	100.0	100.0
FEMALES					
Goods	17.4	21.0	17.1	18.2	28.9
Distributive services	7.7	6.7	6.1	7.9	7.3
Consumer services	27.9	27.3	16.7	21.9	18.5
Business services	14.6	14.0	3.7	6.2	4.0
Health, education, and welfare	29.8	25.7	50.0	39.7	34.4
Public administration	5.9	5.3	6.5	6.0	5.5

SOURCE: Comparative Class Structure Project.

and Sweden).[7] The distinctive feature of the Canadian and US labour markets is the large share of employment in the low-wage, low-skill personal services.[8] The distinctive feature of the Nordic countries (especially Sweden) is the large share of employment in the comparatively high-skill, high-wage welfare state industries. There are also substantial differences in the share of employment in business services: 11 per cent in Canada and the United States compared to 4 to 6 per cent in the Nordic countries.

The point of the comparison is to show that the mix of services is not the product of some ineluctable "logic of post-industrialism." Service economies come in a variety of sizes and shapes. And as Esping-Andersen argues, the welfare state, in its capacity as employer, has a critical role in shaping the structure of employment.

The consequences of these national differences in the composition of services are experienced mainly by women (see Table 16.2). Goods production, distributive services and, to a lesser extent, public administration tend to be male industries. Consumer, business, and social services – where national differences are most pronounced – are female industries. Among these, social services is the only sector where women have access to a large number of middle- and high-level jobs as measured by both wages and skills. The quality of female employment is directly related to the share of jobs in health, education, and welfare and inversely related to the level of employment in consumer and business services. As a result, the shift to a service economy means something far different to Swedish than to North American women.

The quality of employment in a service economy is not simply a matter of the mix of services, however. The same service can be provided in radically different ways. For example, there are two alternative models available for the daycare industry to emulate: low-wage, unskilled baby-sitting services, or high-wage, skilled, educational services. Daycare can be provided by highly qualified teachers with advanced degrees in child development, or by minimum-wage child-minders. First and foremost, job quality in the service economy (as in goods production) is a question of public policy and national standards. There is nothing "technical" about the care of young children to dictate the choice. In sum, there is nothing intrinsic to a service economy dictating that it will be dominated by low-wage, low-skill jobs and intermittent employment *or* their opposites.

THE SERVICE ECONOMY AND THE DECLINING MIDDLE

What of actual trends in job skills and wages? Has the shift to service employment and knowledge-intensive goods production resulted in a more polarized wage and skill structure as often claimed?[9] The answer is yes and no. The results of our research at Statistics Canada in 1988 indicate that the Canadian wage structure has become more polarized over time (more low and high paying jobs and fewer jobs in the "middle").[10] Changes in the industrial and occupational composition of jobs had something to do with this but not much. At most 20 to 25 per cent of the total change in wage structure is explained by changes in industrial and occupational composition. In the 1980s the main source of change has been a shift in the age-wage profile: a very sharp decrease in the relative wages paid to young (age sixteen to twenty-four) workers and a small rise in the relative wages paid to "middle-aged" (thirty-five to fifty) workers. The downward drift in relative youth wages characterizes *all* industries and occupations. The reason we have tended to identify wage restructuring as a "McJobs" phenomenon is because of the concentration of young workers in consumer services.

This trend is disturbing because it occurred over a period when the labour supply of young workers was declining, when their educational qualifications were rising, and in a period of economic recovery. In sum, the relative wages of young people should have been rising, not declining, over this period. What accounts for this change? One, optimistic, scenario is that the change is temporary. The current generation of young people are entering the labour market in the backwash of the baby boom generation ahead of them. As the baby boomers age and stop clogging up the labour market, youth wages will begin to rise again. The more pessimistic scenario is that a more general wage restructuring is under way that is showing up first among entry-level jobs, a change that Canadian (and American) Labour is unable to resist. Two-tier wage contracts, increased use of part-time labour, and contracting out of production to new and smaller work sites are more likely to have their impact on new labour market entrants than on older, established workers with seniority and union rights to protect them. One indication of this is a decline in the percentage of young people in unionized jobs in all industries. The decline is not attributable solely to the fact that young workers are finding employment in sectors where union levels are traditionally low (such as retail sales). Between 1981 and 1986, the share of unionized jobs held by young workers fell from 52 to 30 per cent in resource and resource-based industries, from 35 to 28 per cent in other manufacturing, from 46 to 40 per cent in construction, and from 49 to 40 per cent in social services.[11]

Trends in skill levels are more ambiguous, due in part to measurement problems. But again, the trends in recent years do not appear to be industry-specific.[12] The 1950s and 1960s brought substantial skill upgrading, largely because of the rapid growth in public administration in the 1950s and the welfare state industries in the 1960s. In the 1970s, changing industry mix accounted for little change in the skill composition of the labour force (that is, most change took place within industrial sectors). In the 1980s, measurable skill change has been modest. There is some evidence of a polarized labour market for skills, but not of the sort described by Braverman, with the dividing line between professionals and managers, on the one hand, and the "mass" blue and white collar occupations on the other. Rather, the polarization is within these "mass" occupations, between high and low skill clerical workers, high and low skill blue collar workers, high and low skill sales workers and the like.

REFLECTIONS AND OBSERVATIONS

"Manufacturing Matters"

The shift to a service economy does not mean that our economic well-being no longer depends on our ability to produce goods. Declining *employment* shares in manufacturing does not necessarily mean that manufacturing accounts for a smaller share of the total *wealth* produced in

Canada. Between 1981 and 1988, the share of all jobs accounted for by manufacturing fell from 19.3 to 17.2 per cent but the manufacturing share of total output remained virtually constant at about 20 per cent.[13] The reason that employment shares in manufacturing have declined while manufacturing has maintained a constant share of total output is higher productivity gains in goods production than in services. If there is a reason for concern among Canadian workers, it is that Canadian productivity gains were not larger. Over the decade, Canada has lagged behind most advanced capitalist countries in this respect. For labour, the issue is not productivity gains per se but rather how the benefits of rising productivity – more wealth or less labour time – are distributed.

Manufacturing also matters for employment growth and the quality of employment in the service sector. Both distributive and business services depend directly on the goods sector for their economic health. Some of the growth in these sectors simply represents the contracting out of services once performed "in-house" by manufacturing enterprises. Canadian competitiveness in the international market for business services depends directly on areas of production, such as telecommunications and energy, where Canada has historically had a competitive advantage. And this advantage is often a direct result of government intervention. The success of Lavalin, for example, is a direct result of its experience with Hydro-Québec in the construction of the James Bay project.

The transition to post-industrialism, then, does not mean that goods production matters less, any more than the shift from an agricultural to an industrial economy meant a decline in the importance of food production. The transition to industrialism did not mean that food production declined or was shipped offshore. On the contrary, the ability to produce vast quantities of food with very little labour was a precondition of industrialization, and a significant number of our manufacturing firms continue to depend on agriculture both as a source of inputs and as a market for their products. In the same way, post-industrialism does not mean that we can afford to abandon manufacturing to offshore producers and put everyone to work selling services to one another. As Akio Morita, president of Sony, warns, an economy which has lost its manufacturing base has no engine to drive it. As with services, the critical issue for the future is not *whether* to manufacture but *what* and *how*.

"So Does the Welfare State"[14]

Historically, the relative mix of "bad jobs" and "good jobs" in the service sector is reflected in the size of the personal service sector (bad jobs) on the one hand, and public services (good jobs) on the other. This mix in turn depends on the way national expenditure is divided between personal consumption and government spending. Big welfare states tend to "crowd out" low-wage consumer services. If people pay high taxes for comparatively luxurious social services, there is less discretionary income for other things. Esping-Andersen estimates that employment in food and accommodation services is over 7 per cent in the United States but less than 2 per cent in Sweden.[15] A large, high-wage public sector simply makes it difficult for low-wage personal service industries to compete. As a result, in a post-industrial labour market the welfare state can contribute as much or more to economic well-being through its role as employer as through its role as income redistributor. The issue for the future is not whether we will have a service economy but what kind of service economy. But to date, Canada's rather modest welfare state has resulted in a service economy that is more American in its contours than Scandinavian (see Table 16.1).

The role of the welfare state is important for more than distributive reasons, however; it does more than create jobs that pay high wages. Competitive advantage also depends on the quality of other services in obvious and not-so-obvious ways. An obvious example is the quality (or the lack thereof) of our educational institutions. Less obvious, perhaps, is Canada's competitive advantage vis-à-vis the American labour market because of our ability (through national health insurance) to contain health care costs. The great irony of the free trade agreement is that, if anything, it has led American business leaders such as Lee Iaccocca to call for harmonization of American health care with Canada's, more efficient, national health insurance system. Universality takes advantage of a basic law of all insurance programs – namely, that the effective cost is inversely related to the size of the insured group.

Finally, a growing body of economic opinion indicates that to compete at the high end of the market for goods and services requires more economic security, not less. At least since the Myrdals, it has been part of social democratic lore that the welfare-efficiency trade-off would be a positive sum precisely because of the labour flexibility and responsiveness to innovation more equality and security would bring. Insecure workers threatened by job loss or a shift from high- to low-paid work will naturally (and correctly) resist innovation and further development of the productive forces. In contrast, workers confronted with an egalitarian wage distribution, active labour market policies, and security of employment will welcome and promote structural change. A growing body of neo-institutionalist economic analysis suggests the Myrdals were correct.[16] In this respect Canada's competitive disadvantage lies in the fact that its welfare state is too small (and often of the wrong sort), not because it is too large.

The Service Economy Is Not the Enemy

Historically, the service economy has been the source of as many "good jobs" as "bad jobs". This is not to say the "McJobs" economy is nothing to worry about. The personal service industries do provide bad jobs and, in relative terms, these jobs have got worse in the 1980s. The point is rather that the dualization of the labour market into a primary and secondary sector is symptomatic of most sectors of the economy, including the public sector. The disproportionate growth of the low end of the service sector is a symptom, not the cause, of the problem.

Pfeffer and Baron describe this trend in terms of the growing use of "contingent labour." For example, IBM, like Sweden, runs on a full-employment, high-wage labour strategy *inside* the firm. The resulting labour costs are high, so that IBM only wants to provide the "rights" of corporate "citizenship" to their most skilled and valued workers. As a result, IBM attempts not only to contract out the less-skilled aspects of production, such as warehousing and distribution, but also actively assists in the establishment of small firms to do this work. Similar stories and examples can be found in both social services and government.[17]

In effect, the problem is not the service economy per se but the changing "rules" of the labour market in general. Bluestone and Harrison's recent description of the United States situation could apply to Canada as well.

Among the "rule changes" we have in mind ... are erosion of the real minimum wage, the uneven diffusion of wage freeze and concession demands among firms, the growth of two-tiered wage systems, the transformation by employers of full time into part time jobs, and the continued outsourcing of production from work sites whose wage schedules are characterized by relatively high means and low variances (thanks in part to the presence of unions) to suppliers with wage distributions having on average lower means and higher variances.[18]

Policy matters in all of this to the extent that labour market, industrial relations, and social policies all either stimulate or accommodate this situation. In other words, they make it profitable for employers to invest or to shift production into the low end of the wage and skill distribution, a point to which I return in the conclusion.

The Youth Labour Market

The growth of low-wage employment is not idiosyncratic to the service sector but is taking place across the whole of the economy, including manufacturing. The main reason we have come to identify the expansion of low-wage employment as a McJobs phenomenon is simply because so many young people are employed there. Transformations in the labour market (including both the shift to services and the dualization of the labour market) tend to show up primarily among new labour market entrants such as women and young people. Expanding industries (as in services) tend to recruit from new labour market entrants and employ more young people and women. Stable or declining sectors have few new recruits and, hence, tend to have a disproportionate number of older, predominantly male, workers. Older, established workers are also more likely to be protected against wage cuts by seniority and other contractual provisions. With female labour force participation rates peaking in the 1980s, the primary victims of dualization have been younger workers who experienced a 15 to 20 per cent wage drop relative to older workers in all sectors of the economy.

The results are manifest in a number of ways: rising enrolments in post-secondary institutions as competition for good jobs increases: return to the family home and rising welfare rates as the supply of good jobs declines. For young people this means later career starts, delayed family formation, and generally postponed adulthood. For the economy it means we are not fully involving the next generation of workers, either socially, politically, or economically, in finding our way through the current transition.

If wage rates are indicative of other aspects of job quality such as the skill content of work (as human capital theory would suggest), then trends in youth wages are indicative not only of short-term social problems for youth but also of long-term problems for the economy as a whole. The early years in the labour market are typically when critical jobs skills and work attitudes are acquired. If, as the wage data suggest, we are excluding our youth from the more complex jobs requiring capacity for self-direction and creativity, they are less likely to become the innovative and responsible employees that we are told the next generation of production systems will require.

It is not clear that any of our social institutions are paying much attention to this development, including political parties, labour unions, or the social movements. The "sixties generation" that is now middle-aged and at the head of these institutions seems to have written the next generation off as "conservative" and disinterested even as their own material conditions have improved. The first political party to make the "youth issue" its own is likely to reap windfall gains; those national economies that prove capable of mobilizing the energies of their youth are likely to enjoy unanticipated dividends in the new global marketplace.

CONCLUSION: POST-INDUSTRIALISM'S FUTURES

The question raised by the post-industrial transition is not whether we will or should have a service economy but what kind of service economy. Actually existing patterns in post-industrial labour markets suggest three emergent scenarios.

1 The first might be called a "high-wage–low-employment" strategy. The exemplar is West Germany. Productivity gains are not translated into a shift of employment into services but into less employment. This does not mean rising unemployment but simply fewer people in the labour market. Here the welfare state is used to implement a labour market "exit" strategy. The pension system, disability and unemployment insurance schemes are used to absorb surplus labour. The main result of such a strategy is to create a cleavage not between high- and low-wage workers but between those inside and those outside the labour market. Age, sex, immigrant, and family status are the typical divisions along which such boundaries have been constructed in the past.

2 The second alternative is a "high-wage–high-employment" strategy. The exemplar in this case is Sweden. Here the welfare state's main role is that of employer and manager of labour market transitions as employees shift from declining to expanding industries. Work-time reductions do not take the form of reinforcing old or creating new divisions between those who are and are not employed but by reducing working time across the whole of the labour market in the form of paid work absences (sick leave, maternity leave, retraining, vacations). With high levels of employment, this strategy depends critically on a capacity to restrain inflation-generating wage growth, especially at the top of the labour market. This means not just containing wage increases but actually bringing down the relative earnings of the "new middle class" of managerial, professional and technical workers.

3 The third strategy is the "dualization–high-employment" strategy. Canada and the United States are the exemplars here. Both have been successful in creating a large number of new jobs but mainly at the bottom of the labour market. Here, the emergent role of the welfare

state appears to be that of "wage subsidizer," providing various kinds of income subsidies to the working poor to keep those at the low end of the labour market alive. Hence the popularity of various guaranteed income proposals not only among social policy experts but also in business circles.

The logic of each system is somewhat different and resolves similar problems in different ways. The way each system solves the employment-inflation trade-off seems especially important. The dualization strategy allows for strong growth in total employment levels without inflation-generating wage pressure by encouraging employment growth at the bottom of the labour market. Many conservatives see this as desirable; many liberals and social democrats see it as inevitable. This seems to be the dominant rationale for the current popularity of a variety of guaranteed income schemes to supplement the incomes of the working poor.[19] We might call this a strategy of "accommodating dualism."

The alternative to accommodation is to institutionalize labour market and social policies to skew investment into the high end of the wage and skill distribution and discourage investment and employment at the bottom. The labour market exit strategy achieves this at the cost of lowering total employment levels. In West Germany inflation-generating wage pressure can be avoided not only for historical and institutional reasons (a political economy organized around the principle of inflation avoidance) but also because a growing share of the population – pensioners – are effectively subject to the "wage controls" of the welfare state.

The Swedish combination of high wages and high employment works to the extent that wage and salary growth at the top of the labour market can be contained. Employers continue to invest to the extent that wages and salaries at the top of the Swedish labour market are lower than they otherwise would be. One might think of this as a strategy where the economy "competes" with the top of its labour market – including the new middle class – rather that its bottom. At the same time, elimination of the opportunity to use low-wage labour compels employers to increase productivity both through technological change and by utilizing a labour force with a higher skill mix.

Either variant of the high-wage strategy requires a strong commitment to continuous productivity growth. High wages are both cause and consequence of rising productivity. Low wages provide no incentive for employers to increase productivity or push their labour mix up the skill gradient, since increases in output can be had more cheaply by hiring more labour. Dualization may enhance productivity for individual firms but not for the economy as a whole. IBM simply exports its problems when it contracts out low-productivity jobs.

A strong commitment to continuous productivity growth ("revolutionizing the forces of production") also requires a strong commitment to the welfare state. A dynamic economy is one that by definition produces change, and change inevitably produces winners and losers among firms, industries, and regions. To make economic change acceptable, the welfare state is required in order to redistribute the costs and benefits of change. Otherwise, workers (and local politicians and often employers) will quite correctly resist change. By providing pathways out of the labour market, the German labour market exit strategy deals with this in one way. By providing employment inside the welfare state and managing labour market transitions within an active labour market, the Swedish model provides another.

In contrast, the dualization strategy – where the welfare state is used to subsidize the victims of low-wage employment – is likely to work against large gains in productivity. With a ready supply of low-wage labour, employers have little incentive to "revolutionize the forces of production" by eliminating low-skill, low-productivity jobs. This is not to say that dualization cannot succeed as an economic strategy in the current transition, but rather that it is a sub-optimal strategy. It brings with it labour market flexibility and the capacity to adapt and change, but it is a flexibility of a particular sort. The capacity to change and innovate may mean that skilled workers equipped with the appropriate technologies are able to apply these skills ans technologies on a continuous basis to improve product quality, to change products to accommodate changing markets, and to adopt – even to create – new technologies. But flexibility may also mean the ability to lay off workers, lower wages, and contract out to non-unionized firms. The first – dynamic flexibility – is defined by Cohen and Zysman as the ability to increase productivity steadily through improvements in production processes and innovation. The second – static flexibility – they define as the ability of firms to adjust operations at any moment to shifting conditions in the market.[20] Whereas the former requires a high-skill, high-wage workforce with security of employment, the latter requires a low-wage, unskilled labour force. The flexibility it offers is characterized as static because of a tendency to adopt new technologies at a slower rate (low labour costs reduce incentives to innovate) and because innovation occurs in a series of successive plateaus rather than on a continuous basis. This fact more than any other provides the political leverage for those who would prefer an alternative future for Canada's post-industrial labour market.

NOTES

1 Portions of this paper are drawn from John Myles, "States, Labor Markets and Life Cycles" in Roger Friedland and A.F. Robertson, *Beyond the Marketplace: Rethinking Economy and Society* (Aldine de Gruyter 1990).

2 On industrialism see Clark Kerr *et al.*, *Industrialism and Industrial Man* (New York: Oxford University Press 1964); on post-industrialism see Daniel Bell, *The Coming of the Post-Industrial Society* (New York: Basic Books 1973).

3 Fred Block, *Revising State Theory: Essays in Politics and Postindustrialism* (Philadelphia: Temple University Press 1987), 27.

4 Ibid., 99–100.

5 John Myles, Garnett Picot, and Ted Wannell, "Wages and Jobs in the Eighties: Changing Youth Wages and the Declining Middle," Research Paper 17 (Ottawa: Statistics Canada 1988), 52.

6 Locating public administration is of course more ambiguous than my classification suggests. A significant part of public administration consists of "producer services" – inputs made into the production of goods and services.

7 Data are from the Comparative Class Structure Project. Identical national surveys were conducted in the early 1980s in the five countries by independent national research teams. For further information see Don Black and John Myles, "Dependent Industrialization and the Canadian Class Structure: A Comparative Analysis of Canada, the United States and Sweden," *Canadian Review of Sociology and Anthropology* 23 (1986): 157–81.

8 See also Gosta Esping-Andersen, *Post-Industrial Employment Trajectories: Germany, Sweden and the United States* (Florence: European University, Department of Politics 1987).

9 Bob Kuttner, "The Declining Middle," *Atlantic Monthly* (July 1983): 60–72.

10 Myles *et al.*, "Wages and Jobs."

11 Ibid., 96.

12 John Myles, "The Expanding Middle: Some Canadian Evidence on the Deskilling Debate," *Canadian Review of Sociology and Anthropology* 25 (1988): 335–64.

13 Canadian Labour Market and Productivity Centre, "Restructuring in Canadian Manufacturing in the 1980s," *Labour Research Notes* 7 (May 1989): 1–12.

14 The couplet "Manufacturing Matters – And So Does the Welfare State" is shamelessly stolen from Leon Muszynksi's superb paper with the same title, given at a conference to consider the de-industrialization of Toronto, September 1988.

15 Esping-Andersen, *Post-Industrial Employment*.

16 For example, Rune Aberg, "Market-dependent Income Distribution: Efficiency and Legitimicacy" in I. Goldthorpe, ed., *Order and Conflict in Contemporary Capitalism* (Oxford: Clarendon Press 1984), 209–30; and Stephen Cohen and John Zysman, *Manufacturing Matters: The Myth of the Post-Industrial Economy* (New York: Basic Books 1987).

17 Jeffrey Pfeffer and James Baron, "Taking the Workers Back Out: Recent Trends in the Structuring of Employment" in Barry Straw and L.L. Cummings, eds., *Research in Organizational Behavior* (Greenwich, CN: JAI Press 1988). One can also find examples of firms using contingent labour at the high end of the labour market (e.g., professors) to avoid long-term commitments to employees and so maintain a flexible labour market.

18 Barry Bluestone and Bennett Harrison, "Increasing Inequality and the Proliferation of Low-wage Employment in the U.S.: A Review of the Debate and Some New Evidence," mimeo 1989.

19 In view of prevailing forms of family organization, emergent labour market trends, and the growing importance of competing in international markets, it is unrealistic, many argue, to expect the labour market to provide everyone with the high and rising real wage levels we came to expect in the past. Under these conditions, the state cannot afford to "waste" scarce transfer dollars on the middle classes (i.e., on social insurance and public services). A fundamental requirement of the welfare state of the 1990s and beyond, according to the Canadian Council on Social Development, a major anti-poverty lobby, is "to find acceptable ways of accommodating this form of economic development." See Canadian Council on Social Development, *Proposals for Discussion: Phase One – Income Security Reform* (Ottawa 1987), 5. The welfare state must be adjusted to the new reality of a service economy, single-parent families, and flexible low-wage, labour market through better targeting of benefits on the poor. Instead of a universal system of income security for a nation of high-wage workers, the welfare state of the future will have to provide subsistence to a growing number of low-wage workers. There is nothing wrong with a guaranteed income of course, if it is introduced under conditions where it is largely unnecessary, that is, where there is full and high levels of employment, high minimum wages, and strong unions to defend wage levels. Under these conditions the working poor are an anomaly rather than an institutionalized feature of the economy. Otherwise, a guaranteed income becomes an industrial strategy to encourage investment into the low end of the wage distribution: wage supplements for the working poor are also wage subsidies to low-wage employers.

20 Cohen and Zysman, *Manufacturing Matters*, 131.

17 Canada in a High-Tech World: Options for Industrial Policy

MERIC S. GERTLER

As Canada moves into the era of continental and world market restructuring it should not be surprising to find that industrial policy is back at the top of the policy agenda, at least in those regions where manufacturing has traditionally figured prominently. In Ontario the much-publicized Premier's Council on Technology has been striving to formulate plans to give producers there the technological wherewithal to meet and beat the foreign competition. In Quebec the Bourassa government continues to mobilize local sources of financial capital, using large pension funds and tax breaks to invest in Quebec-owned businesses, exploiting industrial policy mechanisms put in place by previous administrations. However, as the winds of change sweep through the manufacturing heartland of Canada, governments at all levels remain confused and uncertain about what model to pursue in formulating new industrial policies. They are also unsure of the role of high-technology industries in such a strategy.

Recent studies indicate that high-tech industries' output has grown relatively more quickly than that from other industries, and that high-tech industries have exhibited superior rates of productivity improvement. However, as direct employers of Canadian (or American) workers, these industries leave something to be desired (see Appendix on p. 389 for alternative definitions of high-tech, and a review of their performance in various national studies). Nevertheless, their potential contribution to the Canadian economy can be considerable in a number of areas. First, as industries whose output may expand more quickly than other sectors of the economy, high-tech firms stimulate demand for the output of other sectors to which they are linked, thereby also indirectly creating employment. Secondly, the new technology can be used by firms in other sectors to improve their competitiveness, profitability, and employment creation record. Old, mature sectors may rejuvenate themselves by changing the contents of their products, or by restructuring the process used to manufacture their product. The case of the automobile sector is most vivid here (see the papers by Holmes and Morris in this volume), though there are many other less dramatic examples.

Hence, the impacts of high-tech industry for the overall economy are more profound as the technology is adopted and applied than in the actual firms where production of such technology occurs. Perhaps in recognition of this, there has been a temptation on the part of some industrial policy analysts and formulators – most notably the Economic Council of Canada – to suggest that the best route to technological sophistication for Canadian industry is to import it from abroad, usually through the foreign multinational corporation producing in Canada.[1] It is alleged that this strategy would also reduce the significance of Canada's chronically pathetic R&D effort by allowing other countries to perform this function for it indirectly, as embodied within technology-intensive imports.

Yet this strategy does not seem to have served Canada well. Canadian industry's general export performance and productivity growth has left much to be desired (see, for example the chapters in this volume by Donner and Cohen). It will become evident in this chapter that a large part of the explanation for this lacklustre performance can be found in the rather underdeveloped technological state of Canadian producers. This sector is in desperately poor shape by world standards, with its trade performance actually weakening since 1971. The Economic Council was led to conclude: "The gravity of this situation demands that Canada urgently undertake a major review of its science and technology policies," continuing "that the problem must be addressed soon if it is not to severely affect Canada's productivity, international competitiveness, and standard of living."[2]

In the sections that follow, I examine the recent experience of high-tech activity in Canada, focusing on its sectoral characteristics, geographical distribution, trade performance, and ownership structure.[3] I then assess the degree of success of Canadian firms in general, in adopting innovative technologies imported from foreign sources. This is followed by the elaboration and critical appraisal of three alternative industrial policy strategies, including options which have hitherto not been considered within the Canadian context. In this way, I hope to

reopen the Canadian industrial policy debate to an international literature that has raised serious new questions for Canada to consider.

APPRAISING CANADA'S HIGH-TECH PRODUCERS

In their recent study of Canadian industrial structure, Charette *et al.*
note that the manufacturing sector's share of Canadian GDP has
remained more or less constant between 1947 and 1981, at around 22
per cent. During the same time, its share of employment declined from
around 25 per cent to just under 18 per cent, despite an increase in
the absolute number of workers in all manufacturing sectors combined. For individual industry groups within manufacturing, the pattern of employment change was rather uneven. Between 1961 and
1981, those groups with significantly expanding shares of manufacturing employment included transportation equipment, machinery,
rubber and plastics, and metal products. Significant losers included
food, textiles, and apparel, with the latter two sectors registering absolute declines since 1973.

Sectoral Characteristics

A picture of Canadian manufacturing as it currently exists, based on
the most recently available statistics (1985), is presented in Table 17.1.
Those industrial groups that have been classified as being of high or
medium technology intensiveness by the Science Council of Canada
(based on R&D expenditures as a proportion of sales) are shown in bold
face. At this rather gross level of industrial aggregation, only electrical
and electronic products and chemicals and chemical products qualify as
being highly technology-intensive, the rest being medium technology.
Of the top five employers, only two groups are from the technology-
intensive category – transportation equipment (ranked 1) and electrical/
electronic products (ranked 4). Taken together, the technology-intensive
industrial groups accounted for 46.1 per cent of all manufacturing
employment in 1985. However, since the level of aggregation used here
is still very great, this figure is of questionable meaning. For instance,
in the electrical/electronic group, only 53 per cent of jobs are actually
found in those specific industries that one would reasonably classify as
being high tech.

The need to disaggregate industrial sectors more finely in order to
analyse high tech's prominence in Canada manufacturing is demonstrated more fully in Table 17.2, which shows the top 25 sectors within

Table 17.1
Canada's Sectoral Distribution of Manufacturing Employment and Establishments

SIC*	Major industrial group	Rank	Employment No.	%	Estab- lishments	Employees per estab- lishment
10	Food	2	192,000	10.9	3,228	60
11	Beverages	16	31,903	1.8	304	105
12	Tobacco products	22	7,097	0.4	25	284
15	Rubber products	19	25,366	1.4	148	171
16	Plastic products	15	38,182	2.2	1,091	35
17	Leather products	20	23,129	1.3	384	60
18	Primary textiles	18	26,758	1.5	215	125
19	Textile products	17	31,110	1.8	802	39
24	Clothing	7	110,910	6.3	2,497	44
25	Wood	8	107,560	6.1	3,476	31
26	Furniture & fixture	14	49,868	2.8	1,727	29
27	**Paper products**	**6**	**114,187**	**6.5**	**688**	**166**
28	Printing & publishing	5	117,062	6.6	5,443	22
29	**Primary metals**	**9**	**106,808**	**6.0**	**435**	**246**
30	Fabricated Metal products	3	139,698	7.9	5,537	25
31	**Machinery**	**11**	**74,732**	**4.2**	**1,815**	**41**
32	**Transportation equipment**	**1**	**210,984**	**11.9**	**1,471**	**143**
33	**Electrical & electronic products**	**4**	**137,165**	**7.8**	**1,379**	**99**
35	Non-metallic mineral products	13	50,605	2.9	1,532	33
36	**Refined petroleum & coal products**	**21**	**16,739**	**1.0**	**121**	**138**
37	**Chemical and chemical products**	**10**	**87,224**	**4.9**	**1,256**	**69**
39	**Other manufacturing**	**12**	**67,676**	**3.8**	**3,280**	**21**
	TOTAL Manufacturing		1,766,763	100.0	36,854	48

SOURCES: Statistics Canada (1988), Catalogue 31–203 (1985 Census of Manufactures).

Boldface sectors are designed as high or medium technology-intensive by the Science Council of Canada. See Charette et al., for discussion of classification methods.

"Evolution of Canadian Industrial Structure: An International Perspective" in D.G. McFetridge, ed., Canadian Industry in Transition. Vol. 2 of Background Studies for the Macdonald Royal Commission (Toronto: University of Toronto Press 1986), 116.

* Standard Industrial Classification code used by Statistics Canada to identify each major industrial group.

manufacturing using a more finely disaggregated industry breakdown, ranked by value of shipments of goods of own manufacture in 1985. Once again, high-technology sectors (defined according to R&D intensity and proportion of employees in scientific and technical occupations)

Table 17.2
Canada's Top Twenty-five Manufacturing Industries Ranked by Value of Shipments,
1985

Rank	SIC	Industry	Shipments ($'000,000)	Employment
1	3611	Petroleum products	23,991	5,545
2	**3231**	**Motor vehicles**	**23,723**	**44,358**
3	1011	Meat and meat products	8,248	24,099
4	2919	Other primary steel industries	7,347	33,458
5	2512	Sawmill and planing mill products	6,863	49,616
6	2712	Newsprint	6,631	28,786
7	**3712**	**Industrial organic chemicals**	**4,709**	**5,982**
8	2958	Non-ferrous smelting (incl. aluminum)	4,596	21,443
9	3251	Motor vehicle engines and parts	3,809	13,255
10	2819	Other commercial printing	3,751	39,047
11	1049	Other dairy products	3,593	8,237
12	2711	Pulp	3,545	13,999
13	3259	Other motor vehicle accessories & parts	3,348	20,573
14	1041	Fluid milk industry	2,817	6,283
15	**3211**	**Aircraft and parts**	**2,729**	**21,053**
16	1053	Feed	2,624	5,842
17	**3199**	**Other machinery and equipment**	**2,619**	**20,036**
18	1098	Other food industries	2,581	8,773
19	3192	Construction and mining machinery	2,529	15,277
20	3049	Other stamped & pressed metal products	2,515	11,792
21	2841	Newspapers, magazines and periodicals	2,442	16,124
22	1598	Other rubber products (incl. tires)	2,340	16,341
23	**3741**	**Pharmaceuticals and medicine**	**2,230**	**7,490**
24	**3711**	**Industrial inorganic chemicals**	**2,187**	**5,731**
25	**3351**	**Telecommunication equipment**	**2,018**	**10,834**

SOURCE: Statistics Canada (1988) *Manufacturing Industries of Canada: National and Provincial Area, 1985*.
    Catalogue 31–203.
Bold face sectors are high-technology as defined in Charette, *et al.*, "Evolution of Canadian
Industrial Structure," 116–17.

are highlighted in bold face. Here, one finds a somewhat less impressive
picture. Only two industries crack the top ten (motor vehicles and
industrial organic chemicals)[4] and the latter sector is highly capital-
intensive and a notoriously poor provider of direct employment. The
archetypal high-tech sectors, such as those associated with microelec-
tronics and biotechnology, are scarcely represented on this list. The only
hint of such a presence is in two of the last sectors shown here – phar-
maceuticals and medicine, and telecommunication equipment. If the list
were expanded to the top forty industries, it would add other electronic
equipment, and electronic computers and peripherals in the thirty–fifth
and thirty-seventh spots respectively.

Table 17.3 presents some basic statistics on a selection of seven specific high-tech manufacturing industries. While these are drawn largely from within the electrical products industry, they also include aerospace and machine-tool firms. A number of interesting features are evident from these data. For industries such as machine tools, computers and office equipment, electronic components, and other electronics, employment grew more rapidly than it did for all manufacturing activity over the post-recession period of 1982–85. However, within this group were some apparent laggards: aircraft and aircraft parts, consumer electronics, and most notably, telecommunications equipment, which actually showed an absolute decline during this period. These lagging industries happened to have the highest average establishment sizes amongst the seven-industry group. Indeed, there is an almost perfect inverse relationship between establishment size rank and employment change rank across the seven industries, implying superior employment creation performance within the smaller plants. Whether such a relationship holds true within a single industry remains an open question.

Spatial Characteristics

Table 17.3 demonstrates the marked geographical concentrations within most of these sectors. While Canadian manufacturing as a whole is already highly concentrated in the two central Canadian provinces of Ontario and Quebec (a total of 80 per cent), all the high-tech sectors but one (telecommunications equipment) are even more strongly clustered in central Canada than manufacturing as a whole. These concentrations reach particular extremes in the case of consumer electronics (100 per cent) and machine tools and tooling (98 per cent).

It is more difficult to document the spatial distribution of employment for these more finely disaggregated industries at the smaller scale of individual metropolitan areas, due to the confidentiality regulations which govern the reporting of industrial data in Canada. Nevertheless, one is able to piece together a partial picture for Canada's two largest census metropolitan areas, Toronto and Montreal, and to a lesser extent for Ottawa-Hull, thereby capturing a reasonably large proportion of central Canadian employment (see Table 17.3).

Again, one gets a sense of strong spatial concentration in most of the sectors. For example, Toronto's share of all manufacturing employment was 21 per cent; only in the case of telecom/electronic components did Toronto's share (13 per cent) fall below its overall share of national manufacturing employment. Furthermore, these figures tell us that more than three-quarters of Ontario's employment in the aircraft and aircraft parts industry was located in the Toronto metropolitan region.

Table 17.3
National, Regional, and Metropolitan Statistics for Selected High-Technology Manufacturing Industries in Canada, 1986

	Canada (all manufacturing)*	Aircrafts & parts (3211)	Machine tools & tooling (3062)	Computers & office equip.* (336)	Consumer electronics (3341)	Telecom equip. (3351)	Electronic components (3352)	Other electronics (3359)
EMPLOYMENT	1,766,763	38,409	10,708	18,582	3,462	16,563	11,364	22,007
% change, 1982–86	n.a.	15.4	52.3	17.5	19.1	-19.1	38.1	29.2
% change, 1982–85	3.8	1.6	29.7	10.2	3.5	-0.1	30.1	20.3
ESTABLISHMENTS	36,854	198	578	148	19	44	251	206
AVERAGE NUMBER OF EMPLOYEES PER ESTABLISHMENT	48		19	126	182	376	45	107
REGIONAL SHARES OF EMPLOYMENT (%)								
Atlantic	5	3	0	0	0	9	2	2
Quebec	28	43	10	18	32	20	17	32
Ontario	52	44	88	63	68	46	68	53
Prairies	8	9	1	13	0	20	5	5
B.C.	7	1	1	6	0	5	8	8
METROPOLITAN AREA SHARES OF EMPLOYMENT (%)							(335)	
Toronto CMA, 1985	21	34	30	24			13	
Montreal CMA, 1985	14	43	8				14	
Ottawa-Hull CMA, 1983	1			7			8	

SOURCES: Statistics Canada, Catalogues 42–251B, 41–251B, 43–250B, 31–203 (1985 and 1986), 31–209 (1983, 1985, 1986).

* 1985 Statistics.

NOTE: Figures in parentheses are the SIC code numbers identifying each industry. SIC 335 incorporates within it SIC 3351, 3352, and 3359. Metropolitan area data were not available at the more disaggregated (four-digit code) level.

Similarly, Montreal's 43 per cent share of national employment in the aircraft industry far exceeded its 13 per cent share of all manufacturing employment, and we can see that virtually all of Quebec's aircraft industry employment falls within the Montreal metropolitan area. Likewise, of the rather small proportion of Canada's machine tool industry in Quebec, some 80 per cent is located within the Montreal area. Only in the telecom/electronics industries do we see much geographical dispersal. Toronto's share of national employment is only a paltry 13 per cent (despite the fact that Ontario possesses between 46 and 68 per cent of the national employment in the constituent industries which make up the telecom/electronic components grouping). The implication here is that this sector is comparatively rather dispersed, both nationally and within the province of Ontario. Part of the Ontario employment is accounted for by Ottawa-Hull, which had 8 per cent of national employment in this sector in 1983.[5]

Hence, apart from the telecom sector nationally and telecom/electronics regionally, which seem to exhibit rather "footloose," locational tendencies, the rest of the seven high-tech industries appear from these limited data to be highly concentrated within central Canada. Furthermore, Toronto and Montreal emerge as major high-tech agglomerations.

Trade Performance

One key indicator of the performance of Canadian high-tech manufacturers is their success in competing on a world scale. If one of the alleged benefits of a high-tech economy is export competitiveness and the advantages assumed to be associated with that, how have high-tech industries actually performed?

Table 17.4 gives us some indication of how successful certain Canadian high-tech industries have been in the world market. For a subset of the sectors examined in Table 17.3, plus scientific and professional instruments, one finds a rather depressing situation. All of the industries but one (aircraft and aircraft parts) show large deficits in their 1986 trade balances. Furthermore, all of the industries have experienced a downturn in their trade balances during the recovery period since the 1981–82 recession. Prior to 1982, the performance of individual sectors was somewhat uneven. The aircraft sector experienced a significant decline between 1966 and 1975, with improvement since then.[6] Scientific instruments and consumer electronics (largely television, radio, and phonograph equipment) also dropped between 1966 and 1975, with only marginal and inconsistent improvement since then. The trade picture for office and business machines, and communications equipment brightened in the earliest period, but has consistently and successively worsened since then.

Table 17.4
Trade Balances for Selected High-Tech Industries (as a percentage of exports plus imports)

Industry	1966	1975	1980	1982	1986
Aircraft and parts	14.5	−19.0	−8.8	19.8	4.2
Scientific and professional instruments	−39.1	−61.2	−56.6	−51.7	−55.2
Office and business machines	−56.6	−39.6	−40.8	−48.0	−52.6
Consumer electronics	−39.3	−80.4	−77.4	−72.6	−79.8
Communications equipment	−43.1	−24.8	−25.2	−13.7	−25.0

SOURCES: Adapted from D.G. McFetridge, "The Economics of Industrial Structure: An Overview," in McFetridge, ed., *Canadian Industry in Transition*, p. 11, Statistics Canada catalogue 65–001 (December 1986), and Industry Profiles prepared by Industry, Science and Technology Canada.

All in all, there appears to be little cause for optimism on the trade front. It should also be noted that these findings run directly counter to the blithe claims made by contributors to background reports of the Macdonald Commission (based on 1970s trade data) that "there is no evidence that [Canadian] high technology industries have been unable to keep pace."[7] Based on the numbers reported here, domestic high-tech products have not found a ready market for their goods outside of Canada, and their position appears to have deteriorated in recent years. Furthermore, even the generally conservative, pro-free trade Economic Council of Canada has acknowledged in a recent study that Canada's share of world export markets in high-tech goods has declined markedly since 1971, as has its share of US high-tech imports during a period when Americans were importing more high-tech goods than ever before.[8]

Ownership of High Technology

The above discussion has demonstrated the tendency for Canadians to import far more high-tech goods than they export to the rest of the world. The only possible exception to this practice, for the industries surveyed here, is the aircraft and aircraft parts industry. This image is further reinforced by Table 17.5, which shows the international balance of payments for technological services purchased or sold by all Canadian firms performing or funding R&D. This reflects payments or receipts for research and development, patents, licences, and technical know-how. In 1981–82 balances were negative for all of the technology-intensive industries sampled here, as well as for all other manufacturing and manufacturing as a whole. In some high-tech sectors, most notably scientific equipment, receipts for Canadian technology were dwarfed

Table 17.5
Technological Balance of Payments for Selected Manufacturing Industries, 1981 and 1986

	1981			1986		
Industry	Payments	Receipts	Balance[1]	Payments	Receipts	Balance[1]
	($1981 millions)		%	($1981 millions)		%
Aircraft and parts	16*	9*	−47*	13	14	4
Telecommunications equipment	70	33	−36	61	184	50
Business machines	144	31	−65	146	92	−23
Scientific and professional equipment	21*	1*	−91*	12	1	−11
Refined petroleum & coal products	37	7	−68	30	2	−88
Chemical products	56	24	−40	81	20	−75
All other manufacturing	156	35	−63	200	78	−44
Total manufacturing	463	130	−56	518	377	−16

SOURCES: Adapted from Statistics Canada, Catalogues 88–202 (1986) and 88–502E (1984).

1. Balance is expressed as a percentage of payments plus receipts.

* 1982 figures.

by payments for foreign technology. By 1986 the picture had improved significantly for total manufacturing, although many of the individual sectors (and total manufacturing) still showed negative balances. Producers of chemical products and refined petroleum and coal products actually made proportionally greater use of foreign technology. Producers of scientific and professional equipment were importing less foreign technology than before, but selling no more to the rest of the world. On the other hand, in business machines, telecom equipment, and aircraft and parts, receipts for Canadian technology appear to have risen, even producing net "exports" by 1986 in the latter two sectors.[9]

Here, then, the results are mixed. Canadian manufacturers, including many in the high-tech sector, are still net importers of foreign technology. For some sectors the size of the negative balance is declining or has turned positive, while for others the trade deficit has worsened or changed little. However, as will be seen below, interpretations of these phenomena may not be as straightforward as they first seem.

UTILIZING HIGH-TECH INPUTS AND PROCESSES: THE STRUGGLE TO ADOPT

Canadian manufacturers' sizeable appetite for foreign technology has been viewed by the mainstream of the Canadian economics fraternity as a positive phenomenon. Writing in a background study for the Macdonald

Commission, McFetridge expresses approval of the situation, viewing it as a relatively easy way for Canadian producers to appropriate new technologies without having to develop them themselves. He cites evidence to show that, indeed, Canadian firms are as quick to adopt technologies as producers in other countries, noting as well that a principal vector for such technologies is often the multinational corporation.[10]

There can be no doubt that adoption of product and process innovations (rather than exclusive reliance upon self-generation) is an intelligent and essential strategy for manufacturers everywhere to pursue. Nevertheless, while there might be abundant evidence to demonstrate that Canadian producers are quick and hungry to adopt foreign technologies, this does not necessarily prove that Canadian firms are applying these new technologies effectively on the shop floor. Indeed, there is a growing body of data to show that Canadian manufacturers are experiencing considerable difficulty in attempting to apply new process technologies within pre-existing production systems, or in trying to set up entirely new production systems.

I refer here particularly to the advent of various forms of "flexible" technologies, which may range from computerized, reprogrammable machines capable of producing a wide range of products, to clusters of such machines linked together and co-ordinated by computer networks (flexible manufacturing systems or FMS), to networks of computerized flexible machines which integrate producers and their suppliers, often using "just-in-time" systems of assembly, delivery, and inventory management. Along with such new "hard" technologies are the "soft" technologies, consisting of a more flexible use of labour, in both a quantitative and qualitative sense.

Despite the many claims that we have irreversibly entered an era dominated by such post-Fordist production methods, the evidence within the productive sphere of Canadian economic life is still rather inconclusive.[11] A recent study conducted by Meurer *et al.* demonstrates that some of Canada's most advanced manufacturers are encountering difficulty in implementing new flexible forms of production. New production processes have taken much longer to put in place, and at a far higher cost than was originally imagined. Operating costs of production have not declined to the extent expected due to the high cost of malfunctioning equipment. Labour displacement has been far less than was originally imagined. While there have been qualitative changes in firms' labour forces, as they seek multi-talented generalists to work alongside multi-purpose machines, overall numbers of workers have declined hardly at all. Problems are frequently encountered as firms try to mesh new forms of fixed capital with pre-existing plant and equipment. Firms also find it difficult to graft new ways of organizing production and new

roles for labour and managment onto pre-existing practices and employment relations on the shop floor.[12] These findings echo those of other
Canadian studies, such as that of Fertey *et al.*, focusing on the automotive
industry, the federal government analysis of recent trends within the
machine tools and tooling industry, and Mansell, looking more generally
at workplace innovation in a variety of sectors across the country.[13]

In highlighting the frailties and failings of Canadian producers, this
is not to imply that they are unique among world producers. Jaikumar
has described the difficulties that American producers have encountered
in trying to implement FMS technologies, largely imported from Japan,
noting how the US producers have tended to apply the same technologies
in rather Fordist, non-flexible ways, with predictable results. More
recently Kelley and Brooks have documented the rather sorry state of
computerized automation in general within American manufacturing.
They observe a similar litany of costs and other problems, including a
tendency for firms to overlook the training requirements for both management and labour in order to adopt successfully these new production
technologies. Finally, the halting progress made by British firms in
attempting to adopt more flexible forms of production, including their
use of flexible labour and subcontracting, has recently been described
by Pollert and Pinch *et al.*[14]

There are, of course, other countries whose producers appear to have
had far more success in making this transition, Japan, West Germany,
and Italy foremost among them. Interestingly, all of these countries are
major innovators and producers (rather than adopters) of machine tools,
particularly flexible, computer-numerically controlled (CNC) machine
tools, one of the key process technologies underlying the flexible automation of manufacturing. Japan has 24 per cent of the world market,
West Germany 16 per cent, and Italy 5 per cent, as opposed to the
United States with 10 per cent, and Canada with less than 1 per cent.
Hence, these countries have been successful in producing the tools with
which their other leading commodities are produced. In contrast, the
Canadian machine tool industry is small and closely linked to a single
sector, the automotive industry. In 1986 the total volume of Canadian
machine tool production of $682 million was swamped by the value of
imports ($853 million). Hence, some 68 per cent of Canadian con-
sumption was served by imports, which came largely from the United
States and, increasingly, the European Community (Germany and Italy)
and Japan.[15]

The Canadian machine tool industry is also relatively underdeveloped
in technological terms. To quote from the recent federal government
survey of the industry: "Canadian firms have limited capacity in strong
growth areas such as CNC machine tools ... In addition, there is no

capability in Canada in computerized-machine controls, or in general-purpose robots, which are being increasingly integrated with machine tools into production systems."[16] It appears, then, that one of the factors contributing to the lack of success that plagues Canadian producers in implementing computerized automation is the lack of an indigenously developed advanced machine tools industry. Should this conjecture prove to be true, it casts a more negative light on Canadian manufacturers' demonstrated willingness to import technologies from other countries, since it would appear that the more advanced process technologies in particular are not easily adopted in places at some distance from their invention.[17]

ALTERNATIVE STRATEGIES FOR
PROSPERITY: ''MILLIONS'' VERSUS
''EMILIANS''

We can see by now that Canada's high-tech manufacturing economy is underdeveloped, in terms of the presence of producers of products, and also in the application of the products themselves within other sectors of manufacturing that might be able to benefit from their use. It is appropriate now to shift attention to a discussion of industrial policy strategies that might be employed to enhance the competitive position of these Canadian producers within the emerging world economy. There are two different industrial strategies that come to mind: one which has received a great deal of attention of late from both the business community and government, another which has not received much notice within the Canadian context, although it has become increasingly prominent in industrial policy debates outside Canada.

"Millions"

The first might be described as a strategy based largely on achieving larger scales of production – the well-known search for internal economies of scale and specialization, based on a larger market in which to sell one's output. The logic of this strategy is to reduce average costs of production by spreading fixed costs over larger internal scales of output, thereby enabling a lowering of prices to increase sales.

It has been a familiar refrain for some time in Canada that the country's biggest handicap has been the limited size of the domestic market and the excessive diversity of products produced in Canadian plants. The solution to such ills, according to this view, is to promote greater specialization for individual producers and to seek larger markets on a world scale by promoting trade liberalization. Of course, it is precisely this strategy that has figured prominently in the Mulroney government's push for a free trade agreement (FTA) with the United States.[18] Indeed, such a strategy has been prescribed not only as a solution to the ills of normal and mature industries, but also as a boon to would-be Canadian users of high-tech production methods. McFetridge writes:

New technologies may be scaled inappropriately for small firms. Fixed acquisition and installation costs may also be proportionately more burdensome for small firms. If ... tariff reductions have the effect of increasing the length of production runs of Canadian firms, they may also have the added benefit of increasing the extent to which these firms can make use of the newest technologies and increasing the speed with which they can do so.[19]

McFetridge may be half-right. Many new technologies are prohibitively expensive for small firms to employ economically. However, the difficulty for these firms is not so much production runs of insufficient length as lack of access to capital with which to acquire, develop, or adapt advanced production equipment appropriate for serving the smaller, more specialized markets in which they might feasibly compete with technologically sophisticated products.

Since the logic of the above approach focuses exclusively on price competition (given its emphasis on increasing internal scale to reduce average cost, hence price), there is continual pressure on producers to keep costs of production (including labour costs) as low as possible. If past experience is any guide, this will likely lead to an assault on wages and work conditions as a further means to reducing Canadian costs of production. However, this strategy also assumes the existence of a large and stable market for the output from industries' longer production runs. There are growing claims that such an assumption is no longer valid for many important industries.[20] Furthermore, to argue that an assault on foreign markets is the cure for our economic ills would seem to be somewhat misguided when it is apparent from earlier discussion that Canadian producers cannot command their own domestic market, even in sectors for which one might expect a domestic comparative advantage.

"Emilians"[21]

The alternative strategy to consider takes a somewhat different tack, in that it assumes demand to be more qualitatively fragmented, hence unlikely to be served effectively by large, rigid, specialized producers. I refer here to the strategy of flexible specialization, in which producers operate more effectively at smaller *internal* scales by servicing smaller niches in the market and/or are able to respond rapidly to changing market tastes through the use of both flexible, computer-automated machinery and flexible subcontracting arrangements with other small firms and individual workers in the same area. Hence, competition is no longer based solely on price (internal economies of scale), but on the ability of firms to identify and serve quickly changing niche markets (economies of scope). This strategy exploits *external* scale economies that abound within clusters of interlinked firms which have come to be referred to as "industrial districts" or "territorial production complexes."[22] What is most important to this strategy is the proximity of transacting producers, whose geographical concentration allows them to work effectively together in the face of rapidly changing products. It also facilitates the very process of linkage formation and change itself, as different subcontractors may be used for different jobs.

This strategy has been advocated increasingly as a solution to the ills of mature, uncompetitive manufacturing sectors in countries such as the United Kingdom and the United States.[23] It also holds an obvious attraction for Canadian manufacturers, as it has the potential to free them from the need to produce at large volumes of output – the "tyranny of the millions." But it is also a strategy that accommodates effectively changing demands in the market place. Interestingly, in countries such as Italy, which inspired Piore and Sabel originally, producers in the area referred to as the "Third Italy," centred in the regions of Emilia-Romagna, Veneto, Tuscany, Umbria, and the Marches, have used this strategy to rise to industrial prominence in their own country, and also to export manufactured commodities very successfully to the rest of the world. Furthermore, these exports are in advanced sectors such as computerized machine tools, packaging machines, agricultural machinery, oleodynamic machines and components, woodworking machine tools, and food processing machinery, as well as in consumer goods sectors such as knitwear and other garments, ceramic tiles, cycles, motorcycles, and shoes.[24] Similar kinds of territorial production complexes populated by technologically advanced, exporting firms, have been identified in places as diverse as Japan, Silicon Valley, Orange County, California, and elsewhere.[25]

While exporting seems to be an integral part of both strategies outlined above, it should be pointed out that in the first strategy, exporting is seen as an end in itself (greater sales, hence profits for Canadian capital, employment for Canadian labour), as well as the only means to achieving that end (larger production scales, hence markets, are required to bring down unit costs and prices). In the case of the second strategy, exporting is a consequence of successful product development, quality, customization, and modification, (achieved through important innovations to production processes and organization), though not strictly a necessity for successful industrialization of this sort.

Canada has already committed itself to the first strategy, without having seriously considered the second. In fact, if the pages of the Macdonald Commission reports are any indication, the second strategy has not even penetrated the consciousness of the large majority of Canadian economists or policy advisers.[26] And yet, the "Emilian" model and other similar experiences underscore that the secret of successful, technologically dynamic economic growth does not necessarily lie in achieving internal economies of scale. Rather, there is a fundamentally territorial basis to industrial development that has hitherto gone unappreciated in this country. Hence, it is a model that Canadians ignore at their peril. At the very least, it would seem a worthwhile venture to consider the potential applicability of this model to the Canadian realm.[27]

In his 1986 analysis of the Italian industrial districts, Brusco notes a number of characteristics and conditions of the firms and regions in which the most dynamic of these districts is found. First, there is a preponderance of small firms, with many selling directly to the market for the finished product. Secondly, subcontractor firms tend to work for many different clients. Lastly is the presence of firms producing the machines that other firms in the region use to make their products.

In attempting to explain the proliferation of such districts in the Third Italy but not elsewhere in the country, Brusco alludes to the importance of: (i) a local history of entrepreneurship, based on the past dominance of independent farming; (ii) the prior existence of one or more large firms which have served as learning sites for workers who then spin off to form small and artisan firms producing similar goods; (iii) the dominance of productive processes that could be easily divided into separate phases, thereby accommodating subcontracting activity; (iv) the longstanding presence of technical schools in the region; and finally (v) what Brusco calls a general state of "diffused competence" in managerial, technical, and commercial matters across all social strata in the region. The local state (controlled by the Italian Communist party) has also played a role in supporting the development of these districts, through the provision of family-support services such as daycare, and land-use planning procedures to allow small workplaces to be located at the owner's place of residence and to discourage land speculation from displacing small manufacturers.[28] Piore and Sabel add to this list by drawing attention to the history of artisanal goods production in the region, as well as a longstanding mercantile tradition that has established and maintained direct links to the needs and tastes of the market of end users.

Table 17.6
Percentage Distribution of Manufacturing Employment for Canada and Italy
(by size of establishment)

Establishment Size	Canada 1985	Canada 1971	Italy 1971	Emilia 1971	Ontario 1971	Ontario 1985	Toronto CMA 1985
<10	4.0	3.2	23.4	27.8	2.4	3.0	3.6
10–19	5.1	4.6	8.4	10.4	3.8	4.1	5.0
20–49	12.0	10.4	12.5	14.7	8.7	10.1	12.9
50–99	13.4	12.3	10.2	12.7	10.8	12.6	15.8
100–499	37.8	37.6	22.2	23.7	36.6	38.0	39.8
500+	27.7	31.9	23.3	10.7	37.7	32.2	22.9

SOURCES: Statistics Canada (1974 and 1988), Catalogue 31–203 (1971 and 1985 Census of
Manufactures); Brusco, "The Emilian Model."

Could such a strategy work in Canada? There is probably little prospect for replicating the Third Italy in particular regions of Canada.[29] The limited extent of the indigenous Canadian machine tools and machinery industries and the difficulties encountered by Canadian manufacturers in trying to implement flexible, computer-based (and largely foreign) technologies have already been discussed. Furthermore, Canadian manufacturers have practised the time-honoured tradition of importing most of their skilled workers rather than developing fully their own system of technical colleges.

One must also recognize the fundamental differences between the Canadian economy as it currently exists, and that of Italy. Consider, for example, the degree of prominence of small businesses of the sort that Brusco describes. One indicator of this is found in Table 17.6, which shows how manufacturing employment is distributed across different-sized establishments in Canada and Italy. One is immediately struck by the immense differences between the two countries, with Italy showing a far greater preponderance of small firms (especially in the under-ten employees class). While Canada's size distribution has changed somewhat in favour of smaller firms between 1971 and 1985, the differences are still huge.[30]

Similar data are also provided for the region of Emilia and, for comparison, the province of Ontario and the Toronto CMA (which appeared in our earlier analysis to possess Canada's greatest spatial concentration of manufacturers in advanced technology sectors). Emilia shows an even greater prominence of small shops, while Ontario is more heavily biased towards large establishments than the country as a whole. Even in Canada's predominate manufacturing region of Toronto, which falls somewhere between Ontario and the nation, the size distribution of establishments resembles nothing like that of Emilia.

These differences in establishment size certainly underscore the fundamentally different nature of these two economies. Yet it is worth pointing out that Italy's performance in the world trade of manufactured goods has been much superior to that of Canada. Similarly, in terms of productivity growth over the period 1960 to 1982, according to one measure, Italy ranked second behind Japan, while another measure put Italy third behind Japan and France, but still ahead of such industrial powerhouses as West Germany and Sweden.[31] Given the small average scale of Italian manufacturing establishments, these trade and productivity data clearly call into question the importance of *internal* scale economies in providing competitive advantage to producers in a world market place. As such, they challenge the basic rationale underlying recent Canadian economic policy initiatives.

It is clear from the preceding discussion that, despite some appealing characteristics, the Emilian model may not be suitable for Canada. In addition to the rather different structure and history of Canadian manufacturing that may render it a difficult context in which to support such an approach, there are some currently developing changes within the Third Italy itself that may prove instructive for Canadian industrial policy. Based on the most recent data available, Amin and Harrison report that firms in the most successful Italian industrial districts are losing their competitive position as they encounter certain barriers to growth that threaten their leadership in their established markets. These firms are being outcompeted because they have been overtaken by larger firms which have more successfully introduced new product and process technologies. Not surprisingly, the small firms of the industrial districts have become vulnerable to takeovers, mergers, and other forms of reorganization, so that control of their activities is passing to large Italian and foreign firms attracted to the technologically dynamic and market-sensitive Third Italy firms.[32] Meanwhile, the small firms themselves are keen to gain better access to crucial investment capital required to upgrade their production technologies. It remains to be seen whether the current round of industrial reorganization in the districts will restore these firms to their former successful position.

At the same time, there is further evidence that even large firms are discovering the virtues of competing on the basis of product attributes other than price alone. Harrison reports the recent rush by big American and European companies to instill more flexibility in their operating procedures in order to be more responsive to changing market demands. This has been sought primarily through the greater use of more flexible interfirm relations (subcontracting, strategic alliances) and labour practices. He also provides figures to show that product diversification is an increasingly common strategy among large American and West German manufacturing firms.[33]

PROSPECTS FOR A THIRD OPTION
IN CANADIAN INDUSTRIAL POLICY

Despite the fact that the Third Italy experience now appears to be somewhat tarnished by recent events and may have been discredited as a paradigmatic model for technology-intensive development policies elsewhere, there are certain valuable lessons to be learned from the recent industrial policy debate outside Canada. First, it has become clear that firms can compete successfully in international markets based on attributes other than the simple price of their product. This is not to say that price is no longer important, but rather, that quality and distinctiveness ought not to be overlooked as a basis on which to serve more specialized markets. While there can be no denying that mass production and consumption of standardized commodities remains dominant in many product sectors, it does make sense to question whether Canadian manufacturing can *ever* be internationally competitive in such markets, and indeed, whether it should even try. After all, large firms in many other countries already dominate mass product markets and have the market power to undercut new entrants.

Secondly, both the successes and the failures of the Italian experience are instructive. The successes are important because they demonstrate the potential for innovative growth based on locally clustered and interlinked small and medium-sized enterprises, supported by indigenous production of compatible machinery for their use. The failures highlight the problems that arise when access to development capital is limited, and show the constructive role played by industrial policy in ensuring that such key barriers are overcome before the firms involved lose their markets.

Given these lessons, what forms might industrial policy take in improving the lot of technologically sophisticated manufacturers in Canada, and how does it compare to the present activities of the federal and provincial governments? Obviously, some awareness of the territorial nature of technologically dynamic growth is a first step for policy makers, as it has been in places such as Japan. However, there is little evidence that this kind of awareness exists in Ottawa, which not long ago dismantled its Department of Regional Industrial Expansion (DRIE) and replaced it with the Atlantic Canada Opportunities Agency and the Western Economic Diversification Fund. These newer agencies have already been criticized for a lack of coherence to their various activities, an absence of theoretical logic to direct their initiatives, and a limited understanding of the process of technological change.[34] Meanwhile the Prime Minister's Office orchestrates the regional location of major federal contracts for defence-related aerospace and shipbuilding manufacturing and servicing, to serve largely political purposes.

Furthermore, while regional policies lack sufficient sensitivity to technological issues, technology policies have been framed largely in a manner oblivious to the importance of spatial context. This remains true, despite the fact that technology-intensive manufacturing in Canada already exhibits considerable spatial clustering that could be utilized as the basis for expanded and intensified industrial development, and that the Science Council of Canada went on record in 1984 with recommendations to set up metropolitan technology centres to stimulate territorially based, technology-intensive growth. While the federal government does operate a number of programs to enhance the technological capabilities of individual manufacturers,[35] none of these have been designed to exploit the possibilities for territorially based growth in Canada. Nor do they acknowledge the potentially key role to be played by an indigenous machinery and machine tools industry. The lion's share of federal funds have accrued to large, mature firms, which are often branches of foreign-owned multinational enterprises in traditional sectors. This assistance has come either in the form of loosely controlled and much criticized tax expenditures for performing R&D activity, or as outright grants for "modernization" and "restructuring." While the dollars devoted to such uses are small by international standards, they are nevertheless considerable. Furthermore, because they are poorly targeted, both in terms of firm size and location, these expenditures have achieved far less than they could have in the development of Canada's technological capabilities.[36]

At the local level, Canadian municipalities are generally preoccupied with decisions pertaining to land-use issues or the well-worn tradition of attempting to attract outside firms to set up in their vicinity. In Ontario the Davis Conservative government was active in setting up various sector-specific advisory centres to assist in the dissemination and implementation of product and process technologies in areas such as computer-aided design and manufacturing, automotive parts, robotics, farm machinery and food processing, and micro-electronics. However, these centres were dispersed around the province for largely political reasons, and it is doubtful that they have contributed to the forming or strengthening of new territorial production complexes. In the automotive industry, the Ontario Conservatives also took steps to assist local parts producers upgrade their technological capabilities so that they might obtain contracts from the increasingly sophisticated

North American and Asian producers setting up new plants in Ontario. The Peterson Liberals continued some of this assistance, while at the same time privatizing the technology centres. They chose instead a more high-profile way of pursuing the goal of technological renewal through the creation of the tripartite Premier's Council on Technology. While the documents produced by this organization dispense admirable rhetoric about the need for higher-value-added production in Canada and the necessity of government intervention to ensure a sound technological future, there is precious little evidence of tangible impact from this much-publicized initiative.[37]

The bottom line appears to be that Canadian governments at all levels have been rather inactive, with perhaps most activity occurring at the provincial level. Yet international experience suggests that there is a role to be played by governments in promoting both the production of new technologies and their diffusion and use throughout the rest of the economy. Indeed (as other chapters in this volume have made clear), governments can make a choice between two fundamentally different industrial strategies – one, such as in the United Kingdom currently, in which competitive advantage in manufacturing is predicated largely on keeping wages low, and one, such as the direction followed in Sweden and West Germany, based on the desire to keep wages high. The viability of the latter option depends fundamentally on firms' ability (with strategic assistance from the state) to develop and implement new product and process technologies.

One area would be to support the development of a more technologically capable machinery and machine tool industry, given the strategic importance of this sector. If the arguments in this paper are correct, it is crucial that Canadian manufacturers be afforded better opportunities to interact frequently with a dynamic, indigenous group of machinery producers. Even the federal government, in its own 1988 review of this industry, notes the significant role that public sector assistance has played in the technological development of the Japanese and West German machine tool industries. However, it continues myopically to point to the small internal scale of Canadian producers as the domestic industry's major handicap. One very powerful impetus to the further development of this industry would come from the kind of public assistance given to small Japanese manufacturers wishing to adopt computerized numerically controlled (CNC) machine tools and other advanced process equipment. Instrumental in achieving this objective have been easily available low-interest loans and active assistance in the transfer of such technologies.[38]

Another form of intervention would be in the area of improving the standard and availability of technical education and labour (re)training.

While the Canadian system of technical schools has been neglected for many years, other labour market programs fail to provide the adjustment assistance required by Canadian workers and firms alike. This is especially troublesome for Canadian firms trying to develop and implement new technologies. Yet the experience of labour market programs in Sweden and West Germany indicates both the importance of training in creating the conditions for effective production and rewarding work, and the crucial role played by trade unions in encouraging employers to empower workers through training.[39]

Assuming that Canadians wish to protect and enlarge their manufacturing base by ensuring its technological renewal, then government should seriously consider taking action in some of the new directions suggested by this paper. While it is true that a "managed trade" strategy – based on the Auto Pact, with its domestic content safeguards – has likely helped the top tier of Canadian auto parts producers to become more technologically advanced (see Holmes's chapter in this volume), it is highly unlikely that the Canada–US free trade agreement, in the absence of concerted policy efforts, will do much to enhance Canada's domestic technological capabilities. Indeed, as Wilkinson (in this volume) points out, implementation of the FTA is likely to place serious constraints on Canadian government's abilities to enact the aggressive industrial policies discussed above, as many of these are likely to be construed as countervailable subsidies to Canadian producers. Even though the subsidy codes have yet to be determined through negotiation, it is highly unlikely that Canadian business, which seems to have privileged access to economic policy-makers in Ottawa, will lobby on its own accord for such reforms.

It is difficult to conceive of a successful industrial strategy that does not aspire to promoting the sale of Canadian products abroad. Again, this is not because producers in all sectors necessarily need large markets and long production runs to be competitive; there are other bases for competitiveness. Rather, the motivation for seeking larger markets is simply to sell more goods, thereby providing more employment opportunities at home. And indeed, part of the success of the Third Italy in its heyday was based on many of its firms maintaining strong, direct links with export markets, thereby remaining in touch with consumer demands.

If Canada wishes to pursue a technology-based, high-wage industrial strategy, it must look beyond the American market and court markets in Europe and Asia. The rationale behind this strategy is simple. The record until now is clear on the failure of Canada's current implicit industrial strategy, which is based on importing technology through the medium of the foreign multinational. As long as the United States insists that the host countries of foreign firms selling in its market desist from engaging in the kinds of strategic industrial assistance described above (construed by the Americans as countervailable subsidies), then Canada will be unable to develop a technologically sophisticated economy.

On the other hand, the major industrial players in Europe and Asia have employed these kinds of strategies for decades, to great effect, and are unlikely to alter their strategies significantly in an era when global competition is increasing. For this reason, under the new reciprocal treatment rules for admitting foreign-made products tariff-free into the European market (for a summary of these, see Wilkinson's chapter in this collection), Canadian producers wishing to sell in the European market are unlikely to be penalized because their own government happens to engage in meaningful industrial assistance.[40]

There are undoubtedly significant barriers to overcome before Canadian manufactures command a presence in Europe and Asia – particularly the sheer physical distance separating Canada from these markets, and cultural (including language) differences that make marketing abroad more difficult. Nevertheless, producers in Europe and Asia have themselves overcome such barriers to sell successfully in the North American market. Furthermore, there is evidence that English is rapidly becoming the *lingua franca* of international business. Additionally, specialization in export products with a high ratio of value to weight (such as many technology-intensive goods) would minimize the prominence of transportation costs as a proportion of total costs. What remains clear is that Canadian manufacturers will pay a high price for their lethargy by continuing to rely so exclusively on the US market.

Given the prevailing attitude of the Canadian business community (dominated as it is by the interests of American multinationals), the task of ensuring a progressive technological future for Canada may thus fall on Canadian labour. Understandably, organized labour in Canada has been wary of technological change – more for the nonconsensual way that it has usually been introduced than for its consequences for employment. If their natural aversion is to be overcome, unions must necessarily be centrally involved in presiding over the conception and administration of training programs, and the overall technological renewal of Canadian manufacturing.

APPENDIX
UNDERSTANDING ''HIGH-TECH''

A.R. Markusen, P. Hall, and A. Glasmeier, in *High-Tech America: The What, How, Where and Why of the Sunrise Industries* (Boston: Allen and Unwin 1986), discuss four alternative ways of distinguishing high-tech from other activities within the economy. These include basing one's definition on: 1. the perceived degree of technical sophistication of an industry's product; 2. the rate of growth of employment in a given sector (based on the rather tautological reasoning that "if it grew quickly, it must have been high-tech"); 3. an industry's expenditures on research and development expressed as a proportion of the industry's sales; and 4. the occupational structure of the industry (e.g., the prominence of engineers, technicians, computer scientists, life scientists, and mathematicians relative to other sectors). For a variety of practical and theoretical reasons, Markusen *et al.* prefer the last method, and have used this to designate twenty-nine manufacturing sectors (representing one hundred specific industries) within the US economy.

Canadian studies, including those by the Science Council of Canada, have employed similar criteria, focusing especially upon R&D intensity as the critical determinant of technology intensity. Combining the definitions of a number of different studies, Charette *et al.* examine the changing share of national output and employment, as well as productivity growth, over the period 1961 to 1979 for the high-tech industries so defined. Their results confirm some, though not all, of the generally held notions about high-tech industry. While these industries increased their share of national GDP (implying a rate of output growth between 1.2 and 1.5 times that for all sectors of the economy taken together), their share of national employment was either stable or declined during this eighteen-year period. For most sectors, absolute levels of employment increased, but at rates below the all-industry average. However, for some specific three-digit sectors (e.g., television and radios), absolute employment declines were registered. This finding parallels the uneven results obtained by Markusen *et al.* in their American study at the three- and four-digit level. Finally, Charette *et al.* did find that productivity was growing faster in the high-tech industries than for the aggregate economy as a whole (between 1.22 and 1.52 times faster, depending on the definition of high technology actually used).

NOTES

The author wishes to acknowledge the financial assistance of the Humanities and Social Science Committee of the Research Board, University of Toronto. He would also like to thank Neil Wrigley and Phil Cooke of the Department of City and Regional Planning at the University of Wales College of Cardiff, and David Harvey and Erik Swyngedouw of the School of Geography and St Peter's College at Oxford University, all of whom provided generous institutional and collegial support during the author's sabbatical leave when much of this chapter was written. Thanks are also due to Daniel Drache, David

Wolfe, and John Britton for helpful comments contributing to this chapter. The usual disclaimers apply.

1 For an overview of this and other industrial policy positions in postwar Canada, see A. Blais, "The Debate on Canadian Industrial Policy" in A. Blais, ed., *Industrial Policy*. Vol. 44 of Background Studies for the Macdonald Royal Commission (Toronto: University of Toronto Press 1986), 55–82.

2 Economic Council of Canada, "High-Tech Trade: Serious Weaknesses to Solve," *Au Courant* 10, no. 2 (1989): 10.

3 In what follows, I take it as axiomatic that goods production (which in Canada also includes resource exploitation and refining) continues to be the essential foundation of the economy, despite the rise of the service sectors as providers of new jobs in Canada.

4 Motor vehicles likely qualify as "high-tech" by virtue of the nature of inputs and processes used, although we still tend to think of automobiles as being not particularly technology-intensive compared to computers or the biotechnology industries. In this sense, the automobile sector does not properly belong in the discussion in this section.

5 Although this CMA straddles the Ontario-Quebec border, the large majority of this region's high-tech firms in this sector are in fact located on the Ontario side of the Ottawa River. See G.P. Steed and D. DeGenova, "Ottawa's Technology-Oriented Complex," *Canadian Geographer* 27 (1983): 263–78.

6 The improved performance of this industry is due largely to increased exports of small turbofan and turboprop aircraft to markets such as the United States, where airline deregulation has fuelled demand for smaller craft for commuter lines, and other markets such as Asia, Africa, and South America.

7 M.F. Charette, R.P. Henry, and B. Kaufman, "The Evolution of the Canadian Industrial Structure: An International Perspective" in D.G. McFetridge, ed., *Canadian Industry in Transition*. Vol. 2 of Background Studies for the Macdonald Royal Commission (Toronto: University of Toronto Press 1986), 61–133.

8 Economic Council of Canada, "High-Tech Trade."

9 The positive 1986 technological balance of payments for the telecommunications industry may seem puzzling, given that it was shown in Table 17.5 to have suffered absolute employment losses between 1982 and 1986. One plausible explanation is that large producers in this sector – primarily Northern Telecom – have moved some of their production and research facilities outside of Canada, and now "sell" proprietary technology from their Canadian operations to their foreign branches. Hepworth documents

the growing international structure of Northern Telecom, which has been doing business in the United States for some time and has recently expanded into the European market. See M. Hepworth, "The Geography of Technological Change in the Information Economy," *Regional Studies* 20, no. 5 (1986): 407–24.

10 D.G. McFetridge, "The Economics of Industrial Structure: An Overview" in McFetridge, ed., *Canadian Industry in Transition*, 45.

11 Leading proponents of the post-Fordist vision within the recent economic geography literature include P.N. Cooke, "Flexible Integration, Scope Economies and Strategic Alliances: Social and Spatial Mediations," *Environment and Planning D: Society and Space* 6 (1988): 281–300; D. Harvey, *The Condition of Postmodernity* (Oxford: Basil Blackwell); and E. Schoenberger, "From Fordism to Flexible Accumulation: Technology, Competitive Strategies and International Location," *Environment and Planning D: Society and Space* 6 (1988): 245–62. For the dissenting view, see M.S. Gertler, "The Limits to Flexibility: Comments on the Post-Fordist Vision of Production and Its Geography," *Transactions, Institute of British Geographers* New Series 13 (1988): 419–32.

12 S. Meurer, D. Sobel, and D. Wolfe, *Challenging Technology's Myths* (Toronto: Labour Council of Metropolitan Toronto 1987).

13 M.C. Fertey, P.J. Lavelle, and R. White, *Report of the Automotive Industry Human Resources Task Force* (Ottawa: Supply and Services 1986); Industry, Science and Technology Canada, *Industry Profile: Machine Tools and Tooling* (Ottawa: Supply and Services 1988); and J. Mansell, *Workplace Innovation in Canada* (Ottawa: Economic Council of Canada 1987).

14 R. Jaikumar, "Postindustrial Manufacturing," *Harvard Business Review* 64 (1986): 69–74; M.R. Kelley and H. Brooks, "The State of Computerized Automation in US Manufacturing," Project Report, Center for Business and Government, Kennedy School of Government, Harvard University 1988; A. Pollert, "From 'Core-Periphery' to 'Flexible Specialization'," paper delivered at the Conference on the Labour Process, Aston/UMIST, March 1988; and S. Pinch, C. Mason, and S. Witt, "Labour flexibility and Industrial Restructuring in the UK 'Sunbelt': The Case of Southampton," *Transactions, Institute of British Geographers* New Series 14 (1989): 418–34.

15 ISTC, *Industry Profile*, 2.

16 Ibid., 4.

17 Evidence in support of this argument is beginning to mount. Lundvall shows how the successful use of complex industrial machinery depends crucially upon the frequent interaction between machine user and supplier, both when the machinery is first being developed and when it is being used in its ultimate application. See B-A Lundvall, "Innovation as an Interactive Process: From User-Producer Interaction to the National System of Innovation" in G. Dosi *et al.*, eds., *Technical Change and Economic*

Theory. (London: Frances Pinter 1988), 349–69. Similarly, based on his recent ten-country study, Porter concludes that a nation's international competitive advantage is strongly enhanced by close interaction between manufacturers and the firms which produce their key machinery, particularly when these two entities are spatially clustered. See M.E. Porter, "The Competitive Advantage of Nations," *Harvard Business Review* 90, no. 2 (1990): 73–93.

18 It is also well represented in the background studies supporting the final report of the Macdonald Commission whose authorship was largely dominated by traditionally trained economists. See, for example, the articles by McFetridge, Baldwin, *et al.*, and Daly in McFetridge, ed., *Canadian Industry in Transition.*

19 McFetridge, "Economics of Industrial Structure," 45.

20 On this point, see for example the chapters by Holmes, Morris, and Mahon in this collection. On the assault on wages, see the chapters by Drache and Mahon.

21 This name refers to the inhabitants of the Emilia-Romagna region of Italy, who have developed a distinctive form of industrialization based on clusters of closely interacting producers. See S. Brusco, "The Emilian Model: Productive Decentralization and Social Integration," *Cambridge Journal of Economics* 6 (1982): 167–84.

22 On industrial districts see S. Brusco, "Small Firms and Industrial Districts: The Experience of Italy" in D. Keeble and E. Wever, eds., *New Firms and Regional Development in Europe* (London: Croom Helm 1986), 184–202; on territorial production complexes see A.J. Scott, *New Industrial Spaces* (London: Pion 1988).

23 See, for example, M.J. Piore and C. Sabel, *The Second Industrial Divide: Possibilities for Prosperity* (New York: Basic Books 1984), and P. Hirst and J. Zeitlin, eds., *Reversing Industrial Decline? Industrial Structure and Policy in Britain and Her Competitors* (Oxford: Berg 1989).

24 Brusco, "The Emilian Model."

25 Scott, *New Industrial Spaces.*

26 I am grateful for John Holmes for first bringing this point to my attention. Interestingly, Wilkinson (this volume) cites evidence of nascent awareness of the possibilities associated with this second strategy in recent documents emerging from the Department of External Affairs in Ottawa.

27 See Mahon's chapter in this collection, in which she discusses the merits of this option and its hybrid variant, "diversified quality production."

28 However, according to Brusco, "Small Firms and Industrial Districts," this role cannot be said to have been decisive since such districts have also flourished in places where the local state has not been very efficient or active.

29 In many important respects, Canada would not wish to replicate the Third Italy experience. F. Murray documents the "dark side of flexible specialization" as it has developed in this region, noting that the use of information technologies has enhanced the abilities of management to supervise, control, and exploit workers. "The Decentralisation of Production – The Decline of the Mass Collective Worker?" *Capital and Class* 19 (1983): 74–99; and "Flexible Specialisation in the 'Third Italy'," ibid. 33: 84–95. Furthermore, the extensive use of contracting out, which characterizes many of the interactions between firms in the Italian industrial districts, has been motivated by the desire to exploit dualistic wage structures between firms, as well as to accommodate changes in the number and type of labour demanded by externalizing the costs of uncertainty (threat and cost of layoff) to numerically and functionally flexible workers in smaller, non-unionized firms. And fragmentation of production into many smaller shops has served to undermine workers' efforts to organize effectively. Finally, small-scale industrialization has encouraged the proliferation of the "black economy," in which firms operate outside of government industrial regulations over health and safety, minimum wages, work hours, and other issues of immediate importance to workers' well-being.

30 Brusco reports that the 1981 Italian industrial census revealed an even greater proportion of small firms, both nationally and in regions like Emilia. See "Small Firms and Industrial Districts," 194.

31 McFetridge, "Economics of Industrial Structure," 48.

32 A. Amin, "Flexible Specialization and Small Firms in Italy: Myths and Realities," *Antipode* 21 (1989): 13–34. Harrison refers to this process as "concentration without centralization" because, while the superficial spatial form of the industrial districts has not changed significantly, power has become increasingly concentrated in the hands of fewer large firms. See B. Harrison, "Concentration without Centralization: The Changing Morphology of the Small Firm Industrial Districts in the Third Italy," working paper, School of Urban and Public Affairs, Carnegie Mellon University, Pittsburgh 1989.

33 B. Harrison, "The Big Firms Are Coming out of the Corner: The Resurgence of Economic Scale and Industrial Power in the Age of Flexibility," working paper, School of Urban and Public Affairs, Carnegie Mellon University, Pittsburgh 1989.

34 J.N.H. Britton, "A Policy Prospectus on Regional Economic Development: The Implications of Technological Change," *Canadian Journal of Regional Science* 11, no. 1 (1988): 147–65.

35 For a summary, see ISTC, *Support for Technology Development: A Summary of Federal Programs and Incentives.* (Ottawa: Supply and Services 1989).

36 J.N.H. Britton and M.S. Gertler, "Locational Perspectives on Policies for Innovation" in J. Dermer, ed., *Competitiveness Through Technology: What*

Business Needs From Government (Toronto: Lexington Books 1986), 159–75. For a comprehensive recent argument along similar lines see G.P. Steed, *Not a Long Shot: Canadian Industrial Science and Technology Policy.* Background Study 55 (Ottawa: Science Council of Canada 1989).

37 Ontario, Premier's Council, *Competing in the New Global Economy*, vol. 1 (Toronto: Government of Ontario 1988).

38 See R. Florida and M. Kenney, "High Technology Restructuring in the USA and Japan," *Environment and Planning A* 22, no. 2 (1990): 233–52.

39 L. Muszynski and D. Wolfe, "New Technology and Training: Lessons From Abroad," *Canadian Public Policy* 15 (1989): 245–64.

40 Indeed the same logic renders Harris's industrial strategy problematic. Harris favoured an approach combining free trade with an aggressive technology policy. Yet, with the hindsight possible now that the actual FTA has been signed, such a policy would be unworkable (for the reasons just given) as far as trade with the United States is concerned. See R.G. Harris, *Trade, Industrial Policy and International Competition.* Vol. 13 of Background Studies for the Macdonald Royal Commission (Toronto: University of Toronto Press 1985).

PART SIX

Democratic Alternatives: Rebuilding from the Ground up

18 Canada and the Global Crisis in Resource Development

FRANK J. TESTER

The evidence that global ecosystems are in imminent danger of collapse is overwhelming. The Worldwatch Institute, which publishes an annual report on the state of the global environment, noted in its 1988 report that eight million acres of forest burned in the Amazon basin in 1987 – an area the size of Austria; a decline in the ozone layer of the atmosphere such that at certain times of the year the ozone concentration over the South Pole was down by 50 per cent from its historical level; and about six million hectares of land lost, worldwide, to desertification, with another twenty million becoming so impoverished that it is unprofitable to farm. The global environmental crisis is extensive, including air and water pollution, the greenhouse effect,[1] the threat posed by toxic wastes and the continued use of herbicides and pesticides, soil degradation, the depletion and contamination of groundwater supplies, the extinction of species and extensive global deforestation.

Canadians are certainly not immune from the emerging global developmental and environmental crisis. We have become accustomed to a continually rising standard of living and the abundance of material goods and opportunities which have accompanied it. At the same time, in the midst of the affluence Canadians have produced from the sale of natural resources, there is poverty for Native people, for single-parent families, many headed by women, and for many Canadian children.

The social and regional disparities experienced by Canadians are in serious danger of being exacerbated. We are on the leading edge of a resource crisis with serious implications for government finances, social programs and differences in opportunities and incomes for many Canadians. Canadian forest resources are in decline, fish stocks on both coasts are threatened by serious overfishing, prairie agriculture is reeling from depressed grain prices, soil erosion, over-use of fertilizers and staggering farm debts.

These are problems which modern technology cannot ultimately address. In fact many so-called technical fixes give rise to a series of new environmental problems. Thus, fish farming on the west coast has created new water pollution hazards, larger machinery on the prairies has compacted soils and contributed to the farm debt load, and mechanized logging techniques have allowed us to increase the rate at which forests are depleted while eliminating jobs. The evidence suggests that we cannot continue our current standard of living, let alone hope to constantly increase it on a limited natural resource base. This reality runs counter to the experience of generations of Canadians, especially those who currently occupy positions of economic and political power. Most importantly, it runs counter to the commercial messages directed at, and expectations generated in, the minds of most Canadians. Sustainable development – perhaps better expressed as sustainable living – requires that we seriously rethink Canadian developmental prospects and seriously confront a mentality which expects too much from a country and planet of finite resources. The crisis is one of mind as well as matter. The environmental implications are a deep concern.

THE WORLD COMMISSION ON ENVIRONMENT AND DEVELOPMENT

In this regard, the Brundtland Commission established by the General Assembly of the United Nations in 1983 and chaired by Gro Harlem Brundtland, the prime minister of Norway[2] was asked to propose long-term environmental strategies for achieving sustainable development by the year 2000 and beyond.

The World Commission on Environment and Development (WCED) is concerned with making development sustainable, the implication being that current forms of economic practice have disastrous implications for the global environment. Even if sustainable development is not a new idea, nonetheless it is a crucial concept whose time has come. In its simplest form, sustainable development refers to practices which can be maintained indefinitely without jeopardizing the resource base and ecological systems upon which they depend.

The WCED report advocates increasing the "economic pie" of developing countries both through environmentally sensitive growth and a mild redistribution of income. Redistribution can only operate if there are increases in income, and the report suggests that a desirable target for redistribution is 25 per cent of the incremental income of the wealthiest one-fifth of the population in a developing country with a growing per capita income.[3] But is the Brundtland Commission's conceptual framework a viable blueprint for the future?

As evident from the following quote, the commission appears to be soft on any structural analysis of the global environmental problem.

Nature is bountiful, but it is also fragile and finely balanced. There are thresholds that cannot be crossed without endangering the basic integrity of the system. Today we are close to many of these thresholds; we must be even mindful of the risk of endangering the survival of life on Earth. Moreover, the speed with which changes in resource use are taking place gives little time in which to anticipate and prevent unexpected effects.[4]

While the authors appear to address the problem, this statement, typical of many others in the report, says nothing about causes. The authors are concerned with the rate at which changes in resource use are taking place and the urgency of acting. But the speed with which resource use is changing needs to be addressed, in and of itself. In truth, the motives and manner in which the production/distribution and consumption/disposal of the planet's resources are organized lies behind the speed with which resources are developed and consumed, as well as other problems which confront human survival on the planet.

Given that the global production, distribution, consumption, and disposal of commodities and manufactured goods is increasingly in the hands of transnational corporations (TNCs), their relationship to the global environmental problem merits considerable attention. Between 1960 and 1980 the revenues of the top two hundred TNCs rose as their combined share of the world's gross domestic product increased from 18 to 29 per cent.[5] Furthermore, transnational banks (TNBs) have become important in international development. In 1985 the combined assets of the world's twenty-five largest banks were $2.6 trillion – triple the sales of the twenty-five largest industrial firms.[6] Developing nations accounted for two-fifths of Japanese foreign investment and Japanese banks included five of the top ten largest banks in the world.[7] Foreign revenues have also become an increasingly large proportion of the revenues of American TNCs and TNBs. Despite the incredible growth of TNCs since the 1960s and their rapidly expanding role in the global economy, they receive relatively little attention from the Brundtland Commission.

The western environmental movement has also been slow to identify the importance of TNCs in understanding the global environmental crisis. Consequently, solutions are often seen as a matter of changing public attitudes and values, of arguing that species and landscapes have values other than "use" values, of protecting species and landscapes from development, and of subjecting development to assessment of environmental and social impacts. These responses, while contributing to debates about what our relationship to living and non-living nature should be, often assume that capitalism can be "adjusted" to meet new environmental realities: that it is possible to retain capitalist modes of production while practising a form of moral restraint which recognizes the limits of world ecosystems. These are the same sentiments which inform the WCED report.

Increasing global trade may not be a viable alternative either for industrial nations or the Third World if the environmental crisis is to be taken seriously. By not proposing ways to hobble the growing influence of the MNCs, it fails to comprehend the limitations of trade liberalization as a growth strategy for both rich and poor nations alike.

Limits to Sustainable Development

The chief culprit undermining the viability of world ecosystems are the low prices developing countries receive for their commodities. This causes developing countries to push production to the limit so that volume compensates for the low unit price of commodities. Such a policy is necessary if they are to make payments on mounting foreign debts and attempt to maintain existing meagre standards of living. The evidence shows that most debtor developing nations have fallen behind on both accounts. The WCED report uses the example of the current exploitation of tropical timber, a problem most acute in the Amazon River basin: "The trade in tropical timber, for example, is one factor underlying tropical deforestation. Needs for foreign exchange encourage many countries to cut timber faster than forests can be regenerated."[8]

Furthermore, the commission argues that the decline of markets in which such countries would otherwise have a competitive advantage generates unemployment and poverty at home, forcing the poor to rely more heavily on the natural resources of the country for sustenance and hence, degrading the environment further.

Two other effects of the existing economic situation on developing countries are cited by the commission in making its case for trade liberalization.

Austerity programmes inevitably include government cutbacks in both staff and expenditure of fledgling, weak environmental agencies, undermining even the minimal efforts being made to bring ecological considerations into development planning.

Conservation always takes a back seat in times of economic stress. As economic conditions have worsened in developing countries and debt pressures have mounted, planners have tended to ignore environmental planning and conservation in both industrial and rural development projects.[9]

To counter this tendency, the commission appears to assume that freer trade would be coupled with better controls on development aimed at making production more sustainable. This ignores the logic of the global economy. With higher prices and greater profits to be made, why wouldn't developing countries push the environment to the limit, producing more, using more fertilizers, herbicides, and pesticides in order to take advantage of "good times"? In fact, this is the logic which has operated historically and continues to operate in many industrial countries.

For example, in the 1970s and early 1980s, when wheat prices were rising, western Canadian farmers did not cut back on their use of fertilizers and herbicides. The use of nitrogen fertilizers in western Canada increased 1,000 per cent over this period. Farmers often put every hectare available into production, ploughing under coulees and natural areas in order to take advantage of favourable economic conditions and to pay off debts. Farmers went heavily into debt acquiring additional land and modern, bigger machinery in order to take advantage of rising grain prices. The resulting degradation of soil has been considerable. Current losses to the agricultural economy of western Canada from all types of soil degradation are in excess of $1 billion annually.[10] The dramatic drop in international grain prices, environmental problems, and record farm bankruptcies in the late 1980s suggest that, as currently practised, western Canadian agricultural production is not sustainable.[11] Similar developments and logic have brought the east coast fishery to the brink of complete collapse.

If this is true of a developed country with sophisticated policy devices for dealing with environmental matters during times of plenty, is it reasonable to suggest that developing countries with limited resources and fledgling or non-existent departments of environment would do better under similar circumstances?

The real issue that both environmentalists and concerned policymakers have yet to face is the unevenness of economic growth globally. Dismantling trade barriers has not improved the lot of Third World producers, rather it has accentuated the growing gap between the rich and poor nations worldwide.

INTERNATIONAL TRADE AND TRANSNATIONAL CORPORATIONS

Since the 1960s the growth in world trade has been considerable. The share of trade for developing countries has risen from 18.1 per cent of total world exports in 1970 to 25.0 per cent in 1980. The composition of the trade of developing countries is revealing. Primary products accounted for 65.6 per cent of the total exports of developing countries in 1985. Food, beverages, and tobacco accounted for 12.7 per cent of these exports, while the same products accounted for 10.2 per cent of imports. This shows the extent to which an international division of labour has been achieved in agricultural production – to the point where crops for domestic consumption have been neglected by developing countries. The economies of most developing countries have become very dependent upon single commodities.

Neo-classical theory claims that trade liberalization and an international division of labour leads to a higher standard of living in developing countries and ultimately addresses the disparities that exist between so-called developed and developing countries. However, as the data on commodity trading reveal, trade liberalization and an international division of labour leave developing countries vulnerable to the vagaries of a narrow range of commodity prices and subject to the activities of transnational corporations trading in the commodities in question. Given that poverty contributes to environmental degradation, placing a national economy in such a precarious position is to invite the possibility of recurring bouts of poverty.

During the 1970s loans to developing countries were readily available. Furthermore, developed countries had not yet put in place extensive protective measures discriminating against the exports of developing countries. Nevertheless, with the exception of countries exporting oil, the economic growth which neo-classical theory would predict under such circumstances appears not to have happened. The terms of trade for non-oil exporting developing countries for the period 1973 to 1980 were, on average, −2.6 per cent a year, while export volumes increased an average of 3.8 per cent a year. What is particularly revealing is that the volume of exports for non-oil exporting developing countries increased considerably in the period from 1980 to 1985 (7.7 per cent), while the purchasing power of exports increased an average of 5.4 per cent a year. This supports the claim that many developing countries have increased the volume of their exports in order to compensate for lower unit prices. As noted, this increased volume has particularly negative consequences for the environment and for sustainable development.

During the period from 1973 to 1985 there were major differences in the extent to which developing countries participated in international trade. For developing countries exporting mostly primary products, their share of total world exports fell from 6.9 to 5.2 per cent. For major developing country exporters of manufactures, their share of world exports grew from 3.7 to 8.3 per cent.[12] The extent to which domestic economies and the general population of developing countries – as opposed to TNCs headquartered in Japan, North America, and Europe – benefited from these increased exports is open to question.

Writing in *Trade and Development: An UNCTAD Review*, Frederick Clairmonte and John Cavanagh identify a number of problems with the global economy which can be related to the behaviour of TNCs. Some of these also have implications for the global environment. The relevant considerations are unemployment, industrial stagnation, indebtedness, and economic rivalries of major developed market economies.[13] To this list can be added the rivalries among developing countries anxious for the foreign investment and development essential to addressing their debt problems. The mergers and acquisitions of TNCs in recent years have further decreased the power of national governments in dealing with TNCs and in coming to grips with the social and environmental issues associated with their activities.

In developing countries the advantages to TNCs depend on keeping production costs low. As elsewhere, increasing labour costs lead to technology substitution. In the forest industry worldwide the technology used for harvesting and processing trees has reduced the labour input considerably. The volumes which can be harvested have also increased significantly. Where TNCs have access to such equipment and where developing countries have a need to increase their commodity exports, the resulting pressure on the environment is obvious. Wrongly, the Brundtland Commission suggests that increased commodity exports will provide employment and thereby relieve pressure on the natural environment as a source of subsistence living. However, an enhancement of world trade in commodities or manufactures, given the realities of international competition, the need to reduce labour costs, and technology substitution, may have exactly the opposite effect. The industrial stagnation which characterizes developed market economies has been attributed by neo-classical economists to protectionist policies which counter pressures to introduce new production methods and technologies in a competitive, internationally open market. However, TNCs have increasingly transferred production to developing countries because the production costs in these countries are lower. The volumes of engineering and metal products, including machinery and transportation equipment, exported from developing countries increased steadily in the period from 1973 to 1985. As noted, major developing country exporters of manufactures saw their share of world exports grow from 3.7 to 8.3 per cent.[14]

In developing countries, as in developed ones, keeping production costs low includes externalizing the environmental costs of production. The Bhopal gas tragedy, in which three thousand lives were lost and another two hundred thousand people suffered disabilities, is a clear example of what happens when TNCs adopt safety standards below those acceptable in their countries of origin.[15] Globally, hundreds of plants have been shifted to developing countries to avoid the health and pollution standards and the higher labour costs found in developed countries.[16] The industrial stagnation of developed countries is therefore related to the deterioration of the environment in developing ones, as industrial processes are transferred to locations more favourable to the interests of TNCs.

For "deep green" environmentalists, it is the connection between the marketing strategies of TNCs, the consumerism of the developed market economies of the world, and the debts of developing nations which is the crucial one and which is not part of the Brundtland Commission's theoretical framework. What it failed to grasp is that the fiscal crises of developed countries are related to the way in which corporate interests develop within the welfare state. Personal indebtedness in developed countries is currently high as their economies have increasingly grown around the purchase of goods and services on credit. Both personal and national indebtedness put pressure on interest rates, with disastrous implications for debtor developing countries.

As well, the worldwide drive to form conglomerates has facilitated intra-firm transfers. These buying and selling arrangements within the branches of a firm make transfer pricing possible and enhance corporate ability to undermine national economic policies. The manipulation of prices in intra-corporate trading allows corporations to maximize profits in countries with lower tax rates and to minimize them in countries with higher rates. In a world where trade is increasingly conducted by TNCs, developing countries can be beggared relative to one another. Environmental standards and controls are one item which can be bargained away in the process of attracting investment.

THE NEED FOR INSTITUTIONAL, REGULATORY, AND LEGAL REFORM

New national and international institutional and legal reforms are needed to address structural questions related to power, the ownership and control of natural resources, and the role of TNCs in international development and the deterioration of the global environment. This is difficult given the goals of TNCs and their role in international trade. The fact that the vast majority of these corporations are located in developed countries while doing extensive business in developing ones cannot be overlooked. The examples which follow are intended to be illustrative of the challenge to regulatory reform.

Corporations can only behave morally, and can only consider the environment, to the extent that it is profitable for them to do so, or to the point where they are not disadvantaged relative to competitors.[17] Modern industrial capitalism is characterized by a high mobility of capital and diversification of corporate interests. These all serve to hold national governments hostage. Therefore, in making public policy as Schrecker indicates, the public/private distinction is critical:

We should therefore think about conflits between governments and megacorporations over environmental policy, and about latent conflicts which fail to reach the state of open invocations of threats or sanctions, in terms of the shifting boundary between the domains of the two sets of institutions. That boundary is in a state of constant change and redefinition depending both on the general historical context and on the particular actors and situations involved.[18]

Thus the rules under which such profits can be accumulated are clearly important. Frequently environmental controls do not contribute to the short-term interests of capital. For example, in Canada, pulp and paper mills are consistent violators of water and air quality standards.[19] That they can continue to be so in violation of federal and provincial standards across the country is indicative of the importance of the industry to the overall Canadian economy and a reflection of the exemptions granted it in many circumstances.

In the longer term, environmentally sound policies require new tough legislative measures to force the private sector to radically change its production techniques as well as its short-term profit horizon. This will require increased activity by institutions and international agencies such as the United Nations and its Environment Fund.[20] Yet this is not likely to happen if international organizations do not have the funds to carry out their new regulatory activities. The sad reality is that programs addressing the global environmental crisis are mostly cash-strapped, reflecting the ongoing fiscal crisic of the governments which fund or contribute to them.[21]

In a fiscally restrictive environment, it is social and environmental programs which are often first to be sacrificed by cost-driven policymakers. This is nowhere more evident than in the management of Canada's forests. Canada's standard of living is very much dependent on this single resource which, in 1986, accounted for $14.6 billion in exports, 11.4 per cent of the total.[22] Forest products have come to dominate the Canadian economy. They play a major role in protecting the country's balance of trade and currently account for more of our net foreign exchange earnings than all other segments of the economy combined. The forest industry and forest products generate over $2 billion a year in provincial and federal taxes.

The problem is simple. Canada is running out of trees. Who is to pay for reforestation? The contest is between the federal and provincial governments and the industry. The federal government, despite the recent appointment of a forestry minister, is inclined to see forestry as a provincial matter. Much replanting has been carried on since 1982 under federal–provincial forest agreements, recognizing that the federal government has an economic interest in, and benefits from, the industry. With many of these five-year agreements coming to an end, and with pressure on the federal government to reduce its deficit, forest replanting is the site of struggles characteristic of those between social expenditures and creating the conditions for accumulation within the welfare state. Similar problems exist in developing countries which have had to cut back on social expenditures in order to address national debts. What lies behind these limits to protecting the environment and the resource base of the country are structural problems related to power, ownership, and the organization of production.

Canadian forest companies illustrate the exigencies of a system of production that increasingly dominates both the world and national economies. They are off in other parts of the world, using environmental blackmail to secure terms and conditions for the development of forestry operations which make it profitable for them to be there. For example, Noranda, under the chairmanship of Adam Zimmerman, attempted, in 1989, to get approval for a pulp mill at Wesley Vale, Tasmania, Australia. The Tasmanian government had originally established environmental criteria for the plant so restrictive, according to Zimmerman, that the mill could not operate. After negotiations, the Tasmanian government introduced a new interpretation of the criteria to Parliament, entitled the Doubts Removal Bill. The legislation was supposedly intended to address the company's concerns.[23] However, the Australian federal government insisted that the guidelines for environmental matters related to the project be rewritten and tightened. Noranda announced that it was withdrawing from the project as a result. This may be regarded as a victory for the environment, but such "victories" are often hard-fought, hard-won, and uncommon in developing countries hungry for capital investment. It is clear that countries taking environmental standards seriously must be willing to live with the investment consequences.

If governments in developed countries are subject to such pressure, what are the real possibilities for the governments of developing nations to tackle the environmental crisis in their backyard, desperate for foreign investment and capital? As was the case with northeast coal development in British Columbia, the governments of many developing countries are more than willing to become partners with TNCs in the exploitation of national resources. For example, in the Philippines, the government has allowed a mine partly owned by Placer Dome, a Canadian mining corporation, to continue to dump thirty thousand tonnes of mine wastes, daily, in Calancan Bay, despite a "cease and desist order" from the Philippine Department of Environment and Natural Resources. The order was recently overruled by the president's office. The copper mine is 40 per cent owned by Placer Done and 49 per cent by the Philippine government. The mine supplies power to the residents of Marinduque Island, who have been without power since it shut down. Job and revenue loss were used as arguments for allowing the operation to continue.[24]

The forest industry in many developing countries also operates subject to few regulations. Tropical forests are currently disappearing at an alarming rate. A 1985 report by the World Resources Institute indicated that, at the time, 40 per cent of the world's tropical forests had been cleared. The ongoing destruction of the forests of the Amazon basin have received recent and worldwide attention. It is hard to ignore the role of multinational logging companies and wealthy land-owners in this destruction. The Amazon basin is being cleared by cattle ranchers and plantation-owners as well as by smaller landholders. But the failure of the Brazilian government to redistribute land elsewhere in the country is a major factor in considering the current behaviour of Brazilian peasants. The contribution of each to the demise of the Amazon forest is complex.[25] However, the Amazon basin is not simply being deforested by desperate peasants, as is sometimes portrayed by the western press.

Forestry officials in the Amazon have been quoted as admitting privately that low penalties and lax inspection mean that environmental laws are ignored: "Although the forestry agency requires that all lumber companies maintain a reserve of standing forest, one high-level official [of the Brazilian Institute for Forestry Development] returning from an inspection tour in southern Brazil said, '90 percent of the lumberers didn't have any reserve at all. They cut everything down'."[26]

The government of Thailand in January 1989, in recognition of the demise of its tropical forests, banned all logging. This dramatic move was taken after 350 people died as a result of flooding caused by illegal logging. Some 70 per cent of Thailand was covered by forests at the end of World War Two; forests currently cover only 18 per cent of the country. As a reporter for the British newspaper, the *Guardian*, noted: "Enforcement of the decree begs questions about corruption both among the law enforcement authorities, royal forestry department officials and politicians who are funded by logging tycoons."[27]

Alternative directions are needed. There can be little doubt about the need for legal and institutional reform. However, such reforms are only possible and will only work if the problem of international capital and the behaviour of TNCs as the ultimate embodiment of international capital are confronted.[28] Thus, governments which do not want to be held hostage by corporations wishing to invest and operate within their borders, have to be in a position to regulate realistically the behaviour of economic and civilian interests. Otherwise, the dynamics of fiscal crisis are increasingly likely to affect social expenditures, with direct consequences for the environment and any possibility of achieving sustainable forms of human activity.

In the search for alternatives, the western world has much to learn from indigenous populations who, prior to the imposition of a capitalist world order on global patterns of production and consumption, had developed integrated social, cultural, and economic systems which ensured survival, often on marginal lands and in difficult environmental circumstances. While the viability of these systems is affected today by population growth, indigenous principles and practices provide alternatives to the notion of economies based on the generation of surplus and the division of labour. The traditional practices of pre-capitalist societies can provide us with clues as to how to organize production/distribution and consumption/disposal in a way which preserves the basic ecology of a specific region. However, social and cultural systems must also accompany these forms. Sustainable development necessitates paying attention, not only to biological and environmental considerations and to economics, but also to social and cultural systems. In the 1990s it will be imperative to integrate ecological principles with economic considerations. Sustainable development requires the integration of economic, biological, and social/cultural systems.

In this connection, the concept of bioregions is promising. A bioregion is a geographically and socially defined area characterized by shared and interdependent ecosystems and cultural practices. In moving towards sustainable development, the redefinition of national and other political boundaries is important. For example, the geography of northern California, Oregon, Washington State, and coastal British Columbia constitutes a bioregion within which there are common and interrelated ecosystems and environmental concerns. Much can be done to promote the development of such regions by developing political economic and social relations at the local or municipal level. Not only do municipalities need to think globally and act locally, but regional-based communities have to seek counterparts in their bioregions. In developing countries, some movement in this direction is already obvious in the case of those countries which share the ecosystems of the Amazon basin. In the development of programs and in the restructuring of management institutions, the United Nations could do much to encourage bioregional development.

Furthermore, we must do more to consider culture, social factors, and gender balance in the development of theory and policies affecting international development. In most so-called Third World countries, women account for 60 to 80 per cent of all agricultural production as well as almost all the labour associated with reproducing the workforce. Development theory has a strong gender bias. Much of it has been reductionist and biased, compartmentalizing social, political, and economic life. As in much feminist theory, these distinctions need to be questioned. Many of the alternative and informal systems of social and economic organization used by women in developing countries need to be given more recognition. The example of the Kenyan Green Belt movement is one striking instance of the prominent role women can play in development. Women have, of necessity, organized around co-operatives and community-based programs which hold out hope for solving the problem of sustainable development using alternative perspectives and frameworks. Dealing with the issues of land tenure, political power, and channelling more resources to women are significant strategies for sustainable development.

CONCLUSION

Since the publication of the Brundtland report, the concept of sustainable development has spawned many debates. In this article I have avoided them – until now. The stark fact remains that, when all is said and done, the term development is itself problematic. The notion of development is culturally biased towards a world view which predominates, not only in developed countries, but increasingly in developing ones. The reason is that it regards progress, the accumulation of more material goods, and the acquisition of power as the ultimate goals of personal and social life. What the globe desperately needs are forms of human activity – social, cultural and economic – which leave a world to be passed on to our children and our children's children. Whether or not these forms constitute "development" is debatable. If development means extracting more from a planet limited both in its resources and in the ability of its ecosystems to survive developmental activity, then development is the wrong word to use in conjunction with sustainability. If development means the evolution of a human consciousness which places us gently on the planet and in caring relationships with each other and a world we have inherited, then it is time to get on with it.

NOTES

1 The authors estimate that in 1987, humanity added about eight billion tons of carbon to the atmosphere, of which 2.5 billion tons were from deforestation. This, it is maintained, has contributed significantly to global warming trends. See Lester R. Brown *et al.*, *Annual Report* (Washington Worldwatch Institute 1989), 9.

2 World Commission on Environment and Development, *Our Common Future* (New York: Oxford University Press 1987), 35.

3 Ibid., 50–51.

4 Ibid., 32–33.

5 Frederick F. Clairmonte and John H. Cavanagh, "Transnational Corporations and Global Markets: Changing Power Relations," *Trade and Development: An UNCTAD Review* 4 (Winter 1982): 151.

6 Charles W. Kegley and Eugene R. Wittkopf, *World Politics; Trend and Transformation*, 3rd ed. (New York: St. Martin's Press 1989), 166.

7 WCED, *Our Common Future*, 83.

8 Ibid., 68.

9 Ibid., 70.

10 The Senate Standing Committee on Agriculture, Fisheries and Forestry, *Soil at Risk: Canada's Eroding Future* (Ottawa 1984), 2; and the Science Council of Canada, *A Growing Concern: Soil Degradation in Canada* (Ottawa 1986), 7.

11 F.J. Tester, "Capitalism and Prairie Agriculture," *Canadian Dimension* 23, no. 2 (1989): 10–13.

12 United Nations Conference on Trade and Development, *Revitalizing Development, Growth and International Trade; Assessment and Policy Options* (New York: United Nations 1987), 127.

13 Clairmonte and Cavanagh, "Transnational Corporations and Global Markets," 169.

14 UNCTAD, *Revitalizing Development*, 127.

15 Sehdev Kumar, "The Three Legacies of Bhopal," *Alternatives; Perspectives on Society, Technology and Environment* 13, no. 4, (1986): 3–10.

16 Khor Kok Peng, "Polluting the Poor," *New Internationalist* 171 (12–13 May 1987).

17 For example, concern has recently been expressed about the takeover of Consolidated-Bathurst Inc., a Canadian-owned forest products firm, by Stone Container Corporation of the United States. The Canadian forest industry is now (1989) 40 per cent foreign-owned. Roger Stone, Stone Container's president, left the public with little doubt about the goals and priorities of his firm's operations in Canada. Since 1982, sales of Stone Container have increased tenfold and profits twenty times. Said Stone, in commenting on his company's takeover, "Our job is to make our shareholders rich. That's what we're here for." *Globe and Mail*, "Stone Container Reflects Life in Corporate Fast Lane," 2 March 1989.

18 Ted Schrecker, "Resisting Regulation: Environmental Policy and Corporate Power," *Alternatives: Perspectives on Society, Technology and Environment* 13, no. 1 (1985): 16.

19 A recently released Environment Canada study shows that 83 of Canada's 122 pulp mills dump more toxic chemicals in the water than allowed for by national standards. Mills built prior to the 1971 Fisheries Act are exempt from the standards contained in the act. The report states that virtually every mill in Canada would be charged if federal regulations were enforced. The department is in the process of revising current regulations. It remains to be seen as to whether or not these will produce higher standards, but the problem of enforcement is obvious. See *Globe and Mail*, 16 March 1989, "Mills Exceed Toxic Limits Report Says," A1.

20 WCED, *Our Common Future*, 322–23.

21 The fiscal crisis in Canada has had direct implications for environmental protection. Despite its rhetoric on the environment and its apparent response to the Brundtland Commission report, the Mulroney government cut the budget of Environment Canada soon after coming to office in 1984. In a department with about ten thousand employees, the government cut 511 jobs. On 16 September 1988, the government announced it would cut 361 more jobs over the next two years (*Globe and Mail*, 17 September 1988: A5). The federal government has also failed to give Canadians better access to information, as it promised to do before it was first elected. Freedom of information legislation has always been regarded by environmentalists as critical to their efforts in addressing environmental issues.

22 Statistics Canada, *Canada's Trade Statistics*, 2nd ed. (December 1987).

23 *Globe and Mail*, "Battle Heats up over Pulp Mill in Tasmania," 4 March 1989.

24 Alex Cunningham, "Government Ruling Allows Dumping," *Alternatives; Perspectives on Society, Technology and Environment* 15, no. 4 (1988): 11.

25 Michael Redclift, *Sustainable Development; Exploring the Contradictions* (London: Methuen 1987), 119–25.

26 *Sunday Star* (Toronto), "Reducing the Rain Forest to Ashes," 2 October 1988: H6.

27 *Toronto Star*, "Thailand Trying to Save Forests with Dramatic Ban on Logging," *The Guardian*, 12 January 1989.

28 Barbara Dinham, co-author of *Agribusiness in Africa*, makes this point with unusual clarity. The plantations of TNCs such as Unilever add to the problem of landlessness and poverty. She goes on to succinctly list the problems. The plantations of TNCs involved in agribusiness take the attention of governments of Third World countries away from the needs of small farmers. Plantations take the best land and attract investment away from food crops grown for local consumption. Development funds are channelled towards export crops at the expense of local food production (and, it must be added, given the herbicides, pesticides, and fertilizers used, at the expense of the environment). Producing crops for export has become increasingly important to meeting foreign debts. Development funds so directed, contribute not to environmentally sustainable forms of production, but to the accumulation of capital by financial interests in developed countries. See "Planting Poverty," *New Internationalist* (June 1987): 24.

19 For a Second Economy

ABRAHAM ROTSTEIN AND
COLIN A.M. DUNCAN

Globalization creates an accelerated pace of footloose economic activity. Goods, services, currencies, and capital move out of their traditional moorings among nation states, regional authorities, and international supervisory bodies, and travel in wider and faster circuits beholden to no one.

Higher productivity and greater output are the ostensible benefits of these frenetic transformations of the economy. But there is a downside as well – the increased risk and vulnerability to which the whole system is subjected. The possibility of massive systemic disruption on a global scale is the reverse side of the coin.

Intermittently, the entire global economy seems to be placed in jeopardy, as for example in the stock market crash of 19 October 1987. When so much rides on the outcome at one global gaming table, the precarious underside of globalization becomes apparent. In the circumstances, planning for contingencies is increasingly important.

More than ever, states seek to protect themselves from global shocks by introducing industrial strategies. These strategies aim to co-ordinate macro-policy with micro-economic activity across a broad policy field. Industrial strategy is conceived principally as a state-centred device to strengthen industrial performance in an increasingly interdependent world. But there is also the need for a kind of industrial policy "from below" that is not state-driven but protects the economic and social space of individuals and communities from the growing uncertainty of the currency and capital markets, that tie all countries to the vicissitudes of this single global process.

This is the thrust of the present proposal: to explain how some small economic enclave can be secured against the turmoil and unpredictability of these economic tides. We argue that it is possible to have an industrial strategy from the "grass roots up" which permits communities to disengage from the currency mainstream without moving out of a money economy altogether to a barter economy. The vehicle for this is the informal economy, which refers to exchanges between individuals and communities at the so-called periphery of the formal economy. Usually, the informal economy is seen separate and apart from the global economy. In fact, today the global economy has given new relevance to a broad family of so-called barter networks that provide some defence against the fickleness of increased capital mobility and the internationalization of production.

We argue that such admirable, albeit modest, achievements should not be dismissed lightly, even by economists. It is possible to add a second medium of exchange that is not linked to a global system but is generated by and enhances the local economy. What we discern in the monetary experiments described below are the stirrings of a fundamental challenge to the ubiquitous monetary credo of the nation-state: "One state. One economy. One currency!"

Until recently, it has been axiomatic that currencies must be national in their scope of operation and that the state retain exclusive jurisdiction over this currency. In fact, it appears that many of these ongoing monetary experiments that we shall discuss, that are incapable of working in theory, seem to be reasonably effective in practice. Our primary interest is not in revamping monetary theory. Rather, these practical, small-scale, monetary ventures deserve more widespread attention because of their implications for economic policy and economic pedagogy.

These networks are unusual, if not unique, in relying on "special-purpose" monies, that is, in having incidentally created a new form of "currency." We will be using the term currency broadly to denote monetary media in general, not just notes and coins. Our focus here is exclusively on this unusual money as a device for enhancing economic activity. This restriction in function to a means of exchange[1] reduces the extent of the impact of these currencies but, at the same time, increases the likelihood of their success. Given our limited concerns, it should be clear that we are not implicated directly in the current debates on monetary reform. For example, the attacks on current banking practice associated with the revival by John Hotson of interest in the "100% money" scheme do not fall within the purview of this article. The same holds for the recent proposal by Milton Friedman for reform of the Federal Reserve system. Nor are we taken, as Hayek has been, with plans for allowing in a floodtide of other national and private currencies so as to be able to punish national governments for alleged monetary sins against the value of money.[2] Such proposals for reform tend to grapple with the standard dilemma of monetary policy: how to reconcile two of the often warring functions of money, a means of exchange, and a store of wealth. We prefer to settle for one problem at a time.

The prospect of sub-national currencies may come as a shock to some. We will first examine some of the instinctive reactions against such proposals. We will then outline the historical origins of modern currencies as national-scale, "general purpose" currencies. A brief, schematic treatment is all that can be attempted here. For contrast we will touch on some ancient and medieval monetary arrangements, even at the risk of alarming those evolutionists who regard the current system as the late harvest of a centuries-long process of gradual improvement. Once the general case for currency pluralism is laid out in historical retrospect, we will pass to a descriptive account of the operation of two current varieties of local currency systems which we think could be usefully applied more widely. We will then give an account of several of their precursors, noting the superiority of the contemporary schemes.

THE MONEY VISE

The field of monetary reform has had more than its share of cranks and charlatans. But even innovative and credible proposals are usually given short shrift. Why is it that proposals for reform of the currency system fall so unfailingly on unsympathetic ears?

Part of the reason is that in modern times a currency is expected to fulfil at least four purposes simultaneously: a means of exchange, a means for making (one-way) payments to discharge formal obligations, a store of wealth, and a standard of value. These four functions welded together give us what we refer to as "general purpose money." The fear is that a weakening or adjustment of the currency in any one of these functions threatens the entire monetary system and hence the total fabric of the economy. Although many do not object to paying taxes and fines in depreciated currency, it is very unpopular to weaken the function of the currency as a store of wealth (i.e., inflation) when so many of our assets such as pensions, for example, are denominated in fixed nominal values.

Many economists are apt to view our modern type of general purpose money as some final pinnacle of progress. While such an evolutionary perspective is rarely acknowledged, it is an underlying leitmotif in modern economic thinking. Witness Richard Cooper, railing against the current and widespread phenomenon of international counter-trade:

"But human beings spent millennia developing money as an efficient medium of exchange, and unless there are very special reasons for not doing so, those who engage in countertrade will rediscover that it is better to sell for money."[3]

We will not try to determine just how many questions are begged in Cooper's pronouncement. But for those to whom it appears self-evident that general purpose money represents progress, any currency reform which might lead to a new balance among the various functions of money tends to be dismissed out of hand. Neither Keynesians nor neo-conservatives would be enthusiastic about weakening the control over the economy that can be wielded through the central bank's monopoly. The fact that control has been eroding rapidly since the collapse of the Bretton Woods system in 1973 hardly encourages them to soften their attitudes on this score.

This welding of the four monetary functions into a single monetary unit has created some modern anomalies. The anti-inflation measures of recent years that have been taken to stabilize money's value as a store of wealth and as a standard have only been accomplished at the expense or impairment of money's ability to serve as a means of exchange. A malfunction in one area could only be dealt with by exerting pressure in another – for example, the restricting of the rate of increase in the money supply that gave rise to the recession of the early 1980s. Conventional Keynesian policies of monetary reflation have been considerably muted during this period of large fiscal deficits.

An examination of some historical evidence would suggest, however, that the reflation/deflation dilemma which causes us so much agony need not so completely tie our hands if only we would stop trying to meet simultaneously all four functional requirements of money.

A more modest goal is often easier to attain. Perhaps monetary devices tailor-made to the sub-national scale could help in the present situation. Historical precedents may be illuminating.

ON THE ORIGINS OF NATIONAL CURRENCIES

The gradual emergence of a state monopoly on the creation of currencies (through the state's proxy, the central bank), was the result of a lengthy and untidy process. At the heart of the process was the convergence of hitherto distinct currencies, with their own unique or special functions, into one general purpose currency. An analytical rather than a comprehensive historical account must suffice here. The starting point is the insight of the anthropologist/economic historian, Karl Polanyi into the separate and independent origins of the various money functions listed above.[4]

Money as a means of exchange was a latecomer in this process. Polanyi showed that in both ancient and so-called primitive societies quite distinct objects were frequently employed for the various functions of money. In the empires of antiquity a radical separation existed between the circuits of long-distance trade and the local markets for domestic essentials. It was customary to employ different monies for the transactions involved in the two respective spheres of exchange. The use of distinct monies for the two different spheres helped ensure that traffic in the basics of everyday life was not jeopardized. It is not too much to say that what we find in such ancient civilizations is, in effect, two different economies existing side by side. Perhaps the same could have been said of those eastern bloc countries that required the use of dollars to purchase luxury goods from abroad. Likewise, it was not unusual in the ancient world for different monies to be used for different functions within the same "economy." As in ancient Babylonia, the means of payment might be one kind of money, barley, with the universal standard being another kind, silver.[5]

In medieval and early modern times this separation continued. Fernand Braudel has recently received much attention for his insistence on a three-tiered structure for analysing the economies of West European societies.[6] Braudel's "capitalist" sphere of long-distance (luxury) trade and international finance was segregated from the broad base of local markets dealing in everyday goods. These goods formed part of the rich layer of non-monetized, everyday, material life. Many problems of economic development (as we would now call them) were solved by having segregated currencies for domestic markets and for international trade respectively. It was tolerable to debase the local coins (thereby causing inflation) because domestic trade and enterprise were stimulated without jeopardizing long-distance trade. Here the accounts were settled in an altogether different currency. Ingenious arrangements were in widespread use which allowed the expression of the value of any kind of coin whatsoever in units of an "ideal" money. This had no physical existence anywhere but had a defined and recognized value within every local area which adopted its use for the purpose of denoting contract prices. It would lead us too far afield to attempt to give full accounts of these ingenious arrangements. The overall point is that although they must have kept the accountants busy, these multi-currency systems worked reasonably well for many centuries.

Under the impetus of the growing powers of the mercantilist state in early modern times however, pressure grew to unify the currency system within a given military jurisdiction. The state acquired a strong interest in having only one currency (its own) acceptable throughout the nation. But this led to conflicts about money, rooted in the uneasy relations among the distinct and separate purposes served by money.

The problems that were previously solved by having different monies for different functions (and levels of trade) necessarily resurface in different guise once economies come to be integrated under national "general purpose" monies. For example, in the early modern era periodic shortages of currency used as a means of exchange were often severe. Throughout the early development of capitalism in Europe there had been a continuous problem with the steady flow of silver from Europe to the East. Imports from the Orient had to be paid for in silver. Direct East-West exchanges of commodities were rarely acceptable.

As Braudel explains it, the problem was considerably exacerbated by the penchant for hoarding among early capitalists and early bankers. In 1751, for example, the total value of hoarded precious metals in Naples is estimated to have been four times the value of the currency in circulation there.[7] Whenever there was widespread concern about the currency, the problem grew worse. Gresham's law about bad money driving out good money is, unfortunately, too vague. The fact of the matter is that in early modern times bad money drove good money into hoards. Here we see one unusual instance of the tension between money as a means of exchange and money as a store of value. Bad money can be used for trade so long as it turns over rapidly, but only good money holds its value over time.

With the development of the national currency system, the problem of hoarding underwent a subtle transformation, but it by no means disappeared. The holders of wealth pressured the state not to inflate the currency. The poor and those in trade, by contrast, often tended to wish otherwise. A supposed resolution was achieved by appealing to the gold standard system. As an external and thus seemingly objective actor in the field, the gold standard was taken to be the best possible arbiter in this dispute. All national currencies were to have their value both for local and for long-distance trade related to the value of gold. Gold thus provided, as it were, an automatic solution to the question of how much money to allow. Intelligent statesmen the world over came to adopt a solution to a pressing political problem which only swept that same political problem out of their immediate jurisdiction.

It followed from the adoption of the gold standard that the more gold a country happened to have, the more domestic currency it could allow itself. Countries lacking gold simply had to stay backward until they could acquire it. The gold standard implied that the amount of money for domestic trade might at times be quite inadequate to finance it properly.

For domestic economic activity, an increase in the money supply was a good thing. For the holders of financial assets, the opposite was true. So the battle between the means of exchange function and the store of value function took place in the arena of banking policy with regard to the setting of the gold value of the currency.

Central banking arose to solve the quite different problem of bank failures. But as central banks emerged in the major countries, the ultimate decision-making power over the matter of the money supply also came to be ever more centralized. The state came to have a direct interest in this question and the thrust of its policy varied. At times, concerned not to antagonize the holders of wealth, from whom it might need to borrow to finance a war, the state might favour restricting the amount of money. If more impressed by the need for economic development or by the depredations of trade crises, it might favour expansionary policies. Governments, fearful of social upheaval whenever a shrinking of the money supply led to a serious shrinking of trade and employment, got in the habit of putting pressure on central banks to try using monetary policy to control the economy at times of crisis. Central banks provided a buffer between the world economy and national domestic economies with the aim of maintaining control during the expansive phase of the world economy, particularly in the latter part of the nineteenth century.

World War One and the Great Depression underlined the responsibility of the state to manage the economy. Keynes provided the intellectual foundations. When the gold standard collapsed with the emergence of a permanently lopsided pattern of world trade, the responsibility to control currencies reverted exclusively to the state.

After World War Two, the social "safety net," begun during the Great Depression, was entrenched and extended with the establishment of the welfare state. With so much hanging on government monetary policy by then, it began to seem self-evident to economists that to compromise the state's exclusive control of the money supply was to invite disaster.

Currently, however, the uncertainties due to high-speed electronic banking as well as the new abilities of the banks to increase the effective money supply in a stagflationary way, threaten to overwhelm the existing commitments made by the state. It is a difficult climate in which to attempt to construct an industrial policy. The decision to hold the line against deficits amidst high global unemployment constitutes a declaration by the state that it is suspending some of its obligations and that it will try to reduce them. In such a context the monopoly powers of the state in the area of currency increasingly appear as an anachronism. The case for amending this monopoly has been strengthened by the abnegation by the state of some of its social responsibilities.

The novel phenomena of the current international financial scene, may suggest to some that the state's exclusive power over money is already a thing of the past, and not without reason. It was when the United States reluctantly turned to controls over the exportability of dollars, and abandoned Bretton Woods, that the world's private bankers responded by creating, by accident as it were, our new international monetary system, if indeed it can be called a system. The new scheme is reminiscent of some of the medieval arrangements in some respects, despite the use of computer technology. It became common for international traders to make use of Eurodollars (that is, US dollars held outside the United States) and other similar Eurocurrencies. This credit money is not directly subject to any governmental control. While it is true that world trade is denominated in US dollars, it is not the case that the supply of them is under the control of American officials or indeed of any government or central bank. There currently is no committed lender of last resort in this scheme. Such "stateless money" is a far cry from the self-regulating gold standard. Instead of domestic economies being less vulnerable to the vagaries of the world market, they are more so. Having no one in control is arguably worse than having tight-fisted central bankers at the helm. A catastrophic banking crisis could happen at any time and no one is quite sure how it could be resolved or by whom.

With the additional problem of Third World debt hanging over us, it is arguable then that the world economy is poised to unravel again, since all the domestic economies remain extremely vulnerable to the shifting tides of international trade. Given that it seems politically impossible to control international speculation in currencies, the question arises as to the advisability of some contingency planning. Could we moderate a possible disaster by at least partially separating the international and the local economies, by to some extent reseparating "trade and market," to revive Polanyi's phrase?

Looking at the range of economic policy tools currently available, many commentators today see national currencies as anachronisms, but few can envisage any monetary solution which is not launched on a national scale at least. The error they make is to look for a single solution to what can more usefully be regarded as several problems. To the problems of international trade we have nothing particular to contribute here. To the specific problems of decaying or vulnerable local economies, however, the experiments we champion in this paper do have something to offer. We will show in the next section how groups and communities can resort to a simple, non-convertible means of exchange backed 100 per cent by goods and services operating in local circuits. In the developed countries they could be particularly useful for the unemployed and for the poorest strata, those that are hardest to reach by conventional macroeconomic policy measures.

BARTER NETWORKS AS LOCAL CURRENCIES

Over the last twenty years, in hundreds of cities and communities across North America, there have appeared various so-called barter networks.[8] "Barter" here is strictly speaking a misnomer. These networks are multilateral trading circuits or clubs, in each of which exchanges are marshalled by means of the group's own, internal currency, the "trade dollar." Typically, however, the federal dollar is used as the standard of value. In almost all cases, credit balances within these systems do not accrue interest, so they are not attractive as devices for storing wealth. The currencies moreover are generally non-convertible.[9] The "money" is supplied to the seller's account and taken from the buyer's account as each transaction occurs. So far, no taxes or fines are payable in funds from these networks, so it is clear that we have here a pure exchange currency, devoid of the other three functions of money.

Barter networks largely fall into two main categories, each suited to its particular kind of clientele. What we may call the commercially oriented or business network ("retail exchange" being another term used in the trade) is set up as a profit-making enterprise in its own right. It serves as a type of clearing house or brokerage service, to business firms, professionals, and self-employed tradesmen. Such a network is organized and controlled by the owner (usually) in accordance with rules regarding credit limits and other features of the system. While these networks usually comprise small businesses, several of the largest transnational corporations in the world are members of their own barter networks.

The growth of this phenomenon in the United States was due in part to some ambiguities in the anti-trust laws, which may forbid direct barter between firms, but allow barter to be mediated through a third party. It became clear to many of these firms that a multilateral network offered more opportunities than one-to-one barter. In Canada networks have been created in the last decade to serve retail businesses in the large urban conglomerations.

By contrast, the community-oriented networks are generally run on a break-even basis. They aim to facilitate exchanges of all sorts of goods and services among private individuals, families, and local businesses. Community networks typically serve a variety of purposes that reflect local goals and objectives. In many cases they have arisen to meet some form of economic stringency, such as low local cash-flow levels, but they are by no means a phenomenon entirely contingent upon "bad times."

Though the two kinds of barter networks differ in their clientele, the common reason for participating in either kind of network is to supplement income from the regular economy. There was a period when much of the membership in commercial networks was motivated by a desire to evade taxes, but this loophole is essentially closed now. As suggested above, the nominal prices used in these transactions generally mirror those in the economy at large. The currency units are typically called trade dollars or green dollars. Depending on the circumstances, there is sometimes a small premium, sometimes a small discount, relative to prevailing market prices in the federal currency. Formally the denominated prices tend to be the same numerically, although expressed in the alternative currency unit.

In the mechanics of day-to-day operation, several interesting differences between the kinds of networks manifest themselves. In the business–oriented barter networks there are typically several hundred member firms and the annual volume of trade can be large (in the millions of dollars). The network is generally founded by an entrepreneur seeking to make a profit and he or she runs it as a business enterprise with that end in view. The members are required to pay entrance fees of several hundred dollars in cash. In some cases these are automatically "refunded" in the system's internal currency (its trade dollars) as a way of stimulating spending, but they are always succeeded by annual membership fees (generally non-refunded) thereafter. There is a cash charge on each transaction calculated as a percentage of the dollar volume of the transaction (typically around 10 per cent), which builds in a substantial incentive to the operator to stimulate trading by becoming an active "barter broker." He or she may negotiate deals by serving as an intermediary, in addition to being a network administrator, keeping the accounts, providing a directory of members and their offers, and hosting get-togethers. Although these networks usually start with a relatively narrow geographic base (a city or local community), in the United States the most stable and active networks have tended to become members of inter-network exchanges.

The chief flaw in these networks is that the members are prone to crises of confidence. Business networks generally start off very well and then enter a period of uncertainty when the members begin to have qualms and anxieties about the stability and durability of the network. A network that has sound regulations and is carefully administered can usually survive such waves of doubt. These systems almost invariably include limits on the extent to which an account can be in debit, and penalties are administered accordingly. A fund is built up to provide for bad debts. In most of them there is a rule that forbids the proprietor from trading within the network on his or her own account. There are usually limits placed on the number of memberships in each category of business at any one time so as to preserve a "balanced economy." This reinforces the position of the first-comers and reassures them. The membership consists overwhelmingly of small incorporated businesses, with some self-employed tradesmen and professionals such as lawyers and accountants. The greater part of trading is in services rather than goods, but the latter are present as well, for example, auto parts, stereo equipment, and so on.

There are three typical motives for joining: to get access to what is in effect cheap credit, particularly if there is a cash-flow problem; to take advantage of unused business capacity; or to move excess inventory onto a more easily accessible market. Since in many cases firms join for the last two reasons and have typically covered their usual overheads in their normal business operations, a high marginal "profit rate" is enjoyed in these transactions.

The community-oriented barter network, on the other hand, has quite different features. The members are ordinary private individuals and the membership grows slowly, but can attain several hundred in number. Not surprisingly, the annual volume of trade is small, being in the order of tens of thousands of dollars. A community network is usually set up by a small group of citizens concerned about unemployment (for example, during periods of tight money), but sometimes the initiative reflects a desire for an alternative (that is, more personal) socio-economic framework. Membership fees are nominal (tens of dollars for life-long membership) and the transaction charge is assessed on the basis of accounting costs only (typically less than one dollar per deal and usually denominated in the internal currency). These systems appear as local community ventures. The level of activity is strongly dependent on the attitudes and initiatives of the individual members themselves, since so far they have tended to be without benefit of a full-time administrator.

Community systems often get off to a very slow start and tend to stagnate during a "wait and see" period before commencing solid and steady growth. Since there is less pressure to grow than in a commercial network, the community systems are often structurally capable of idling for long periods at a low level of activity. The problem of large debit balances – that is potential bad debts – is approached through "moral suasion," in other words, the ostracizing of any member who is on the way to becoming an offender. At the time of a transaction, both parties have access to the current balance and volume of trade of their partner. A large negative balance of long duration is regarded with suspicion.

It is unusual for there to be restrictions on who can join. Most of the members typically are persons with more time than cash, but that includes a wide range of people, such as single parents, unemployed persons, retired persons, workers in seasonal industries, disabled persons, self-employed craftsmen, retailers, and farmers. As in the commercial networks, most of the trade is in services (especially personal ones such as baby-sitting where the seller does not want to bother setting up a more formal business). Used goods are also traded as well as items which are simply unavailable or rarely available in the market economy, such as organically grown farm produce, special handicraft items, custom baking, and so on.

The differences in the mode of operation between the two types of networks originate in the different intentions of the respective founders of these networks. Many commercial networks have been started and many have gone under. The community-oriented variety is a rarer species, but probably somewhat hardier. Strikingly, neither type provides more than some fraction of the income of its participants. Most firms would be reluctant to try to do all their trading within the confines of a barter network because of the constant fear of collapse. Members of community networks are still unable to find all the things they need for their day-to-day existence within such networks, so members must, to some extent, rely on other income. This situation will likely continue, but it is not as severe as it sounds because of one further difference between the two varieties of networks.

In business networks it is generally forbidden for members to trade with each other through some private barter arrangement without using trade dollars; in other words, they must operate through the central office. By contrast, in the most prominent form of community network, the family of Local Exchange Trading Systems (LETS), a transaction need only consist in part of an exchange of the system's so-called green dollars. There can be a cash component as well to most transactions which is not registered by the central office. Interestingly, the accounting usually breaks down into the local value-added part, which is largely labour, paid for "in green," and the externally purchased materials whose value is recouped by the seller in federal dollars. This allows a much wider range of activities to occur since people can offer services without having first acquired capital.

The two sorts of system differ markedly in their effects on the rest of the economy. The commercially oriented networks take up some slack in specific businesses and among some professionals and facilitate trade that otherwise might not occur during recession or out of season.

They undoubtedly contribute some indirect stimulus to the economy via the usual multiplier effect. Their contribution may be significant in maintaining employment levels in, for example, the hotel and restaurant trades, and in certain lines of retail business. But commercial networks have little impact on those unemployed and underemployed persons who are currently standing outside the economy's mainstream. Community networks tend to have more to offer these categories of people.

The barter industry in the United States used to suffer from a bad reputation due to the presence of some spectacularly dishonest operators. It is currently attempting to improve its image by having legislation passed which contains guidelines aimed at making the industry self-regulating.

A sensitivity to the charge of "tax scams" exists (richly deserved in some notorious cases), but it has now been obviated in the United States by the stipulation of the Internal Revenue Service in 1983 that copies of the particulars of each barter transaction must be filed by the network operator with both parties and with the IRS. Prior to this amendment to the tax laws, the IRS had been obliged on occasion to use a third-party summons (the "John Doe" summons) to request information from a network on its membership and their transactions and it had to show there were reasonable grounds for suspicion. Now barter exchanges are explicitly defined as a type of broker and the whole problem is approached under the rubric of the tax law relating to brokers.[10] Their "trade dollar" transactions are treated, for tax purposes, exactly as if they were normal transactions in federal dollars.

In Canada there have not yet been instituted any special procedures for reporting (or collecting) information on barter transactions. The law has always been clear on the point that money need not be involved in order for a transaction to count as one that generates income and is in principle taxable. Revenue Canada did, however, issue an Interpretation Bulletin on barter transactions in 1982.[11] Non-regular exchanges between neighbours and/or friends have been defined to be exempt from consideration as income. The greater simplicity of the Canadian provisions may result from the fact that fewer Canadian commercial exchanges exist.

The barter industry in the United States is sufficiently developed for there to have emerged a company specializing in, among other things, the salvage of barter exchanges about to collapse. This firm, for a consideration, "converts" failing networks over to its own, more failsafe, system of accounting. The American networks are very aggressive and expansionist and already the idea of a common currency for all of them has been tabled by one group.[12]

THE ANTECEDENTS OF LOCAL CURRENCIES

Those who are involved in contemporary barter networks are not particularly concerned with the historical precedents for the arrangements they utilize. There was however, a substantial wave of similar activity in the "barter and scrip movement" during the Great Depression. The twentieth century provides a number of other examples of similar systems. A comparison with these historical cases highlights the interesting innovations that can be found in the current networks.

Certain of the 1930s barter networks constitute the nearest precedents. But because this whole period is now a forgotten episode in American history, it is worth providing a sketch here of some of the local currency experiments.

Because the welfare system as we know it was not in place at that time, the early years of the Great Depression witnessed a great many socio-economic experiments of diverse types. Among them were local or community networks using barter and/or various kinds of non-legal tender (generically known as scrip) to facilitate self-help economic activity amongst the unemployed. The organizations generally embraced a wider social philosophy and typically aimed to encompass the whole of the life of the unemployed person and his or her family in a new structure of economically meaningful activity. In many cases these included alternative institutions for credit, landholding, labour remuneration, and so on. They aimed to be much more than a supplementary currency system.

The movement was not negligible. Early in 1933 it was reported that there were 159 barter organizations in 127 cities of twenty-nine states in the United States.[13] At least one million people were thought to be using them (this figure includes the members of the families of those in the networks). At that time there were seventeen million unemployed and nine million more were working only one or two days a week.[14]

Most of the schemes used in the 1930s were actually revivals of (and variations on) the late nineteenth century "labour exchanges," or "mutual credit organizations" as they also had been called. They had been common during the so-called years of panic in the mid-1890s, but the groups had subsequently lapsed. They were designed to integrate the self-help economic activity of the distressed with the rest of the community.

They worked in the following way. The local organization issued tokens to the local unemployed and indigent, either as loans (in the case of those in desperate immediate need), or in payment for labour services rendered to the organization. The organization gathered raw materials so that various useful items could be produced by the members of the exchange and sold among themselves for tokens. Depending on the degree of community trust in these monetary instruments, they could also be redeemed for goods at local retail outlets. It was also possible for a person to perform work for others in the community and be paid in tokens which could then be used to repay original loans taken out in tokens.[15]

The danger with such schemes (and their 1930s reincarnations) was that tokens would be issued in an amount greater than the value of goods produced (and/or services performed) by persons working under the rubric of the scheme. As soon as they became seriously inflated, these local means of exchange lost favour in their respective communities.

An altogether different kind of exchange was exemplified in the Midwest Exchange (of Antioch, Ohio), a network oriented to the problems of sizeable, capital-intensive business firms and thus rather like today's commercially oriented variety of barter network. The brainchild of Antioch College president, Arthur Morgan, Midwest Exchange was essentially a device to stimulate trade among regular manufacturers with immobile surplus inventory, and it ran on barter principles as a credit clearing house. The firms were invited to "deposit" goods with Midwest Exchange in return for credit in the system. The amount of credit given out depended on the ease of marketability, as well as on the quantity of the product so deposited. The system contained a complementary group of enterprises and was kept in balance so as to keep the surpluses moving, and to stimulate production by co-ordinating the inventories of the various materials. Strikingly, Midwest also ran a retail outlet for its members, the Yellow Springs Exchange, which used scrip. Employees of the member firms of Midwest could be paid in scrip. The scrip in the system was backed by foodstuffs put up by the members. Presumably the Exchange hoped that, as with banks, not everyone would come demanding conversion of their scrip on the same day.[16]

The current generation of barter networks cannot trace its origins directly back to the prewar era because the war so profoundly altered the economic situation that the prewar networks did not continue operations afterwards. The institutional lineage is broken and indeed there seems to be little intellectual continuity either. Through the 1950s and 1960s the whole phenomenon was a forgotten episode.

The change in overall economic context must be borne in mind when assessing the significance for the present of the prewar movement. Many of the 1930s networks were more like intentional communities and suffered from the usual advantages and disadvantages of social experiments along such lines (greater trust and effectiveness within, and greater irrelevance and impotence externally). Many of the rest were more in the nature of government or semi-governmental relief organizations.

The recent networks are less ambitious than their predecessors and not paternalistic, as were the earlier ones. It is a telling irony that the recent renaissance of barter networks is in part due to the faltering of the very macro-economic policies whose success in the 1940s through to the 1960s was behind the death of the earlier generation of networks.

CONCLUSION

It ought by now to be abundantly clear that the scheme we are discussing differs sharply from those of earlier proponents of monetary reform. This is so in two respects. Within the camp of monetary reform we are clearly in the wing inhabited by spenders. But, unlike run-of-the-mill Keynesians, we favour this type of focused spending on the ground floor of the economy in the first instance, as being cheaper, more democratic, and more likely to work. Let us pursue this point with further reference to contemporary economics.

Even heterodox ideas in the camp of monetary reform still take the nation state as the starting point. The striking and characteristic omission in economic thought these days concerns the matter of the local economy.[17] We have alluded to Fernand Braudel's three layer theory of economic life. His focus on the role of the non-monetized, informal sector of everyday life is salutary and in tune with some innovative thinking from the environmental movement. Hazel Henderson has proposed some new terms for realistic economic discourse: "the long loop" and "the short loop," distinguishing international economic transactions from local ones. Henderson's concern is with rebuilding the economy from the local level up, in effect, rebuilding from within.[18] In this post-sixties period such an idea may be misunderstood as the counsel of utopian autarky, but that would be quite mistaken. It is not our purpose here to argue for the recreation of autarkic local economies. Rather we would emphasize that the separation of local from global economies can only be a matter of degree, but the degree is important. Goods originating in a given locale can then embark on either short or long loops out into the wider economy. A healthy economic structure includes both kinds of circuits. Our intention is to help foster additional local circuits.

Small, less formal, economies, partially insulated by having their own currency, could offer relatively sheltered enclaves where continuity and local control could thrive in this age of frenetic international markets. We think this idea has good prospects. We advocate it chiefly because it is self-starting and an inexpensive instrument for public policy. At worst it can do little harm, even if it subsequently fails to develop or even fades away. All that would be needed is a little educational work and some further clarification of legal and tax issues (for example, the rules for welfare recipients).

We cannot enter here into these matters, but we suspect that many people would prefer to enhance their economic well-being in this way. We would like to see, in particular, the reincorporation of the unemployed in a pattern of revived, voluntary local economies exhibiting a reasonably complex intra-local division of labour. This alternative is superior in our view to the ills of the one-company town and its various distressing analogues.

In the many pockets of unemployment in Newfoundland, northern New Brunswick, Quebec, and in virtually every other province, few options are presented to revive productive activities in these stagnant areas. Self-help is already present in a reciprocal, informal fashion and is part of the way of life of these areas. But the creation of the networks suggested here may provide additional scope for this self-help tradition through these multilateral networks of exchange.

We suggest that the term "the second economy" be used to refer to the totality of transactions mobilized by this second currency system. The notion of an adjunct second economy may appear as heresy to those conditioned by the classical view of the economy as an unbounded, integrated general equilibrium system. Such a fracturing of the economy, it will be maintained, must be a less efficient deployment of resources than the classical, pristine vision offers.

We do not wish to dispute this as a theoretical point, but draw attention to the practical issue. The choice today is among alternative forms of assistance to those who fall on the wrong side of the "natural rate of unemployment." We may have reached the limits with traditional and expensive welfare systems in an era of high budgetary deficits. A less expansive alternative fostering local initiative and greater output of useful goods and services should not be dismissed categorically. In the absence of such a second currency it is safe to assume that more idle capacity and unused resources will prevail.

Local currency networks can be expected to wax and wane as the general well-being of the wider economy varies. They may well recede markedly if we re-enter something like the long postwar boom, but that is not a compelling objection to them for the foreseeable future.

What can economists do in the mean time? For a start they can upgrade the parable about barter and money in economics texts. They might take note of the fact that sometimes barter is a way to bypass the constrictions of a national, general-purpose money rather than the reverse. As noted, there are things happening in practice that could not occur in theory. Quietly and inconspicuously, the state's monopoly on currency has been challenged.

NOTES

We gratefully acknowledge the help received from Michael Linton of Courtenay, British Columbia, Dick Racey of Schumacher, Ontario, and Makoto Maruyama of the Programme in Social and Political Thought at York University. David Sobel of Toronto, Ontario, carried out excellent research on barter networks. Some preliminary ideas on the theme of this paper were set out by Abraham Rotstein, *Rebuilding from Within, Canada's Ailing Economy* (Toronto: Lorimer 1984), ch. 5.

1 We are conscious of the existence of related forms of money such as "monies of account" and "fictitious currencies." Without offering a comprehensive review of these, it may be pointed out that monies of account are generally used in trade, especially long-distance trade. Such monies serve as accounting devices to reconcile specific transactions between two different groups of people using different units, weights or measures. The "means of exchange" monies discussed in this paper have a longer-term purpose in so far as debits and credits are honoured in future transactions.

2 John Hotson, "Professor Friedman's Goals Applauded, His Means Questioned," *Challenge* (September/October 1985). Milton Friedman, "The Case for Overhauling the Federal Reserve," *Challenge* (July/August 1985): 4–12; and F.A. Hayek, *The Denationalization of Money* (London: Institute of Economic Affairs 1976).

3 Richard N. Cooper, "The Future of the International Trading System" in David W. Conklin and Thomas J. Courchene, eds., *Canadian Trade at a Crossroads: Options for New International Agreements* (Toronto: Economic Council of Ontario 1985), 412–13.

4 Karl Polanyi, "The Economy as Instituted Process" in Karl Polanyi, Harry Pearson, and Conrad Arensberg, eds., *Trade and Market in the Early Empires* (Chicago: Gateway 1957).

5 Ibid., 266.

6 Fernand Braudel, *Civilization and Capitalism: 15th–18th Century*, 3 vols. (London: Collins 1981).

7 Ibid., II: 395, I: 463.

8 In the course of our research we interviewed the people running the following barter exchanges: Tradesource, 179 Carlton Street, Suite 200, Toronto, Ontario; Bartercard (Greater Vancouver), 4463 Lougheed Highway, Burnaby, British Columbia; Barter Advantage, 1571 Second Avenue, New York; LETS, Comox Valley, Courtenay, Vancouver Island, British

Columbia. We would like to thank all the persons involved for their helpful co-operation.

9 It is true that in some networks barter credits may be sold by individual
members for cash to and from outsiders. This is in effect nothing more
than a transfer of titles to goods. These currencies are in that sense trans-
ferable, but we maintain that they are not convertible in the sense that
there will be no institution prepared to purchase any amount of these
credits for cash, or alternatively to sell any amount of these local currencies.

10 The relevant parts of the legislation can be seen in the *Standard Federal Tax
Report* of 3 September 1983. The legislation is PL 97–248, amending section 6045 of the 1954 code. The relevant paragraph number is 5093.

11 See interpretation Bulletin IT-490, dated 5 July 1982. The reference is to
sections 3, 9, and 69.

12 The information reported here on recent developments was culled from
various articles in the 1985 issue of the trade journal, *Barter News*.

13 Malcolm Ross, "The Spread of Barter," *The Nation* (1 March 1933): 228–
29.

14 Wayne Weisharr and Wayne Parrish, *Men Without Money: The Challenge of
Barter and Scrip* (New York: Putnam's 1933).

15 Many of the self-help networks of the Great Depression operated without
any form of currency. At the time these were classed as the "pure barter"
groups. Typically a group that started out using no tokens or scrip
resorted to the use of a currency as means of exchange when the book-
keeping task involved in recording enormous series of minute transactions
became too unwieldy. How widely the scrip was accepted varied. Some
states forbade self-help groups from selling their produce on the open
market to protect those business enterprises that were still operating during the depression. In some communities, local companies and even
municipal authorities were enabled to use a local scrip to pay wages.
Firms were obliged, however, to earn this privilege by depositing a quantity of goods with the overseeing organization which would then allow
the recipients of scrip to use it to buy these goods. The system of relative
prices used in such a mixed set-up was once again a mirror of prices in
the economy at large. The standard of value was the federal dollar but the
actual means of exchange was the scrip.

16 The problem of trust with respect to local monetary instruments was
severe within some exchanges. One in Minneapolis backed its scrip with
"gold reserves" consisting of nine hundred barrels of sauerkraut. Attempts
to set up exchanges in New York City failed due to the heightened sense
of urban anonymity that undermined confidence in such schemes.

17 John Hotson may count as something of a developing exception, since in
addition to his recent interesting work reviving Fisher's concerns, he has

been advocating LETS (Hotson, "The Case for Financial Reform," paper presented at the Atlantic Economic Association meetings, Washington, DC, 30 August 1985). Shann Turnbull has also been suggesting locally based currencies but of a type wholly different from the ones advocated here. See Turnbull, "Selecting a Local Currency," *Options* (Australia) (June 1983): 1–10.
18 Hazel Henderson, "Post-Economic Policies for Post-Industrial Societies," *ReVISION* 7 (Winter 1984/Spring 1985): 20–29.

BIBLIOGRAPHIC APPENDIX

The following bibliography will assist those interested in the further study of barter networks and a second economy.

Amberg, Julius. "Scrip-wise and Pound Foolish: the Story of a Community that Surveyed its Own Relief Situation." *The Survey* (Nov. 15, 1932): 595–97.

Arrington, Leonard J. "The Mormon Tithing House: a Frontier Business Institution." *Business History Review* 28 (1954): 24–58.

Baker, Jacob. "Making Money." *Survey Graphic* (February 1933).

Cipolla, Carlo M. *Money, Prices and Civilization in the Mediterranean World – 5th–7th Century*. Princeton: Princeton University Press 1956.

Einaudi, Luigi. "The Theory of Imaginary Money from Charlemagne to the French Revolution." In Lane and Remiersma, eds., *Enterprise and Secular Change*. London: Allen & Unwin 1953.

Fisher, Irving. "The Stamped Scrip Plan." *The New Republic* (21 December 1932): 163–64.

Gesell, Silvio. *The Natural Economic Order*. London: Peter Owen 1958.

Graham, Frank. *The Abolition of Unemployment*. Princeton: Princeton University Press 1932.

Johnston, Marlise. "Back to Barter." *Review of Reviews & World's Work* (May 1933): 34–45.

Journal of Taxation. "I.R.S. Clarifies Reporting on Broker and Barter Dealings" (September 1983): 181–82.

King, Murray. "Back to Barter." *The New Republic* (4 January 1933): 211–13.

Monthly Labor Review. "Cooperative Self-Help Activity Among the Unemployed – General Summary." 36 (1933): 1229–40. See also 38 (1934): 312–19; 43 (1936): 349–55; 47 (1938): 1–17; 49 (1939): 1335–47; 53 (1941): 438–43.

Neale, Walter. *Monies in Societies*. San Francisco: Chandler & Sharp 1976.

Rall, Udo. "Appraising Self-Help." *The Survey* (May 1936): 134–36.

20 Beyond the Market and the State: How Can We Do Better?

DUNCAN CAMERON

Most observers of the Canadian economy take as a starting point that it can be divided into a private sector and a public sector. From this simple distinction flow many important consequences. In order to rethink the economy it is necessary to introduce a broader perspective than the one implied by the two-sector model.

THE TWO-SECTOR MODEL

The private sector operates on the profit principle. Producing more product with less resources (increasing productivity) is deemed by economists to be the basis of economic success (efficiency) and results in profit maximization. By a process of circular reasoning, efficiency is claimed to be the result of reliance on price signals that emanate from competitive market forces, and that themselves produce efficiency. In this way, both the economic goal – efficiency – and the method of achieving it – the price system – are understood by accepting that each be defined in terms of the other.[1]

Questions of what should be produced, how, and with what mix of resources are answered by referring back to internal definitions of profit maximization within the market system of competitive pricing. Indeed, much that is external to the market (for example, government, environment, labour and social relations) is taken to be non-economic by definition and is therefore not valued in market terms. Much that is important to human life is excluded from the economic framework used in the analysis of the private sector.

In simplest terms, we talk of a private sector because private owners of capital produce goods and services that are offered for sale and profit in the market. Production is distributed through purchases of goods and services by consumers, including other producers, at prices determined by competition among producers, including foreigners. Purchases are financed through the banking system either by transfers from income or through credit. The private sector is assumed to provide the source of wealth that allows us to finance the public sector.

The public sector operates on the service principle. Fulfilling the needs of society is deemed to justify government programs. There is no generally accepted measure for judging the effectiveness of government. But many criteria are used to justify programs. These include equity or fairness in distribution of needed services, the need for public authority to assume control of natural monopoly situations, and acting to ensure security and welfare. That such measures are introduced by representatives elected through democratic choice is important for legitimizing such action. Government spending is financed through taxation and public borrowing. The public sector is assumed to be non–productive of wealth.

This two–sector model is widely accepted among economic observers. Yet in many ways this way of thinking is incomplete, inaccurate, and misleading. The bias against the public sector is clear. Yet in fact little private sector "wealth" could be created without the provision of the infrastructure of schools, roads, postal service, among other things. An important repercussion of this bias is that private-sector criteria and rationality are often imported into the public sector. Private-sector thinking is then incorporated into public sector operations. As well, such policies as privatization and deregulation are based both on the supposed superiority of the private sector and the presumed burden of the public sector on society.

Once the logic of the two–sector model is accepted, many policy options are constrained and the ability to rethink the economy severely limited. Moreover, the two–sector model is often accepted as the starting point for analysis not just by social and business liberals, for whom the wisdom of the market is unquestioned, however their views of government may differ, but by social democrats as well.

In rethinking the two–sector model, a number of propositions need to be highlighted. When business groups defend the profit motive they do so from a perspective of self-interest: they want more profits. When they charge that the public sector is inefficient they have in mind widening the scope for profit-making activity. Indeed, when business groups call themselves the private sector they are dressing themselves up in neutral language in order to present business concerns as abstract appeals to reason rather than concrete desires for more financial power.

The financial system is the heart of the economy and the key points on which economic debate turn have to do with money. Business groups have effectively used arguments about the role of the public sector in creating inflation and saddling future generations with debt in order to discredit government as a service provider. It is even argued that too much government spending diminishs international competitiveness and causes balance of payments deficits to appear. When you consider that government services meet human needs, it is no mean feat to discredit government spending. Above all, this illustrates the force of financial arguments and suggests that they need to be faced head on.[2]

Refuting the financial arguments used by business groups to discredit the public sector is beyond the scope of this paper. But it should be pointed out that the control of inflation requires limiting the power of corporations to set prices, not limiting public spending. Public debt problems are overstated because of leakages in the tax system and ineffective public control over monetary policy, while, especialy when social and environmental costs are factored in to the economic equation, private sector debt problems are understated. And balance of payments problems arise because of a weak structure of domestic industry, not because Canada can't compete abroad.

THE NATURE OF WEALTH

The nature of wealth is an important question for critical analysis. Notions of efficiency and economic performance are based on market ideas of what constitutes wealth and how it is best produced. It is generally accepted by liberals that the market creates wealth in an even-handed manner. People are rewarded for their efforts and talents. Money serves to recognize success in the market place. In this conception monetary gain is an all-important incentive for economic activity. Individuals and firms are driven to perform and compete efficiently for monetary reasons.

In a market economy wealth is viewed as the capacity to consume goods and services. For a society as a whole, it is measured by the annual calculation of the flow of goods and services (Gross Domestic Product). This, of course, is given in monetary terms, which is the chief advantage of a measure that is crude in the extreme, given that no qualitative changes are reflected in the numbers. As a measure of wealth creation, GDP is a poor surrogate for broader measures of well-being.

Classical political economy understood that the source of wealth was human labour. Goods could be exchanged because they had been transformed by human effort and toil. Economists such as Adam Smith and David Ricardo attributed value to labour time. Though this notion was never refuted, it was set aside and replaced by the narrower (and statistically easier) practice of equating "value" with market prices. By changing the perspective to one of price formation from that of the classical labour theory of value, economists became preoccupied with the marginal productivity of various factors of production. In the marginalist perspective the understanding of labour changes in an important way. Labour becomes a cost of production, something that can be substituted for, or replaced by capital.

What Harold Innis called in another context "the penetrative power of the price system" has had a profound influence on the way we see and understand the economy. In fact, this dominant economic perception is a large obstacle to seeing how things actually happen. The focus on prices and cost tends to obscure the fact that the economy is about people creating goods and services and agreeing to distribute them amongst themselves.

While the market forces of supply and demand are all too real, the competitive price model is an abstract construct that represents only one dimension of economic reality. By making supply and demand for goods and services the central economic focus, and then assuming that the supply and demand for anything can be regulated by movements in prices, economists first narrow the range of economic questions that can be asked, and then limit the type of answers that can be given. Rethinking the economy means broadening the approach so as to focus on the fulfilment of economic needs; it means seeing analysis couched terms of perfectectly competitive markets as ideological in nature. Indeed, it is a short step from an analytical approach that posits the existence of perfect competition to policy prescriptions which call for market "liberalization" so that price competition can bring about greater efficiency.

Much can be learned about the ideological bias of the competitive price model of the economy by looking at major issues that have arisen in the labour market in the 1980s. Feminist analysis has shown how the so-called market economy is in fact dependent on the unpaid labour of women. It is clear that corporations have benefited by consistently underpaying women for work of equal value to that performed by men. For years women have been joining the paid labour force in increasing numbers but the feminization of labour has also seen the creation of job ghettos of low-paying work, and many new jobs are in fact involuntary part-time jobs. Labour market analysis that assumes that wages are determined by price competition fails to recognize that market outcomes may be rigged by discriminatory hiring practices. A focus on labour with a market price excludes the important economic role of non-market labour.

DE-MYSTIFYING THE FINANCIAL ECONOMY

Curiously enough, economic analysis often separates consideration of the real economy of physical products and services from consideration of the monetary aspects of the economy. Money is considered to be neutral or, in the jargon, a veil for real activity. A better way to look at the economy is to recognize that money indeed "makes the world go around." Workable alternatives to current economic practice require de-mystifying the financial economy. The problem with many important alternative perspectives – those that recognize the importance of the informal economy or the role of unpaid household labour, for instance – is that while they broaden our understanding of the social nature of economic life, they fail to come to grips with the power relations inherent in the financial economy.

In monetary terms the economy can be seen as a stream of spending decisions. Expenditures are either financed out of income, including past accumulated income, or by credit. Income comes from wages and salaries, government transfers, and from interest, dividends, and profits. Income is assumed to be determined by labour and capital markets but in fact, as with other prices and costs, it is subject to bargaining and negotiating processes that are social in nature. The unequal distribution of spending power ensures that social inequalities will be perpetuated. Since borrowing power is linked to the ability to pledge marketable assets against loans, access to credit is linked to the existing distribution of wealth and income.

Traditionally, social democrats have argued that government should redistribute income in order to make the market system more fair. In addition, public credit could be used in a variety of ways: to create social wealth (schools, hospitals, housing, and so on); to underwrite major projects, such as transportation systems, that are beyond the scope of private owners; and to develop enterprises based on natural resources that belong to the community. Whether natural resource development takes place under state ownership and control or whether public authorities rely on regulation and taxation, the goal is to derive social dividends from market activity.

There is no good reason to believe that this reasoning should be abandoned. It is worth noting that Canada has had great difficulty in affecting the distribution of wealth and even income. The progressive income tax, minimum wage, unemployment insurance, and welfare system have had no great impact on the distribution of income, which remains as unequal as it was after the Second World War. Of course, social democracy has not made great inroads in Canada either. But the experience of European nations suggests that the critique of social democratic thinking – that the way wealth is produced determines income distribution, and that therefore new ways of producing wealth are required – seems to be upheld. Managing the capitalist economy in a more fair way has significant limits. As well, the public sector, by importing private sector management techniques and forgetting social goals, has done much to undermine support for its activities.

The key to understanding the workings of the economy is to see that so-called economic activity actually has a much broader content than simply the image of an individual producing and consuming. Economic activity has social and environmental content and the economy is an integrated whole. Society as a whole produces and consumes, but it also creates, educates, provides care, nurtures, conserves, and explores other dimensions of life. Society attributes social roles as well as income. Individuals act alone or together with others to improve their economic circumstances, but society validates choices. Many individuals and families have few options and fewer choices about what they do.

Economic control is exercised through ownership. The two-sector model implies two types of owners, private and public. Rethinking the economy implies envisaging new types of ownership. In financial terms, private ownership rests on equity, either in the form of marketable shares (stock in so-called publicly traded companies) or direct ownership of production (or services) facilities. Public ownership implies that investments in crown corporations or the like are held by governmnent on behalf of the citizenship at large.

In practice it is sometimes difficult to distinguish between the operations of crown corporations and private companies – Air Canada (pre-privatization) and Canadian Airlines, for instance. The key differences are not in operating procedures, where both are subject to market pricing in a regulated (or increasingly deregulated) environment, conduct employee relations in a similar way, and offer similar services, but rather in access to capital.

To raise investment capital (that is, start-up money or, more normally, funds for expansion), private companies issue shares and sell equity in the market. They also float loans through the issuing of marketable debentures or bonds. Public sector companies receive grants from government or borrow in the market on the basis of government guarantees. Both public and private sector companies have recourse to the banking system for commercial credit.

In a market economy any enterprise can continue to operate so long as it can recover costs of its production through sales. The financial structure of the organization is key. Private ownership of capital requires that financial return on equity be considered a cost of production. The logic of the private sector requires that return on equity be maximized for investors. Debt and equity instruments must be considered as substitutes so that the return on share investment must at least equal the return available from holding debt (once risk and tax considerations are accounted for). Putting all this together means that many activities are rendered "uneconomic" because they can't meet the return on equity requirements of investors. This is the case, even if they can recover the costs of direct production. At other times, financial constraints such as high interest rates limit new investment possibilities.

THE COST OF CAPITAL

In another light, the cost of capital in Canada is very high. Here equity investors have depressed the value of ownership shares so that they represent no more than about ten to thirteen times that amount in earnings. In Japan this price/earning ratio per share has been as high as one to sixty. At similar rates of return on investment, the cost for each company of servicing each investor is much higher in Canada, since each dollar of earnings is divided among ten to thirteen shareholders rather than among sixty as in Japan.

Moreover, central bank lending rates below 4 per cent in Japan, and barely above that in West Germany, compare most unfavourably with rates in Canada above 12 per cent. This benchmark rate sets the financial context and influences what is profitable and therefore worth doing, and what is not. The implications of high-cost capital for Canada's economic future are seldom given the attention they deserve. Creating conditions under which low-cost ownership capital can be provided for cost recovery activities is a major challenge. The way in which the co-operative sector has become much like the private sector under terms of market competition outlines the difficulties of doing things differently.

Though ownership and control within the Canadian private sector is tightly concentrated, much of the capital invested in marketable securities is pension fund money. Pension fund investment stands at about $180 billion in Canada. Since ownership capital represented by pension contributions represents current income foregone by employees in return for deferred payment of that income, the potential for breaking down the distinction between owners and employees within the private sector (about which much more could be said) is quite large.

Extending control of pension funds for investment purposes represents the major potential lever for affecting private sector economic activity in Canada. Though changes to the current system of pension trusteeship that effectively lodges control with the financial sector and its managers would require government action, the grounds for acting would have to be determined outside government. The scope for trade union involvement should be obvious. Broadening the role of unions to include direct stewardship of investment capital could be the most important step since the right to strike.

Talk about the global economy often obscures the need to explore alternatives to the private ownership model of economic development. While funds are easily moved around the world in search of maximum returns, within the market sector there is considerable scope for alternative ownership schemes to be introduced in Canada. Marshalling pension funds, both public and private, and introducing new models of worker ownership seem suitable options when compared to the global casino approach to corporate finance.

BROADENING THE ECONOMIC VISION

Real economic power lies behind the stylized perception of a private sector and the limited vision of links between it and the public sector. While it is invaluable to see the economy in new terms, as something more than a two-sector model, it should be clear that actually to transform the economy requires empowering subordinate groups. It is assumed here that a different vision of the economy is a part of this empowering process.[3]

Dividing the economy into a public and a private sector has the effect of ignoring much economic activity that doesn't fit neatly into either sector. In fact there is a third sector, which can be called the popular sector, and it deserves greater attention. Creating more space for the popular sector could have the effect of transforming the economy from within by emphasizing areas of activity undervalued at present. As will be seen, this could be done by modifying some public sector practices and limiting some of the authority of the private sector. Canada needs legislative, spending, and taxation initiatives at every level of government to promote voluntary organizations, associations, and cost-recovery enterprises. Seeing the economic role for popular sector groups as being an important alternative to the private sector is the starting point.

The popular sector exists because people see themselves in more than one dimension. They are employees, but also have identities as women, Catholics, environmentalists, peace activists, humanitarians, to mention only a few. Labour, church, and women's organizations have overlapping membership. Thousands of voluntary associations and community organizations of various types operate in Canada. The economic significance of the popular sector has yet to be analysed and to do so would require that new statistics be collected.[4] But some conceptual observations can be made. The way in which the sector is financed distinguishes it from both the private and public sectors. Though some organizations operate through sales of products and services, it is important to understand that popular sector organizations do not have owners that demand the distribution of profits. Though many receive government grants, they do not have access to taxation or borrowing guarantees in the way the public sector does. Labour unions collect dues, churches receive donations, other groups rely on voluntary labour, supplemented by fund-raising through charitable tax credits and other means. Many organizations rely on government funding.

Popular sector organizations employ people, meet needs (broadly defined), purchase goods and services, provide services and sometimes goods, and involve millions of people in activity that is thought to be non-economic because it is not directed to profit-making. Much of our cultural and artistic expression is popular sector activity rather than for-profit commercial activity. Its political potential is enormous and has just begun to be tapped in an conscious way. The Pro-Canada Network's fight against free trade is the best example of how the business/government alliance and its control of the economic agenda can be challenged through public debate. In this respect Canada is further ahead than other industrialized countries.[5]

By working together in coalitions, popular sector groups give each other credibility. While business is still widely seen as the sole legitimate actor on economic issues, this is due as much to a process of "manufacturing consent" through control of major media as it is to the real power conferred by ownership of the means of production. Such consent can be undermined through the use of popular sector media and the power of ownership diminished. The amount of resources expended on communications by the popular sector probably far exceeds amounts spent on all other activities put together. To a great extent popular sector organizations are communications vehicles.

Each of the major elements of the popular sector has its strengths and weaknesses. Labour has organization, churches communicate with great sophistication, and women's groups mobilize their membership effectively. Native and farm organizations have strong identities. Social welfare organizations have great legitimacy. Cultural and artistic groups have high visibility in their communities.

The economic clout of the popular sector could be considerable. The job creation potential cannot be underestimated. If organizations were properly financed, much good work being done by the popular sector could be transformed into thousands of interesting paid jobs. While important issues need to be addressed, such as the current tendency to farm out public sector jobs to voluntary groups, the important thing is that the popular sector be seen for what it is: a force for political, economic, and social transformation that is unparalleled.

WITHOUT THE MARKET OR THE STATE

Pulling together the elements of the foregoing presentation suggests certain avenues for the future. The old left thought that economic transformation would occur either through a popular revolt or by parliamentary action. It should be obvious that neither prospect should be awaited. Working–class consciousness has not developed the means to produce political transformation of the economy through either a revolution or the ballot box. But there is no point in simply struggling within a private sector framework either. Instead, the resources of the popular sector need to be mobilized for some concrete action, some of which requires legislative changes and therefore support through the formal political process, some of which requires intervening in the market system. But in both instances the aim is to go beyond the choices imposed by market and state rationality.

While questioning the representation of economic wealth as increasing GDP per capita, it can be accepted that the economy exists to serve people's needs and that the organization of work is the critical factor in wealth creation for common use. Full employment defined as paid work for all that seek it remains a primary objective. The means of achieving it need to be rethought, but it remains the case that a viable economy fulfills needs through meaningful work. Some propositions follow.

1 The economy is a monetary economy. Wages, salaries, pensions, and social transfer payments are the means through which material needs are met. The private market functions because income created through production of goods and services, and provided through public sector taxation, is expended on goods and services. Equity in meeting needs requires *equity in remuneration*. In the workplace, this means more unionization, employment and pay equity legislation and bargaining, and solidarity wage policy for companies. No executive should earn more than, say, three times the wage of the lowest paid employee.
2 *Redistributing existing income* would go a long way to satisfying many basic material needs that now go unmet. The model for wage bargaining should be based on need through the life cycle. Younger workers should receive rapid increases at a time when they need to

set up homes and establish themselves. Pay should be normalized across skill areas – that is, not based on historical differences by craft, trade, or qualifications. Obviously this is only attractive if lower-paid groups receive increases and privileged groups in society are denied excessive compensation either through legislation (maximum wage as well as minimum wage). A truly progressive income tax would reduce the incentive to pay executive benefits in the $200,000 to $1 million (and up) range.

3 *Control over pension funds* must be a primary objective for labour organizations. Direct ownership of companies should not be avoided on the spurious grounds that workers are not investors. Investment committees of individual unions should work together to ensure maximum financial clout. Worker solidarity funds serve an education purpose and could become an important vehicle in transforming the basis on which equity investment is made; in other words, someone has to support maximizing job creation rather than financial return on investment.

4 Rather than closing down single-industry towns because of corporate financial decisions and then seeing the social costs absorbed by the community and government, new forms of community organization are needed. Let's call them *cost recovery enterprises.* Participants would include workers from existing production facilities, municipal and other levels of government, community groups, perhaps private companies, and even foreign investors. Control would be exercised by local participants. Government infrastructure would be mobilized to assist in marketing, distribution, and production. The goal would be to help people help themselves. The objective of the enterprises would be financial self-reliance. This would be facilitated by an equity loan procedure.[6]

5 Action to create the conditions for cost recovery production under community control means creating *new forms of equity ownership.* Community development banks and a revitalized federal business development bank could be vehicles. Instead of making loans in the form of debt to be repaid, such banks would make equity loans. That is to say, they would issue stock to be held by the bank against the funds provided to a community enterprise. The terms of the stock issue would allow the community enterprise to buy back the stock after a lapse of time. Thus, instead of facing the immediate requirement of retiring a loan and being forced to engage in short-term thinking, such enterprises would have the time to use their money wisely. Cost recovery, not profit, would be the incentive.

6 *Injections of public money* through equity investment rather than through dubious grants to attract multinationals, or tax expenditures and holidays, would at least hold out some prospect of repayment.

Such a policy could also provide the basis for an industrial strategy that did not depend on foreign investors deciding on whether Canadians should have jobs or on the laughable proposition that Canada should set the terms on which it trades as low as possible through the free trade agreement. Effective industrial policy requires instruments such as development banks which are funded by government through grants from money raised through taxation and which, unlike credit unions, are not obliged to compete for funds through the deposit market or borrow at market rates.

7 *Funding for voluntary agencies* could be put on a much more stable basis if a generous 100 per cent tax credit (refundable) were to be established for charitable donations. By setting a universal credit at, say, $300 per tax filer, some $5.1 billion would be available to existing organizations. This would allow them to replace volunteers with paid staff. The basic idea is that instead of individuals sending $300 in income tax money to government, it could be earmarked for a popular sector group instead. The amount of paid work created per dollar expended is undoubtedly higher in this sector than elsewhere. The administrative problems of identifying qualifying organizations would not be insurmountable. Groups would have to justify the worth of their organizations in order to secure funds, as they do now, but the difference would be that all Canadians would have an equal ability to provide direction to the charitable sector through tax-free donations. The present system gives great weight to the wealthy.

8 The question of who should qualify for *income support from government transfer payments* needs to be opened. There are many problems in proposing a guaranteed annual income in the present political environment of unemployment and social cutbacks, though such a program may well make sense in a climate of full employment and adequate social payments. One group that could benefit considerably from specific guaranteed income support is the artistic community of musicians, visual artists, writers, and actors. Through guaranteeing income support for individual artists, such a program would make many cost-recovery cultural projects viable, and create the conditions where communities could benefit from the cultural activities that arts workers provide.

9 In many respects action by the women's movement and the feminist analysis of the economy provide indications of the way ahead. Rethinking the economy so as to include recognition of the significance of unpaid labour is important. Issues that arise around part-time work, job-sharing, employment equity, child care, and the introduction of new technologies and work practices all provide an opportunity to *integrate social and economic policy*.

NOTES

1 Many critiques of market economics have appeared. The most stimulating for this observer remains Karl Polanyi, *The Great Transformation* (Boston: Beacon Press 1944).

2 On the business agenda in Canada, see Daniel Drache and Duncan Cameron, *The Other Macdonald Report* (Toronto: James Lorimer 1985).

3 One of the most powerful statements on the need for a new economic vision comes from Canada's Catholic bishops: see Gregory Baum and Duncan Cameron, *Ethics and Economics* (Toronto: James Lorimer 1984).

4 See David Ross and Peter Usher, *From the Roots Up: Economic Development as if Community Mattered* (New York: Bootstrap Press 1986).

5 See Ed Finn, ed. (with John Calvert and Duncan Cameron), *The Facts on Free Trade* (Toronto: James Lorimer 1988).

6 See Patricia Lane, "Community Based Economic Development: Our Trojan Horse," *Studies in Political Economy* 25 (Spring 1988).

Contributors

Isabella Bakker is associate professor of political science at York University, Toronto.

Duncan Cameron is on the faculty of the Political Science Department at the University of Ottawa and is director of the Canadian Centre for Policy Alternatives, Ottawa.

Stephen Clarkson is professor of political science and a member of University College at the University of Toronto.

Marjorie Cohen is professor of sociology at the Ontario Institute for Studies in Education, Toronto.

Robert W. Cox is professor of political science at York University, Toronto.

Arthur W. Donner is a consulting economist living in Toronto. He is also a regular columnist on economics and business with the *Toronto Star*.

Daniel Drache is chair of political science at Atkinson College, York University, Toronto.

Colin A.M. Duncan lectures in history at Queen's University, Kingston, Ontario.

Meric S. Gertler is associate professor of geography and planning at the University of Toronto.

John Holmes is associate professor of geography at Queen's University, Kingston, Ontario.

Jeanne Kirk Laux is professor of political science at the University of Ottawa.

Rianne Mahon is associate professor in the School of Public Administration at Carleton University, Ottawa.

Michael Mandel is professor of law at Osgoode Hall Law School at York University, Toronto.

Anthony C. Masi is associate professor of sociology at McGill University, Montreal, and director of the Faculty of Arts Computing Laboratory.

Jonathan Morris lectures in the Cardiff Business School at the University of Wales, Cardiff.

John Myles is professor of sociology at Carleton University, Ottawa.

Paul Phillips is professor of economics in University College at the University of Manitoba, Winnipeg.

Abraham Rotstein is professor of economics and a member of Massey College at the University of Toronto.

Frank J. Tester is associate professor in the School of Social Work at the University of British Columbia, Vancouver.

Bruce W. Wilkinson is professor of economics at the University of Alberta, Edmonton.